My Dearest Heart

THE ARTIST MARY BEALE (1633–1699)

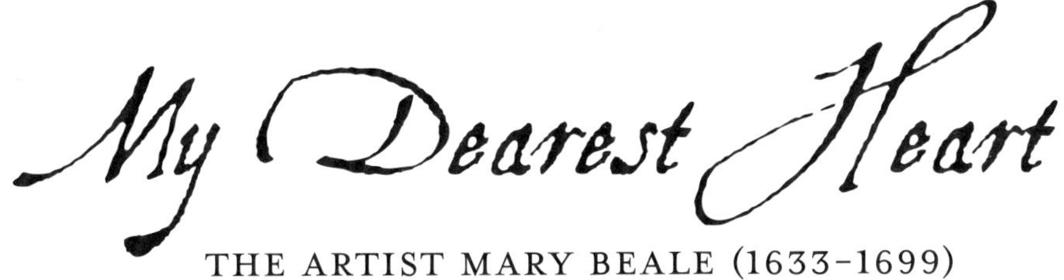

THE ARTIST MARY BEALE (1633–1699)

Penelope Hunting

UNICORN

Published in 2024 by Unicorn, an imprint of Unicorn Publishing Group
Charleston Studio
Meadow Business Centre
Lewes BN8 5RW
www.unicornpublishing.org

ISBN 978-1-916846-19-7
10 9 8 7 6 5 4 3 2 1

Design by Anna Hopwood
Printed in Turkey through Finetone

CONTENTS

FOREWORD BY DR BENDOR GROSVENOR

The fate of most artists working in Britain in the seventeenth century was to be unrecognised by posterity. The dominant subject matter was portraiture, and unsurprisingly the demands of the paying sitter dominated those of the artist. Look at most portraits painted at the time, and you will struggle to find a signature; it was simply not done to add an artist's name to a painting intended to glorify someone else. Consequently, the walls of stately homes across Britain were covered with portraits which in time became either optimistically ascribed to the few major artists anyone had heard of – Sir Peter Lely, or Sir Godfrey Kneller – or described as being by unknown artists in the 'Follower of Lely' or 'Circle of Kneller'.

For centuries, therefore, the paintings of Britain's first successful female artist, Mary Beale, tended to be regarded as the work of men, if they were regarded at all. If art history is about doing justice to artists – recognising their work, and why they did it – then Mary Beale has suffered a double injustice. Very occasionally one finds an old inscription 'Mary Beale' on a portrait, but this too can be in error; my favourite example is the prominent 'by Mary Beale' on a painting actually by Joan Carlile, who briefly preceded Beale as a professional (if less prolific) artist in London in the 1650s. Such has been the fate of Britain's pioneering female painters. And yet Beale was capable of painting not only works of great technical achievement, but of an emotional sensitivity rarely approached by her male contemporaries. Her sketches of children in particular seem to strip away time, and present us with an image of childhood which is movingly immediate. And the wonderful thing is that unlike most artists, we know so much about why and how Beale produced such paintings; thanks to her writings and those of her husband, Charles, Beale is one of the best documented artists Britain has ever produced.

Nevertheless, it has taken too long for art history to turn its attention seriously to the work of female artists at work in Britain before 1900. Recent wider cultural and political changes have now given the subject an added impetus, and at last progress is being made. In Beale's case, institutions like Tate Britain have acquired new works, including a pair of wonderful oil studies of her son Bartholomew. That these were new discoveries – found when the art historian James Mulraine stopped in a Paris street to tie his shoelaces and happened to look up into the window of an antiques dealer – tells us that our understanding of Beale's oeuvre still has much to yield.

One institution in particular has led the way in championing Beale's life and work; the Geffrye Museum in London. Only two exhibitions on Beale have so far been mounted, and both were at the Geffrye. The first in 1975 was curated by Elizabeth Walsh and Richard Jeffree, two tireless Beale enthusiasts and experts, while the second, in 1999, was curated by Tabitha Barber, the pre-eminent connoisseur of Beale's varied work, who can spot the artist's hand at twenty paces. It is especially fitting, therefore, that Penelope Hunting's first ever biography of Beale should have had its genesis in her own work for the Geffrye Museum. This important, absorbing and much-needed book will – finally – help complete our knowledge of one of Britain's most fascinating and under-appreciated artists. May the life and work of Mary Beale be unrecognised no more.

INTRODUCTION

MARY BEALE WAS FIRST RECOGNISED AS AN ARTIST OF MERIT by Sir William Sanderson, the author of *Graphice: the use of the Pen and Pencil or, the most excellent Art of Painting* (1658). Mrs Beale was then at the dawn of her career as a professional portrait painter and was living in the artists' quarter of London, Covent Garden, with her husband and their young son. Mary Beale's husband, Charles, documented her subsequent career in almanacks, two of which survive as a unique record of her patrons, her painting technique and the materials and colours she used. The almanacks for 1677 and 1681 are supplemented by excerpts from several more noted by the art historian George Vertue in the eighteenth century. Mary Beale's life and work is revealed further by the diaries, memoirs and correspondence of the poet Dr Samuel Woodford, the miniaturist Thomas Flatman, Dr John Cooke, Latin secretary to King Charles II, and 'our kind friend', Francis Knollys.

Academic evaluation of Mary Beale's talent commenced in 1706 with Bainbrigg Buckeridge's *Essay towards an English School of Painters*. Writing just seven years after Mary Beale's death, Buckeridge pointed out that Mrs Beale 'work'd with a wonderful Body of Colours, was exceedingly Industrious and her Pictures are much after the Italian Manner, which she learnt by having copy'd several of the Great masters of that Country, whose pictures she borrowed out of Sir Peter's Collection'. Sir Peter Lely was Mary Beale's mentor who, on visits to her 'painting-roome' commended her work. Horace Walpole, historian and patron of the arts, acquired Vertue's notes relating to Mary Beale's career in 1758, prompting his appraisal of her portraits in *Anecdotes of Painting in England* (1762-71). He commented that Lely, 'her master, was supposed to have had a tender attachment to her'.

Mary Hays provided a fresh slant on Mary Beale in *Female Biography or Memoirs of Illustrious and Celebrated Women of all ages and centuries* (1803). Since then Beale has been held up as a feminist icon for her stature as a professional artist and the author of a 'Discourse on Friendship' (1667) which argued for equality of men and women in marriage. Later in the nineteenth century Ellen Clayton's *Directory of English Female Artists* (1876) described Mary Beale as 'a painter who claims respect, not so much for brilliant original talent as for persevering industry and conscientious study'. C. H. Collins Baker devoted a chapter to Mary Beale in *Lely and the Stuart Portrait Painters* (1912). He criticised 'the hardness of her early work', pointed out that she was 'a specially good colourist' and payed tribute to her 'gentle, feminine and not unpleasing individuality' before concluding that she was 'a painter of industry, scant training and slight feeling'. Ellis Waterhouse's judgement of Mary Beale in *Painting in Britain 1530–1709* (1953) dismissed her as 'a drab and unoriginal follower of Lely's manner'.

The reassessment of Mary Beale's portraiture began in 1975 with the first exhibition of her work at the Geffrye Museum, London, and the Towner Art Gallery, Eastbourne. This was inspired by the research of Richard Jeffree and Elizabeth Walsh whose exhibition catalogue, *The Excellent Mrs Mary Beale*, was introduced by Sir Oliver Millar, surveyor of the Queen's pictures and an expert on seventeenth-century British paintings. He drew attention to Mrs Beale's true English quality, to the Beales' circle of artists and intellectuals and, in a subsequent review he praised Mary's 'charm in presenting a character…her freshness of touch and palpable affection' in portraits of family and friends. Interest in Mary Beale quickened, sustained by Jeffree and Walsh who compiled a catalogue of her work, listing 158 verified portraits and forty-one attributions, since when additional paintings by Beale have been discovered and it is likely that more will come to light.

After Richard Jeffree's death in 1991 and the bequest of his collection of portraits by Beale to the Manor House Museum, Bury St Edmunds, an exhibition was organised at the Museum, *Mrs Mary Beale, Paintress 1633–1699*, with an accompanying brochure by Christopher Reeve (1994). The most recent exhibition of Mary Beale's work was held at the Geffrye Museum during the winter of 1999–2000 with a catalogue, *Mary Beale. Portrait of a seventeenth-century painter, her family and her studio* by Tabitha Barber (1999).

This biography of Mary Beale draws together her personal life, her career as a professional artist and her patrons, set in the historical context of seventeenth-century England. Her portraits endure as a visual record of the aristocracy, politicians, bishops, physicians, intellectuals, poets and authors who figured large in the history of the seventeenth century, painted by one of the first women in England to make a living from her art.

Since the publication of *My Dearest Heart* in 2019, Mary Beale has received much attention. Her work has recently been exhibited in Madrid, at Tate Britain, the Philip Mould Gallery, the Weiss Gallery and at Moyse's Hall Museum, Bury St Edmunds, and her portraits have been acquired by the Museum of Fine Arts Boston and the Yale Center for British Art. The Gallery of New Images on pages 186 to 201 illustrates an additional thirty-three of her portraits.

Penelope Hunting

LIST OF ILLUSTRATIONS AND CREDITS

Sir Théodore De Mayerne's notes on painting, 1620–46
© The British Library Board, Sloane Ms 2052, f. 90v **pg. 58**

Wenceslaus Hollar, *Covent Garden* c. 1647
Wikimedia Commons **pg. 62**

William Morgan, Hind Court, Fleet Street, 1682
London Topographical Society **pp. 64 & 67**

Hind Court, Fleet Street, 1675
London Metropolitan Archives, City of London: Collage, the London Picture Archive 22340 **pg. 68**

Thomas Flatman, *Charles Beale*, 1664
Victoria and Albert Museum **pg. 69**

Thomas Flatman, *Samuel Woodford*, 1661
© The Fitzwilliam Museum, Cambridge **pg. 70**

Mary Beale, *Archbishop John Tillotson*, 1687
© The Chapter of St Paul's Cathedral **pg. 73**

Mary Beale, *Dr John Wilkins*, c. 1670–72
© The Royal Society **pg. 74**

Mary Beale's letter to Mrs Tillotson, 1667
The British Library Board, Harley Ms 6828, f.510 **pp. 78 & 85**

Allbrook farmhouse, Hampshire
British Listed Buildings/Rachel Davies **pg. 79**

Mary Beale, *Self portrait*, c. 1666
National Portrait Gallery, London **pg. 83**

Mary Beale, *Charles Beale*, c. 1666
Andrew Beale, Beale Hotels/St Edmundsbury Heritage Service **pg. 84**

Mary Beale, *Sir William Turner*, 1676–7. Bridewell Royal Hospital (King Edward's School, Witley) **pg. 89**

Jan van Leyden, *The Dutch raid on the Medway*, c. 1667–9
Rijksmuseum, Amsterdam **pp. 92–93**

Thomas Flatman, *Self portrait*, c. 1680-88
National Portrait Gallery, London **pg. 94**

William Morgan, Pall Mall, 1682
London Topographical Society **pg. 98**

Thomas Chambers after Mary Beale, *Mary Beale self-portrait with Charles Beale junior*, 1762
National Portrait Gallery, London **pg. 100**

Mary Beale, *Self portrait*, 1672
St Edmundsbury Heritage Service **pg. 100**

Mary Beale, *Lady Leigh as a Shepherdess*, c. 1676
St Edmundsbury Heritage Service **pg. 101**

Mary Beale, *Portrait of an unknown woman*, c. 1675–80
St Edmundsbury Heritage Service **pg. 102**

Mary Beale, *Self portrait*, c. 1680
Isherwood Fine Art **pg. 102**

John Thane after Mary Beale, *Thomas Wentworth, Earl of Strafford*, 1793
National Portrait Gallery, London **pg. 103**

Mary Beale, *Mrs James Long, née Susanna Strangways*, 1672
Private collection **pg. 106**

Mary Beale, *Mrs Thomas Strangways*, c. 1675
Private collection **pg. 106**

Isaac Fuller, *King Charles II and Jane Lane riding to Bristol*, c. 1660–72
National Portrait Gallery, London **pg. 107**

Mary Beale (attributed to), *The Countess of Shrewsbury* c. 1660
The Althorp collection **pg. 109**

Mary Beale, *1st Earl of Berkeley*, 1679
The Berkeley & Spechley Estates, Berkeley Castle **pg. 109**

Mary Beale (attributed to), *Lady Godolphin*, 1675
Andrew Beale, Beale Hotels/Peter Dyer **pg. 110**

Sir Peter Lely, *Bishop Symon Patrick*, 1668
National Portrait Gallery, London **pg. 113**

Mary Beale, *Two children in a landscape*, 1680s
Peter Harrison Fine Art Ltd, London **pg. 196**

Mary Beale, *Richard Goulston*, c. 1677
Wikimedia Commons **pg. 197**

Mary Beale, *A young boy*, c. 1682
© Victoria and Albert Museum, London **pg. 198**

Mary Beale, *Christopher Vane*, c. 1670s
© Raby Estate. Courtesy of Lord Barnard **pg. 198**

Mary Beale, *Elizabeth, Baroness Barnard, née Holles*, 1681. © Raby Estate. Courtesy of Lord Barnard **pg. 198**

Mary Beale, *Elizabeth Adams, née Hirst or Hurst as a shepherdess*, late 1660s. Philip Mould & Company **pg. 199**

Mary Beale, *A woman with jewels in her hair*, c. 1670s. Andrew Beale, Beales Hotels **pg. 200**

Mary Beale, *A woman in a brown dress*, c. 1670
Andrew Beale, Beales Hotels **pg. 200**

Mary Beale, *Barbara, Countess Castlemaine, Duchess of Cleveland*, 1670s. Andrew Beale, Beales Hotels **pg. 200**

Mary Beale, *Portrait of a gentleman*, c. 1670s
Peter Harrison Fine Art Ltd, London **pg. 201**

Mary Beale, *Bishop John Lake*, c. 1685
Wikimedia Commons **pg. 201**

Mary Beale, *A member of the Milton family*, 1670s
Wikimedia Commons. National Trust, Nostell Priory **pg. 201**

———

Recent research raises questions about the attribution to Mary Beale of the portraits on pages 24, 33, 56 lower, 109 top, 110, 153, 157,158 lower.

ABBREVIATIONS

BL: British Library, London

CBA: Charles Beale's almanacks 1677, 1681

DNB: *Dictionary of National Biography*, (1885–1901)

Evelyn: *The Dairy of John Evelyn*, ed. by E. S. De Beer, (2001)

GB: *Gilbert Burnet's History of My Own Time*, ed. by Osmund Airy, (1897–1900)

GVCBA: George Vertue's excerpts from Charles Beale's almanacks, published by the Walpole Society, (1930–38)

NPG: National Portrait Gallery, London

ODNB: *Oxford Dictionary of National Biography*, (2004)

Pepys: *The Diary of Samuel Pepys*, ed. by Robert Latham and William Matthews, (1970–83)

Rawlinson: Rawlinson Letters, Bodleian Library, Oxford

S. Woodford, *Liber:* Samuel Woodford, '*Liber Dolororus*', 1663–65, Ms Eng.misc.381, Bodleian Library, Oxford

S. Woodford, 'Memoirs': 'Memoirs of the most remarkable Passages of my Life long since collected', annotated copy of *A Paraphrase Upon the Psalms of David*, (1678), Ms 9494, New College, Oxford

WCA: Westminster City Archives

ACKNOWLEDGEMENTS

The research notes compiled by Richard Jeffree and Elizabeth Walsh bequeathed to the Heinz Archive and Library of the National Portrait Gallery, London, form the major corpus of information about Mary Beale. These notes fill twenty-seven boxes containing 211 files; I am grateful for access to them. Jeffree and Walsh hoped to publish a book about Mary Beale. The two colleagues died before this was achieved but I hope this biography fulfils the plans they laid some forty years ago.

Richard Jeffree was a partner with a firm specialising in interior design and textiles. He had no formal training in the history of art, nonetheless he acquired an extensive knowledge of British art and seventeenth-century artists in particular. His enthusiasm for Mary Beale was sparked by an article in the *Connoisseur* (1953) written by Elizabeth Walsh, whose own interest in Mrs Beale dated from 1948 when she was planning a series about famous women for the BBC. Subsequently, Jeffree and Walsh collaborated on a study of Beale which culminated in an exhibition, *The Excellent Mrs Mary Beale* (1975-6).

When Jeffree died in 1991 he left his collection of Mary Beale portraits to the National Art Collections Fund with the request that they should join four Beale portraits already owned by St Edmundsbury Borough Council. His executor, Anthony Frater, ensured that Jeffree's wishes were carried out.

This biography was conceived as the result of the purchase from the Geffrye Museum by my husband, Richard Hunting, of two exhibition catalogues featuring the work of Mary Beale: the first was Jeffree and Walsh's *The Excellent Mrs Mary Beale* (1975) and the second was by Tabitha Barber, *Mary Beale. Portrait of a seventeenth-century painter, her family and her studio* (1999). I was persuaded to pursue Mary Beale. Richard's computer skills, comments, proof reading and patience have contributed to this project from start to finish.

Tabitha Barber, curator of British art 1500–1700 at Tate Britain, is the expert on Mary Beale's work and I thank her for her encouragement. I am grateful to Dr Susie West of the Open University who arranged for St Michael's church, Walton, to be open. Andrew Beale was generous with his research and hospitality at West Lodge Park, Hertfordshire. Sheila O'Connell of the British Museum's department of prints and drawings and Ben Ridgeon at St Edmundsbury Heritage Service provided essential support.

I thank Lord Strathcarron, chairman of Unicorn Publishing Group, for his positive approach. Lucy Duckworth at Unicorn, Anna Hopwood, the book's designer, and Julia Casella who helped with picture research, have been a pleasure to work with. Dr Bendor Grosvenor was immediately enthusiastic about this book and I thank him for the Foreword.

Penelope Hunting

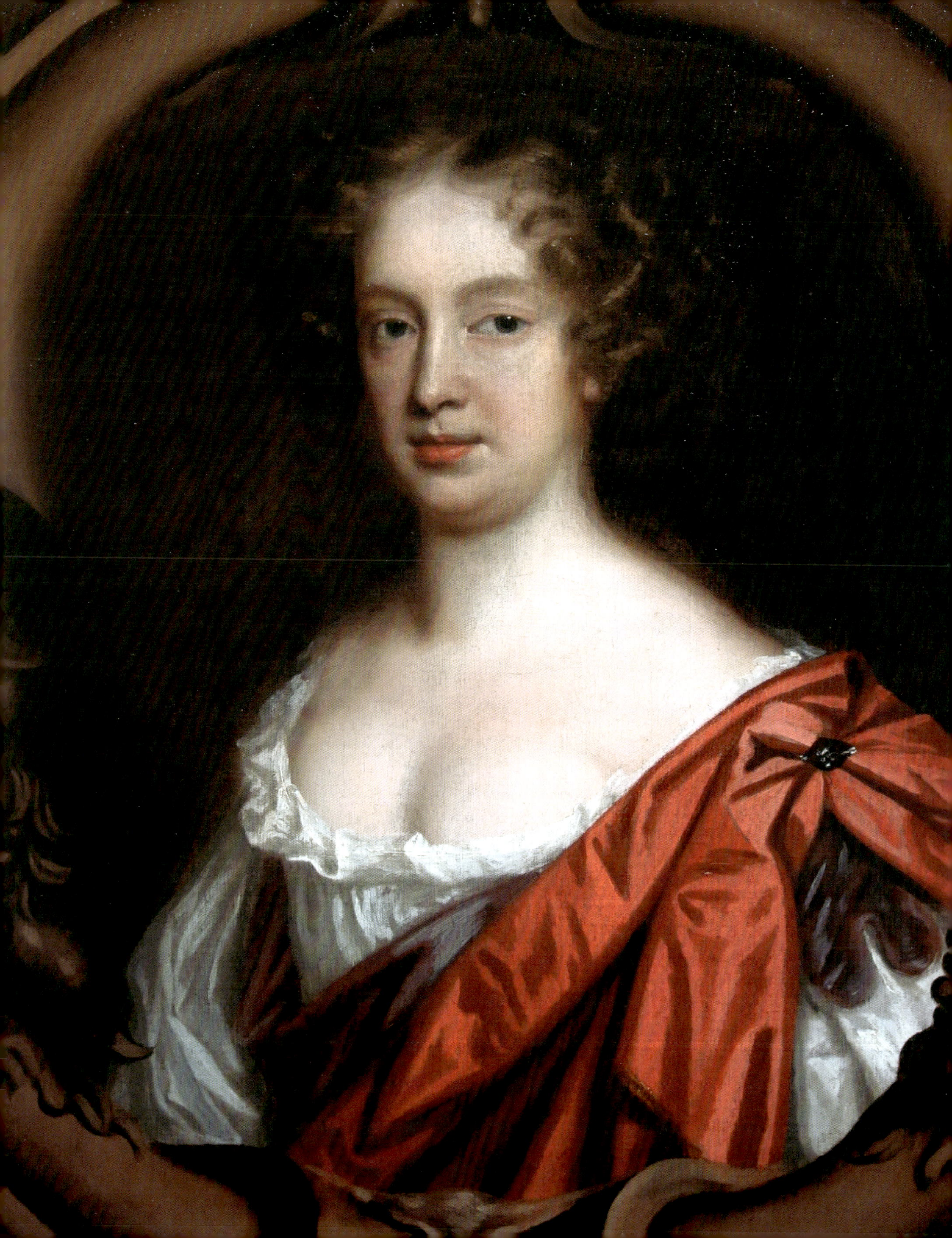

1. THE CRADOCKS AND THE BEALES

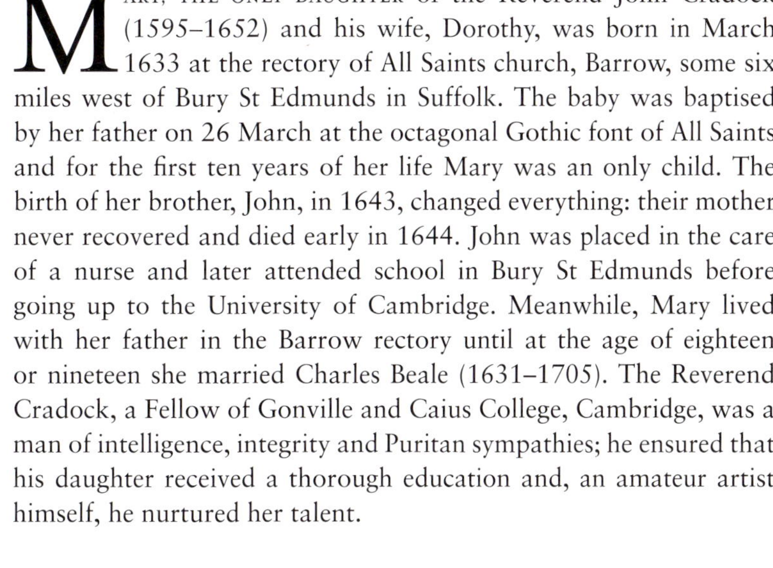

MARY, THE ONLY DAUGHTER of the Reverend John Cradock (1595–1652) and his wife, Dorothy, was born in March 1633 at the rectory of All Saints church, Barrow, some six miles west of Bury St Edmunds in Suffolk. The baby was baptised by her father on 26 March at the octagonal Gothic font of All Saints and for the first ten years of her life Mary was an only child. The birth of her brother, John, in 1643, changed everything: their mother never recovered and died early in 1644. John was placed in the care of a nurse and later attended school in Bury St Edmunds before going up to the University of Cambridge. Meanwhile, Mary lived with her father in the Barrow rectory until at the age of eighteen or nineteen she married Charles Beale (1631–1705). The Reverend Cradock, a Fellow of Gonville and Caius College, Cambridge, was a man of intelligence, integrity and Puritan sympathies; he ensured that his daughter received a thorough education and, an amateur artist himself, he nurtured her talent.

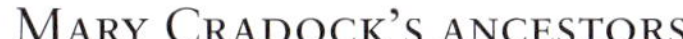

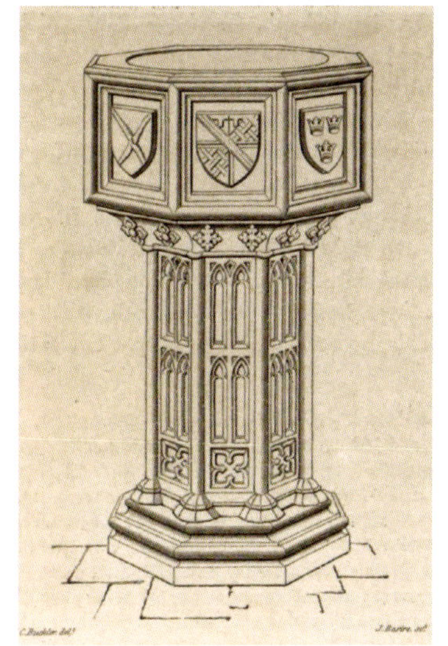

Mary Cradock was baptised by her father, the Reverend John Cradock, at All Saints church, Barrow, Suffolk, in 1633. A drawing of the font by J.C. Buckler, 1838

Opposite: Mary Beale, *Self portrait*, c. 1680

Mary Cradock's ancestors

The Cradocks were prosperous wool merchants from Staffordshire where Thomas and his son, Matthew (1520–c. 1590) owned large estates. In the early seventeenth century a younger Matthew Cradock (c. 1590–1641) embarked on a career in the City of London. His cousin, Elizabeth (1600–1661), cemented Cradock connections with the City and Westminster by marrying Alderman Richard Bennett and secondly Sir Heneage Finch.

In the first decade of the seventeenth century, Matthew Cradock and his brother, Zachary, were apprenticed to Sir Matthew Cockayne (1560–1626), a liveryman of the Worshipful Company of Skinners, number six or seven of the 'great twelve' City livery companies (the Skinners' order of precedence alternates with the Merchant Taylors', hence the idiom 'at sixes and sevens'). The introduction to Cockayne came from William Cradock of Staffordshire, Cockayne's factor at Hamburg and the father of Elizabeth, above. When Elizabeth's husband, Bennett, died in 1628 he left her £30,000, diamonds, chains of pearls and gold, a coach and four grey mares. The wealthy widow attracted several suitors before she chose Sir Heneage Finch, Speaker of the House of Commons, as her second husband in 1629. This Cradock/Finch marriage was to lead to commissions for Mary Beale for portraits of the Finch family.

Elizabeth Cradock's cousin, Matthew, signed his indentures to Sir Matthew Cockayne at Skinners' Hall on Dowgate Hill in 1609. Cockayne was a powerful figure in the City of London, a member of the major international trading companies, Master of the Skinners' Company three times and Lord Mayor 1619–20. Matthew's brother, Zachary, died while still an apprentice but Matthew completed his ten-year apprenticeship, during which time he lived at Cockayne's mansion in Broad Street. Once he had been trained in all aspects of the fur trade and been admitted a freeman of the Skinners' Company, Matthew was poised for a career as a London merchant. He duly made his way up the hierarchy of the Skinners' Company to be elected First Warden in 1640 (therefore in line to succeed as Master had he not died in 1641). While this Matthew Cradock was establishing a reputation as a City merchant, his cousin, also Matthew (1584–1636), MP and Mayor of Stafford, maintained the family's link with Staffordshire where he rebuilt Caverswall Castle.

Matthew Cradock's success and renown as a London merchant brought him wealth. He owned or part-owned eighteen trading vessels and, as a member of the East India Company, the Merchant Adventurers, the Levant Company, the Eastland Company, the Virginia Company and the Russia Company his activities ranged wide. His enterprising spirit prompted him to back the Massachusetts Bay Company on its foundation in 1627 and two years later he was chosen to be the first governor of the colony. His ships (one was named after his wife, Rebecca) transported settlers and provisions to Massachusetts where he founded a plantation on the Mystic River, the base for his trading activities in fur and tobacco, and for ship-building. Cradock must also be credited with contributing £50 towards the foundation of Harvard College (University) in 1636. Despite his interests and investments there, he never undertook the journey to New England, preferring to remain in St Swithin's Lane, within walking distance of the River Thames and the Custom House.

Matthew Cradock was a Puritan and he ensured that ministers accompanied the migrants to Massachusetts. At Westminster he supported his fellow Puritan John Pym in the parliaments of 1640, leading the opposition to King Charles I's taxes and impositions vociferously. Cradock's political career was brief: he died aged fifty-one, leaving a widow, Rebecca, who in 1643 married the theologian Dr Benjamin Whichcote (1609–1683), see page 151.

Matthew Cradock's nephews, Samuel (1621–1706) and Zachary (c. 1633–1695), were distant cousins and contemporaries of Mary Beale. Samuel was an influential tutor at Emmanuel College, Cambridge, from 1645 until 1656, the year he married Honoria, sister of the regicide George Fleetwood, and was presented with the living of North Cadbury, Somerset. His circumstances improved further when in 1657 he inherited the Cradock estate, Geesings (now Gesyns), at Wickhambrook, Suffolk, after the death of Walter Cradock. The Reverend Samuel Cradock was a nonconformist and was ejected as rector of North Cadbury in 1662. Undeterred, he founded an academy to train dissenters (see page 34).

Samuel Cradock's younger brother, Zachary, pursued a less controversial career as chaplain to the English church at Lisbon and later as a chaplain to King Charles II. He was painted by Mary Beale in 1672 soon after his election as a Fellow of Eton College where he was later Provost. He did not endear himself to Etonians, who derided his modest background and objected to his ban on scholars having wine hoisted to their rooms in baskets when they were gated.[1]

Mary Cradock's Suffolk roots

A branch of the Cradocks of Staffordshire settled in Suffolk in 1608 when the Reverend Richard Cradock (1562–1630), Mary Beale's grandfather, was presented with the living of All Saints, Barrow, by Sir John Heigham and Sir Clement Heigham MP, of Barrow Hall, a moated stronghold built by their ancestor, Sir Clement Heigham (1500–1571), Speaker of the House of Commons and a staunch Roman Catholic. On the other hand, his heirs John (1540–1626) and Clement (d. 1634), were zealous Protestants, determined to propagate their faith in west Suffolk and Richard Craddock was expected to play his part in this mission.

After graduating from Clare College, University of Cambridge, Richard Cradock was ordained and married Elizabeth Coney; her family appointed him vicar of Bassingthorpe in Lincolnshire. The Heighams lured him to Barrow and at the time of Sir Clement Heigham's death, the parish was being ministered to by Richard's son, the Reverend John Cradock, Mary Beale's father.

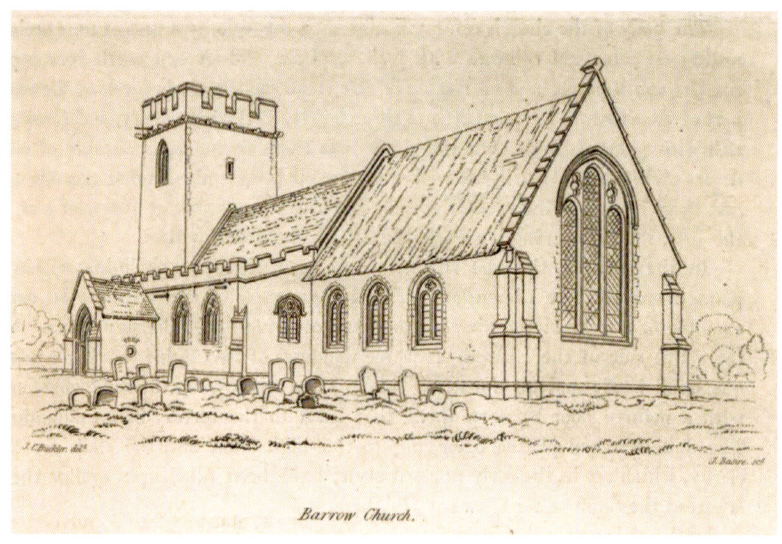

All Saints church, Barrow, Suffolk, drawn by J. C. Buckler, 1838

Of the four surviving children of Richard Cradock and his wife Elizabeth, John was the only son. He was schooled in Cambridge and went up to Gonville and Caius College in 1612, obtaining an MA and a fellowship. At university he formed an enduring friendship with Sir Edmund Bacon Bt (c. 1570–1649), one of a large family of landowners in Norfolk and Suffolk. Once John Cradock was ordained in 1628, Bacon offered him the living of Rickinghall Superior, a parish situated between Diss and Bury St Edmunds. It was probably through the Bacon family that John Cradock met Dorothy Brunton/ Brinton whom he married in April 1629 at the chapel of Botesdale-cum-Redgrave (part of the Bacon domain). On the death of his father the following year, John transferred to All Saints, Barrow, where he served as rector from 1630 until his death in 1652. The fourteenth-century church stands on the edge of a hill, and the rectory where his daughter Mary spent her childhood was nearby, a short distance from the houses that clustered around the village green.

The Reverend Richard Cradock's will of 1630 indicated that Barrow rectory was comfortably furnished; the family owned pictures, books, a treasured bedstead, and the rector kept bees (he left a 'skep of bees' to several beneficiaries). His 'loving son John Cradock of Redgrave' inherited 'all my books and papers in my study or elsewhere'. Richard's three daughters were not forgotten in his will: Priscilla was married to Richard Thach, a chandler of St Martin-in-the-Fields, London, and a member of the Salters'

Company; Mary was the wife of Elias Crabtree, the Puritan rector of Dickleburgh, south Norfolk, and Abigail was married to the Reverend Samuel Baker, the Puritan preacher at St Margaret Pattens and later at St Christopher-le-Stocks in the City of London. Baker was especially favoured by his father-in-law who left him 30s for a ring 'in token of my love to him'. A blind cousin who lived in the rectory, Cradock's godson, servants and the poor people of Barrow were other beneficiaries of Richard Cradock's will.[2]

Robert Beale of Barnes (1541–1601)

Charles Beale, who married Mary Cradock in 1652, was the great-nephew of the Elizabethan diplomat, Robert Beale, 'a political intellectual of remarkable erudition and sophistication'.[3] International scholar, linguist, Councillor of the North and Clerk of the Privy Council to Queen Elizabeth I, Robert Beale persuaded the Queen to sign the death warrant of her cousin, Mary Queen of Scots, judged guilty of plotting the assassination of Queen Elizabeth by the Court of the Star Chamber in October 1586. Robert Beale personally read the death warrant to the Queen of Scots prior to her execution at Fotheringhay Castle, Northamptonshire, in February 1587. Beale and Sir Francis Walsingham were convinced of Mary's guilt and that she posed a threat to the throne of England. Ironically, Beale had long been in negotiations with the Scottish Queen and had earned her respect: she presented him with a gold chain worth £65, little suspecting that he was engineering her execution.

Robert Beale was at the core of Elizabethan diplomacy, along with Lord Burghley and Walsingham. The latter was a neighbour of the Beales at Barn Elmes (Barnes, south of the Thames) and Walsingham's will (witnessed by Beale in 1589) mentioned twelve acres in Barnes already passed to Beale.[4] Milbourne House, Barnes Green, where the Beale family lived from 1592 and where Robert died in 1601, survives (the eighteenth-century façade hides late-sixteenth and seventeenth-century features). Robert Beale also owned an estate at Priors Marston, Warwickshire.

As Secretary to Sir Francis Walsingham, Queen Elizabeth I's ambassador at the French court, Beale was in Paris from 1570, returning to London in July 1572 to take up his appointment

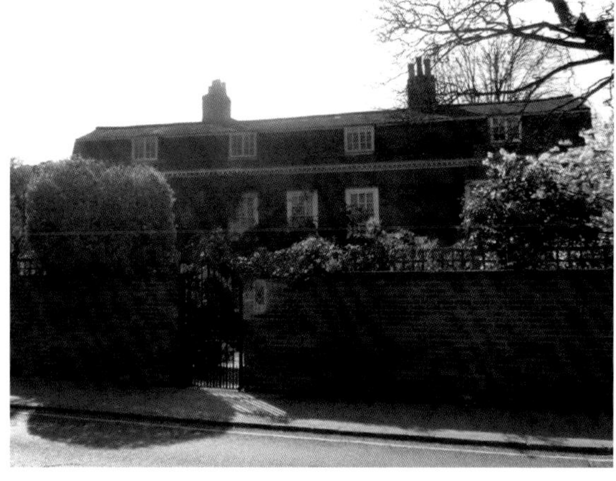

Milbourne House, Barnes, the home of Robert Beale, Clerk of the Privy Council to Queen Elizabeth I

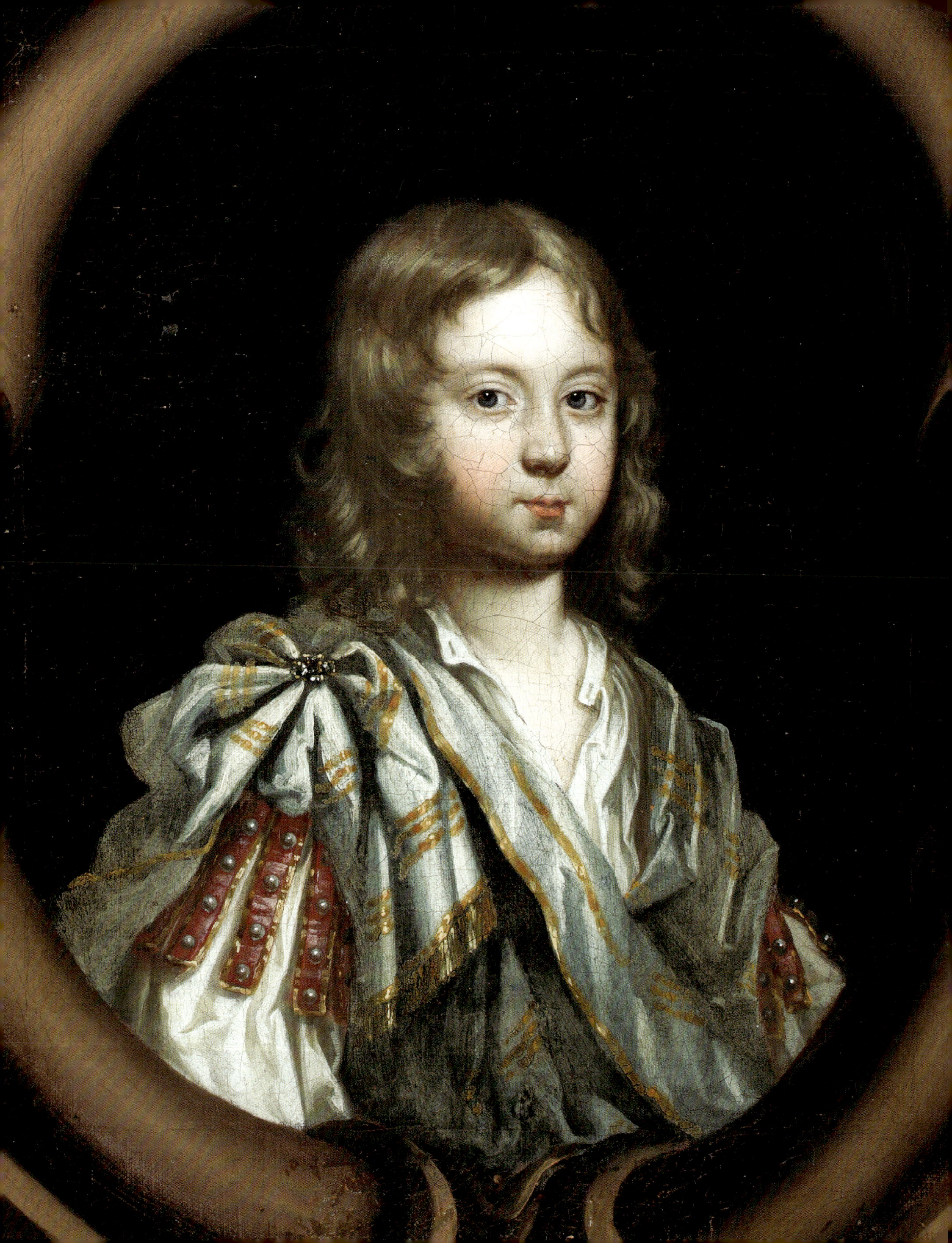

as Clerk of the Privy Council, which gave him personal and regular access to the Queen. It is not clear whether he was still in London or had returned to Paris by 24 August when the massacre of St Bartholomew's day took place. His wife Edith, née St Barbe, was certainly in Paris, sheltering at Walsingham's embassy (her sister Ursula was Walsingham's second wife and they were accompanied by the courtier and poet, Sir Philip Sidney who was to marry Walsingham's daughter). Edith Beale's 'Boke of Medecines' with a 'Book of Receipts of Cookerye' (1576-1693) provides the evidence. It is inscribed 'this is Eadithe Beales boke, vii of Aprill 1576', and on the second page, 'Grace Strode, Her book, Aprill the 29 1693 – This book was my Grandmother FitzJames Grandmother Beales who was at Paris in the Massicar of St Bartholumus day in the rain of Charles the 9th of France'.[5] Grace, who inherited the recipe book, was the daughter of Sir George Strode and Grace FitzJames. In 1695 she married the Hon. Henry Thynne (1675–1708), heir to Longleat House, Wiltshire, bringing with her a dowry of £20,000. Mary Beale painted Henry Thynne as a boy with chubby cheeks; as an adult he became obese, causing his sudden death at the age of thirty-three (a post mortem revealed that his heart was a lump of fat and blood and his liver was wasted). His mother Frances, Viscountess Weymouth, and several more members of the Thynne family sat for Mrs Beale in the 1670s and 1680s.[6] Likewise, the FitzJames/Beale connection led to Mary Beale's portraits of Katherine FitzJames, her sister Eleanor and Eleanor's husband, William Freeman, in 1677.[7]

The matriarchs of the Beale family handed down their medicinal and culinary recipes, from Edith Beale to Katherine Beale to Grace Strode, and the recipe book was inherited in due course by Grace's granddaughter, the 1st Duchess of Northumberland.

The killing of Protestants on St Bartholomew's day in 1572, when at least 2,000 were massacred in Paris alone, was seared in the collective memory of the Beale family whose sons were regularly given the name Bartholomew. For the time being, Robert Beale applied his mind to the events of the day and the possible repercussions by writing 'A Discourse after the great murder in Paris and other places in France, August 1572', probably intended for Lord Burghley's eyes.[8] More personal was Beale's 'Treatise of the office of a counsellor and principall secretarie to her majestie'[9] which advised his successors how to manage Queen Elizabeth I: 'when her highness is angry or not well disposed, trouble her not with any matter which

Opposite: Mary Beale, *The Hon. Henry Thynne, eldest son of 1st Viscount Weymouth*, c. 1680

you desire to have done',[10] (although if the business was urgent Beale insisted on her attention, headache or no headache). Beale's brilliant career faltered after 1587 on account of his involvement with the execution of the Queen of Scots: 'my name was made odious to the whole world for carrying down the commission for the execution of the Scottish Queen,' he wrote to Sir Robert Cecil in 1599, pleading for 'relief of his necessities'.[11] After twenty-eight years' service, Beale claimed he received mean fees and was not able to pay his debts or provide for his wife and children; he denied rumours of double dealing and dissembling. To add to his difficulties, Beale's outspoken puritanism and opposition to Bishop Whitgift led to his expulsion from Court and the House of Commons in the 1590s when he was placed under house arrest. He died at Barnes and was buried at All Hallows, London Wall, where the family maintained a pew.

Robert and Edith Beale had two sons and nine daughters;[12] the widowed Edith was living with their daughter, Katherine Stephens (b. 1587), at Eastington manor, near Stroud, Gloucestershire, at the time of her death in 1628 and she is commemorated at the local church, St Michael and All Angels. Another daughter, Margaret (1583–1625), married Sir Henry Yelverton, judge and politician. She inherited Robert Beale's invaluable documents for the history of Elizabethan diplomacy, now in the safekeeping of the British Library.

Charles Beale's parents

The family tradition of public service continued with Bartholomew Beale (1583–1660), nephew of the Elizabethan diplomat, who held a position in the Clerk of the Signet's office. Bartholomew's marriage to Katherine (c. 1590–1657, daughter of Edward Beale, a London merchant) in 1611 is recorded on an impressive marble monument by Thomas Burman at St Michael's church, Walton, Buckinghamshire. As the inscription points out, Bartholomew and Katherine were 'the Happy Uniters & Restorers of Two Ancient, but almost extinct Familys who till then were Different Houses, though bearing the same Name'. While Bartholomew traced his ancestry to Robert Beale, Katherine was descended from William (d. 1600) and Alice Beale (d. 1629, née Parkington) of Boxford, Suffolk, who were married at St Dunstan in the East, London, in 1588. William and Alice had three children: Theodore (the royalist curate of Boxford, rector of Ashbocking and finally of St Michael's, Walton), Sara (who married Cockayne, a Goldsmith) and Katherine, the wife of Bartholomew

Beale, hence Mary Beale's mother-in-law. The inscription pays tribute to the couple:

> They enjoyed each other in Wedlock XLVI yeares III Monthes. Happy longer then others use to live. The Religious Parents of VII Sonnes and II Daughters. By their Death may bee seen the Triumphs of the Grave, as those of Piety & Virtue were in their lives. Hee dyed at London XV June MDCLX, aged LXXVI years. Shee dyed at Walton XVI August MDCLVII aged LXVII years. Henry Beale & Charles Beale The Eldest & Youngest Sonnes of them who survive, To the Pious & Beloved Memory of their Honoured Parents, Erected this Monument.

The eldest son, Henry, died before the monument was completed

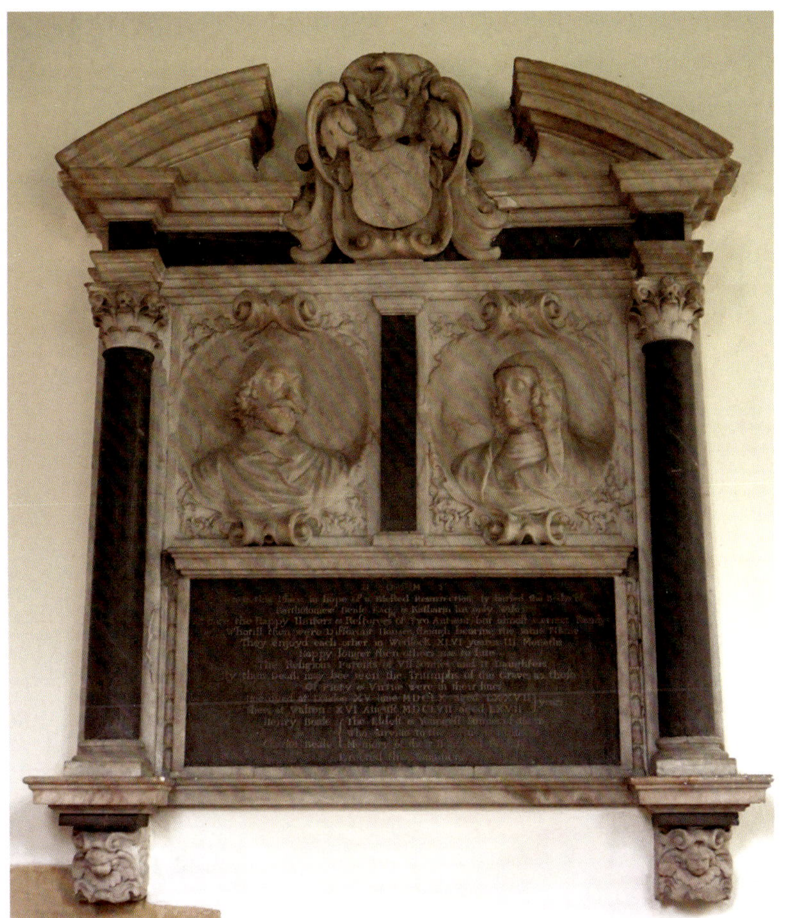

Monument to Bartholomew and Katherine Beale at St Michael's church, Walton, Buckinghamshire. It was commissioned from Thomas Burman by Henry and Charles Beale in 1672

and Burman himself died in March 1674, whereupon Charles Beale paid £45 owing to Burman's widow, Rebekah, then in charge of the Burman workshop in Drury Lane, Covent Garden.[13]

Bartholomew and Katherine Beales' second son, Bartholomew, also died before his parent's monument was completed. He pursued a lucrative career as an Auditor of the Imprests of the Treasury with responsibility for expenditure at the Navy Office, in which capacity he liaised with Samuel Pepys, a distant relation. 'Cousin Auditor' as the family called him, and his wife, Elizabeth, lived in Hatton Garden when in London and maintained a country estate on the Shropshire/Herefordshire borders where Elizabeth's family originated. 'Cousin Auditor' sat for his portrait by Mary Beale in 1664, 'very happily' and the result was pronounced to be 'exceeding like'.[14]

The youngest surviving son of Bartholomew and Katherine Beale, Charles, lacked prospects and ambition. He indulged his artistic tastes by touring Italy and then married a vicar's daughter who aspired to be a professional artist. Charles's only appointment, as Deputy Clerk of the Patents Office, ended in his dismissal in 1664. Having inherited a joint interest in his parents' manor house at Walton, he surrendered this in 1668. Thereafter Charles devoted himself to the career of his wife, Mary, 'My Dearest Heart'.[15]

Suffolk artists

Mary Beale's father, the Reverend John Cradock, was one of a côterie of early seventeenth-century Suffolk artists. His patron, Sir Edmund Bacon, was an amateur artist who bequeathed two paintings and his artists' tools to Cradock. Sir Edmund was one of the dynasty descended from the lawyer Sir Nicholas Bacon (1510–1579), Lord Keeper of the Great Seal and Privy Councillor to Queen Elizabeth I. Sir Edmund and John Cradock held similar political and religious views and were both amateur artists. Bacon's will of 1648 left to 'Mr John Cradock, minister of Barrowe my great grinding-stonne of purfure with the muller to it, and the little grinding-stonne of purfure with the muller to it' (a stone and muller were used to grind and mix pigments); 'purfure' (porphyry) was a valuable red/purple stone. 'I give him alsoe my two perspectives of Saint Marke hanging in the chamber of my laboritary'.[16]

Sir Nathaniel Bacon of Culford (1585–1627) was the most talented of this group of Suffolk artists. The grandson of the Elizabethan lawyer, and Sir Edmund Bacon's kinsman, Nathaniel grew up at Redgrave Hall, which his family had purchased from the Crown in 1542. He inherited Brome Hall after his marriage in 1614, also Culford Hall, four miles from Bury St Edmunds, where he chose to live. Privileged and gifted, Bacon's still lifes and portraits of the 1620s have earned him recognition as 'the most accomplished English amateur artist of the seventeenth century'.[17] He was a gardener, particularly knowledgeable about the colours to be derived from plants. He is credited with 'inventing' a 'pinke' (yellow) pigment, with assistance from John Fenn in London, the colour seller who also supplied Mary Beale's father and her husband, Charles, with pigments. Charles 'was told by Mr Ffen when he once ground some of my father Cradock's pink that he did grind for Sir Nathaniel Bakon a rare green colour which he called Green pink and I imagine it was made of Greenweed [*Genista tinctoria vulgaris*] before it came into flower'.[18] 'Bacon's pink' was used by the miniaturist Peter Oliver, and Charles Beale experimented with the pigment in order to supply Mary with the best colour.

Mary's father admired the work of Robert Walker (1599–1658), portraitist to John Evelyn, Oliver Cromwell and parliamentarians of the 1640s, so he commissioned Walker to paint his portrait. This was inherited by Mary and Charles Beale who owned other portraits by Walker and several by Sir Peter Lely.[19] Walker and/or Lely have been identified as the most likely drawing masters to the young Mary Beale (see pages 31, 37, 38). Lely's family name was van der Faes and he assumed the pseudonym Lely from a sign or decoration of a lily on a family property in The Hague (contemporaries sometimes spelled his name 'Lilly'). He was in London by 1643 and was soon 'face painting' courtiers and beautiful women, despite the civil war. He is

Sir Nathaniel Bacon Bt, *Self portrait*, c. 1620

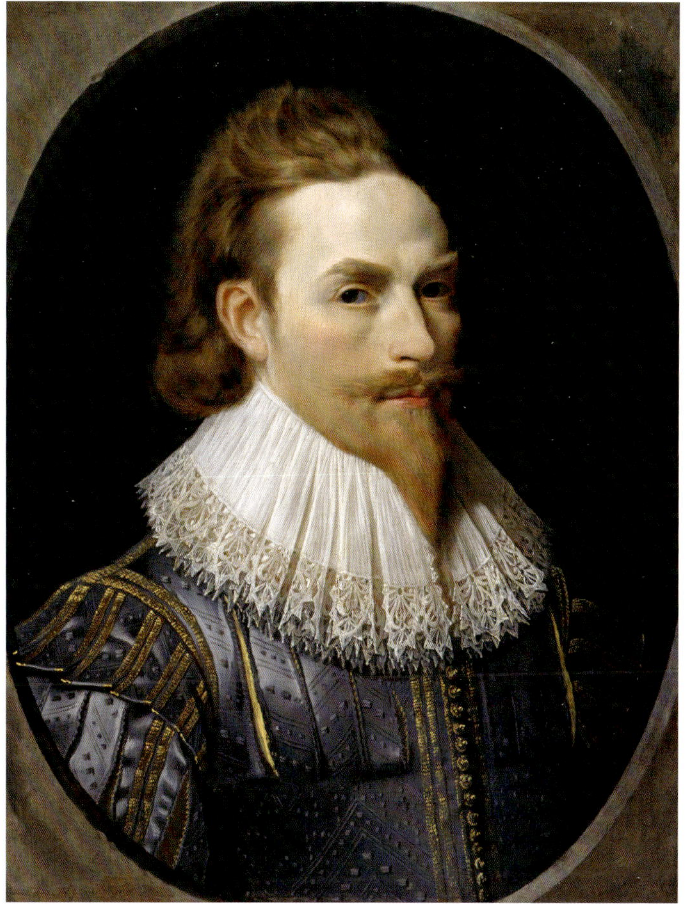

said to have visited Suffolk when he may have met John Cradock and his daughter, Mary. Lely, Walker and Cradock were freemen of the Worshipful Company of Painter-Stainers' of London: Lely was admitted to the Company in 1647, followed by John Cradock (1648) and fellow artists Robert Walker (1650), Francis Barlow (1650) and John Baptist Gaspars (1653).

The Reverend John Cradock was in London in July 1648, visiting Painters' Hall in Little Trinity Lane in order to take up the freedom of the Company and to present 'a piece of painting of his owne makeinge wch he gave unto this company consisting of variety of fruits, viz. apricocks, quinces, ffilberts, Grapes, Apls and sortes of fruites and was also at this Court made free of the said company'.[20] In an otherwise bleak environment the Painter-Stainers' Company increased its art collection by accepting the work of newly admitted freemen. Unfortunately, Cradock's still life perished, either when Painters' Hall burnt down in the great fire of 1666 or in May 1941 when the Hall was destroyed by enemy action.

Matthew Snelling (1621–1678) was another Suffolk artist who may have influenced Mary Cradock. Snelling lived at Little Horringer Hall, Horringer, following the marriage of his widowed mother, Mary, to Ambrose Blagge in 1625. Mary was one of the Norths of Mildenhall, while the Blagges were related to the Herveys of Ickworth House, and were neighbours of the Jermyns of Rushbrooke. These Suffolk families were geographically close and personally connected. Horringer was in the adjoining parish to All Saints, Barrow, where John Cradock lived with his children, so it is highly likely that Snelling knew Mary Cradock before her marriage to Charles Beale. Possibly Snelling gave Mary drawing lessons – he taught drawing to members of the Gawdy family in Bury St Edmunds from around 1655 and was renowned as 'a gentleman & seldom painted unless for ladies, with whom he was a mighty favourite & a gallant'.[21] When Mary was endeavouring to establish herself as a portrait painter in the 1650s, Snelling presented her with two packets of 'pinke'.[22]

Sir John Gawdy Bt of West Harling, Norfolk, (1639–1709), having been instructed by Snelling, progressed to Sir Peter Lely's studio in London with the intention of becoming a professional portrait painter. Responsibilities to the country estates he inherited in 1660 precluded this, although Gawdy continued to paint occasionally. He was a deaf mute, handsome and sociable, as John Evelyn reported after enjoying a dinner in his company at Euston Hall in September

1677, 'a very handsome person, but quite dumb; yet very intelligent by signes & a very fine painter'.[23] It is plausible that Mary Cradock received instruction in drawing and painting from Snelling, along with Gawdy; Gawdy's self portrait of 1674–5, set within an oval surround decorated with bunched fruit, bears comparison to Mary Beale's compositions.

The artist Nathaniel Thach (1617– c.1659), John Cradock's nephew, was baptised by his grandfather, the Reverend Richard Cradock, at All Saints, Barrow, in July 1617. Nathaniel would have stayed at Barrow rectory on visits to his grandparents, uncle and cousins, and John Cradock thought well enough of Thach as a 'picture drawer' to leave him his artists' materials. Brought up by his parents Richard and Priscilla, in London, Thach fled to The Hague during the civil war, where he found work (see page 34). He fades into obscurity after 1652 when his father left him £10 (had he returned to London he would surely have been part of the Beale/Woodford/Flatman circle).

A Suffolk artist called Thomas Blemwell/Bramwell of Bury St Edmunds was said to have been a friend of Sir Peter Lely. He painted the Hon. John North (one of ten children of Baron Dudley North of Suffolk) when John (a contemporary of Mary Cradock's brother) was a boy at King Edward VI's grammar school, Bury St Edmunds. The North family found Blemwell 'a civil and well-bred gentleman, very well accepted and employed in the town and neighbourhood'.[24] Elizabeth Walsh, whose research into Mary Beale dated from 1948 when she was planning a series about famous women for the BBC, thought it possible that Blemwell was Mary Cradock's first drawing master.[25]

Encouragement from her father, the example of her father's patron, Sir Edmund Bacon, possibly instruction from Robert Walker, Matthew Snelling, Thomas Blemwell or Nathaniel Thach, stimulated Mary Cradock's interest in painting. The art historian George Vertue (1684–1756) claimed that Sir Peter Lely 'first put his pencil in her hand before she was married',[26] and that she may have received instruction from Walker.[27]

Royalists versus parliamentarians

At the outbreak of civil war in 1642 the county of Suffolk supported Oliver Cromwell, and Bury St Edmunds was established as the centre of the parliamentarian Eastern Association. Nevertheless, the majority of the county's landowners were royalists, and confrontations between the opposing parties were violent, fuelled by politics, religion and the financial demands of Cromwell's regime. The Stour Valley riots broke out in August 1642 and in the same month Long Melford House was sacked by parliamentary troops. In this threatening situation, the Reverend John Cradock was fortunate to be approved by the parliamentarian party and given the title of Elder, with licence to raise troops and supplies locally if required.

In January 1643 Cromwell's troops stormed Hengrave Hall, near Bury St Edmunds, the seat of the Earl and Countess Rivers and a stronghold of Catholic royalists. The Rivers' daughter, Penelope, Lady Hervey of Ickworth (1593–1661), defended her family's properties. When parliamentarian soldiers invaded Hengrave Hall, forced open the armoury and confiscated the contents, she confronted them, and during the civil war she managed both the Hengrave and Ickworth estates which were vulnerable to sequestration and severe taxes. A portrait of her wearing widow's weeds is attributed to Mary Beale (see page 56).

In the spring of 1644 Cromwell's forces tightened their hold on East Anglia with raids on Little Saxham. This only served to provoke the royalist Henry Bennet, 1st Earl of Arlington and Viscount Thetford (1618–1685), a neighbour of the Cradocks. Arlington fought for King Charles I at Andover in 1644 and was wounded on the nose, giving him a scar he was proud to display. Arlington's only daughter, Isabella (1667–1723), was pledged in marriage at the age of five to Henry FitzRoy (1663–1690), the illegitimate son of King Charles II and Barbara Villiers. In 1679 when Isabella was twelve, the pair were 'remarried' at the King's insistence: 'there was no going back & this sweetest, hopefullest, most beautifull child & most virtuous too, was Sacrificed to a boy, that had been rudely bred, without anything to encourage them but His Majesties pleasure'.[28] FitzRoy, later 1st Duke of Grafton, died after being wounded at the storming of Cork, and in 1698 Isabella married Sir Thomas Hanmer Bt (1677–1746), Speaker of the House of Commons and a Shakespearian scholar. Isabella's portrait by Mary Beale is at Euston Hall, Suffolk, the estate she inherited from her father. The Earl of Arlington's mother, Dorothy Croft of Little Saxham Hall, allied with the neighbouring Jermyn family of Rushbrooke Hall and the Herveys of Hengrave to oppose the parliamentarians in Suffolk. In May 1648 opposition became widespread with a royalist uprising at Bury St Edmunds where the townspeople set up a maypole and shouted 'for

Opposite: Mary Beale, *Isabella, 1st Duchess of Grafton*, c. 1688-93

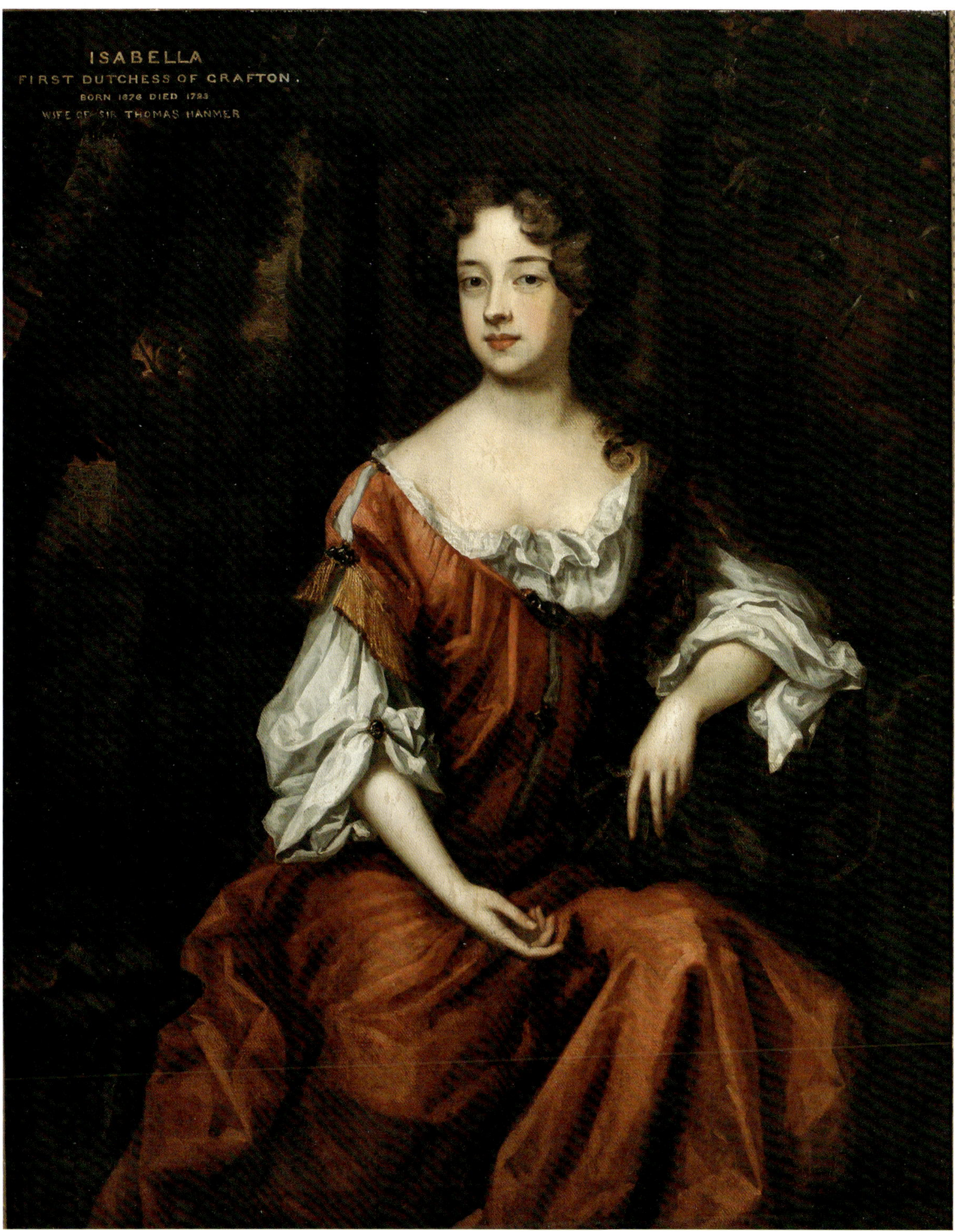
ISABELLA
FIRST DUTCHESS OF CRAFTON.
BORN 1676 DIED 1723
WIFE OF SIR THOMAS HANMER

God and King Charles'.

Mary Cradock was nine years old when parliamentarian soldiers first reached her neighbourhood. Riots, skirmishes, the confiscation of property, arrests and strict surveillance pervaded the county but the major battles of the civil war raged elsewhere. By the time the newly married Mary Beale left Suffolk in 1652, King Charles I had been executed and his son Charles II had been defeated at the battle of Worcester. In December 1653 Oliver Cromwell was made Lord Protector of the Commonwealth. The monarchy and the House of Lords had been abolished and power lay with Cromwell's Council of State.

The Cradock family was divided by personal loyalties to the King or to the Lord Protector. The Puritan/parliamentarian contingent was headed by the Reverend John Cradock's sister, Mary, and her husband, the Puritan Elias Crabtree (1591–1662). The Reverend Samuel Cradock (1621–1706), a nonconformist, married Honoria Fleetwood (1628–1709) whose family included a regicide and the mainstay of the parliamentarian army, General Charles Fleetwood. Following ejection from his living under the Act of Uniformity in 1662, Samuel Cradock founded an academy to train dissenting young men in philosophy and theology at Badmondisfield Hall, near Geesings in Suffolk.

Other members of the Cradock family defied their Puritan/nonconformist relations by supporting the royalist cause. The Reverend John Cradock's sister, Abigail, married the Reverend Samuel Baker in 1623, rector of St Christopher-le-Stocks in London and a canon of Windsor until he was forced to resign in 1640. He retreated to Essex but did not escape the censure of the Puritan party, which sequestered his living and confined him to the Tower of London in 1645.

Nathaniel Thach, Mary Beale's first cousin, felt threatened by the civil war, so fled to The Hague, where he found patrons, notably Elizabeth Stuart, Queen of Bohemia, (1596–1662), sister of King Charles I, who married Frederick V, Prince Palatine of the Rhine in 1613. Thach painted high quality miniatures of their children and was employed by several royal families resident at The Hague.

The Cradock's neighbour in Suffolk, Matthew Snelling, shared the political views of his step-brother, Colonel Thomas Blagge (1613–1660), groom of the bedchamber to Charles I and Charles II. Blagge was active during the civil war as Governor of Wallingford

Castle and he fought with the King at Worcester. His daughter, Margaret, who married Sidney, 1st Earl of Godolphin, was painted for the Countess of Berkeley in 1674, and the portrait has been attributed to Mary Beale (see page 110).

The Beale family was likewise split by differing political and religious views. Charles Beale's two sisters married men of opposite persuasions. His eldest sister, Margaret, married John Bridges/Brydges in 1636, a Colonel in the parliamentarian army and Governor of Warwick Castle in 1645 (he was alleged to have captured twenty-five waggons of the King's treasures valued at £50,000). Charles's sister-in-law, Elizabeth, shared these affiliations. She was the daughter of Colonel Thomas Hunt of Shropshire, a parliamentary soldier. The Colonel and his son kept thirty horses ready for combat at their house, which was a hotbed of Presbyterianism.

On the royalist side of the family, Charles Beale's sister Katherine was married to Nicholas Smythe of Theddlethorpe, Lincolnshire, a barrister whose estate was impounded by the parliamentarians as a result of Smythe's 'delinquency' in assisting the royalist garrison at Mablethorpe. Mary Beale painted several of the Smythe family, beginning with John in 1664, followed by Charles, Mary and Nicholas in 1681.

Charles Beale's uncle, the Reverend Theodore Beale (1566–1652) was a rampant royalist and suffered for it. He was rector of Boxford in Suffolk, then from 1639 to 1644 of All Saints, Ashbocking, near Ipswich, where he hung the royal arms on the church wall with the inscription 'God save the King', a bold statement of allegiance to Charles I. As a result he was sequestered of his living and faced fifteen charges levied by the parliamentarians for, among other offences, his support for the Earl of Strafford, for 'inveighing against the rebellion and the Parliament... and for being disguised in Drink'. To the Puritans, Beale was 'a Solemne Cringer and bower' to the altar; he had refused to lend money to the cause and was accused of being 'an alehouse-haunter'.[29] Deprived of his living Beale took refuge at a chantry, then found a home at Walton as rector of the Beale's parish church, St Michael's, where he was buried in 1652.

Dr William Beale, Master of St John's College, Cambridge, in 1633 and Vice Chancellor of the University 1634–35, was related to Charles Beale and was another blatant royalist who fell foul of the Cromwellian regime. Troops surrounded his college in 1644 when he was arrested, accused of giving the college plate to finance King

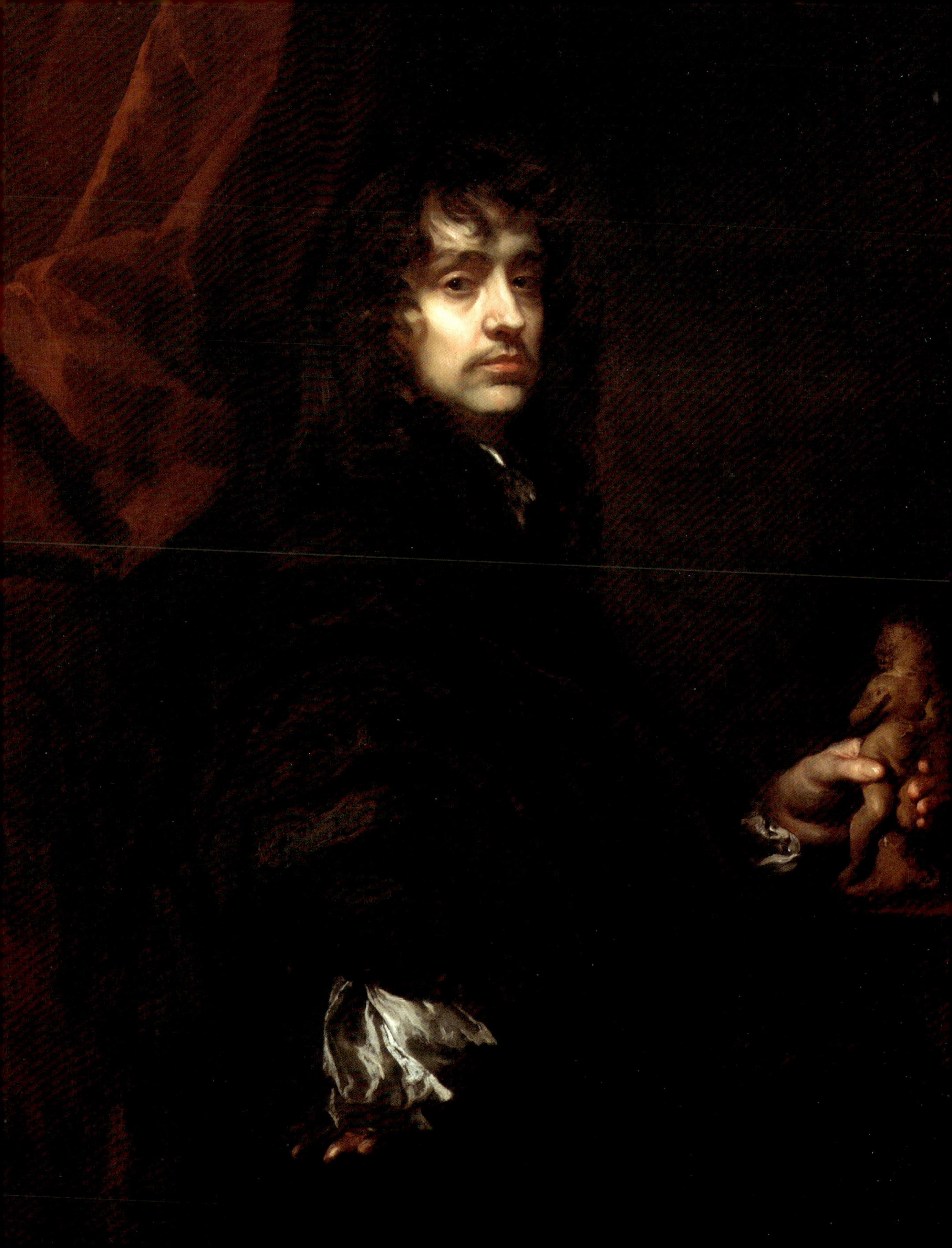

Charles I's forces and of enriching the college chapel with 'Romish' adornments. Dr Beale and his colleagues were confined to the Tower of London. On release, Beale joined King Charles I at the royalist headquarters in Oxford in 1645; he was briefly Dean of Ely before going into exile and dying in Madrid in 1651.

Mary Beale's mentors

After the death of Sir Anthony Van Dyck in 1641, William Dobson (1611–1646) came into his own as the favourite portrait painter of the royal family and cavaliers who were shored up at the royalist stronghold in Oxford. Dobson was soon outshone by Peter Lely whose success as a 'face painter' to the royal family and courtiers attracted numerous pupils and assistants: Prosper Henry Lankrink, Frederick Sonnius, Joseph Buckshorn, Thomas Hawker, Nicholas Largillière, Jan van der Eyden, Bartholomew Fleshier, Henry Tilson, John Greenhill, John Baptist Gaspars and William Wissing are known to have worked in his Covent Garden studio. On arriving in London in 1655 or early 1656 Mary Beale became a neighbour of Lely in Covent Garden but there is no evidence that she was his pupil at that time. On the contrary, the fact that she was keen to watch him at work and learn from his methods in the 1670s indicates that she had not previously had this opportunity. She certainly studied his portraits and admired his style, imitating the postures of his figures and accepting commissions for copies of his original portraits.

George Vertue claimed that Lely's encouragement of Mary Beale commenced before her marriage when she was living in Suffolk. Lely's half-length portrait of Mary, with 'several pictures of the Family of Beals by Mr Lilly' were hanging on the walls of their house at Hind Court by 1661.[30] Mary's portrait by Lely was in the sale of Peter Cross's collection of paintings in December 1722, when it was described as 'a fine original picture of Mrs Beal, a small half-length painted by Sir Peter Lilly in his best manner. She was a great favourite of his'. The portrait was sold to Mr Raynard for £16 10s.[31]

The claim that Lely first met the young Mary Cradock in Suffolk gains credibility with Roger North's account of a visit Lely made to Suffolk. North (1651–1734), lawyer and MP, owned several paintings by Lely and loaned him money from time to time. North lived in Suffolk not far from the Cradocks, with interludes at Kirtling in Cambridgeshire. He was Lely's solicitor and executor, and was painted by Mary Beale around 1677 and by Lely in 1680.

Opposite: Sir Peter Lely, *Self portrait*, c. 1660

In his autobiography North remembered that Lely visited Bury St Edmunds to see his sister and 'shewd himself, in all his beaux-aires at church and so was the subject of all the afternoon visits to be canvast [scrutinised] and read upon'. If not on this occasion, Lely could have met the Reverend John Cradock at Painters' Hall in London, or through the artist Thomas Blemwell of Bury St Edmunds or during one of his sojourns 'at gentlemen's houses thereabouts'.[32] The art connoisseur Horace Walpole supported Vertue's claim that Lely knew Mary Cradock before her marriage to Charles Beale in 1652. 'The master was supposed to have had a tender attachment to her but as he was reserved in communicating to her all the resources of his pencil, it probably was a gallant passion, rather than a successful one'.[33]

The author and art historian C. H. Collins Baker shared Vertue's view that Mary Beale might have studied under Robert Walker, who painted her father, her husband and herself.[34] Walker was highly regarded by parliamentarians and he enjoyed the patronage of Thomas Howard, Earl of Arundel (1585–1646), a major art collector who provided lodgings for Walker at Arundel House in the Strand. Could Walker have instructed Mary after her arrival in London in 1655/1656, prior to his death in 1658? Vertue was inclined to think 'she had some instructions by Walker at first in drawing & painting'.[35]

A marriage and a death

Charles Beale's ancestors and Mary Cradock's forebears shared Suffolk roots and connections with the City of London. The coat of arms of 'Beale of Woodbridge, Suffolk' was drawn up in 1572, the year Robert Beale was appointed Clerk of the Privy Council to Queen Elizabeth I.[36] Robert Beale travelled widely and settled at Barnes, Surrey, while maintaining a strong connection to All Hallows church, London Wall, where Charles Beale's parents were married in 1611. Charles's maternal grandmother, Alice, married William Beale of the Salters' Company and William left his Suffolk estate to Alice, who was buried at Boxford in 1629. As for the Cradocks, the name was well-known in the City due to the merchant Skinner, Matthew Cradock. His grandson, Walter (1584–1657), inherited Geesings, Wickhambrook, Suffolk, from his mother, and in 1608 the Reverend Richard Cradock became the first of five Cradock rectors of Suffolk parishes.

While Mary Cradock was living at the Barrow rectory with her father, the patriarch of the family was Walter Cradock of Geesings,

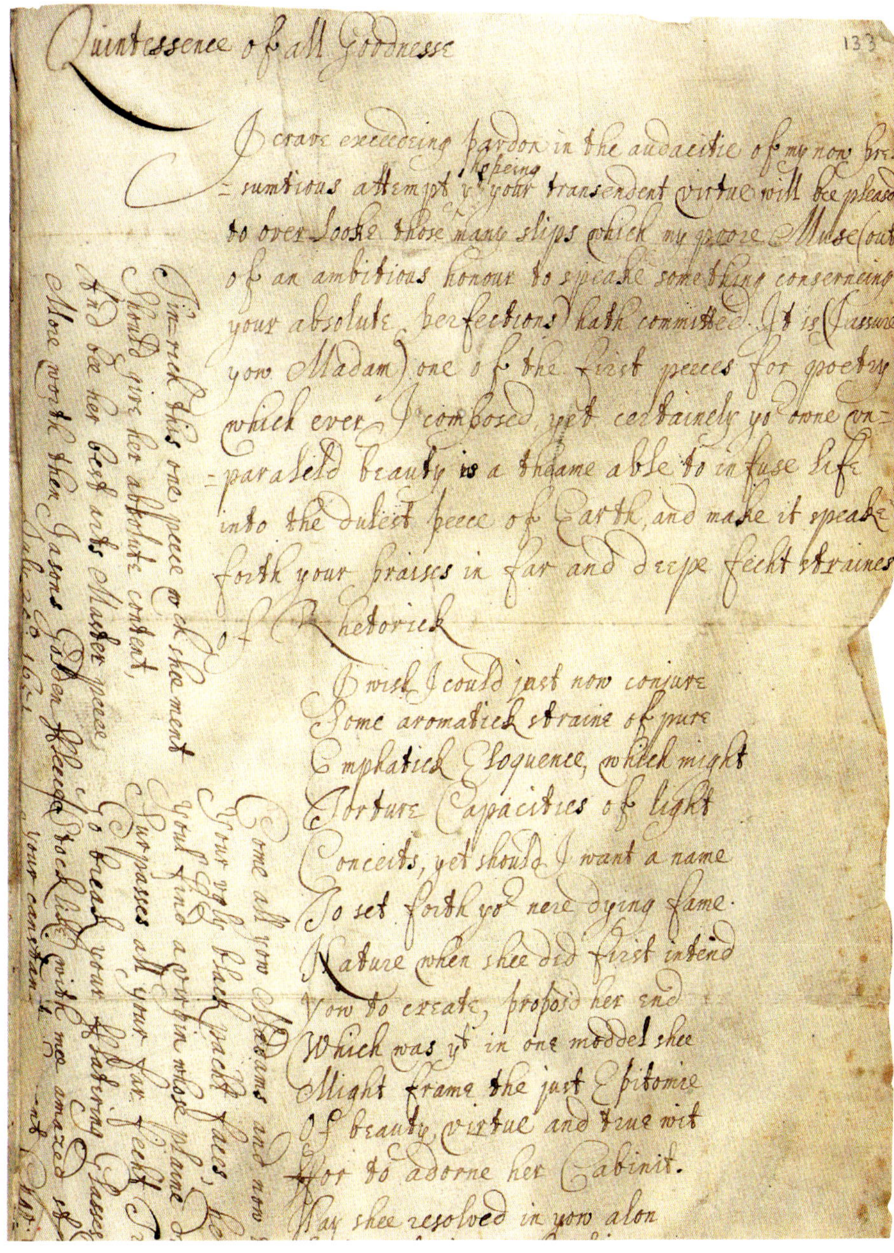

Quintessence of all Goodnesse

I crave exceeding pardon in the audacitie of my now pre=
=sumtious attempt hopeing yt your transendent virtue will bee pleased
to over looke those many slips which my poore Muse (out
of an ambitious honour to speake something conserning
your absolute perfections) hath committed. It is (I assure
you Madam) one of the first peeces for poetry
which ever I composed, yet certainely yor owne un=
=paraleld beauty is a theame able to infuse life
into the dulest peece of Earth, and make it speake
forth your praises in far and deepe fecht straines
of Rhetorick

I wish I could just now conjure
Some aromatick straine of pure
Emphatick Eloquence, which might
Torture Capacities of light
Conceits, yet should I want a name
To set forth yor nere dying fame.
Nature when shee did first intend
You to create, propos'd her end
Which was yt in one moddel shee
Might frame the just Epitomie
Of beauty, virtue and true wit
For to adorne her Cabinit.
Nay shee resolved in you alon

Charles Beale's love-letter to Mary Cradock, 25 July 1651

an ancient moated manor house. This was the likely backdrop for the meeting of Charles Beale and Mary Cradock (Walter would have known all the local families and their connections). By July 1651 Charles was courting Mary, to whom he wrote a love-letter, addressed to the 'Quintessence of all Goodnesse. I crave exceeding pardon in the audacitie of my now presumtious attempt hopeing yt your transendent virtue will bee pleasd to overlooke those many slips which my poore Muse (out of an ambitious honour to speake something conserneing your absolute perfections) hath committed'. Charles praised Mary's 'unparaleld beauty…a theame able to infuse life into the dulest peece of Earth and make it speake forth your praises in far and deepe fecht straines of Rhetorick'. There follows a rambling poem extolling Mary's virtues and 'her best arts Master peece, More worth then Jason's Golden ffleece', (a reference to her artistic talent?).[37] For Charles and Mary, painting and poetry went hand-in-hand: Mary, a woman 'of an estimable character and very amiable manners… had among her contemporaries some reputation as a poet'.[38]

Charles Beale's love-letter was well received and the marriage of Mary Cradock and Charles Beale took place at All Saints, Barrow, on 8 March 1652. Mary's father died in April. His will, dated 1644 (soon after the death of his wife), states that he owned land in the parish of Barrow 'called by the name of Beales' (pointing to a local connection with Charles's family). His money, books and household goods were bestowed upon 'my deare & sweete children', John and Mary, to be equally divided between them under the supervision of his executor, Walter Cradock. Nathaniel Thach, late of London, 'picture drawer' was left Cradock's 'empastered rounds as wee call them' (the round cards were secondary supports for the vellum used in miniature painting, suggesting that Cradock painted miniatures in addition to still lifes). Mary inherited her late mother's watch and linen; her aunt Priscilla received 'a Tabby gown' (of silk taffeta) that had belonged to Mary's mother.[39] The rectory was soon vacated and Charles and Mary Beale found a home on the Beale estate at Walton, Buckinghamshire, where Charles's parents lived in the manor house. Bartholomew, the first son born to Charles and Mary, died in infancy and was buried at Walton in October 1654.

Looking to the future, Charles and Mary Beale decided to move to London where opportunities beckoned, although the political situation was unstable. The capital was in the hands of the Lord Protector's Council of State, supported by the army, and the situation was to deteriorate in 1659 when troops surrounded the Palace of Westminster. Optimistically, Charles and Mary Beale took up residence in the artists' quarter of London, Covent Garden, during the winter of 1655 to 1656. The presence of Lely and his studio in the piazza and a vibrant community of artists attracted the young couple who had little to gain by remaining in Buckinghamshire.

1. ODNB

2. Richard Cradock's will, March 1629 (1630 new calendar), IC500/1/87/52, Bury St Edmunds Record Office

3. Patrick Collinson, *Servants and Citizens: Robert Beale and other Elizabethans*, (2004), p. 17

4. John Cooper, *The Queen's Agent. Francis Walsingham at the Court of Elizabeth I*, (2011) p. 324

5. The Archives of the Duke of Northumberland at Alnwick Castle, DNP: Ms 560

6. GVCBA 1676–7

7. Katherine Fitzjames's portrait was framed in 'leatherwork gilt', CBA 23 February 1677

8. Cotton Ms Titus III, ff.302-08, BL

9. Add Ms 48,161, BL

10. Patrick Collinson, *op.cit.*, p. 23

11. *Papers at Hatfield House*, Historic Manuscripts Commission, (1902), IX, pp. 377–9

12. One of Robert and Edith Beale's sons, Robert (b.1590) cannot have been the Robert Beale of Whittlesey who married Susannah Pepys in 1601

13. GVCBA July 1674. Burman executed monuments for the Duke of Bedford and the Earl of Shrewsbury

14. S. Woodford, *Liber*, 29 December 1664

15. Charles Beale's almanacks refer to Mary as 'My Dearest Heart' or 'My D. Ht' frequently

16. Camden Society 49 (1850), p. 217

17. *The Treasure Houses of Britain. Five Hundred Years of Private Patronage and Art Collecting*, ed. by Gervaise Jackson-Stops, (1985), p. 150

18. Charles Beale, 'Experimental Secrets found out in the way of Painting,' (1647-63), Ferguson Ms 134, f.14, Glasgow University Library

19. GVCBA 1661

20. 7 July 1648, Court Minutes Painter-Stainers' Company, Ms 5667/1, Guildhall Library, London. Mary Beale's father, John Cradock, does not seem to have been related to the artist Luke Craddocke (c. 1660–1717) from Somerset, a painter of still life

21. 'Vertue Note Books 1', *Walpole Society* 18 (1930), p. 116

22. GVCBA 4 March 1672

23. Evelyn, IV, p. 113, 2 September 1677

24. *The Lives of the Norths*, ed. by Augustus Jessopp, (1890), II, p. 273

25. Elizabeth Walsh, 'Mrs Mary Beale, Paintress' in *Conoisseur* 131 (1953), pp. 3-6

26. 'Vertue Note Books I', *op. cit.*, p. 108

27. GVCBA 1661

28. Evelyn, IV, pp. 184-5, 6 November 1679

29. A.G. Matthews, *Walker Revised. Being a revision of John Walker's Sufferings of the clergy during the Grand Rebellion 1642-60*, (1948), p. 327

30. GVCBA 1661

31. 'Vertue Note Books I', *op. cit.* p.108. This portrait was exhibited at the South Kensington Museum in 1866

32. *Lives of the Norths*, *op. cit.*

33. Horace Walpole, *Anecdotes of Painting in England*, (1762–71), III, p.68

34. C.H.Collins Baker, *Lely and the Stuart Portrait Painters*, (1912), III, pp. 34-36

35. GVCAB 1661

36. Harley Ms 1560, f. 348 rev, BL. A note records that John Beale was descended from this family, possibly referring to John Beale FRS (1608–1683), rector of Yeovil, Somerset, or to John Beale of the Stationers' Company (1587–1643)

37. Rawlinson Letter 104, f.133r, Bodleian Library, Oxford

38. DNB (1885-1901), II, p. 3

39. Will of 1644, probate 25 August 1652, IC500/1/109/4, Bury St Edmunds Record Office

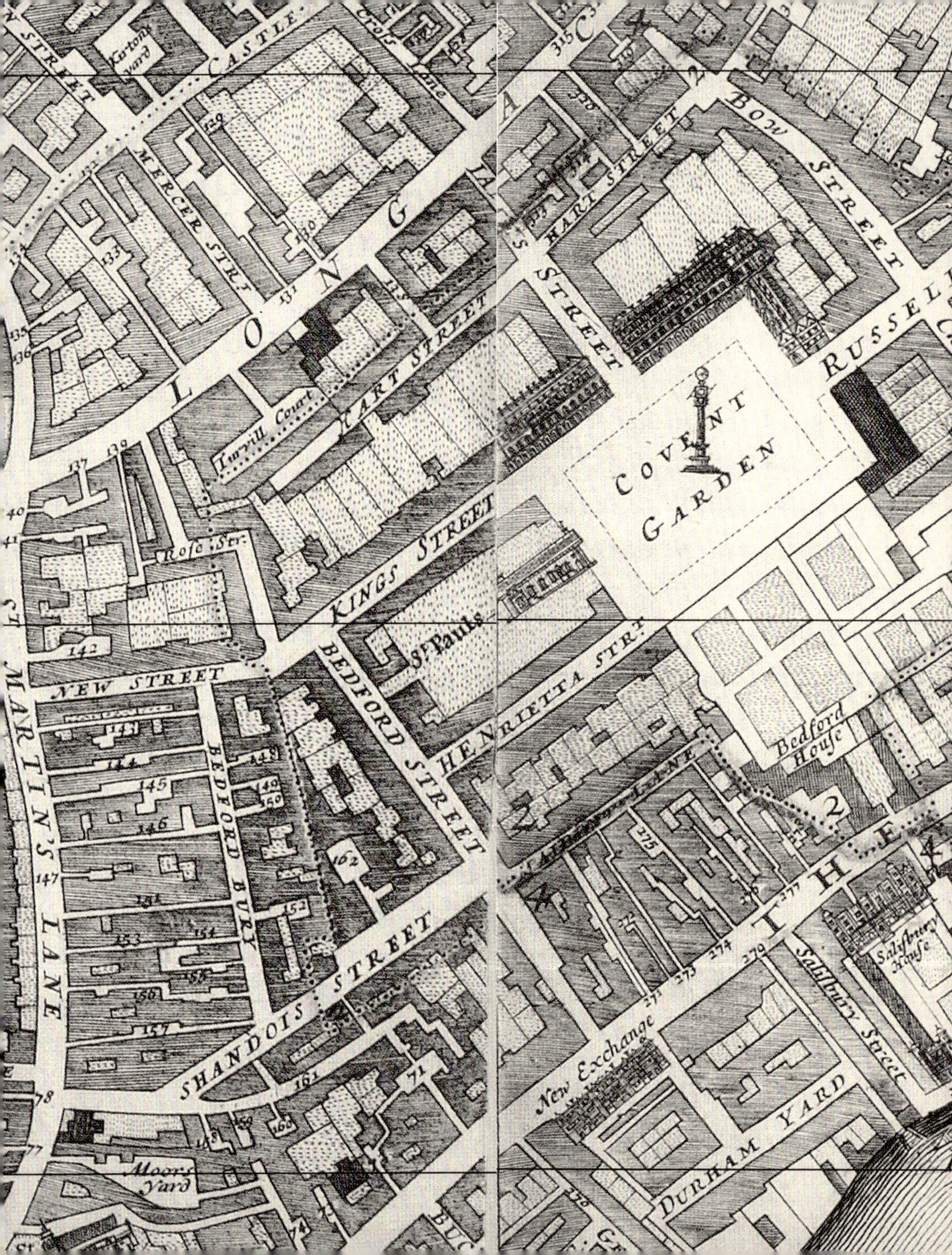

COVENT GARDEN
LONG ACRE
BOW STREET
HART STREET
RUSSELL
KINGS STREET
BEDFORD STREET
HENRIETTA STR
St. Pauls
Bedford House
NEW STREET
BEDFORD BURY
MARTIN'S LANE
SHANDOIS STREET
Turvill Court
Rose Str
MERCER STR
CASTLE
Kirtons yard
Crols lane
Salisbury House
Salisbury Street
New Exchange
DURHAM YARD
Moors yard

2. THE CRUCIBLE OF COVENT GARDEN

THE FIRST HINT OF MARY BEALE'S ARTISTIC TALENT might be gleaned from Charles Beale's love-letter to her composed in July 1651, which refers to 'her best arts Master peece'.[1] A more convincing note occurs in Charles's almanack recording that the Suffolk artist Matthew Snelling (1621–1678) sent her a packet of 'pinke' in 1654 and again in 1658 Snelling presented her with 'a parcel of Pink…of the weed before it flowered' ('pink' was the prized yellow pigment made from greenweed, a variety of broom).[2] These were the gifts of one artist to another and suggest that Mary was painting by 1654. Despite the death of her infant son in 1655, a second pregnancy and the disruption of moving from Buckinghamshire to London, Mary Beale pursued her art and was rewarded by her first commissions for portraits in the late 1650s.

While Charles Beale's parents occupied Walton manor house, the family home in Buckinghamshire, and with his two elder brothers alive, Charles's prospects were not promising. Traditionally, younger sons entered the Church or relied on relatives to provide a sinecure. Charles might have expected his father or his brother Bartholomew, an Auditor of the Imprests at the Treasury with responsibility for government expenditure, to find him an appointment but for the time being this was not forthcoming. Opportunities for employment for Charles and the fulfilment of Mary's potential as an artist lay in London, so late in 1655 the Beales took lodgings with Mrs Stubbs at Clerkenwell while they searched for permanent accommodation, preferably in or near the artists' quarter of London, Covent Garden. By the time of their son Bartholomew's birth in February 1656, Charles and Mary Beale were settled at 13 King Street, Covent Garden.[3] This was a respectable residential street to the north-west of the piazza where numbers 1–14, built by Thomas Turney in the 1630s, overlooked Inigo Jones's church, St Paul's, and its churchyard.[4]

Opposite: When they arrived in London during the winter of 1655-6 Charles and Mary Beale lived at Kings/King Street, Covent Garden. A detail from William Morgan's map of 1682

The Beales' move to London was cushioned by the presence of relatives. Charles's brother, Bartholomew, and his wife Elizabeth lived in Hatton Garden; Charles's sister, Katherine, was married to John Smythe (1612–1675) of Gray's Inn; Mary's aunt, Priscilla, lived in the parish of St Martin-in-the-Fields.

The artists' quarter of Covent Garden

Covent Garden took its name from the convent garden belonging to the monks of Westminster Abbey. Following the dissolution of the monasteries in King Henry VIII's reign, the former convent garden was granted to the Earl of Bedford whose descendant, the 4th Earl, obtained a licence from King Charles I to develop the land in association with Inigo Jones. From the middle years of the seventeenth century, as the grandees of London society moved west to Piccadilly and St James's, artists moved into Covent Garden. The Court painter Sir Peter Lely established his studio on the north-east corner of the piazza in 1650 where he lived in style until his death in 1680. The diarist Samuel Pepys, who found Lely so busy that he could only offer an appointment before 8am, thought the artist arrogant and was astounded 'to see what pomp his table was laid for himself to go to dinner'.[5] Lely's house and studio was a magnet for London's artistic community, attracting disciples, pupils, assistants and patrons. The Beales' frame-maker, Tobias Flessier, lived in Lely's house for a time. The Swedish artist Michael Dahl (1659–1743) and Henry Tilson (1659–1695) worked in Lely's studio before they embarked on a tour of the Continent (Tilson later shot himself in the heart while suffering from unrequited love). If not at Lely's, Frederick Sonnius (d. 1721) could be found in Henrietta Street where he lodged with an apothecary, two doors away from the Rummer Tavern. The miniaturist Samuel Cooper (1608–1672), judged by Charles Beale to be 'the most famous Limner [miniature painter] in the world for a face',[6] was living at King Street during the early 1640s, later moving to Henrietta Street where he died (a Roman Catholic, it was rumoured). Cooper's uncle was the miniaturist John Hoskins (1589–1664) whose family was living at 29 Bedford Street by 1634. The physician Sir Théodore Turquet De Mayerne (1573–1655) was in St Martin's Lane before he moved to Chelsea. He was fascinated by the artists' workshops of Covent Garden and, having commissioned his portrait from Hoskins and met Samuel Cooper at Hoskins's house in 1634, he persuaded Cooper to share his secret methods of preparing white lead, bice (blew bice or Bremen blue, derived from a poisonous copper compound), massicot (yellow monoxide of lead used as a pigment), red lead and vermilion. The miniaturist Peter Cross (*c.* 1645–1724), originally from Suffolk, lived in Henrietta Street at the sign of The Blue Anchor. Charles Beale (who borrowed money from Cross) commissioned Cross's brother-in-law, the sculptor Thomas

Burman, for his parents' monument at St Michael's church, Walton. Peter Cross's neighbours in Covent Garden were the Carters, colour sellers to Charles and Mary Beale.

Long Acre, to the north of Covent Garden piazza, was particularly popular with artists: John Hayls (1606–1679), who painted Samuel

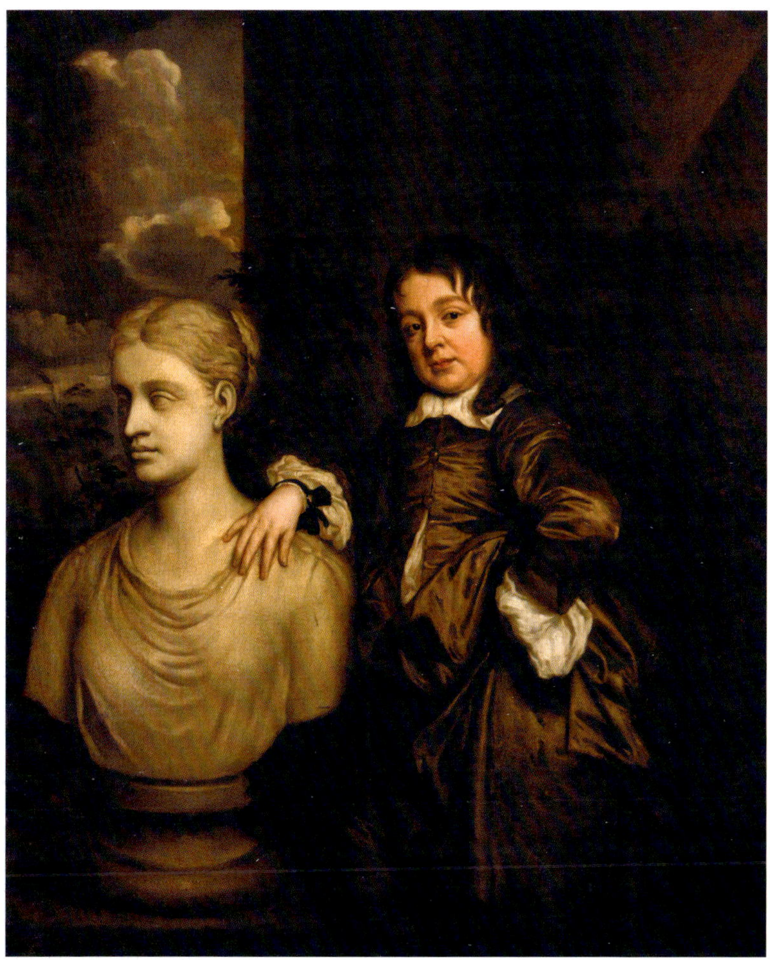

Sir Peter Lely, *Portrait of Richard Gibson*, known as Dwarf Gibson, 1658. Lely and Gibson visited Mary Beale's painting-room in 1672

Pepys and his wife, lived there from June 1668 and died there in 1679 dressed in a velvet suit, about to attend the Lord Mayor's banquet in the City. The art dealer and Court limner from 1673 to 1678, Nicholas Dixon (1645–1708), was based in Long Acre before moving to St Martin's Lane. Richard Gibson (1605 or 1615–1690), known as 'Dwarf Gibson' due to his diminutive height (1m 17cm), was in Covent Garden during the 1640s, returning in 1688 to live with his daughter, the artist Susannah Penelope Rosse, in Henrietta Street. Gibson was the King's favourite miniature painter after the death of Cooper in 1672, the year he accompanied Lely to Mary Beale's painting-room and praised her work (see pages 102, 103). Miniature painters were numerous in this neighbourhood, the Anglo-French David Des Granges (1611–1672) being one (he married Judith Hoskins, who must have been a relative of John Hoskins and Samuel Cooper). During the Interregnum Des Granges was at the Court of King Charles II; latterly Des Granges and his family were at Elm Street, Long Acre, where he died. The Flemish painter Remegius van Leemput, known as Remee (1607–1675), who specialised in copies after Van Dyck and Lely, was living in the area in 1635 and was buried at St Paul's church forty years later. His daughter Mary, an artist, married Thomas Streeter, nephew of the serjeant painter Robert Streeter (1621–1679) of Long Acre. Another foreigner attracted to this cosmopolitan neighbourhood was the German painter, engraver and tapestry designer Francis Cleyn/Clein (1582–1658) also of Mortlake. He trained the artists John Michael Wright, Isaac Fuller, William Dobson, John Hayls, and his daughter, Penelope. The Cleyns lived in Henrietta Street during the 1650s, coinciding with the years Charles and Mary Beale lived nearby in King Street.

Matthew Snelling was in London by 1663, living in Long Acre with his wife (the couple were married at St Dunstan in the West, the Beales' parish church after they moved to Hind Court in 1660). Snelling must have known Mary before her marriage to Charles Beale when they lived in neighbouring Suffolk villages and he was still in touch with her when she was an established portrait painter. On one visit to the Beales' house in Pall Mall, Snelling offered Charles 30 guineas for his painting 'Venus and Cupid' by Hans Rottenhammer. Charles thought it was worth 50 guineas and refused to sell[7] (it fetched £121,250 at Christie's in 2012). Charles and Mary Beale collected and commissioned paintings and Snelling's offer raises the possibility that he and Beale were art dealers.

Alexander Browne (*c.* 1630–1706), teacher and author of instruction manuals on drawing and painting, was based at the sign of The Pestle and Mortar, Long Acre, moving to lodgings at the sign of The Angel by 1669 when his *Ars Pictoria* was published. John and Cornelius Bradshaw of Russell Street, Covent Garden, may have been related to

Mr Bradshaw, a churchwarden of the Beales' local church when they lived in Hampshire. The antiquary Richard Symonds saluted one of the Bradshaws as 'the only man that doth understand perspective of all the painters in London'.[8]

The Flemish artist Henry Prosper Lankrink (1628–1692), 'a man of high spirit and profuse',[9] who was employed by Lely to paint landscape backgrounds, was another resident of Covent Garden. John Greenhill, in London from 1662 and a disciple of Lely, was based in Drury Lane from 1669 (he died in 1676 as the result of a fall in Long Acre after drinking). The artist and picture drawer to King Charles II, John Michael Wright (1617–1694), whose group portrait of Sir Robert Viner and family (1673) outdid Mary Beale's pictures of the previous year, spent the last six years of his life in the parish of St Paul, Covent Garden. The portraitist Mrs Joan Carlile (*c.* 1606–1679) lived near Whitehall until 1637, then moved to Richmond; she was resident in Covent Garden from 1654 to 1656, so briefly a neighbour of Charles and Mary Beale.

Pioneering women artists

Women artists were recognised in ancient Greece and during the Italian renaissance but recognition of female artists by the London art world lay centuries ahead. Pliny the elder found a place for women in his work *Naturalis Historia* of the first century AD, and manuscript illustrations of the Athenian Timarete (Thamyris) and of Iaia (Marcia) show them painting their self portraits. Marcia worked in her studio at Herculaneum before the earthquake of AD 79; Giovanni Boccaccio's *De Mulieribus Claris* (*Of Famous Women*, compiled in the 1370s with biographies of 106 women) depicted her painting her self portrait with the aid of a mirror.

The first-century artist Marcia painting her self portrait. An illustration from Boccaccio's *De Mulieribus Claris*, c. 1403

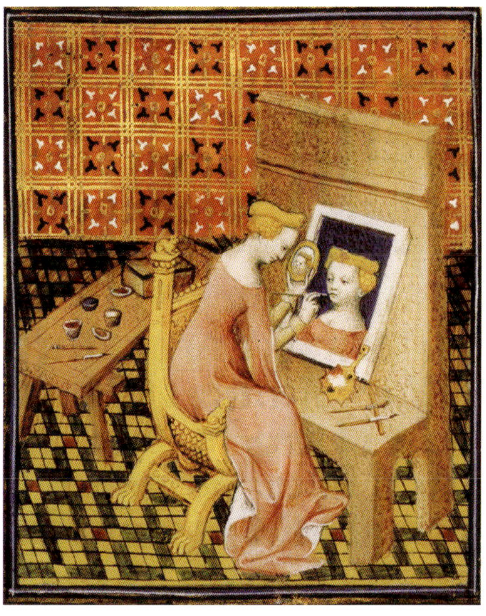

The Italian renaissance of the arts brought the re-emergence of women artists, who invariably owed their success to encouragement from their fathers. In the absence of formal training, denied the study of human anatomy and hampered by the practical problems of working in a male-dominated society, aspiring women artists relied on instruction from their fathers and/or family connections to develop their talent. This was still the case in seventeenth-century England when Mary Beale defied prejudice and established her reputation as portrait painter to the

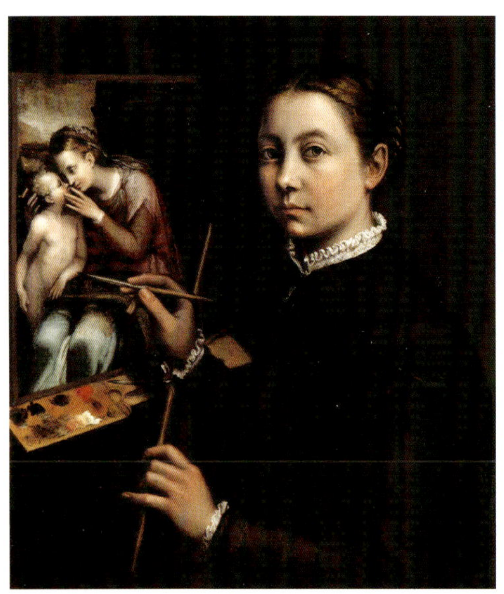

Sofonisba Anguissola, *Self portrait*, 1556

aristocracy, clergy, physicians and fashionable ladies.

The Italian Sofonisba Anguissola (*c.* 1532–1625) was fortunate that her talent was fostered by her father, Amilcare, by Bernardino Campi and by the fresco painter Bernardino Gatti. Sofonisba's father was sufficiently well-connected to bring her to the attention of Michelangelo. His confidence in Sofonisba was justified: she earned the respect of the Pope, Van Dyck (who painted her portrait) and the art historian Giorgio Vasari, whose *Lives of the Artists* (1568 edition) acknowledged 'that women have always succeeded and become famous in all the exercises to which they have devoted themselves', from domesticity to war. Vasari commended one sculptress and three women artists, especially Sofonisba Anguissola, who 'has done more in design and more gracefully than any other lady of our day'. Vasari names another dozen women painters but without details of their achievements.[10]

The career of Lavinia Fontana (1552–1614) from Bologna was promoted by her father and supported by her husband, the artist Gian Paolo Zappi, by whom she had eleven children. She charged substantial sums for her portraits, and her self portrait with palette and brushes (1579) was a prototype for Mary Beale a century later. Fontana gained academic recognition as a *dottoressa* of the University of Bologna and in 1603 she was elected to the Accademia di Belle Arti di Roma.

This miscellany of sixteenth and seventeenth-century Italian women artists should include Barbara Longhi (1552–1638) who assisted her father, and Marietta Robusti (1560–1590), daughter of the Venetian artist Tintoretto (she was said to have disguised herself as a boy while working in the studio). Robusti maintained the tradition of women's self portraiture that originated with Marcia and Timarete in the first century AD. Likewise Elisabetta Sirani (1638–1665), who was running her father's workshop and training other women artists at the age of twenty-two. Sirani's self portraits presented her in various roles; the last defined her status as an artist wielding her palette and brush (1664).

Several Flemish women pursued careers as painters of still lifes, portraits and miniatures during the sixteenth century. Catharina van Hemessen (1528–1588) proclaimed her metier with a self portrait featuring her palette and canvas in 1548, and her work was popular

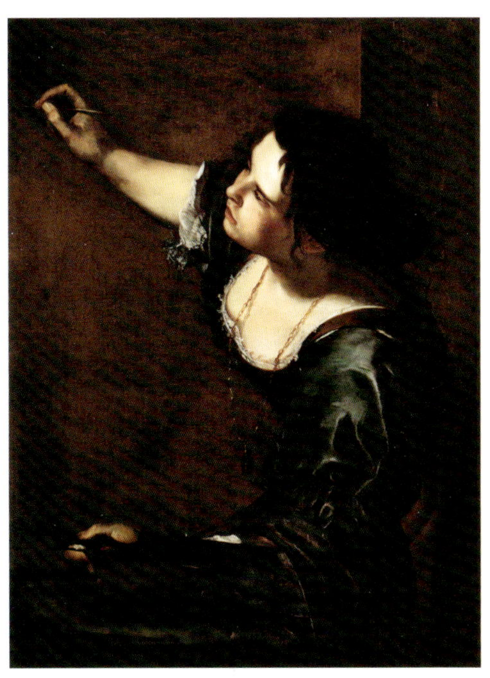

Artemisia Gentileschi, *Self portrait as the Allegory of Painting*, c. 1638-9

with the courtiers of Queen Mary of Hungary. Susanna Horenbout (1503–1554) was given a guilder by Albrecht Dürer for a small religious work in 1521 and she was in London by 1529. She married an Englishman and was employed by King Henry VIII; her success enabled her to build a mansion in Stepney where she died. Horenbout and Levina Teerlinc (1510 or 1520–1576) made 'a seminal impact on the introduction and development of the portrait miniature' in England.[11] Miniature painting being delicate and a less cumbersome process than oil painting, was an attractive option for women artists. Originally from Bruges, Teerlinc accompanied her husband to the English Court where she came to the notice of King Henry VIII who provided her with an annuity of £40 (more than Hans Holbein had received). She was the favourite miniaturist of four successive monarchs and lived near St Bride's church in London from 1546 until her death. Sir Roy Strong is not an admirer of Teerlinc whom he described as 'an indifferent draughtsman' with 'a spidery style' who 'will never emerge as an artist of major importance'.[12] Nonetheless, her employment by the King and his Court was a milestone for female artists in England.

Artemisia Gentileschi (1593–1653), born in Rome and trained in her father's studio, was painting portraits by 1612; her self portrait as St Catherine of Alexandria, dated 1615-17, has been purchased by the National Gallery recently. She married a Florentine artist and was the first female member of the Accademia del Disegno. Her competence and confidence was apparent: she wrote to one patron assuring him that he would 'find the spirit of Caesar in this soul of a woman'.[13] Artemisia followed the bold style of Caravaggio and assisted her father, Orazio, with large scale murals for King Charles I and Queen Henrietta Maria at the Queen's House, Greenwich. Orazio Gentileschi died in 1639 and Artemisia subsequently returned to Italy.

At the English Court and at their country estates privileged women encouraged artists of both sexes by their patronage. At another level of society, women worked as craftswomen/artists in the family workshop and widows often took responsibility for the atelier. Alice Gemmedge, for example, inherited her husband's workshop in Essex and at her death in 1591 she left frames, pictures and artists' materials to her son.

Amateur women artists added another dimension to the seventeenth-century art scene. Drawing was considered a 'virtuous' accomplishment, along with music, sewing and reading. Wealthy fathers, and husbands, Samuel Pepys being one, employed drawing masters to instruct their daughters and wives. Pepys's wife, Elizabeth, was taught by Alexander Browne, the author of *Ars Pictoria or An Academy treating of drawing, painting, limning, etching* (1669). Pepys soon grew jealous of Browne, so banned the artist from his table. 'Upon this my wife and I had a little disagreement'.[14]

From Holbein and Teerlinc in the sixteenth century, to Van Dyck, Lely, Beale and Kneller a century later, portrait painting in England flourished. Van Dyck's arrival in London in 1632 brought portraiture to new heights of sophistication; he was appointed Court painter, knighted by King Charles I and his magnificent pictures celebrated the Stuart monarchy. The scale, quality and number (some forty of the King alone) of Van Dyck's portraits inspired copyists such as Mary Beale.

King Charles II was a generous patron of artists of both sexes: Anna Maria Carew, working in the 1660s, received £200 a year to copy paintings from the King's collection, in miniature. Peter Oliver's widow, Anne (1593–1672), received an annuity of £300 from the King, albeit for her late husband's miniatures, until payment was halted when she voiced disapproval that the King was giving the portraits to 'whores, bastards or Strumpets'.[15]

A portrait of an anonymous woman signed 'Elizabeth 1619' was discovered in the late twentieth century by Elizabeth Walsh during her research into Mary Beale. Walsh surmised this might be the earliest painting by a professional female English artist.[16] Later in the century a handful of professional Englishwomen painting in oils came to the notice of the historian Sir William Sanderson who commended four contemporary women in his book *Graphice: the use of the Pen and Pencil or, the most excellent Art of Painting* (1658), to which the Beales' friend Thomas Flatman contributed a poem and an essay 'On the noble Art of Painting'. Sanderson's section on English modern masters names Walker, Zowst [Soest], Wright, Lillie [Lely], Hales [Hayls], Shepheard [Sheppard] and de Grange [Des Granges], as 'rare Artizans'. Another category of 'worthy Gentlemen' amateur artists 'ingenious in their private delight, are become juditious practitioners herein, namely Sir John Holland, Mr Guies, Mr Parker, Mr Sprignell and others'. Sanderson then calls attention to four women artists:

'And in Oyl Colours we have a virtuous example in that worthy Artist Mrs Carlile: and of others Mr [sic] Beale, Mrs Brooman, and to Mrs Weimes'.[17] Mrs Weimes remains elusive but Mrs Brooman must be Mrs Boardman who was living near Gray's Inn Gate in the 1650s. She was best known for her copy of Titian's 'Venus' and was also a portrait painter. She favoured 'Harlem ultramarine' for painting the chins of her sitters (this was a blue clay earth pigment which cost 7s an ounce, compared to the finest ultramarine for which Charles Beale charged £4 10s an ounce). Mrs Boardman used cullen's earth to paint rich shadows, and she was proud of the flesh colours she devised to paint the cheeks of women sitters.[18]

Sanderson's list of contemporary women artists is headed by Joan Carlile, followed by Mary Beale who has been cited as the first professional woman artist working in London. The accolade must go to Mrs Joan Carlile (*c.* 1606–1679, née Palmer). Her paintings of women in shimmering gowns and her 'conversation pieces' date from the 1640s when she came to the notice of King Charles I, who presented her and Van Dyck with ultramarine pigment to the value of £500. Described by De Mayerne as a 'virtuous Lady who paints very well', Joan Carlile provided Mayerne with notes about Nicholas Lanier's painting techniques. These Mayerne recorded in his memoranda on materials and methods collected from artists such as Rubens, Van Dyck, Mytens, Cooper, Hoskins and Mrs Carlile.[19]

Joan Carlile's husband, Lodowick, a minor playwright, was a keeper of the royal deer park, Richmond, from 1637. The family (Mrs Carlile bore six children) lived at Petersham Lodge, Richmond Park, before moving to Covent Garden in 1654. Vertue reported that Mrs Carlile taught painting (to at least one lady) and 'drew her own picture sitting with a book of drawings on her lap & this Lady standing behind her'. This and other paintings by Carlile were left to her grandsons, while some belonged to Lady Cotterell.[20] No more than a dozen of Carlile's paintings have come to light, the most recent being the discovery in 2016 of a full length portrait identified as Carlile's work of the early 1650s.

Joan Carlile and Mary Beale were succeeded by a younger generation of women artists working in London. Susannah Penelope Rosse (*c.* 1655–1700, née Gibson) was a resident of Covent Garden from birth to death. She learned her art from her father and from Samuel Cooper, whose pocket-book she treasured. Through her father's connections she gained access to the royal family and

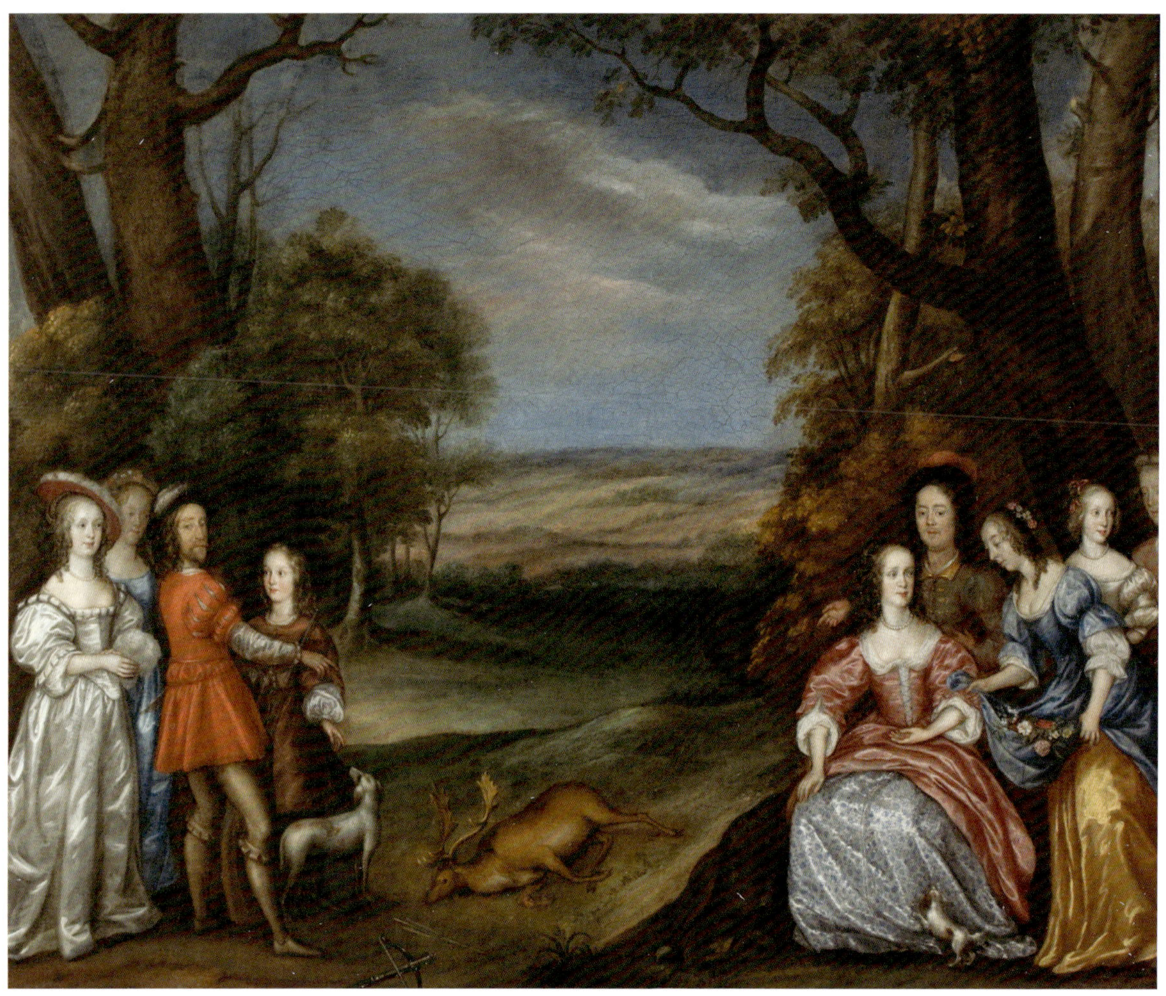

Joan Carlile, *The Stag Hunt*, 1649-50. The painting includes the artist, her husband and son, left

courtiers and was privileged to work alongside Sir Godfrey Kneller while he painted the Moroccan ambassador in 1682. Miss Gibson married a jeweller, Michael Rosse, and died in middle age. The sale of her miniatures in 1723 included nearly forty of the royal family; she also left two self portraits.

The accomplished Anne Killigrew (1660–1685) was born in St Martin's Lane, Covent Garden. Her father, Dr Henry Killigrew, Master of the Savoy and Prebendary of Westminster, was a playwright, as were his two brothers (Thomas Killigrew founded Drury Lane theatre). Through her father Anne was introduced to the Court and was maid of honour to the Duchess of York whose portrait she painted. She completed a full length portrait of King James II shortly after his accession to the throne in 1685, shortly before her own death from smallpox at the age of twenty-five. Anne Killigrew also turned her hand to classical subjects such as Venus and Adonis. Posthumously, she was famed for her poetry, as extolled by John Dryden in his ode 'To the Pious Memory of the Accomplish'd Young Lady Mrs Anne Killigrew. Excellent In The Two Sister-Arts of Poësie and Painting' (1686).

The 'Sister-Arts' of poetry and painting appealed to Charles and Mary Beale; Charles addressed one of his poems to Mary,[21] and he was known by his contemporaries for his elegant prose as much as for his mastery of colours. Mary Beale's skill in the 'Sister-Arts' was acknowledged by Samuel Woodford writing some twenty years before Dryden's elegy to Anne Killigrew. Woodford praised Mary Beale who 'has made Painting and Poesy which in the Fancies of others had only before a kind of likeness, in her own to be really the same'.[22]

Joan Carlile achieved success in the 1650s; Mary Beale, Carlile's junior by nearly thirty years, in the 1670s. If Carlile was the first professional female English artist, Mary Beale was the most prolific. At the peak of her career in 1677, portrait commissions occupied her intensively for six days of the week. Richard Jeffree catalogued 158 verified portraits by her, with another forty-one attributions,[23] since when more paintings have been found. Yet, unlike her French counterpart, Elisabeth Sophie Chéron (1648–1711), Mary Beale achieved no academic recognition. Chéron was taught by her father and at the age of twenty-four was honoured with admission to the Académie Royale de Peinture et de Sculpture in Paris and she was elected to the Art Academy at Padua in 1699. There was no possibility of equivalent honours for Joan Carlile or Mary Beale: the Royal Academy of Arts in London was not founded until 1768 when, among the thirty-four founder members there were just two women, the Swiss-born Angelica Kauffman and Mary Moser, daughter of the Academician, George Moser (whose family also came from Switzerland). These two women were admitted on restricted terms and in Johan Zoffany's painting of 'The Academicians' (1771-2) Kauffman and Moser were represented not in person but by their portraits.

Mary Beale's early portraits

City connections intertwined with religious affiliations led to Mary Beale's earliest formal portrait of a dignitary. Alderman Mark

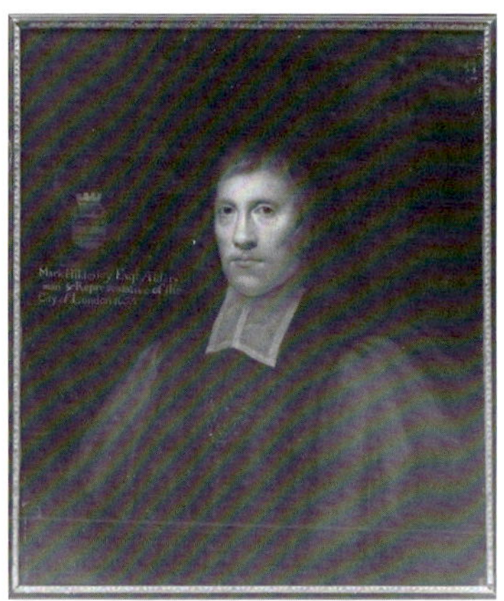

Mary Beale, *Alderman Mark Hildesley*, c. 1656-8

Hildesley was a personal friend of Lord Protector Oliver Cromwell and his commissioner of customs. In 1642 Hildesley was one of those responsible for raising the City of London cavalry, leading to the dominance of Cromwell's army in the City, and as an Alderman and Common Councillor, he put his name to the City's petition opposing King Charles I – the prelude to the King's execution. When the Interregnum came into force, Alderman Hildesley was elected Master of the Vintners' Company (1650), a Member of Parliament for the City (1653) and was in line to be Lord Mayor. His portrait was a prestigious commission for Mrs Beale, still in her twenties, and she took care to emphasise Hildesley's civic status: he posed in his Aldermanic robes and the coat of arms and inscription left no doubt about his importance. The portrait, last seen in 1975, has been dated to around 1656–8 and was certainly painted before 1660, the date of Hildesley's death.

While awaiting further commissions, Mary Beale practised her skills by painting herself, her husband Charles and their eldest son, Bartholomew, in the group portrait of 1659 or 1660 at the Geffrye Museum. Judging by the appearance of the enchanting, curly-haired Bartholomew, two profiles of him discovered in Paris in 1992 must be of a similar date.

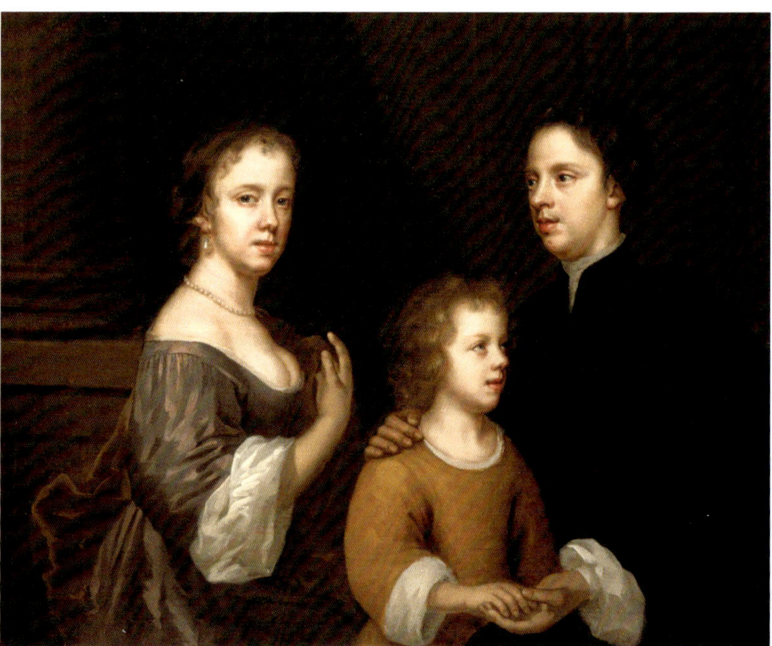

Mary Beale, *Self portrait with her husband, Charles, and son, Bartholomew*, c. 1659-60

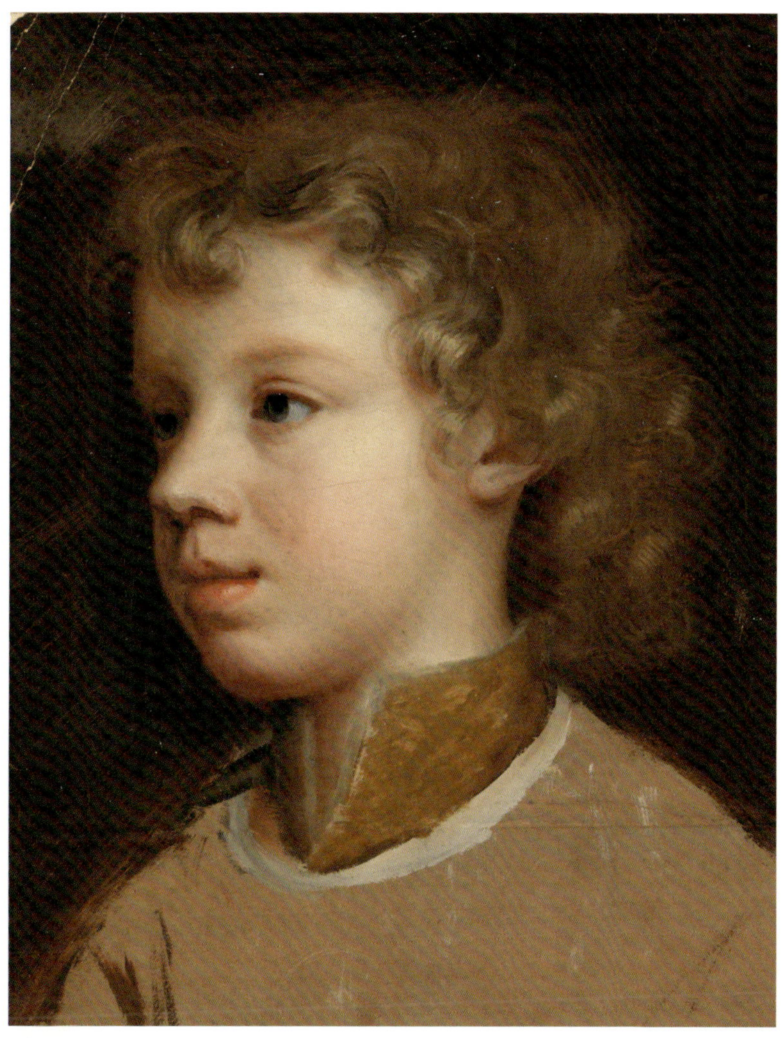

Mary Beale, *Her son Bartholomew*, c. 1660

An intriguing group of three early portraits hark back to Mary Beale's Suffolk roots and may have been painted at Hengrave Hall near Bury St Edmunds, an estate inherited by Lady Hervey from her mother, Lady Rivers. Penelope Hervey (1593–1661) was first married to Sir George Trenchard, secondly to Sir John Gage and thirdly to Sir William Hervey: these eligible bachelors had all sought Penelope's hand in marriage simultaneously and, 'to keep the peace between the rivals she threatened the first aggressor with her perpetual displeasure; humoursly telling them that, if they would wait, she would have them all in their turn – a promise which the Lady actually performed'.[24]

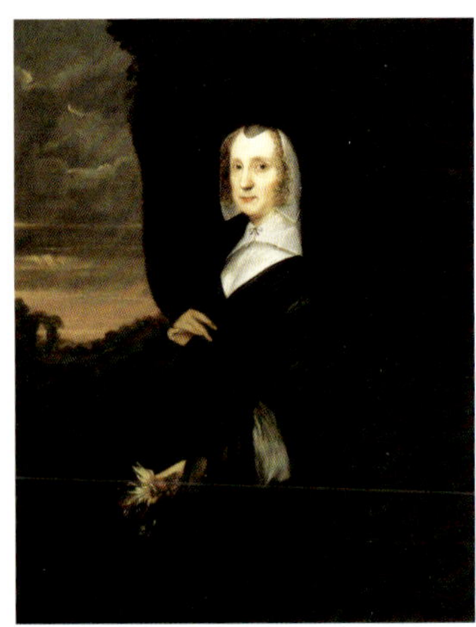

Mary Beale (attributed to), *Lady Hervey*, c. 1660

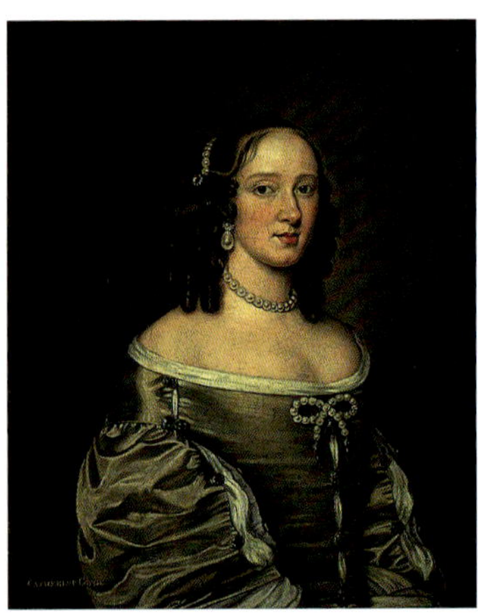

Mary Beale, *Young woman of the Gage family*, c. 1656-8. Although later inscribed 'Catherine Gage', this portrait is more likely to be one of the daughters of Lady Hervey and her second husband, Sir John Gage, rather than Lady Hervey's grand-daughter, Catherine

Lady Hervey's son, Sir Edward Gage Bt (1617–1707), had four sons and two daughters, Catherine and Basilea, whose portraits, said to be by Mary Beale, originally hung at Hengrave Hall. The style of the women's gowns and hair suggests a pre-Restoration date for the portraits and despite the inscription 'Catherine Gage' on one of the paintings, the subjects are more likely to have been the daughters of Lady Hervey, Anne and Frances, rather than her grand-daughters Catherine and Basilea. Lady Hervey's own portrait has been attributed to Beale and dated to around 1650–55. However, she is wearing widow's weeds: her two previous husbands were long dead and her third husband, Sir William Hervey, died on 30 September 1660. She herself died a few months later (her will was proved in July 1661) which gives a date of late 1660 or early 1661 for the portrait.

Personal friends, many of whom were clergymen, posed for Mary Beale after the family had moved from Covent Garden to Hind Court, Fleet Street, in 1660. 'Dr William Bates [was] at Our house all this day sitting to my Cosen Beale for his Picture' on 2 September 1662, and he was followed by the Puritan poet, Dr Robert Wilde.[25] At this early stage of her career, Mary Beale was indebted to the poet Samuel Woodford (1636–1700) for his encouragement and contacts (he lived with the family in the early 1660s). Woodford's mother, Mrs Hannah Guy (1617–1698), whose first husband, Robert Woodford, died in 1654, posed for her portrait in the early 1660s; this is believed to be the first example of Mary's use of a sculptured oval with swags of fruit to frame the head and shoulders of her sitter. The daughter of one of Woodford's father's friends, Mrs Harvey of Northampton, sat for Mary Beale in 1662, and a contemporary of Woodford's at Oxford, Sir William Godolphin, commissioned his portrait in 1664 to mark his fellowship of the Royal Society and auditorship for life of the Exchequer Court (Mary's portraits often marked the sitter's promotion to high office). Samuel Woodford himself posed for her in 1664; 'Shee hath done it very like as all say that see it'.[26]

Charles Beale's 'Experimental Secrets'

Charles and Mary Beale enjoyed a complimentary personal and professional relationship. As a youth Charles described himself as a painter (George Vertue found a copy of *Le Vite de Pittori* by Giovanni Baglione annotated by Charles Beale 'painter' in an inventory of the Earl of Arundel's library).[27] Before his marriage to Mary, Charles painted still lifes and began to write a handbook, 'Experimental Secrets

To paint pewter or plate with
shining glosse to admiration &
very speedily./
First under paint yor sligthly
wth bon black & white then wn it is
throughly dry temp fat oile if it bee
very fat wth oile of poppies and rub
it thin over, then in all the ~~dry~~ dark places
drive it over wth sheere bon black and
hatch it in the lights according to the
coming of the hatches in the plate
and it is don in an instant/ March
11th 1647/8.

To heigthen grapes & plums
the white but wch is about the white
speck must bee white and pure faire
Bice, though the rest of the mealinesse
bee of vine black and white because
the heigthning is pfectly illuminated
and so the meale must bee purer ~~&~~
then the white in the midst & it will
looke passing full of sperit/

Charles Beale, A page from 'Experimental Secrets found out in the way of Painting', 1647-63

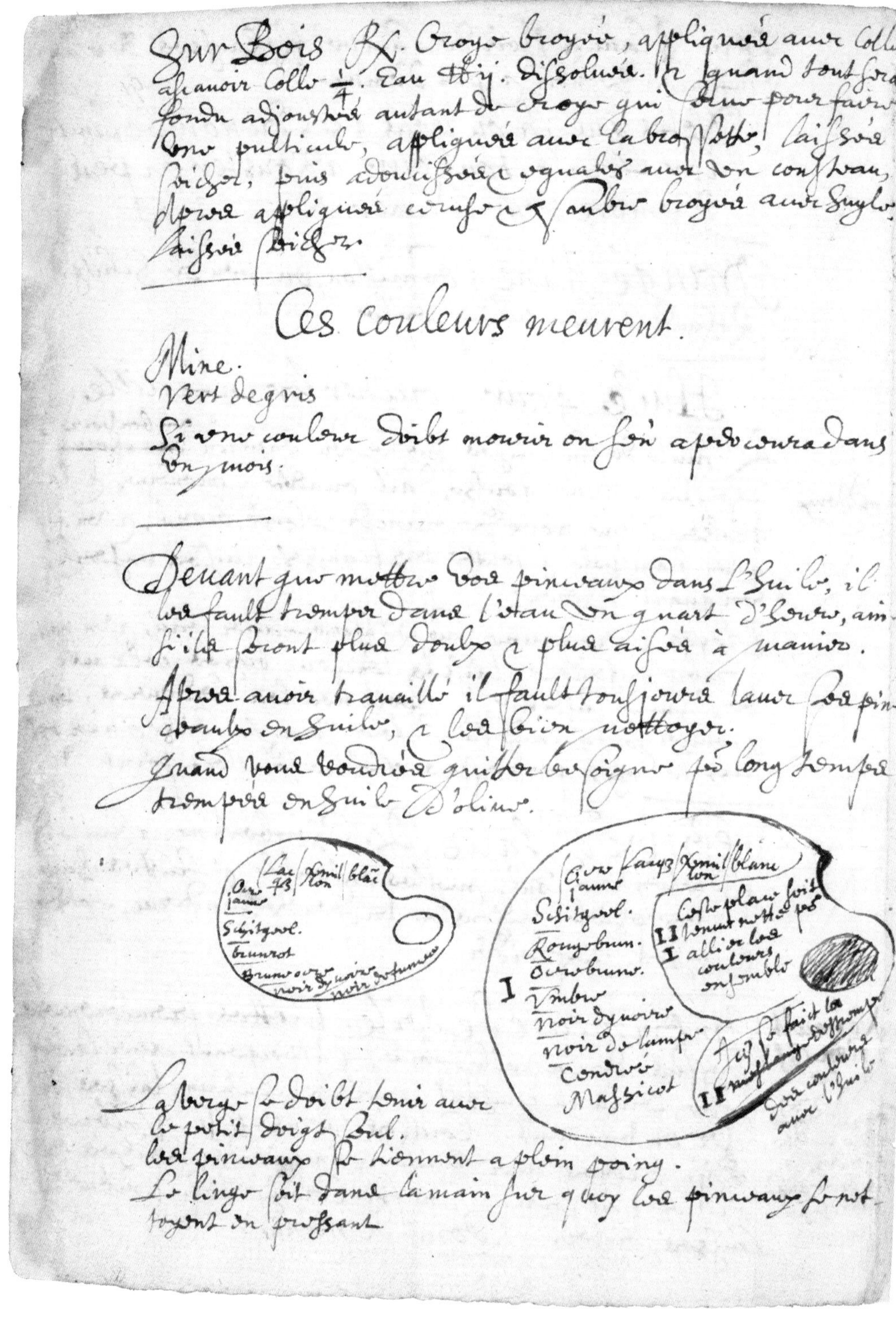

Sur Bois Rx. Croye broyée, appliquée avec Colle a scauoir Colle 1/4. Eau ℥ij. dissolvée. Et quand tout sera fondu adjoustés autant de Croye qui serue pour faire vne pulticule, appliquées avec la brossette, laissés secher, puis adoucissés & egualés avec vn cousteau, apres appliquées encore & l'ambre broyée avec huyle laissés secher.

Ces couleurs meurent.

Mine.
Vert de gris
Si vne couleur doibt mourir on s'en apercevra dans vn mois.

Deuant que mettre vos pinceaux dans l'huile, il les fault tremper dans l'eau vn quart d'heure, ainsi ils seront plus doulx & plus aisés à manier.
Apres auoir travaillé il fault tousjours lauer les pinceaux en huile, & les bien nettoyer.
Quand vous voudrés quitter besoigne pr long temps trempés en huile d'oliue.

La brosse se doibt tenir avec le petit doigt seul.
les pinceaux se tiennent a plein poing.
Le linge soit dans la main sur quoy les pinceaux se nettoyent en pressant.

found out in the way of Painting', sub-headed 'Experimentall Secrets found out in the way of my owne Painting'. From 1647 until the last entry in 1663, Charles described his laborious experiments with colours and materials. His approach was technical and instructive, with recommendations on how 'to heighten and make things shine ... found out in the painting of a raw rabbit...the blewish was pure lake and white'.[28] 'To paint linen very faire and naturall, first dead colour ye linen with white on black and umber', he noted.[29] He discovered a method of making pewter and plate appear glossy[30] and took delight in painting herrings,[31] oranges and colouring 'my great red plums'.[32] From the 1650s he concentrated on the manufacture of colours, especially trials of 'a green pinke',[33] red lake and ultramarine blue. During the summer of 1659 while living in Covent Garden, Charles noted 'my process of making Lake'. He sold his product to Lely and presumably retained some for Mary's use.

Charles Beale's 'Experimental Secrets' drew inspiration from Sir Théodore De Mayerne's researches. Physician to King James I and Queen Anne, De Mayerne was a natural philosopher (scientist) interested in the mineral and chemical properties of colours. He discussed the merits of pigments with John Hoskins the elder, and personally supplied colours to the enamellist Jean Petitot. De Mayerne compiled information from artists about their materials, techniques, recipes for colours, varnishes and directions for painting. This collection, dated to between 1620 and 1646, was acquired by Sir Hans Sloane, another physician with myriad interests.

Charles Beale's trials and experiments with colours formed the basis of Mary's palette, and the sale of his colours to other artists provided a small income. Charles was generous with his knowledge and might have hoped that the results of his experiments would be published. There were several precedents in the genre printed in English, beginning with a *Treatise on limning* (1573) and, more relevant to Beale, *A Booke of Secrets: Shewing Divers Waies to Prepare all Sortes of Inke and Colours* translated from the Dutch in 1596. Henry Peacham's *The Compleat Gentleman* (1622, 1634) was aimed at amateur gentlemen artists, as the title suggests. The most influential work of this era was Edward Norgate's *Miniatura or the Art of Limning,* of 1621–6 (a pirated edition was published as part of William Sanderson's *Graphice* in 1658). Originally written at the request of De Mayerne, Norgate's manual provided 'an excellent receipt for the making of Ultramarine' (Charles Beale's speciality); it

Opposite: A page from Sir Théodore De Mayerne's notes on painting, 1620-46

listed the names and uses of colours 'both for Pictures by the Life, Landscape and History', with an appendix on the 'Art of Painting in Oyl by ye Life', and advice on the sequence of painting portraits in three sittings, a schedule adopted by Mary Beale. Another author Beale would have been aware of was Daniel King whose *Secrets in the noble art of Miniatura or Limning* (*c.* 1653-7) was dedicated to his pupil Mary Fairfax. Alexander Browne's publication, *Ars Pictoria* (1669) aimed at a similar readership with its dedication to the Duchess of Monmouth. Browne advised the artist 'to be very skilfull in the use of Colours, as in that wherein consisteth the whole perfection of his Art', a maxim well understood by Charles and Mary Beale. William Salmon compiled information from previous publications in *Polygraphice* (1672), a handbook that was readily available.

The last entry in Charles Beale's 'Experimental Secrets' is headed 'Observations by MB in her painting of Apricots in August 1663' (the only reference to a still life by Mary although her 'Young Bacchus' held a bunch of succulent grapes). These observations have been interpreted as 'the first known text in English about the act of painting written by a female artist' i.e. by Mary Beale.[35] This may not be so. It is more plausible that Mary's observations were recorded by Charles. Examples of handwriting (Mary's precise and tightly spaced, Charles's loosely formed) indicate that the 'Observations by MB' on the painting of apricots were penned by Charles. He compared Mary's painting of apricots in 1663 to his own still life of apricots executed in 1649, and the notes are written in Charles's inimitable style: 'your dead colour being perfectly dry compose ye severall sorts of Mastics with nut oyl & leave for half an hour. For the greenish colouring mingle white lead, middle masticot, Bury Oker, pinks & a very little Ultramarine together' (massicot was an opaque yellow pigment; Bury ochre was bright yellow). He concludes 'Those apricots I painted before made use of Bury Oker were much harsher coloured and nothing so soft' (as Mary's painting of 1663).[36] The still life which Mary's father had presented to the Painter-Stainers' Company in 1648 included apricots; the colour and texture of the fruit also appealed to his daughter and son-in-law, and Mary was able to capture the fruit's softness.

The manufacture of colours used in oil painting was an intellectual pursuit fostered by the Royal Society, which took De Mayerne's investigations further by promoting research into the fine arts and the sciences. John Evelyn FRS (1620–1706), who planned to write a treatise on engraving, etching and painting, promoted these subjects at the Royal Society, which appointed a committee to investigate painting techniques and colours in 1666. The botanical artist Alexander Marshal (*c.* 1620–1682), renowned for developing new pigments and dyes, and the miniature painter Samuel Cooper were approached for information about their recipes but few artists were co-operative and the Royal Society's initiative floundered. Individual Fellows pursued their researches: Robert Boyle (1627–1691), who built a laboratory opposite the Beales' house in Pall Mall in the 1670s, was the author of *Experiments and Considerations touching Colours* (1664), and Sir William Petty contributed papers to the Society on making painters' colours from earth, chalk and minerals.

De Mayerne, Robert Hooke, Boyle, Petty and Charles Beale were absorbed by experiments with pigments, colours and the scientific aspects of oil painting. For them science and the arts were not two cultures but one, a theme promulgated by the Pre-Raphaelites of the late nineteenth century and by C. P. Snow more recently. Charles Beale was no dilettante: his experiments and trials were scientific investigations which aimed to obtain the best effect in oil painting. A practical man, he purchased pigments, brushes, linen canvas, sacking, onion bags, bed ticking and all the components Mary needed to execute her portraits. He noted the results of using new materials and techniques; one challenge, particularly when 'My Dearest Heart' was inundated with commissions in 1677, was the time oil paint took to dry before another layer could be applied (at least three days). To accelerate this, Charles conducted ingenious experiments with various base coats and glazes painted onto different materials, from linen to onion bags. He was an industrious stretcher and primer of canvases: in the year 1680 to 1681 he primed 172 canvases, mostly of sacking, taking care to apply a mixture of white lead, yellow ochre, cullen's earth, blew black, burnt umber and good red ochre, the colours having been ground by Beale personally or by Carter.[37]

Meanwhile, for Charles and Mary Beale in Covent Garden, future prospects were ephemeral. A few commissions had come Mary's way but her career as a professional portrait painter was in the balance. Charles must have received some financial support from his parents to pay rent and to sustain his family, for he had not fixed on a professional career, so lacked a salary. In 1656, having recently moved to Covent Garden, he enrolled at Trinity College, University of Cambridge, presumably with a view to a career but he never took a degree. He eventually found employment in 1660: King Charles II had recently been restored to the throne and new appointments were being made in official circles. Charles's brother Bartholomew clung onto his post as Auditor of the Imprests, and either he or their father may have secured Charles's appointment at the Patents Office, a department of Chancery. This brought with it a salary, an office, respectability and family accommodation in Hind Court on the north side of Fleet Street. Here the Beales were hosts to clergymen, authors, poets and Fellows of the Royal Society, many of whom commissioned their portraits from Mrs Beale.

Wenceslaus Hollar, *The piazza, Covent Garden*, c. 1647

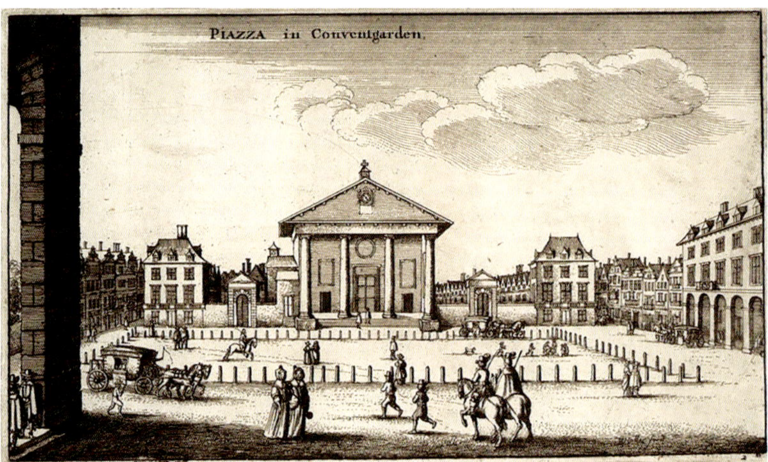

1. Rawlinson 104, 25 July 1651, f.133r

2. GVCBA 4 March 1672

3. *The Registers of St Paul's Church, Covent Garden*, ed. by William Hunt (1906), p. 5. The Jeffree and Walsh research notes, (*c.* 1970–90), 2/2, Ms 128, Heinz Archive and Library, NPG, refer to Charles Beale at number 13 King Street, 1656–7; a recent search at WCA failed to verify this

4. *Survey of London. St Paul Covent Garden*, (1970), XXXVI, pp. 303-5

5. Pepys III, p.230, 20 October 1662

6. GVCBA 5 May 1672

7. *Ibid.*, 4 March

8. Symonds (1617–1660) returned to London from Italy in 1651. For his notes on contemporary artists see Egerton Ms 1636, BL, and Mary Rose S. Beal, *A Study of Richard Symonds,* (1984), p. 311, Ph D thesis, Courtauld Institute of Art

9. 'Vertue Note Books II', *Walpole Society* 20 (1932), p. 69

10. *Vasari. Lives of the Painters, Sculptors and Architects*, ed. by William Gaunt, trans. A. B. Hinds (1963) II, pp. 325-8

11. Susan E. James, *Feminine Dynamic in English Art 1485–1603,* (2009), p. 263

12. Roy Strong, *The Tudor and Stuart Monarchy. Pageants, Painting, Iconography,* (1995), II, p. 213

13. Mary D. Garrard, *Artemisia Gentileschi*, (1989), pp. 390, 394, 397

14. Pepys, VII, pp.115–6, 3 May 1666

15. 'Vertue Note Books I', *op. cit.*, p. 66

16. Jeffree and Walsh research notes (c. 1970–90), 4/2, Ms 128, Heinz Archive and Library, NPG

17. William Sanderson, *Graphice,* (1658), p. 20

18. Mansfield Kirby Talley, *Portrait Painting in England: Studies in the Technical Literature before 1700,* (1981), pp.194, 196, 225

19. Sloane Ms 2052, BL. See also Talley, *op. cit.*, pp. 144, 147

20. 'Vertue Note Books I', *op. cit.*, p.143

21. Letter Charles Beale to Mary Cradock, Rawlinson 104, 25 July 1651, f.133r

22. Samuel Woodford, *A Paraphrase Upon the Psalms of David,* (1667), preface

23. Richard Jeffree, 'The paintings of Mary Beale', Jeffree and Walsh research notes, (*c.*1970–90), 2/11, Ms 128, Heinz Archive and Library, NPG

24. John Gage, *The History and Antiquities of Hengrave in Suffolk,* (1822), p. 224

25. Carol Gibson-Wood, 'Samuel Woodforde's first diary: an early source for Mary Beale', *Burlington Magazine* 147, no 1230, September 2005, pp. 606-8

26. Samuel Woodford, *Liber*, 28 September 1664

27. 'Vertue Note Books I', *op. cit.*, p. 139. Vertue gives a date of 1639 for Baglione's book

28. Charles Beale, 'Experimental Secrets found out in the way of Painting', (1647–63), February 1647, f.1

29. *Ibid.*, March 1647, f.3

30. *Ibid.*, f.4

31. *Ibid.*, March 1648, f.7

32. *Ibid.*, 1649, ff.7, 8

33. *Ibid.*, July 1654, ff.13-17

34. *Ibid.*, 22 July 1659, ff.20-22

35. Helen Draper, 'Her painting of apricots: the invisibility of Mary Beale (1633-1699)', *Forum for Modern Language Studies,* 48, no 4, October 2012, pp. 319–405

36. Charles Beale, 'Experimental Secrets', *op. cit.*, August 1663

37. CBA December 1681. See also Talley, *op. cit.*, p. 286

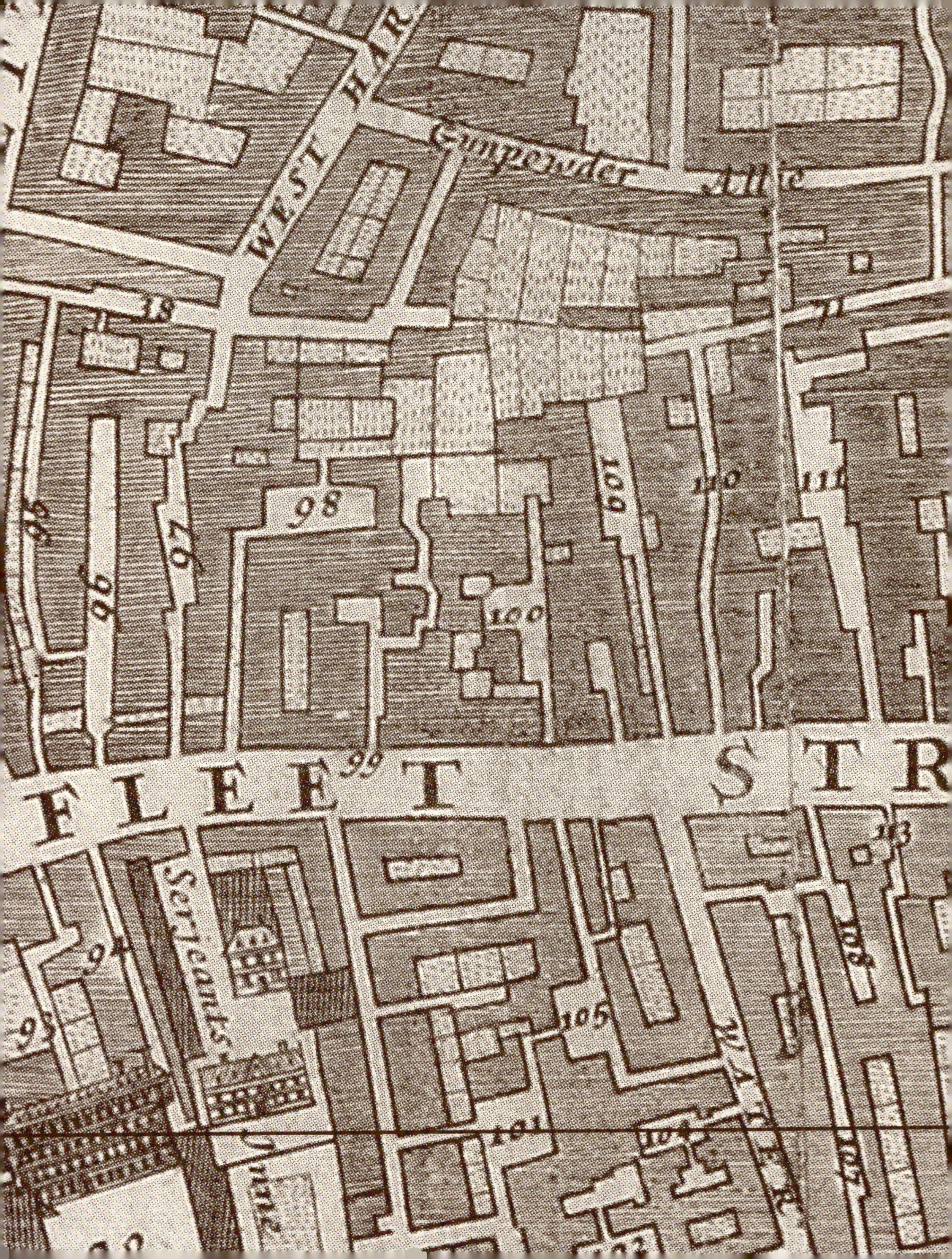

WEST HAR
Gunpowder
Alle
98
100
109
110
111
99
FLEET
STR
Serjeants
Inne
105
108

3. THE BEALES' CIRCLE

THE RESTORATION OF THE MONARCHY IN 1660 was celebrated by Charles II's reception into the City of London on his birthday, 29 May. The King's entourage gathered strength at Southwark and carved its way through the crowds on London Bridge. In the City, opulent Aldermen, Sheriffs and liverymen in their gowns added dignity to the procession of some 20,000 people on horse and on foot. Church bells rang and crowds lined the streets, cheering, refreshed by the wine that flowed from the conduits. The King's ostentatious coronation in 1661 and an extravagant river pageant following his marriage to Catharine of Braganza in 1662 prolonged the festivities that marked the start of an invigorating era in London's intellectual and artistic life.

The arts and sciences were promoted by King Charles II's charter to 'The Royal Society of London for improving Natural Knowledge' in 1662. The Reverend John Wilkins (1614–1672), vicar of St Lawrence Jewry at the time and the most influential founder-member of the Royal Society, chose to be painted by Mary Beale, which brought her to the notice of Fellows of the Society. The years of the Interregnum (1649–60) with the imposition of heavy taxes, 'loans', the sale of the King's art collection, the closure of theatres and general Puritan austerity were over, superseded by the adventurous, sometimes eccentric pursuits of the Royal Society, a revival in patronage of the arts and the flamboyance of the King's Court. The art market recovered, prompted by a 'Proclamation for the Restoring and Discovering of His Majesty's Goods'. King Charles I's magnificent art collection had been sold, dispersed or reserved by Lord Protector Oliver Cromwell, and Charles II was determined to recover his inheritance: by 1685 nearly 1,500 sculptures and paintings had been re-installed in the royal palaces. Art commissions and auctions accelerated, fed by artists such as Sir Peter Lely and his studio, John Greenhill, Gerald Soest, William Wissing, Mary Beale and latterly by Sir Godfrey Kneller, John Riley and Michael Dahl.

Opposite: From 1660 to 1665 the Beales lived at Hind Court, Fleet Street (109 on William Morgan's map of 1682)

For Charles and Mary Beale the summer of 1660 was marred by the death of Charles's father on 16 June. A week later Charles and

Mary's new-born son, Charles, was baptised at St Dunstan in the West by the Presbyterian minister Dr William Bates. The Beales were recent parishioners of St Dunstan's, a short walk from Hind Court, Fleet Street, where they lived between 1660 and 1665.

At the Restoration of the monarchy, diplomats, politicians and civil servants were keen to secure appointments. Thus it was that in July 1660 Samuel Pepys, promised the post of Clerk of the Acts of the Navy Board, made haste to Charles Beale's office in Hind Court. Pepys needed to have his patent written out 'in Chancery hand' and obtain a docket confirming his appointment. Initially, he met with a frosty reception: Beale was busy. 'But he not having time to get it done in Chancery-hand, I was forced to run all up and down Chancery-lane and the Six Clerks' Office but could find none that could write that hand that were at leisure', Pepys complained. Eventually he persuaded a clerk called John Spong to undertake the work (which he did at home in his nightshirt). Pepys took the result to Beale, 'but he was very angry and unwilling to do it because he said it was ill-writ (because I had got it writ by another hand and not by him)'. Beale's petulance was overcome by the gift of 'two pieces...after which it was strange how civil and tractable he was to me' (Pepys paid him £9 in all). Beale then completed Pepys's documentation, 'made it ready for the seal' and met Pepys at the Lord Chancellor's office to have the Letters Patent sealed. Mrs Pepys was overjoyed to hear that her husband's post had been confirmed because it brought with it a large house in Seething Lane and a salary of £350 a year.[1]

The Beale and the Pepys families were related through the marriage in 1601 of Robert Beale of Whittlesey, Cambridgeshire, to Susannah (b. 1580), daughter of John Pepys of Cottenham in the same county. This Robert Beale was a beneficiary of the will of Robert Pepys of Brampton, Huntingdonshire, uncle of the diarist. Samuel Pepys and his father were executors of the will and oversaw arrangements for the funeral in 1661. Therefore, Samuel must have known Robert and Susannah Beale. Furthermore, he dealt with Charles Beale in 1660 (as above) and he enjoyed the company of Charles's brother Bartholomew, Auditor of the Imprests. Auditor Beale was responsible for the Navy accounts, in which capacity he worked with Pepys. In December 1662 Pepys and the Auditors of the Exchequer, John Wood and Bartholomew Beale, dined at The Dolphin, 'We had a good dinner, cost us £5 6 shillings (whereof my share 26 shillings) and after dinner did discourse of our Salarys and other matters'.[2] Auditor Beale and Samuel Pepys continued to do business, perusing ledgers together and indulging in 'a mighty merry evening' at Lord Peterborough's in 1665.[3]

Hind Court, Fleet Street

The artists' quarter of Covent Garden, where Charles and Mary Beale had lived in the late 1650s was more attractive to Mary Beale than the neighbourhood of Fleet Street. Nevertheless, Charles's appointment as Deputy Clerk of the Patents Office came with a salary, an office and accommodation at Hind Court on the north side of Fleet Street. The houses of Hind Court faced each other across the courtyard and the Beales' house was large enough to provide a 'painting-roome' for Mary on the top floor.[4] Below, there was a reception room for musical evenings and a dining-room for entertaining guests such as Dr Bates, Dr and Mrs John Tillotson, Thomas Flatman and Samuel Woodford. This 'Beale-Flatman set'[5] included Dr Thomas Sprat who wrote the history of the Royal Society, and Abraham Cowley,

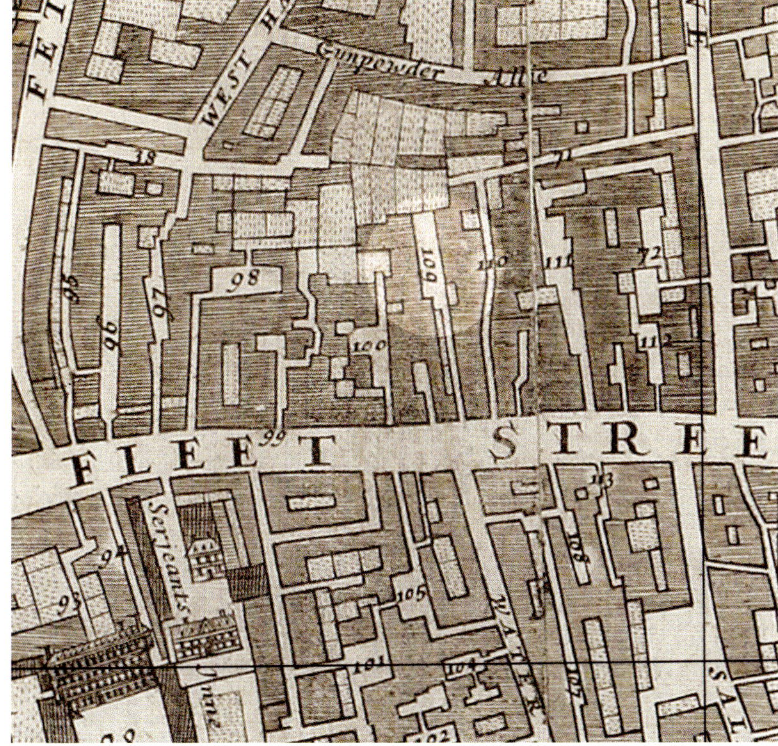

While Charles Beale was Deputy Clerk of the Patents Office, the family lived at Hind Court on the north side of Fleet Street. Hind Court is number 109 on William Morgan's map of 1682

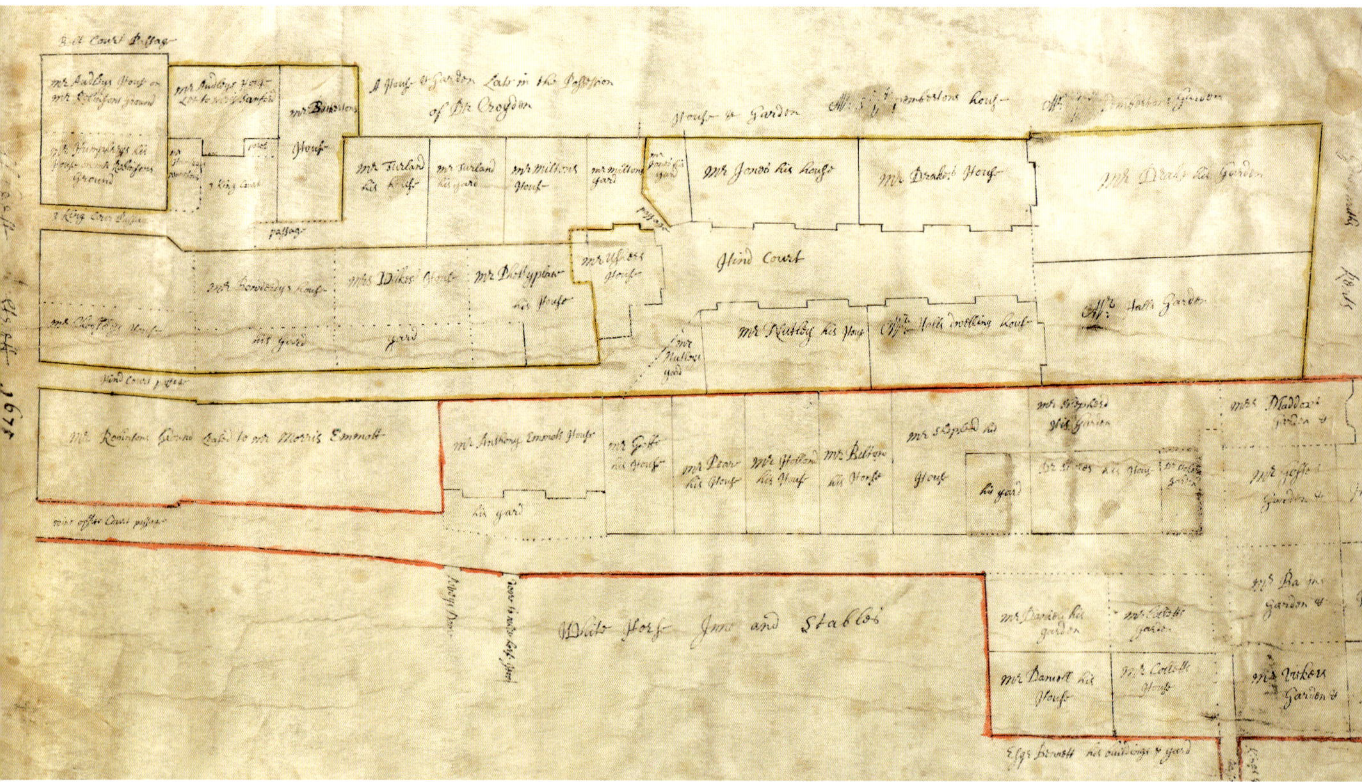

A survey of Hind Court, Fleet Street (top), 1675

the poet, who both dined with the Beales in October 1664 when 'a very agreeable conversation was spoiled by oaths from some of the company'.[6] Mary Beale was both hostess and portrait painter to the Fellows of the Royal Society, clergymen, poets and authors who frequented the house in Hind Court.

The walls of the Beales' house in Hind Court displayed a collection of pictures 'by Rubens and Vandyke several. 3 pictures painted by Mr Walker. Her Father Cradock. Mrs Beale & Mr Beale £18. Several pictures of the Family of Beals by Mr Lilly – Mr Beals picture HL. Mrs Beals HL. Mr Lilly's own picture HL. Each 20 pounds'. A painting by 'Lock' [possibly Nicholas or Rowland Lockey] was worth £12, one by Adriaen Hanneman (portrait painter to exiled royalists including the Prince of Wales) was valued at £18.[7] The collection was to be augmented by a portrait of Bishop Antoine Triest after Van Dyck (Triest, 1576–1655, Bishop of Bruges and Ghent, was a patron of the arts),'Venus and Cupid' by Hans Rottenhammer and Lely's portraits of Tillotson (1672), Brook Bridges (1672), Stillingfleet, (1674), the Beales' son Charles (1674) and 'a double ½ length of Mr Beal &

his wife Mrs Mary Beal by [Vertue copied Lely's monogram here]'. This covetable double portrait was inherited by Carter, the Beales' colour seller.[8]

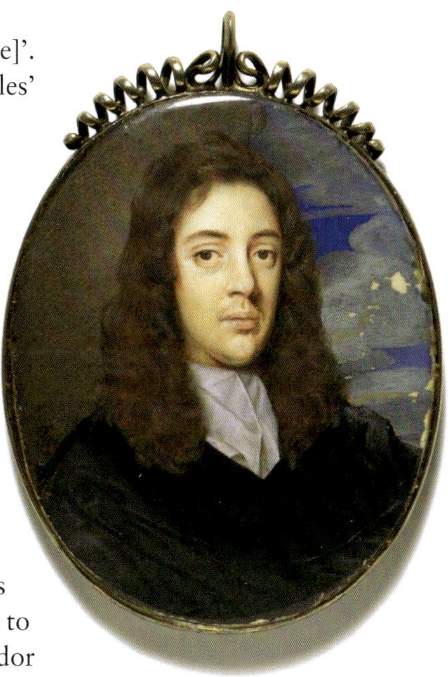

Thomas Flatman, *Charles Beale*, 1664

Charles and Mary Beale were art collectors, connoisseurs and bibliophiles with a library that shelved books on Italian art such as Giovanni Baglione's *Le Vite de' Pittori, Scultori, Architetti* (1642) and a treatise by Leonardo da Vinci, *Trattato della Pittura,* 'which I had from Mrs Flatman' (Suzanna, wife of Thomas Flatman).[9] Leonardo's treatise on painting, originally published in French and Italian in 1651, presented painting as a science, an aspect that interested Charles Beale. His enthusiasm for Italian art was shared by the landscape artist Thomas Manby (*c.* 1633–1695) to whom he entrusted his copy of Leonardo's treatise and 'a little Italian book il partito di Donni about Painting'[10] (Anton Doni's views on design, sculpture, painting and colours, 1549). Charles purchased books for his library from a dealer called Jolivet and at least one volume came to him by courtesy of Francisco de Mello, the Portuguese ambassador who was briefly Lord Chamberlain to the Queen. Recognising that Charles and Mary Beale were bibliophiles, their friends presented them with books: Gilbert Burnet, Bishop of Salisbury, gave Mary the first two volumes of his *History of the Reformation* (1679, 1681); Dr Stillingfleet countered that with a biography of Bishop John Fisher, the sixteenth-century martyr, and 'Our worthy friend Dr Crawford' donated books soon after he had been painted by Mary in 1681.[11]

Before it was lost, Charles Beale's inventory of the contents of the Hind Court house in 1661 was seen by George Vertue. Beale was a methodical diarist and note-taker and his inventory listed paintings, frames, cloths (canvases), utensils, colours, plate, watches, books and furniture. Charles also kept account of the family's expenses which in 1661 included £15 paid to Sir Peter Lely for Mary's late father's portrait and £30 to Thomas Flatman 'for limning my own picture, father Cradock and the Boyes'.[12] Flatman, poet, miniaturist, barrister and a Fellow of the Royal Society, also painted his friend Samuel Woodford and his wife, Alice, soon after their marriage in 1661 when they were living with the Beales at Hind Court. His miniatures of members of the Beale household were multiple. His earliest was of Charles (1660), another of 1662 shows Charles's warts, and a third is dated 1664, not to mention the self portraits he gave to Charles and Mary.

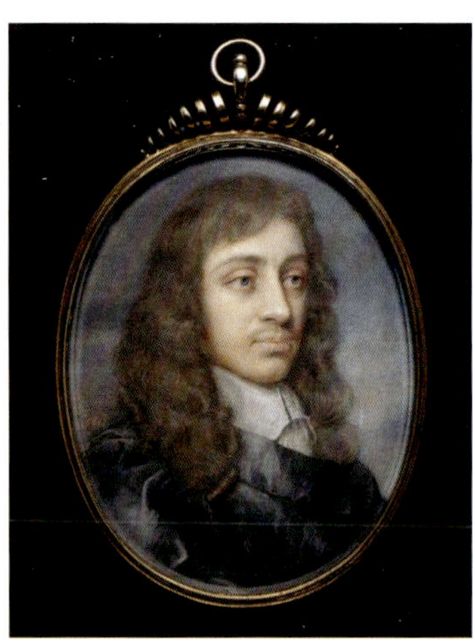

Thomas Flatman, *Samuel Woodford*, 1661

'Cousen Shee Beale'[13]

Despite the distractions of family life, Mary Beale found time to paint. Her portrait of Alderman Hildesley was completed before 1660. Her self portrait which also featured her husband and son must have been painted around 1660 and two profiles of her curly-haired son Bartholomew aged four or five years old must be contemporaneous. A year after moving to Hind Court, Charles and Mary Beale and their two young sons were joined by Samuel Woodford (1636–1700), poet, lawyer, later a rector in Hampshire and Prebendary of Winchester Cathedral. He and his wife, Alice, lived with the Beales between 1661 and 1663; Woodford returned to the household after the death of Alice in 1664 and he accompanied the family to Hampshire in 1665. His relationship with Mary, Charles and their sons was intimate, as his diaries and memoirs reveal. He recorded his deep affection for Mary and Charles, the names of the guests they entertained and those who came to Hind Court to sit for their portraits by 'The Excellent Mrs Mary Beal'.[14]

Samuel Woodford's first wife, Alice (1634–1664), was the youngest daughter of the Reverend Theodore and Mrs Elizabeth Beale. Theodore (1566–1652), vicar of Ashbocking in Suffolk and later of St Michael's, Walton, was Charles Beale's uncle, hence through his marriage to Alice, Woodford was related to Charles Beale, whom he referred to as Cousen or Cosin Beale, while Mary was 'Cousen Shee Beale'.[15]

It is due to Woodford that a description survives of Mary Beale's self portrait as Pallas, goddess of war and patron of the arts and crafts. Woodford's poem 'To Belisa', written in 1664, describes the painting.

> The Excellent Mrs Mary Beal upon her own Picture, done by her self, like Pallas, but without any Arms, except Head-piece and Corselet.
>
> Such would the learned *Pallas* chuse to be,
> With all the Charms of Nature and of Art,
> Tho she had neither Shield nor Dart:
> For if the mighty *Pallas* were like Thee,
> Without those, she to Conquer, need but come, and see.
> And here (alas!) the Goddess nothing can espy
> Except the Garb to own her Figure by;
> The Warlike dress, and that's so Gay,
> Such Terror and such softness does display,

That that as little as the Face she seems to know;
Wishing that her own *Greece* had drawn her so:
Says Fabulous Antiquity;
Ne're gave her half that Grace or Majesty:
That she was never half so Fair
In her own Beauties, or what e're they feign'd
With such clear Limbs, or with so great a Mind,
As in your Draught, *Belisa*, she's design'd,
And were she to be Born again,
Would from your hand desire it rather than *Jove*'s Brain.[16]

By his own admission Samuel Woodford had led a dissolute life as an undergraduate at Oxford. 'I ran into the greatest extravagances imaginable', with 'bad company and naughty acquaintance'.[17] On coming to London in 1658 to enrol as a lawyer at Inner Temple, Woodford shared chambers with his contemporary at Oxford, Thomas Flatman (1635–1688). As Woodford remembered, 'Mr Flatman one day told me he would carry me to an acquaintance of his, a very good house; for novelty's sake I went with him, to my true real and good friend Mr Charles Beale's at the house where I now am. Coming there a second time (I think) I met a Gentlewoman, one Mrs Alice Beale (who since thanks be to Almighty God is my dear and loving wife) and by little and little coming better acquainted with her, continual converse bred an entire affection in me to her and finding in her whatever I desired in a wife I gave over myself to her love'.[18]

In the summer of 1660 Samuel Woodford and Alice Beale were betrothed but opposition from Samuel's widowed mother and his great-uncle, Edmund Heighes (all too aware of Samuel's reckless past), delayed the marriage until 10 October 1661. Samuel was by then employed as solicitor to Sir William Morice, so in receipt of an income, which mollified his family. The couple were married by Dr John Tillotson at St Christopher-le-Stocks, 'none being there but my Cousens Beale & his wife & Tom Flatman my chamber fellow'.[19]

Soon after their marriage Samuel and Alice Woodford visited Lely's studio to have Alice's portrait painted and the couple dined with the artist afterwards. The portrait was unfinished at the time of Alice's death in 1664, so Woodford and Mary Beale, accompanied by 'Cousin Moll', made an appointment with Lely in order to have the painting completed. Mary Beale modelled for the head, Moll for the breast. Woodford was pleased with the result, 'it is exceeding like and by it I am able perfectly to remember her'. At the close of the day Lely entertained the company to dinner.[20] 'Cousin Moll' was Mary Smythe, Charles Beale's niece, who was admired by both Woodford and Flatman. Their friendship stumbled temporarily, over Moll: 'he thinks to traduce me' Woodford wrote, adding 'how false all this is'.[21]

Samuel and Alice's daughter, called Alice after her mother, was born at Hind Court and promptly baptised by Dr Tillotson in November 1662 with Mary Beale as godmother. Samuel, Alice and their daughter moved out of Hind Court in the summer of 1663 when Samuel inherited West Court, Binsted, Hampshire. His wife died there on 14 January 1664, from puerperal fever after the birth of their son, Heighes. Samuel sought comfort with Charles and Mary Beale, returning to live with them at Hind Court. He presented mourning rings to them and to the Smythes and found relief from his grief by writing poems, for example, 'To the Memory of Mrs A.W [Alice] who died in childbed' and 'To Belisa and her Swain' [Mary and Charles Beale]

'Who claimed a share
By love and Friendship in the Pious Care,
Were all his Company and who alone,
Best knew, and judg'd his Sorrow by their own'.[22]

Charles and Mary Beale were Woodford's saviours. He was deeply grateful for the consolation and company of his 'dearest cosin Beales whom my God has raised up to bee my best and most affectionate family since my deare ever deare Alice's death. I have, from all the effects of a most sincere & hearty friendship & ye comfort & agreeableness of society in this solitude'. [23]

While comforting Woodford, entertaining guests and running the household, Mary Beale worked on portraits, expanding the range of her sitters. During 1664 she completed portraits of Woodford, Tillotson, Stillingfleet, Dr John Cooke, Sir William Godolphin, Matthew Hunt (brother of Charles's sister-in-law), Bartholomew Beale (Charles's brother) and Mr and Mrs John Smythe (Charles's brother-in-law and sister).

On the domestic front, four-year-old Charles Beale caught smallpox, a lethal infection which his family managed to avoid by chewing tobacco and dosing themselves with electuaries (mixtures of syrups and powders from the apothecary). In the interests of his physical and spiritual health Woodford decided 'to cut off my hair and putt on a Periwigg – the Lord grant it may be for the health of my body and presenting me in good state to serve him better'.[24] This was a religious household with Puritan leanings but not without merriment. Guests were treated to dinners of venison pie and there were musical evenings starring Signor 'Torriano' (who gave Charles Italian lessons), John Rogers on the lute, Woodford on the viola and Signor 'Pedro' (possibly Pietro Reggio, a music master) whose singing stirred Woodford deeply.[25] Those who made appointments with Mrs Beale to have their portraits painted often stayed to dine when the light faded: Dr and Mrs Tillotson and Dr and Mrs Stillingfleet were regular guests, 'we were very cheerful and I hope without sin'.[26] Dr John Tillotson was related to the Cromwell family by his marriage to Oliver Cromwell's niece, Elizabeth, who was Mary Beale's dearest friend and the recipient of Mary's 'Discourse on Friendship' (see chapter 4). Tillotson, a future Archbishop of Canterbury, was painted by Mary five times (1664, 1672, 1677, 1681, 1687); she was also commissioned for portraits of Elizabeth and their daughter Mary in 1681.

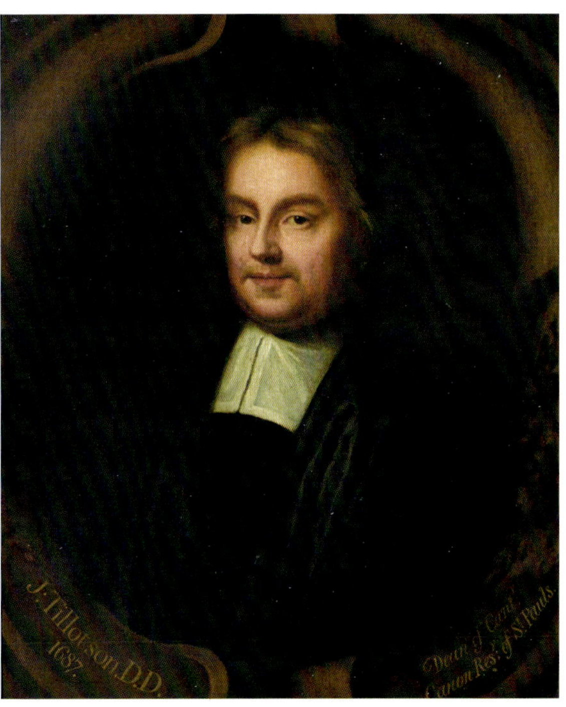

Mary Beale, *Archbishop John Tillotson FRS*, 1687. Tillotson was Dean of Canterbury at that date, advancing to Archbishop of Canterbury in 1691

The influence of Charles and Mary Beale, Tillotson, 'a man of a clear head and a sweet temper', Dr Edward Stillingfleet 'a man of much more learning but of a more reserved and a haughtier temper' who was later Bishop of Worcester,[27] and Dr Bates steered Woodford towards ordination. Personally he credited Dr James Gardiner for 'reclaiming' him (Gardiner and his wife sat for Mrs Beale, who later produced an official portrait of the Bishop to mark his elevation to the see of Lincoln in 1695).

The Psalms

While Woodford lived with Charles and Mary Beale at Hind Court he translated Tasso from the Italian, wrote an ode 'To Belisa' (Mary) and began to work on *A Paraphrase Upon the Psalms of David,* completed in 1666 and first published in 1667. He was inspired by reading a version of Psalm 114 by the poet Abraham Cowley (1618–1667) whom he described as 'a very morose man' on their

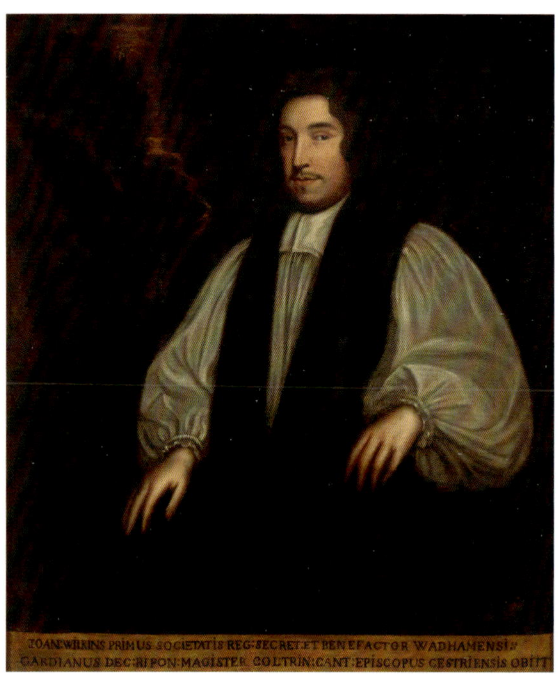

Mary Beale, *Dr John Wilkins, Bishop of Chester*, c. 1670-72

first meeting in 1664.[28] Woodford took advice on his proposed publication from the historian of the Royal Society, Dr Thomas Sprat (discouraging) and from the Society's Secretary, Dr John Wilkins (encouraging). Wilkins loaned Woodford a manuscript translation of the Psalms by the Elizabethan poet Sir Philip Sidney (1554–1586) who, with his sister, Mary, Countess of Pembroke (1561–1621), laboured over 'the Sidney Psalter', completed in 1599 and eventually published in 1823. The Countess's translation of the Psalms (she revised forty-three of her brother's and authored the remaining 107) drew on French, English and Latin translations and commentaries.[29] The autographed copy of her labours was rescued by Woodford, whose brother was using the manuscript as a container for ground coffee.

The precedent set by Sir Philip Sidney and his sister was followed nearly a century later by Samuel Woodford and Mary Beale with a translation that aimed to recapture the poetic quality of the 'Eastern Psalms whose manner of wit seems to be altogether different from ours, and not to be brought under those Laws which the Greek and Latine, and the Modern from them, have assigned verse', Woodford explained.[30] He had been planning a new translation of the Psalms for three years, discussing the project with learned Fellows, Protestant clergy, his wife, and Charles and Mary Beale. The latter's interest in Woodford's project reached fruition with her versions of Psalms 13, 52, 70 and 130 which demonstrated her intellectual, poetic and linguistic skills. Mary must have been taught Latin, possibly Greek and Hebrew by her father and/or by a local scholar while she was growing up in Suffolk. Her version of Psalm 13 which opens with 'How long, O God, shall I forgotten ly', is more forceful than Woodford's 'How long my God, wilt Thou thus hide thy face'. Similarly, Woodford translated part of Psalm 130 as 'Out of the depths unto the Lord I cry'd', whereas Beale's version begins 'Plung'd in the depths of sin and misery'.[31]

Woodford's preface to *The Psalms of David* acknowledged his debt to Abraham Cowley, Thomas Sprat, Sir Philip Sidney, Bishop Hall and the poet/priest George Herbert among other scholars. This is capped by praise for 'That absolutely compleat Gentlewoman, whose leave I very hardly obtained to honour this volume of mine with two or three versions long since done by her, the truly virtuous Mrs Mary Beale, amongst whose least accomplishment it is, that she has made Painting and Poesy which in the Fancies of others had only before a kind of likeness, in her own to be really the same. The Reader I hope will pardon this publick acknowledgement which I make to so deserving a person when I shall tell him that while as a friend and one of the Family, I had the convenience of a private and most delightful retirement in the company of her worthy Husband and herself, I both began and perfected this Paraphrase'.[32] It has been suggested that Woodford was infatuated by Mary Beale;[33] their relationship was certainly close and can be compared to the friendship between John Evelyn and Lady Godolphin (see pages 109-10).

Charles Beale 'in very great trouble'[34]

In December 1663 Woodford heard that Charles Beale was 'in very great trouble...surely he cannot ruin himself into any, being so cautious a man. Religion and the feare of God cannot but be a check on him in everything, especially where duty and loyalty doth also oblige'.[35] Beale was in trouble over 'the George Piggott business'. Piggott, a 'picture drawer' of Blackfriars, had been arrested following the publication of a seditious poem attributed to the Puritan poet, Dr Robert Wilde (1609–1679). Wilde had been ejected from his living in Huntingdonshire in 1662 and his nonconformity, combined with his wit and poems, discomforted the authorities. Piggott and Wilde knew the Beales and the latter was painted by Mary in November 1662 when he stayed 'all daye longe'.[36]

George Piggott claimed that he had found a copy of the seditious verses in the street. His offence was that he had 500 copies printed for distribution.[37] He was a Chancery clerk of twenty-seven years standing, so a senior colleague of Charles Beale, who found himself implicated in the Wilde/Piggott affair. Beale's friends rose to his defence: Woodford pleaded with Dr John Cooke and William Godolphin; Cooke and Sir William Morice thought that Piggott should be imprisoned, and the matter was so sensitive that Cooke added a postscript to his letter, 'Burn this'.[38] Dr Bates approached the Lord Chamberlain and Sir Thomas Vyner on Beale's behalf, to no avail. 'Some base fellows who have by unjust ways sought to undermine him' succeeded in doing so.[39]

As a result of Wilde's seditious verses, George Piggott's rashness and the resignation of Sir Robert Howard, Beale's superior at the Patents Office (by which 'my Cosen is likely to be a great looser'),[40] Charles Beale was dismissed at the end of 1664. This meant the loss of his salary and accommodation. A solution to this dire situation was suggested by Charles's brother-in-law, John Smythe, who drew attention to a house at Allbrook, four miles from Winchester in Hampshire. Woodford inspected the premises and supervised repairs; William Trumbull, a barrister and a distant Beale relation, eased the negotiations and Charles's eldest brother, Henry, laid out £400. [41]

'On ye 26th June 1665 wee went down thither & blessed bee god were preserved from the infection'.[42] Allbrook farmhouse provided a refuge for the otherwise homeless Beales and it allowed them to escape the plague of 1665 and the great fire of London in 1666. As Woodford reported in June, 'The Plague was so much increased in Town, yt all who had convenience of retiring, hastened to escape, & ye family who I was among the rest, to Albrook but they to fix there for good and all being weary of the citty without good employment'.[43]

Woodford thought that Charles and Mary Beale intended to live at Allbrook permanently. This was not to be but for the meanwhile Allbrook provided a relatively inexpensive home and an opportunity for the family to enjoy country life. On the other hand, removal from London meant isolation from friends and patrons, apart from the few who visited or wrote. While at Allbrook between June 1665 and late 1669, the number of Mary's commissions dwindled but she did paint a tender self portrait which included a canvas of her young sons, and a companion portrait of her husband probably dates from the same period. She turned to literary pursuits, writing poems and a 'Discourse on Friendship' (1667). For his part, Charles maintained his interest in pigments and colours, producing his 'best white' for Flatman and doubtless for Mary when required. He may have taken responsibility for the education of his sons and he generated an overwhelming correspondence with Francis Knollys, Dr John Cooke and Thomas Flatman. These letters illuminate the years the Beales spent in Hampshire.

THE BEALES' CIRCLE: NOTES

1. Pepys, I, pp.197–99, 12, 13 July 1660. Mrs Pepys's parents seem to have been neighbours of the Beales in Hind Court at this date

2. *Ibid.*, III, p. 279, 10 December 1662

3. *Ibid.*, VI, p. 68, 27 March 1665

4. S. Woodford, *Liber*, 1665

5. John Murdoch, Jim Murrell, Patrick J. Noon, Roy Strong, *The English Miniature,* (1981), p. 104

6. S. Woodford, *Liber,* 26 October 1664

7. Charles Beale's inventory, GVCBA 1661

8. 'Vertue Note Books IV', *Walpole Society* 24 (1936), p. 65

9. CBA 16 February 1681

10. GVCBA September 1676

11. CBA 1681

12. GVCBA 1661

13. S. Woodford, *Liber*, 27 December 1664

14. S. Woodford, *A Paraphrase Upon the Canticles and some Select hymns of the New and Old Testaments with other occasional compositions in English verse,* (1679), pp. 162-3

15. S. Woodford, *Liber*, *op. cit.*

16. S. Woodford, *A Paraphrase Upon the Canticles, op. cit.,* p. 162

17. Lori Anne Ferrell, 'An Imperfect Diary of a Life. The 1662 Diary of Samuel Woodforde', *Yale University Library Gazette* 63 (1989), pp. 137-144.

18. *Ibid.*, p. 143

19. S. Woodford, 'Memoirs', 10 October 1661

20. S. Woodford, *Liber*, 29 September 1664

21. *Ibid.*, 27 December 1664

22. S. Woodford, *A Paraphrase Upon the Canticles, op. cit.,* p. 157

23. S. Woodford, *Liber*, 4 August 1664

24. *Ibid.,* 10-12 August 1664

25. Lori Anne Ferrell, *op. cit.*

26. S. Woodford, *Liber,* 2 December 1664

27. GB I, pt 1, p. 335

28. S. Woodford, *Liber*, 26 October 1664

29. Theodore Steinberg, ''The Sidneys and the Psalms', *Studies in Philology* 192, no 1, (1995), pp. 1–17

30. S. Woodford, *A Paraphrase Upon the Canticles, op. cit.*

31. S. Woodford, *A Paraphrase Upon the Psalms of David,* (1678), pp. 26–8, 144–8, 195–8, 384–6

32. S. Woodford, *A Paraphrase Upon the Psalms of David,* (1667), preface

33. Nancy Cato, *The Lady Lost in Time,* (1986)

34. S. Woodford, *Liber*, 31 December 1663

35. *Ibid.*

36. Carol Gibson-Wood, 'Samuel Woodforde's first diary: an early source for Mary Beale', *Burlington Magazine* 147, no 1230, (2005), pp. 606-8

37. *State Papers Domestic,* 18, 19 December 1663, pp. 378-9

38. Rawlinson 113, 22 December 1663

39. S. Woodford, *Liber*, 10-12 August 1664

40. *Ibid.*, 1665

41. S. Woodford, 'Memoirs', 3 February 1665

42. *Ibid.*, June 1665

43. *Ibid.*

My Deare ffriend

Though I might bee truly ashamed to send you this my very imperfect draught after that immortall Beauty Friendship, yet considering that ofttimes wee esteem a Picture done by a very unskilfull hand, out of that great affection wee may have for the person whome it was design'd to represent, the work it self being very wretched and inconsiderable; So though you may call these my conceptions rather the Pourtraiture of my own inabilityes, then any true Image of that Divine thing wch I have endeavour'd to describe, yet that wch bears mee up if not in the beleife of your acceptance, yet in the hopes of your pardon, is, that high esteeme which I am assur'd you have for this subject. What I have further to say shall bee only this, That all the errors I have here committed may turn thus farr to your advantage, that they will afford you the opportunity to exercise towards mee all those allowances wch I have hinted must be indulg'd in a Friend. And so I may shorten the trouble of any further apology, by telling you that in the following discourse I have endeavour'd to lay before you my heart, if not what it is, yet what I desire it should bee, and do hope that your Friendship may help to make it; since you have beene pleas'd to admitt mee to the honour of being

Deare Madam

Allbrook. 9 March 1666

your truly affectionate, ffaithfull
Friend and Servant
Mary Beale

4. MARY BEALE'S 'DISCOURSE ON FRIENDSHIP' 1667

Several unfortunate events conspired to persuade Charles and Mary Beale to move to Hampshire in 1665. During the previous autumn 'Poor little Charles Beale had his head cut with a brick that fell on him' in Fleet Street and a month later he contracted smallpox, a deadly disease before the introduction of vaccination.[1] Mary Beale was too ill to 'gett up alone into ye painting roome' during the winter of 1664–65 and the extended family was 'exceeding ill', Woodford remembered.[2] An accident, illness and the cramped conditions at Hind Court caused domestic friction. The appearance of 'a blazing star' in the sky above London during the winter of 1665 was perceived as an evil portent and in the following spring the first fatalities of the plague were reported. Above all, Charles Beale's dismissal as Deputy Clerk of the Patents Office meant eviction from the Hind Court house, prompting the family to move out of London.

Opposite: Mary Beale's letter to her friend, Mrs Elizabeth Tillotson, to whom she sent her 'Discourse on Friendship', March 1667 (new calendar)

Below: Allbrook farmhouse, Hampshire, where the Beales lived from 1665 until late in 1669

Allbrook, Hampshire

In Charles Beale's 'very great trouble'[3] his brother-in-law, John Smythe, found a solution. Retreat to the Beale family estate at Walton in Buckinghamshire was not an option because Charles's elder brother, Henry, occupied the manor house there. Likewise, the Cradock family property, Geesings in Suffolk, was in the hands of the Reverend Samuel Cradock. In these depressing circumstances Smythe alerted Charles Beale to a house at Allbrook in the parish of Otterbourne, Hampshire. Woodford reported that it was 'a good house, it cost £800 building'.[4] The original occupants of Allbrook farmhouse were Gilbert Beare and his wife Anne: the date 1659 and the initials G.A.B. were hammered into the front door with iron nails.[5] The door has since been stolen and the house narrowly escaped demolition when redevelopment loomed in 2007. A campaign for the preservation of the Beales' home led by Sir Roy Strong, Dr Germaine Greer, Tracey Emin and the local MP, Chris Huhne, was

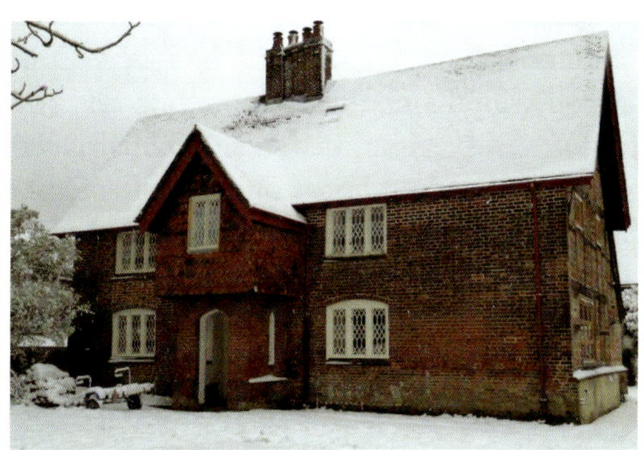

successful and the house is now listed Grade II by English Heritage.

With financial support from Charles's brother, Henry, with practical help from Samuel Woodford who organised repairs and with legal advice from William Trumbull FRS (1636–1716), the house known as Allbrook was acquired for Charles and Mary Beale. Sir William Trumbull, as he became, was related to Charles through the marriage of Elizabeth Trumbull to Charles's nephew, John Bridges/ Brydges. Trumbull was painted by Mary Beale in 1677, prior to his promotion to the office of Clerk of the Signet and his appointment as ambassador to Constantinople in 1685.

The lease of Allbrook farmhouse was sealed in December 1664 and the Beales, accompanied by Woodford, arrived there in June 1665. Mary intended to paint while living at Allbrook where canvases were stored above a false ceiling, and Charles fixed stretching frames to the beams and above the fireplace (drying racks for canvases were still *in situ* in 1950). The family was thankful to be out of London and the threat of infection: 'Great fears of the Sicknesse here in the City, it being said that two or three houses are already shut up. God preserve us all'.[6] Charles and Mary Beale were equally fortunate to escape the great fire of London in September 1666, as did their friend Thomas Flatman, one of the few who appreciated the ruins of the post-fire City. 'When I first entered the town I saw the beuteous ruins of that stately City, not so much as the Sceleton of what it was, *fuit ilium*, but now a glorious heap of ashes'.[7] William Sancroft, Dean of St Paul's at the time of the great fire, worked indefatigably to promote the rebuilding of the cathedral and personally donated £1,400 towards it. He was officially nominated by King Charles II as primate of the Anglican church in December 1677, the day after his appointment with Mary Beale at her Pall Mall painting-room. The Beales' friend Dr Edward Stillingfleet was brought into the debate about plans for the new cathedral – he objected to Sir Christopher Wren's 'Greek cross' design which was abandoned. Several members of the Beales' circle were involved with the rebuilding of St Paul's: Sir William Trumbull was appointed a commissioner in 1692; Dr John Tillotson was Dean of the cathedral from 1689 to 1691, while the lawyer and politician, Roger North (painted by Mary Beale in 1677) liked to spend Saturday mornings at the building site.

Having been part of the Beale household at Hind Court in the early 1660s, Samuel Woodford boarded with the family at Allbrook where he completed his *Paraphrase Upon the Psalms of*

David in March 1666. The next year he married Mary Norton of Binsted, Hampshire, with whom he had six children (his grandson and namesake was an artist and a regular exhibitor at the Royal Academy, 1792–1815). Woodford was ordained in 1669 and was presented with the living of Shalden and Hartley Mauditt, near Alton, Hampshire, by Sir Nicholas Stuart Bt, in 1673. Woodford must have introduced his patron to Mary Beale who was commissioned for portraits of Stuart and his sons, Miles and Charles, in the 1670s. Woodford, now a country vicar, followed the success of *A Paraphrase Upon the Psalms of David* with *A Paraphrase Upon the Canticles and some select Hymns of the New and Old Testaments with occasional compositions in English Verse* (1678, 1679), dedicated to the Archbishop of Canterbury and prefaced by Sir Nicholas Stuart. The publication attracted contributions from Woodford's friends: Dr William Croone FRS (whose portrait by Mary Beale hangs at the Royal College of Physicians) wrote an ode, and Thomas Flatman addressed a poem 'To my dear Old Friend, the Reverend Samuel Woodford on his Sacred Rhymes'. Woodford's own 'occasional compositions' were of a personal nature with sonnets to 'Iärma' (an anagram of Maria/Mary, his wife). Two odes were addressed to Izaac Walton congratulating him on his biographies of George Herbert and Richard Hooker, and a poem remembered 'Clelia', Woodford's late wife, Alice. Woodford referred to 'his owne picture done in water-colours by the Learned Poet and Limner, Mr Thomas Flatman, Fellow student with him and Chamber Fellow at the Inner Temple' (the miniature is illustrated on page 70). Mary and Charles Beale were extolled as 'Belisa and her Swain' (paying tribute to their support while Woodford was in mourning for Alice) and he singled out Mary in 'To Belisa. The Excellent Mrs Mary Beal'.[8] (see pages 70, 71). Woodford's poetry was popular at the time but his reputation has since declined to that of 'a minor bard little remembered today'.[9]

Country friends

Samuel Woodford's friendship with Izaak Walton (1593–1683, author of *The Compleat Angler*, 1653), prompted his prefatory poem to Walton's *Life of George Herbert* (1670). Walton and Woodford knew each other through George Morley, Bishop of Winchester, while Walton and Mary Beale's relatives, the Cradocks, liaised over marriage plans for Elizabeth Cradock. 'Sly Cousin Cradock', 'lawyer Cradock' and the City merchant, Matthew Cradock, plotted with

Izaak Walton to promote the marriage of 'the slippery widow', Elizabeth Bennett (1600–1661, née Cradock) to Sir Edward Dering Bt (she chose Sir Heneage Finch instead).[10] A further Beale/Walton connection was through Matthew Snelling whose step-brother, Colonel Thomas Blagge, ordered Walton to retrieve King Charles II's garter jewel from the battlefield at Worcester in 1651. Another mutual friend was Walton's son-in-law, Dr William Hawkins, rector of Droxford, and a Prebendary of Winchester alongside Woodford. Some years after the Beales had returned to London, Hawkins called at their Pall Mall house to pay £10 that Woodford owed Mrs Beale.[11]

Dr William Lloyd (1627–1717), tutor to the Backhouse family of Swallowfield, six miles south of Reading, Berkshire, introduced Charles and Mary Beale to Lady Backhouse (1641–1700, Lady Cornbury from 1670, Countess of Clarendon from 1674). Lady Backhouse and her first husband, Sir William (1641–1669, an alchemist and astrologer), entertained Charles and Mary Beale at Swallowfield in September 1668. After Sir William's death the next year, Lady Backhouse married Henry Hyde, Lord Cornbury (1638–1709, later the 2nd Earl of Clarendon). The Earl, the Countess and the heir made appointments to have their portraits painted by Mary Beale in the 1670s. Cornbury had known Charles Beale since at least 1662 when he sent 'a whole buck' to the Beales (perhaps repaying a favour from Beale as Deputy Clerk at the Patents Office?).[12]

Bishop Gilbert Burnet made the sceptical remark that the Countess of Clarendon was 'a very weak woman, but a great pretender to learning and devotion'.[13] She was maligned for her bigoted Protestantism, evident in her claim that papists were to blame for the spread of the great fire of 1666. Her second husband, Clarendon, was friendly, good natured and sincere, 'except in the payment of his debts; in which he has a particular art, upon his breaking of promises, which he does very often'.[14]

As friend and tutor to the Backhouse family, William Lloyd 'had great credit with the Countess of Clarendon', Burnet observed. Burnet respected Lloyd's intellect but found him to be 'a jealous, passionate man'.[15] In London from 1672 as vicar of St Martin-in-the-Fields, Lloyd sat for Mary Beale in 1677 and 1681. He was the leader of the bishops who confronted King James II in 1688 and as a result he was imprisoned briefly (see pages 166-8).

As far as Mary's career as a portrait painter was concerned, the period in Hampshire was a hiatus. One patron who tracked her down

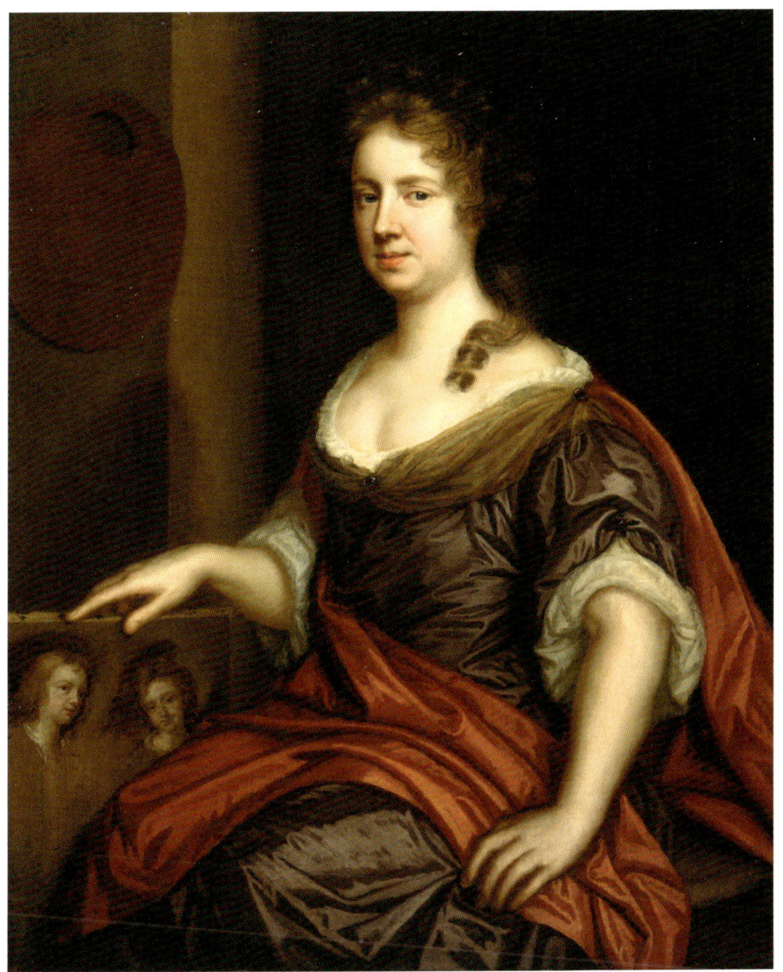

Mary Beale, *Self portrait*, c. 1666. Her right hand rests on a painting of her two young sons

in April 1666 was the learned, disagreeable Dr Robert Creighton, Dean of Wells, who took his picture home with him.[16] Mary's first portrait of Dr John Wilkins, formerly Warden of Wadham College, Oxford and from 1662 vicar of St Lawrence Jewry in the City of London, was painted around 1668, so he too may have visited Allbrook. Mary compensated for lack of sitters with her self portrait of 1665–6 in which her right hand rests on a painting of her sons and her palette hangs on the wall, suggesting that devotion to her sons took priority at this time. Her husband Charles was of course a willing subject, painted at Allbrook wearing an open-necked shirt and informal robe.

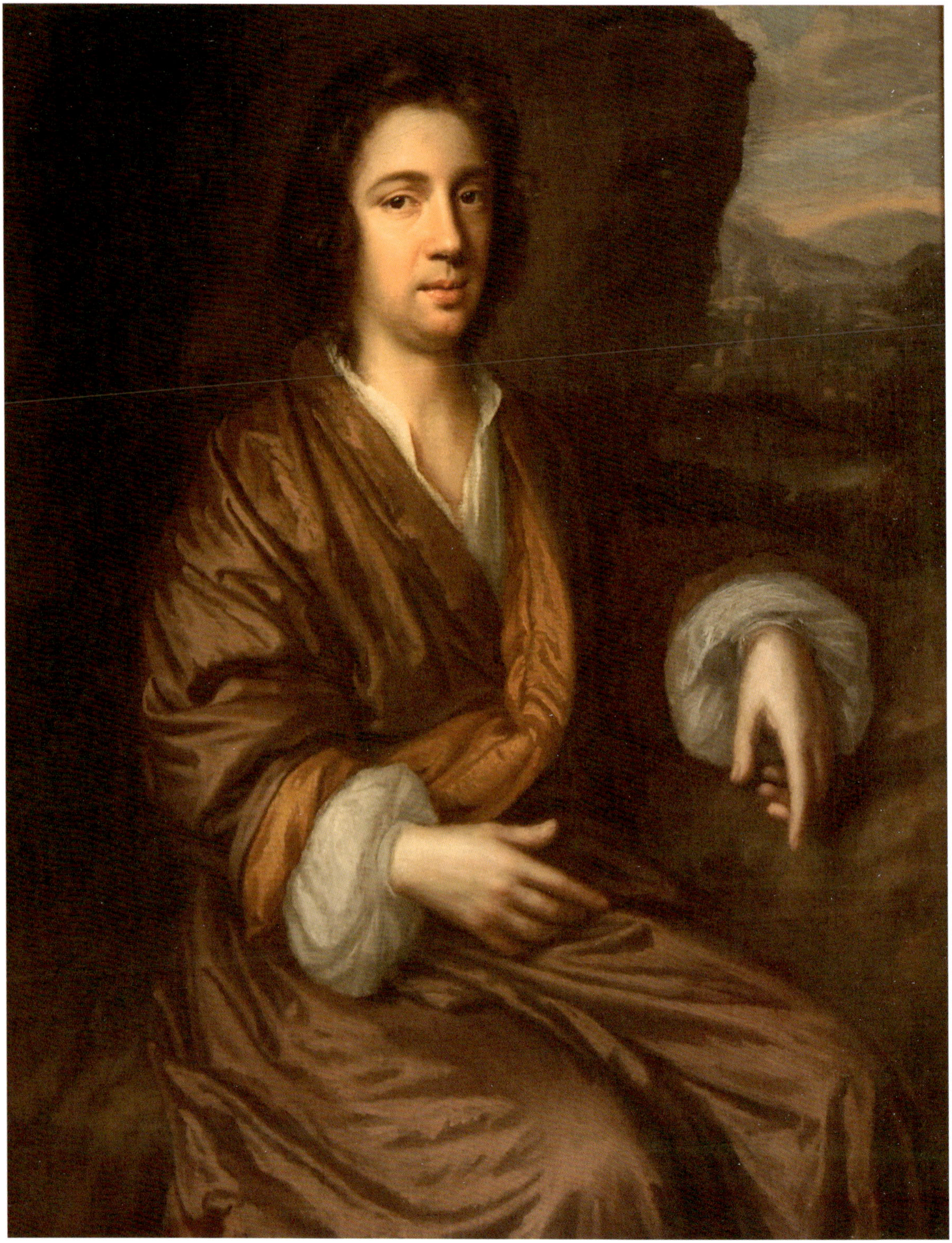

Mary Beale's 'Discourse on Friendship'

While at Allbrook, Mary Beale indulged in literary pursuits. She composed four Psalms for Woodford's publication and she wrote at least one poem, received by Thomas Flatman in 1666. More significantly, she penned a 'Discourse on Friendship' which she sent to 'My Deare ffriend', Mrs Elizabeth Tillotson, dated 9 March 1666 (when the new calendar was introduced on 1 January 1752, this date became 1667).[17] Mrs Tillotson was the daughter of Dr Peter and Robina French (Robina being Oliver Cromwell's youngest sister). After the death of Peter French in 1655, Robina married Dr John Wilkins, who officiated at the marriage of Elizabeth to Dr John Tillotson in 1664. Mary Beale was the personal friend and favourite artist of both families.

Opposite: Mary Beale, *Charles Beale*, c. 1666

Below: A detail from Mary Beale's letter to Mrs Tillotson, with a good example of the artist's signature, 1667

may shorten the trouble of any further apology, by telling you that in the following discourse I have endeavour'd to lay before you my heart, if not what it is, yet what I desire it should bee, and do hope that your Friendship may help to make it; since you have beene pleased to admitt mee to the honour of being

Deare Madam

March 1666

your truly affectionate, ffaithfu
Friend and Servant
Mary Beale

Mary Beale's 'Discourse' exists in manuscript (see pages 186-199 for a transcript). Any ambitions she may have had for publication were unlikely to succeed, given seventeenth-century conventions relating to women authors. It was unprecedented for an Englishwoman to set forth such a treatise and Mary Beale's essay was no sentimental out-pouring but the presentation of friendship as the bedrock of a religious society. Her 'Discourse' expresses her own strong religious beliefs: she insists on the supremacy of religion over 'the misteries of Philosophy'. She cites Socrates, Plutarch and Lord Bacon, evidence of her broad education; she reinforces her argument with metaphors and writes with a memorable turn of phrase: 'Vertue is a Jewell to be admired in an Enemy, praised in a Friend and desired by our selves'.

What inspired Mary Beale to compose a 'Discourse on Friendship'? Her ideas must have been fermenting at Hind Court, nurtured by the Woodford/ Flatman/Tillotson group of authors, Fellows of the Royal Society and clerics who shared Mary Beale's belief in the sanctity of Christian fellowship. Hind Court provided a congenial atmosphere for the exchange of ideas, as Woodford appreciated, 'Wee had frequently about this time at my Cousin Beale's the most agreeable conversation of the town, where and at Gresham College, the place where the Royall Society weekly mett I came acquainted with those persons who are my best and most cordiall friends'.[18] The loyalty of friends at the time of Charles Beale's dismissal from office underlined the value of friendship and, once at Allbrook Mary committed her thoughts to paper.

The idea of marriage as friendship can be traced to Aristotle's *Ethics* and the writings of St Thomas Aquinas. Mary Beale may have been familiar with these texts and with more recent publications such as Thomas Breme's *The Mirror of Friendship* (1584), Daniel Rogers's *Matrimoniall Honour* (1642) and Jeremy Taylor's *Discourse of the Nature and Offices of Friendship* (1657). She echoed Taylor in her insistence that 'Friendship is the nearest Union which distinct Souls are capable of'. She emphasised the divine nature of friendship and insisted that the friendship of husband and wife should be based on equality – a radical concept in the mid-seventeenth century. Her theory was based on the premise that God created Eve to be a 'meet help' to Adam, 'for a ffriend as well as for a wife. A wife and friend but not a slave; For we find her not in the beginning made subject to Adam, but always of equall dignity & honour with him, till by her own great modulity and sinning her self & then seducing her husband, she lost her share in that rule which before they had in common'. Mary questioned how far she was personally qualified to participate in this sacred bond with her husband, a bond that could overcome love of self and the 'Deeps & tempestuous storms' of marriage. True friendship between man and wife should be underpinned by virtue, discipline, consideration and consistent application, she maintained. Mary's principles were put into practice, accounting for the devoted partnership of her own marriage and her close friendships with Flatman, Woodford, Knollys, Cooke and the Tillotsons. Her 'Discourse' also broached the idea that master and servant were equal, although their different circumstances belied true friendship. The sensitive sketches of the Beales' servants and artisans delineated by Charles Beale junior demonstrate the rapport that permeated the Beale household.

In her covering letter to Mrs Tillotson Mary Beale refers to 'a Picture done by a very unskilfull hand out of that great affection she may have for the person whome it was design'd to represent, the work itself being very wretched and inconsiderable'. Modest about her own skills, Mary maintained that affection was an important element in a portrait (some of her best paintings were of those she held in affection).

The theme of friendship between man and woman was taken up by John Evelyn and published as *The Altar of Friendship* (1672) celebrating his platonic relationship with Margaret, Lady Godolphin (1652–1678, née Blagge). Evelyn may have been aware of Mary Beale's 'Discourse': they shared several friends, namely the Earl and Countess of Clarendon, William Lloyd and John and Elizabeth Tillotson. The subject of friendship and equality between a man and woman in marriage was to reverberate in the literature of the future, in Charlotte Bronte's *Jane Eyre* (1847), for instance.

The Knollys letters

The years Charles and Mary Beale spent in Hampshire generated Charles's correspondence with Francis Knollys, Dr John Cooke and Thomas Flatman. Charles Beale's letters to these friends have perished but many of those from Knollys, Cooke and Flatman to Charles survive, providing a picture of the Beale family at Allbrook.

Charles and Mary Beale became acquainted with Francis Knollys (d. 1694) when they lived in King Street, Covent Garden, during the late 1650s. Knollys lived in the neighbouring York Street and was a churchwarden at the local church, St Paul's. Knollys, a descendant of the Elizabethan courtier Sir Francis (1511–1596) was a barrister by profession, employed as the London agent for William Wentworth, 2nd Earl of Strafford (1626–1695) of Wentworth Woodhouse, Yorkshire.

Knollys was an amusing correspondent who kept Mary Beale in touch with Lely, reporting in November 1666 that Lely had not finished 'your picture', for want of a dog (a symbol of fidelity in portraits). So Knollys searched the vicinity of Covent Garden to find one. 'I hunted about ye towne from one end to the other after a dogg…tumbling into many a pretty maid'; he then dragged the animal back to Lely's studio and the completed picture was dispatched to Allbrook.[19] Knollys was with Lely again in 1668 when they had 'some kind discourse of you and Mrs Beale'. Lely wanted Mary to have 'a rarity from his house…it is a sketch of Moses taken out of the water', which was sent to Allbrook with a 'wooden woman' (a figurine).[20] Charles and Mary Beale were missed by their London friends and Knollys urged them to return. Meanwhile, he wrote to Mary, 'Honoured Madame', arranging for the mint water, tobacco and combs she had requested to be sent to Allbrook with Mr Bradshaw.[21]

As a Governor of Bridewell and Bethlem Hospitals from 1674, Knollys commissioned Mary to paint a full length portrait of Sir William Turner, Lord Mayor 1668–9, and President of the hospitals 1669–87, 1690–93. This was an honour for Mary Beale who was content to paint Turner without charge as a gesture of gratitude to Knollys (who regularly loaned money to the Beales). In 1676 Knollys presented the portrait to Bridewell where it hung in the great hall. Bridewell, formerly a Tudor palace on the bank of the Thames was by the seventeenth century a prison, hospital and orphanage. As benefactor, Master of the Merchant Taylors' Company, President of Bridewell and Bethlem, and Lord Mayor during a crucial year in the rebuilding of London after the great fire, Turner was 'the City's Darling and the Orphan's joy', portrayed by Mrs Beale wearing the mayoral chain of office. The Governors of Bridewell then tasked Knollys with responsibility for obtaining portraits of King Charles II and his brother, the Duke of York, specifying Lely rather than Mary Beale as the preferred artist.

Sir William Turner and Knollys liaised over the building of the new Bethlem Hospital (Bedlam) at Moorfields, to designs by Robert Hooke, and Mary Beale's portrait of Turner coincided with this

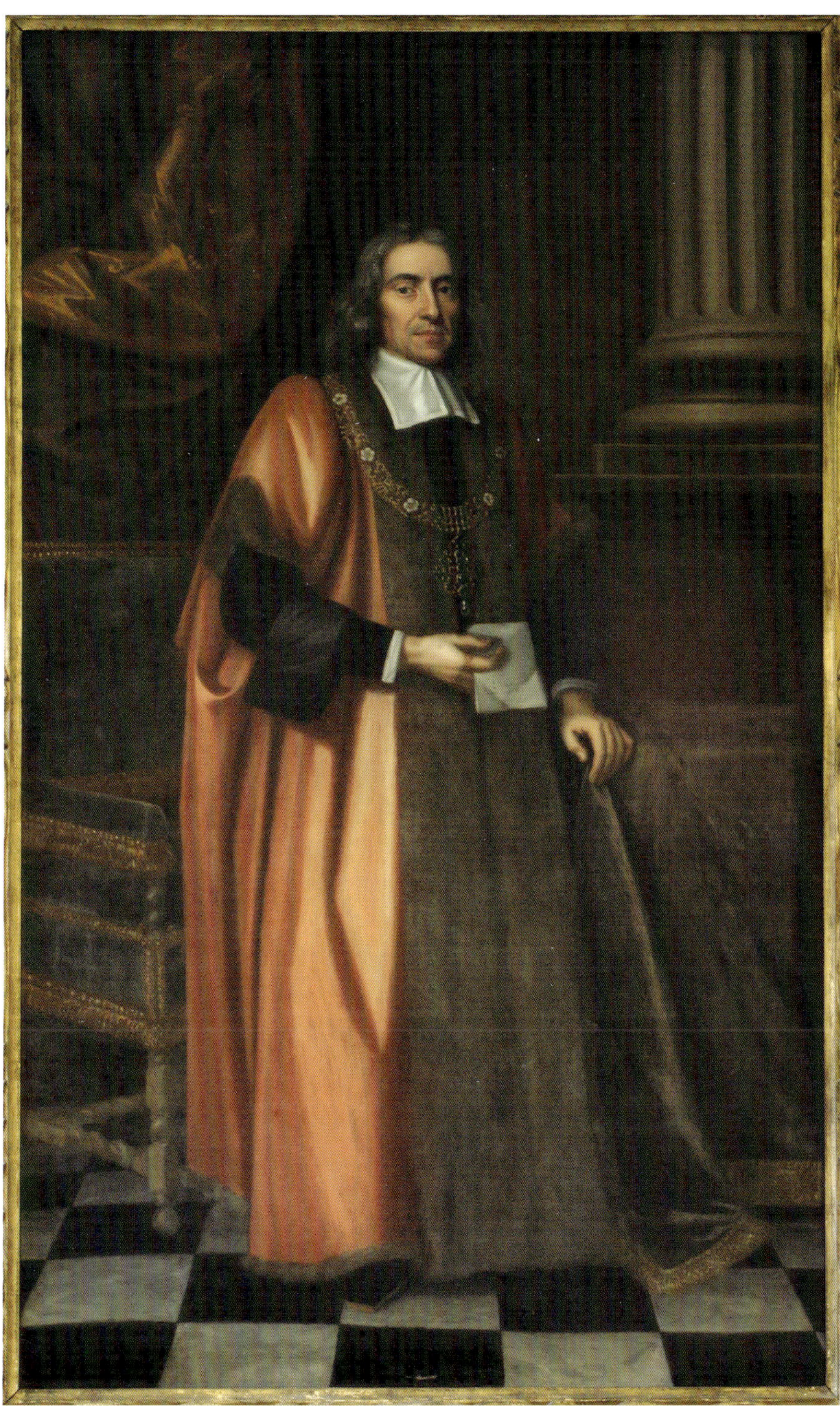

Mary Beale, *Sir William Turner*, 1676–7. Turner was Lord Mayor 1668–9, and MP for the City 1690–93

ambitious project. Knollys was probably responsible for Mrs Beale's introduction to the Countess of Strafford, who sat for her in 1671, and he commissioned her to paint Dr Thomas Lovet, Prebendary of Ely, in 1681.

Dr John Cooke's correspondence

Dr John Cooke (1614–1691) was the subject of one of Mary Beale's early portraits (1664). He lived in Russell Street, Covent Garden, which could account for his first acquaintance with Charles and Mary Beale. After their move to Hampshire in 1665, Charles wrote weekly to Cooke at Whitehall, a mixed blessing to Cooke who felt obliged to reply to Beale's 'violent torrent or overflowing deluge'.[22] Cooke was described by Pepys as 'a sober and learned man' who had served with Colonel Sir William Lockhart, Governor of Dunkirk.[23] Cooke returned to England to be Secretary to Sir William Morice and from 1681 he was Latin Secretary to Charles II, an appointment that prompted his second portrait by Mary Beale.

Dr Cooke was at the centre of Whitehall politics during the 1660s, which wearied him. He sought respite at Allbrook with Charles and Mary Beale. 'I imagine myself almost at Albrook where all things are gay, joyeous and happy. Long may they be so'.[24] 'Poet Sam' Woodford was living with the Beales at Allbrook during the winter of 1666, and the ambience attracted Cooke: 'That place & the Company there strikes me to the heart; and because I cannot come thither as soon as I want, I am over faint and unable to write one word more'.[25] 'I will desire no sweeter lodging till I come to Albrook'.[26]

Samuel Woodford was courting Mary Norton. Cooke (whose own wife is not mentioned) wished them well with some reservation, 'all her graces and excellencies would have grown better if they had been borne planted at Albrook, where she would have had one of the best examples in the world'.[27] 'Samuel is (it seems) gone a-wiving. I wish him and his Dame as much joy as you and yours have'.[28] To their friends, the marriage of Charles and Mary Beale was exemplary but life at Allbrook was not all joyous: in February 1667 Mary Beale was ill with 'an ague'. The news sent Cooke into 'a cold fit'; he promised to visit soon and assured the Beales that at a recent dinner with Woodford, 'you and your lady were not forgotten'.[29]

In June 1667 Cooke conveyed to the Beales the news of the raid by the Dutch Fleet. 'The Dutch have burnt all our great ships at Chatham, threatening to attempt the very Towne itself'. The enemy, 'presuming upon our unprepared river have entered the river at Chatham where their Fleet endeavoured to fire ours lying there unrigged. Yesterday they destroyed three vessels and burnt and carried away out of our best ships indeed, the *Royal Charles*'.[30] The Chatham raid caused panic throughout the nation and Cooke feared that 'a numerous army of French are to be poured in upon us and overwhelm us'.[31] One naval hero of the prolonged campaign against the Dutch was Captain Henry Terne who commanded the *Dreadnought* in 1665 and was killed in action aboard the *Triumph* in 1666 (Mary Beale's portrait of Terne, dated 1674, must be a copy of an earlier work).

By August 1667 peace with the Dutch was being negotiated and Cooke was immersed in credentials, political tracts and the diplomatic negotiations that prefaced the Treaty of Breda. Once peace was secured, Cooke's letters to Charles Beale assume a more relaxed tone, with news of the King hunting at Bagshot, the Countess of Falmouth's smallpox and John Dryden's appointment as Poet Laureate. 'These are the pudding sauces of Court, not half so tastefull as those at Albrook,' where the Beales were expecting the Woodfords as guests. Cooke imagined the preparations: white bread and apple pies to be baked, puddings, butter, carrots and 'a lieutenant shoulder of lamb'.[32] In September Cooke sent a gift of venison to Allbrook with the wish that 'the whole herd in their time and seasons may offer themselves to your knife and mercy'.[33]

On the Beales' return to London, Cooke gave Mary a tankard and, apart from one letter addressed to Charles Beale 'next door to The Golden Ball',[34] no further correspondence has been traced. The Cooke/Beale relationship was doubtless maintained in person, as Cooke's daughters, Mary and Elizabeth, were escorted to Mary Beale's painting-room to sit for their portraits in 1681.

'My incomparable Scholar'[35]

Contrasting with Cooke's political commentaries from Whitehall were the emotional letters written to Charles and Mary Beale by Thomas Flatman, lawyer, poet, literary intellectual and 'easily the most distinguished of the men about town who painted miniatures'.[36] Flatman belonged to the Beales' circle at Hind Court and became personally attached to Charles, his dear friend and master, and Mary, his incomparable scholar.

In 1660 Flatman presented Charles Beale with a miniature

Jan van Leyden, *The Dutch burning the English ships during the raid on the Medway, June 1667*, 1667–69. Dr John Cooke wrote to Charles and Mary Beale with news of the catastrophe

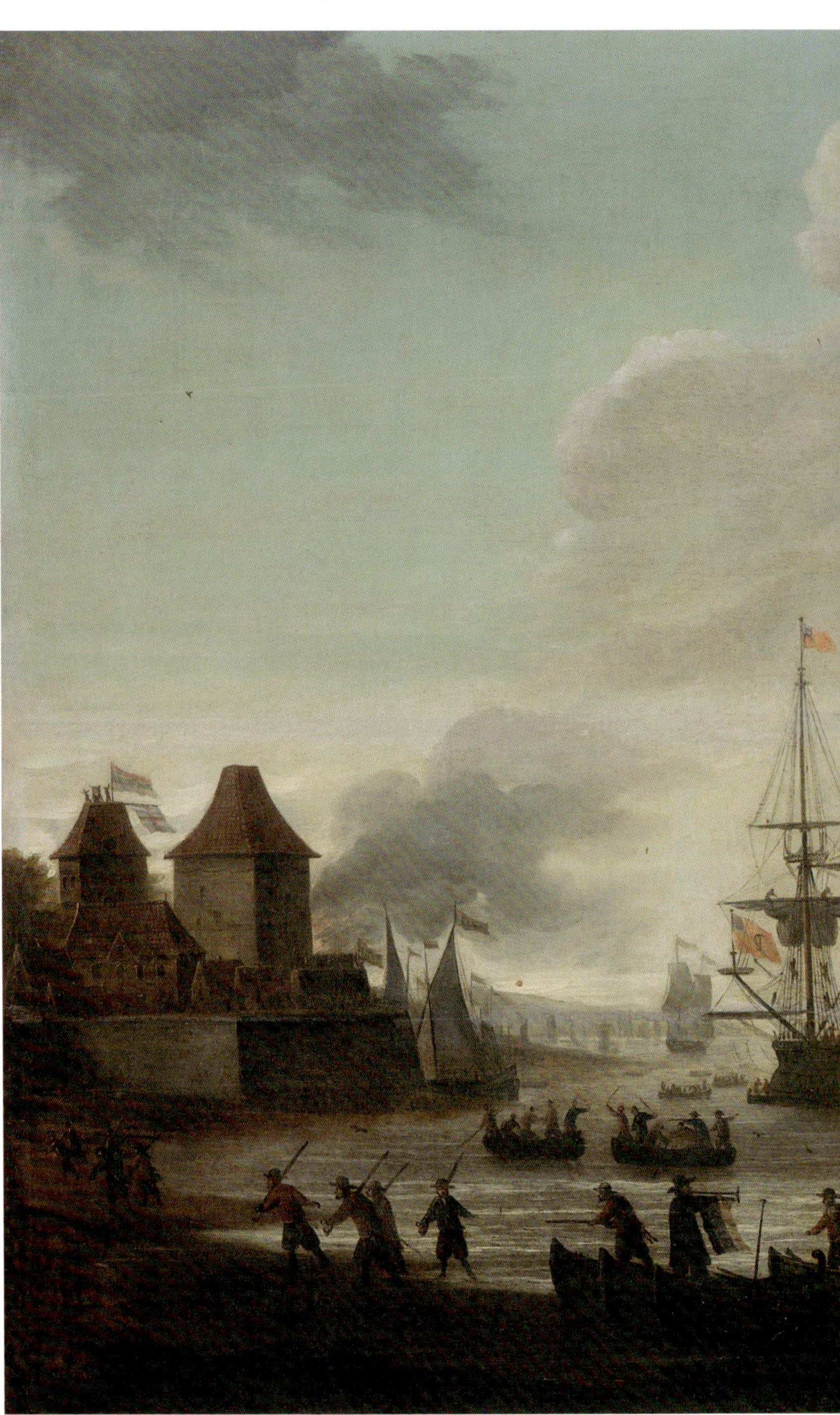

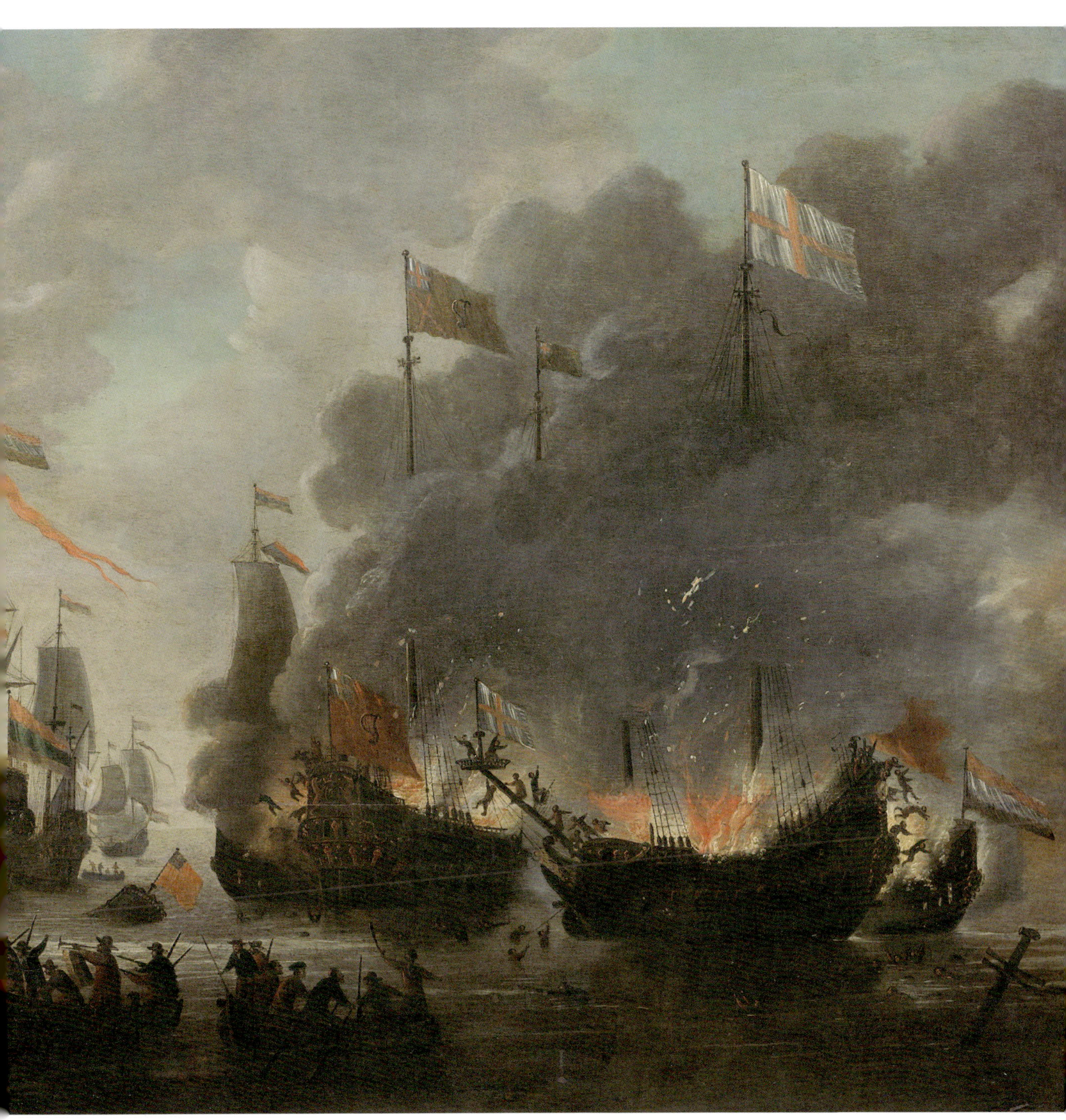

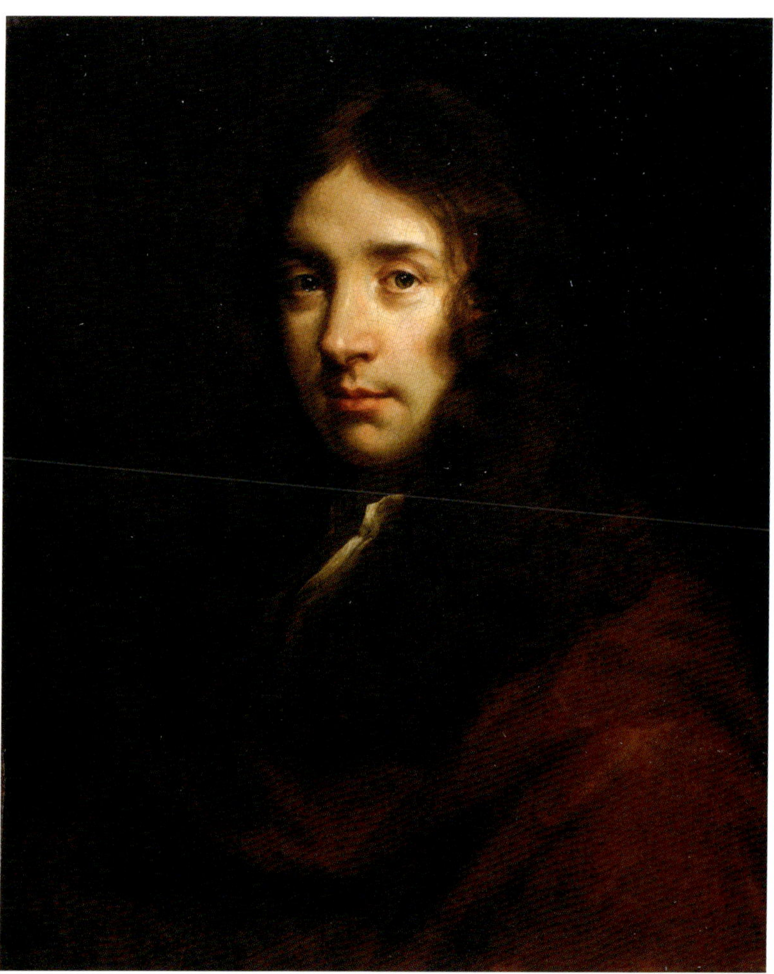
Thomas Flatman, *Self portrait*, 1680–88

inscribed in Latin on the reverse with a dedication that translates 'To his own friend most dear before all, Master Charles Beale this his own likeness. T. Flatman gave and dedicated it as a gift 3 August 1660'.[37] The inscription is ambiguous: is this a portrait of Beale or Flatman's self portrait? John Murdoch, an authority on seventeenth-century miniatures, opts for the former. This was one of Flatman's earliest works and Beale must have been impressed, for the next year he paid 'several wages to Mr Flatman for limning my own picture'.[38] Flatman's miniatures of Charles Beale, Alice and Samuel Woodford (dated 1661, inscribed *Amico suo fideli [ssimo] Samueli Wood[for]de)*, and his self portrait are regarded as 'among the very finest miniatures painted in the seventeenth-century'.[39] In 1669 Flatman gave his 'Honoured Master', Charles Beale, a self portrait accompanied by a letter: 'I am not so vain to think my Face worth drawing nor my Picture worth hanging amongst your other Rarities, yet (such a one as this) I have made bold to send it hoping it may serve at least, for a Foil to the rest, though there be little of Attraction or Pleasure in the Features, yet there is I assure you a great deal of generous kindness and humble deference for you in my Heart'.[40] Flatman's gift was an example of the seventeenth-century portrait as an expression of affection and regard.

Thomas Flatman and Mary Beale shared several patrons, notably the Earl and Countess of Clarendon, the Earl of Shaftesbury and the Earl of Lauderdale. Now renowned primarily as a miniature painter, Flatman was a popular poet in his time. His *Poems and Songs* (1674) went into four editions. His ode on the King's return to Whitehall in 1684 was set to music by Henry Purcell, and the organist Dr John Blow composed a song to Flatman's rousing poem 'My Trembling Song! Awake! Arise!'.[41] Flatman collaborated with fellow authors, contributing to Sir William Sanderson's *Graphice* (1658) and to William Faithorne's *Art of Graveing and Etching* (1662). His skills extended to astrological predictions, matters of profound interest to Charles Beale, Elias Ashmole and John Aubrey, for whom Flatman devised an astrological chart.' It reveals no end of trouble. He has made the figure of my nativity and found it agreeing with all the misfortunes of my life'.[42]

Thomas Flatman's letters to 'My Dear Master' express his regard for Charles Beale as a friend and as a master in the preparation of colours. 'In doing what you have done, Sir, you show yourself rather a Father than a Master and have outfriended all that part of the world which would have ever persuaded me they loved me', he wrote in December 1666 from the ruins of London.[43] Flatman's devotion to Charles and Mary Beale rivalled Samuel Woodford's feelings for 'my best and most affectionate family…for their love and never to be rewarded kindness'.[44]

Gossip relating to mutual friends, complaints about chilblains, the gift of a cake and the memory of an incident at St Bartholomew's fair when a milkmaid was chased by a bull, reveal a lighter side to Flatman's character. His request for some of Charles's 'best white, prepared as formerly',[45] indicates that Charles continued to prepare colours during his Hampshire exile, and Flatman's references to

Mary Beale, 'My Valentine, my Scholar',[46] infer that he instructed her in miniature painting (he trained her son, Charles) and that he adored her. Flatman sent Mary his self portrait, and thanked her for her poem, 'so excellent a Piece of Poetry and if you should hear that I renounce my colours you may conclude me dazzled with your Perfections. Excuse my Boldness in presuming to write to a Lady so every way accomplish'd'.[47] Flatman was in touch with the Beales again in 1681 when he borrowed Mary's copy of the Countess of Newcastle's picture after Lely and 'Mrs Gwyn's drapery'.[48]

The temperamental poet was on the verge of suicide when he confided 'his determinations' to Charles Beale. 'Master I must beseech you by all the endearments of friendship in the world, you communicate nothing of my determinations to any person living but your own brest & my Valentine's', he wrote.[49] Flatman had borrowed £17 from Beale (who was rarely in a position to lend money), even so, he was still in debt for £50. These circumstances stirred suicidal thoughts. 'I think no more light hours are designed for me…Next week (happy week!) presents me with the brave opportunity of quitting all my vexations…the place I go isn't far from the sea' (he owned property at Tishton near Diss, Norfolk). He dreamed that the white billow might serve as his winding sheet or a deep valley as his grave, 'the winds shall sing me asleep forever with ye soft air of forgotten eternity. Well Master! The Dy is thrown. If (after our meeting on Monday morning) you never see me more, pitty me & then forget me. Shame is more than Death. This is all. Happiness attend you & yours whatever becomes of me, dear Master'.[50] Premonitions of suicide by throwing himself into the sea were unfulfilled. However, Flatman 'gave way to fate'[51] at his house in Three Leg Alley near Fleet Street, aged fifty-three in December 1688.

When Charles and Mary Beale moved to Hampshire in 1665 it was anticipated that they would live there permanently. As it was, five years in the country only served to increase the attraction of London. The opportunities the capital afforded for Mary as a portrait painter were irresistible and the couple were fortunate to find a house in Pall Mall, St James's, where Mary was sought out by an increasing number of affluent patrons.

1. S. Woodford, *Liber*, 18 October 1664

2. *Ibid.*, 1665

3. *Ibid.*, 31 December 1663

4. *Ibid.*, August 1664

5. Edward Roberts, John Crook, Linda Hall, Daniel Miles, *Hampshire Houses 1250–1700. Their Dating and Development,* (2003), p. 242

6. Pepys, VI, p.93, 30 April 1665

7. Frederick Anthony Child, *Thomas Flatman. The Life and Uncollected Poems,* (1921), pp. 9-10

8. S. Woodford, *A Paraphrase Upon the Canticles and some Select hymns of the New and Old Testaments with other occasional compositions in English verse*, (1679)

9. Edward N. Hooker, 'The Early Poetical Career of Samuel Woodforde', in *Essays Critical and Historical dedicated to Lily B. Campbell*, (1950), pp. 87-107

10. L.B. Larking, ed., 'Proceedings principally in the County of Kent, in connection with the parliaments of 1640', *Camden Society* 80 (1862), preface

11. CBA 11 January 1681

12. Samuel Woodforde, *Lib. primus*, (1662), Osborne b41 f. 107, Beinecke Rare Book and Manuscript Library, Yale University

13. GB I, pt I, p. 413

14. *Ibid.*, p. 462

15. *Ibid.*, p. 413

16. Rawlinson 113, 19 April 1665

17. Harley Ms 6828, ff. 510-523, BL. A copy is at the Folger Shakespeare Library, Washington, Ms V.a.220. In 1960 a copy belonged to Sir Charles Bunbury Bt of Bury St Edmunds. A transcript is filed under Richard Jeffree's research notes, 6/41, Heinz Archive and Library, NPG

18. S. Woodford, 'Memoirs', 27 January 1665

19. Rawlinson 108, 15 November 1666

20. *Ibid.*

21. *Ibid.*, 1 September 1670

22. Rawlinson 113, 17 January 1667

23. Pepys, V, p.62, 23 February 1664

24. Rawlinson 113, 8 November 1666

25. *Ibid.*, 6 December 1666

26. *Ibid.*, 3 January 1667

27. *Ibid.*, 23 May 1667

28. *Ibid.*, 3 January 1667

29. *Ibid.*, 28 March 1667

30. Rawlinson 104, 13 June 1667

31. *Ibid.*, 13 June 1667

32. *Ibid.*, 8 October 1668

33. Rawlinson 113, 5 September 1667

34. *Ibid.*, 2 November 1671

35. Rawlinson 104, 9 January 1667

36. John Murdoch, Jim Murrell, Patrick J. Noon, Roy Strong, *The English Miniature,* (1981), p. 148

37. John Murdoch, *Seventeenth-Century Miniatures in the Collection of the Victoria and Albert Museum,* (1997), pp. 208-9

38. GVCBA 1661

39. John Murdoch, *op. cit.,* p. 205

40. *Familiar letters of love, gallantry, and several occasions by the wits of the last and present Age,* (1718), I, p. 250

41. Graham Reynolds, 'A miniature self-portrait by Thomas Flatman, limner and poet', *Burlington Magazine* 89 (1947), pp. 63-7

42. Ruth Scurr, *John Aubrey. My Own Life,* (2015), p. 183

43. Rawlinson 104, 13 December 1666

44. S. Woodford, *Liber*, 18 July, 4 August 1664

45. Rawlinson 104, 27 October 1668

46. *Ibid.*, n.d.

47. *Familiar letters, op. cit.,* p. 252

48. CBA 30 December 1681

49. Rawlinson 104, n.d.

50. *Ibid.*

51. Anthony à Wood, *Athenae Oxoniensis,* (1691-2), pp. 244-6

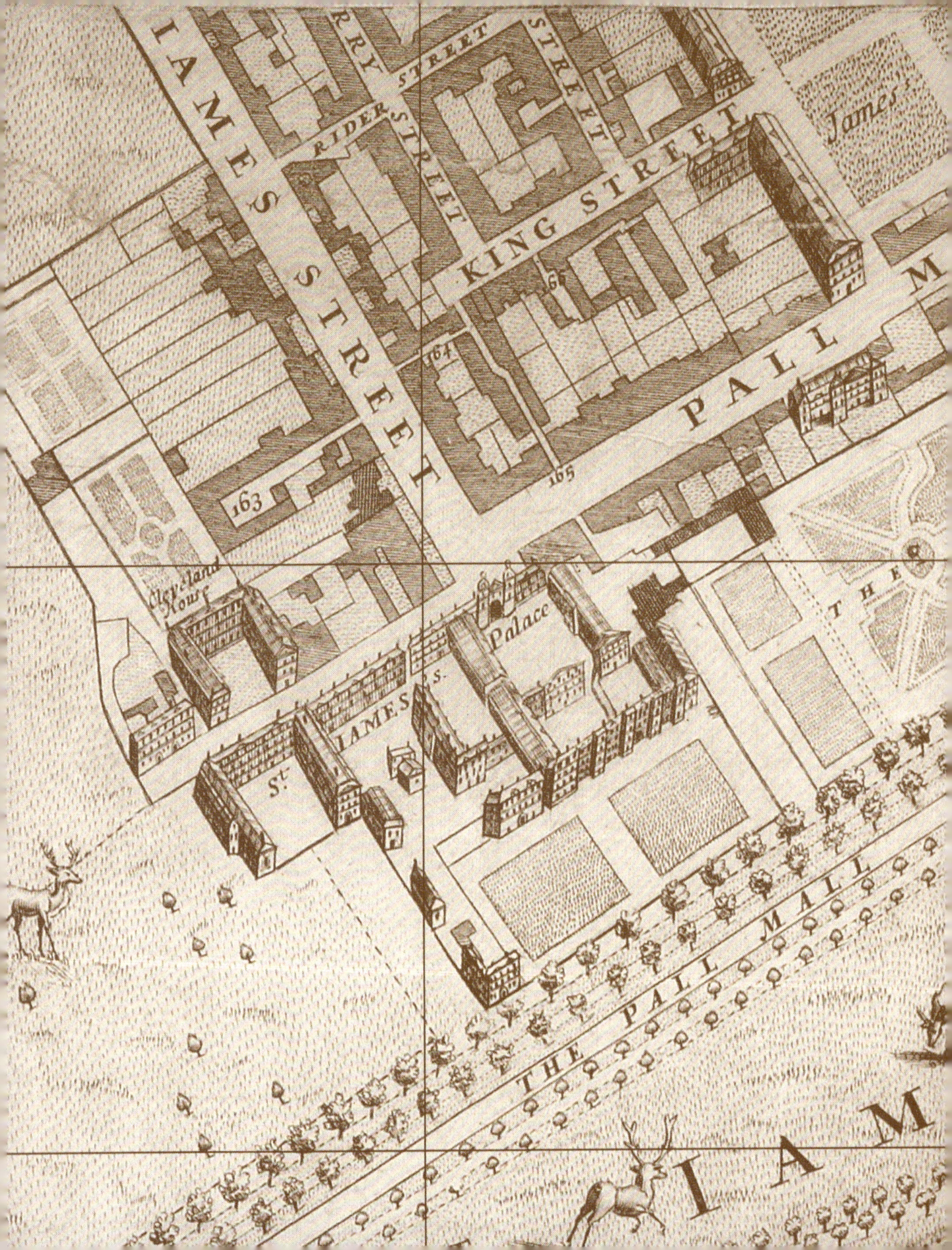

IAMES STREET
RRY STREET
RIDER STREET
STREET
KING STREET
James's
PALL M
163
164
165
Cleveland House
Palace
St. JAMES'S
St.
THE PALL MALL
IAM

5. NEXT TO THE GOLDEN BALL, PALL MALL

WITH THE SOLE PURPOSE OF PURSUING MARY'S CAREER as a portrait painter, Charles and Mary Beale left Hampshire after five years at Allbrook, a remote farmhouse near Otterbourne, and returned to London. In the aftermath of the triumphant Restoration of Charles II, the capital was a magnet for artists and scientists keen to secure the patronage of an indulgent Court. The reign of King Charles II (1660–85), profligate in some respects, encouraged the renaissance of the arts and sciences from which Mary Beale was to benefit.

In order to facilitate their ambitions the Beales travelled to London in November 1669 and took lodgings with Mrs Stubbs in Bow Street, Covent Garden. Hopes centred on a property in the fashionable quarter of St James's, recently acquired by Samuell Symons, a relative of Charles Beale through Symons's marriage to Sara Beale in 1621. Symons was an apothecary of Aldersgate in the City of London who supplied Beale with cochineal, an ingredient which produced the rich, red colour Mary used to enhance lips and eyes in her portraits. Symons (whose daughter Mary was to paint in 1677) was sufficiently prosperous – and astute – to have secured the lease of a plot in 'Pell Mell Field' for forty-five years from midsummer 1669 from the Earl of St Albans who developed the field into a wide new street between 1665 and 1670.[1] St Albans charged Symons an annual ground rent of £5 10s and 'Cousin Symonds' let the 'dwelling house in ye Pall Mall' to Charles Beale for £10 10s a quarter, a sum met in part by rent from the Allbrook house.[2] Thus, late in 1669 the Beales took up residence in St James's,[3] an ideal location as far as Mary's ambitions were concerned. After the great plague of 1665 and the great fire of 1666 those who could afford to moved out of the overcrowded City to the more attractive west end of London – to Piccadilly, St James's Square and Pall Mall, a street which took its name from 'pell mell' (*pallo a maglio),* a game similar to croquet, played at the pall mall alley on the northern edge of St James's Fields.

St James's attracted the aristocracy and the artists they favoured. The conceited Simon Verelst (1644–1721), known as 'the God of

Opposite: A detail from William Morgan's map of 1682. Charles and Mary Beale lived on the north side of Pall Mall, 'next to The Golden Ball' from the winter of 1669/70 until Mary's death in 1699. The house was close to number 165 on this map

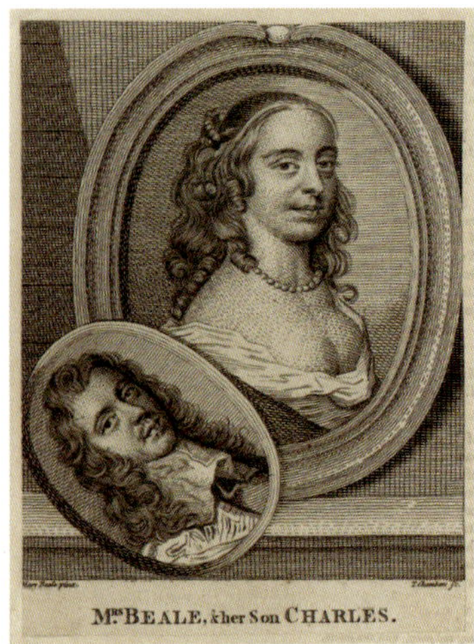

An early self portrait of Mary Beale with a later portrait of her adult son, Charles. An engraving by Thomas Chambers, 1762

flowers' for his still life paintings, lodged in St James's Market (Street) from 1669. He also painted portraits, secured the patronage of Nell Gwyn and rivalled Mary Beale as portrait painter to fashionable ladies before he succumbed to insanity. Jacob Huysmans (1633–1696) was favoured by Queen Catherine of Braganza (a fellow Roman Catholic) and for a time he competed with Sir Peter Lely as Court painter. He died three years before Mary Beale and was buried, as she was, in St James's church, Piccadilly.

While still at Allbrook, Charles Beale prepared for his wife's debut on the London art world by priming thirty-four canvases 'single primed' and 'nine excellent fine canvas double primed',[4] which were transported to the house in Pall Mall. The address, 'next to The Golden Ball in Pall Mall Street',[5] referred to the sign of The Golden Ball, a street sign popular with perfumers and goldsmiths; in this case it may have advertised the perfumer's shop at the south end of St James's Street or alluded to a sign in Golden Lion Court on the north side of Pall Mall. The tall brick house rented by Charles Beale had a 22 feet frontage onto the north-western side of Pall Mall (a site since redeveloped as numbers fifty-nine to sixty-three). The house was large enough to accommodate Charles and Mary, their two sons, one or two servants and Mary's painting-room. Closets in the garret and adjoining the dining-room were stacked with straining frames for canvases, more frames were kept in the attic and there must have been a small laboratory/kitchen where Charles manufactured colours – he specialised in ultramarine, red lake and 'pinke' (yellow).

Mary Beale, *Self portrait*, 1672

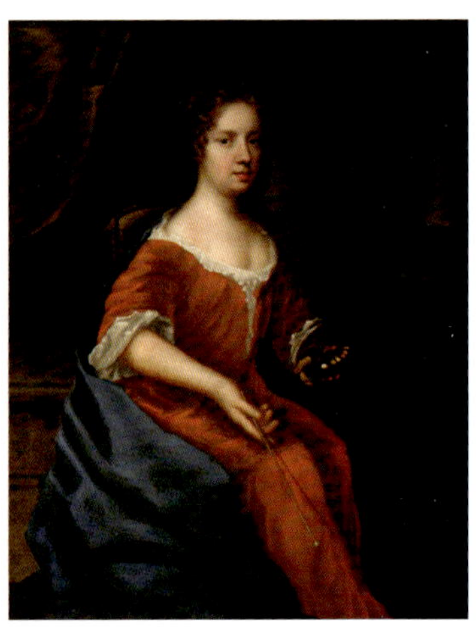

Mary Beale's self portraits

Mary Beale painted herself and her family out of affection, for practice, improvement and as a means of advertising her skills. An early self portrait depicts Mary as a plump, bosomy young woman with long loose curls and wearing a single string of pearls; this was used alongside her portrait of her adult son in Chambers's engraving of 1762. The originals formed part of Horace Walpole's collection at Strawberry Hill, Twickenham, with several more portraits by Mary Beale and her son.[6]

One of the first paintings Mary Beale undertook in Pall Mall was the assertive self portrait in which she grasps her palette; her colours are laid out systematically, ready to be applied. She holds a brush in her right hand and her direct gaze is challenging; no jewellery, dog or child distracts from the image of Mary Beale the artist. The portrait can be dated to 1672 when Charles noted 'Mrs Beale painted her own picture' in July.[7] A companion portrait of her husband was intended to hang alongside, with Charles looking towards his wife (illustrated on the back cover).

In a previous group portrait of herself, her husband and eldest son Bartholomew, painted around 1659 or 1660, Mary looks severe, slightly aloof from her family, and her hand draws attention to herself (she may have been pregnant with her youngest son who was born in June 1660). In contrast to this family group (illustrated on page 54) was the sophisticated self portrait of Mary as Pallas Athena, the Greek goddess of wisdom, the arts and warfare. Lely painted Lady Castlemaine in this guise,[8] and Mary Beale's self portrait endowed her with the same mythological status, demonstrating that she was *au fait* with current trends. This self portrait, which has not been traced, inspired Samuel Woodford's poem 'To Belisa' (1664), dedicated to 'The Excellent Mrs Mary Beal upon her own Picture, done by herself, like Pallas, but without any Arms, except Head-piece and Corselet' (see pages 70, 71).

While living in Hampshire Mary portrayed herself as the devoted mother with her right hand caressing a canvas on which she has painted her two angelic sons. The matching portrait of her husband with an Italianate landscape in the background conveys the relaxed atmosphere of life at Allbrook and refers to his interest in the Italian masters (see illustrations on pages 83, 84).

Once her painting-room was established in the house near The Golden Ball, Pall Mall, Mary presented herself as the working artist with her palette and brush poised for commissions (as above). In 1675 she imagined herself as a shepherdess, although the crook she holds looks more like a spear and the pose echoes the figure of Britannia as it appeared on the new copper coinage of 1672.[9] The pastoral/shepherdess image, signifying the innocence of the sitter, was appealing to Mrs Elizabeth Adams, Lady Mary Watson and Lady Leigh (née Eleanor Watson) who all posed as shepherdesses for Mary Beale.

A woman with pearls in her hair and wearing a blue dress has been cited as a self portrait of around 1675–80 but the face looks too youthful for Mary Beale in her forties. Moreover, the composition includes a terra cotta urn supported by a gilded cupid, an incense burner or brazier which, with the extravagant use of ultramarine for the robe, suggests that the sitter was a wealthy, whimsical aristocrat

Mary Beale, *Lady Leigh as a Shepherdess*, c. 1676

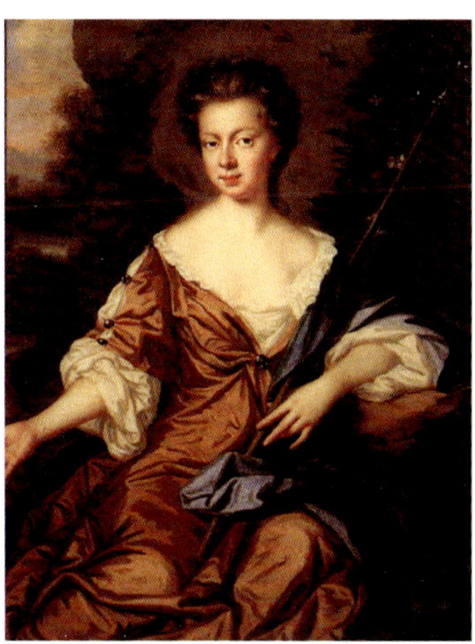

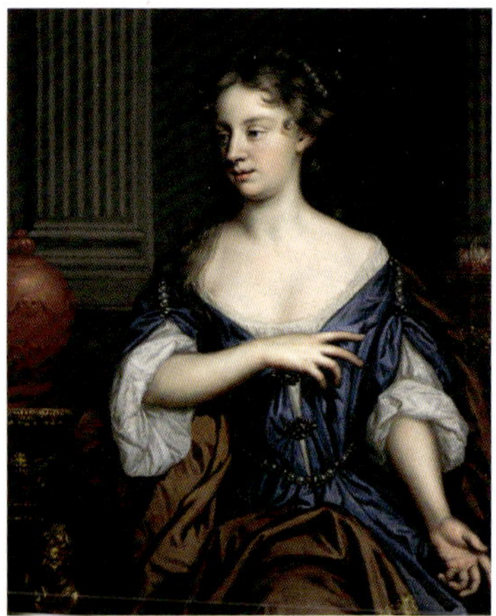

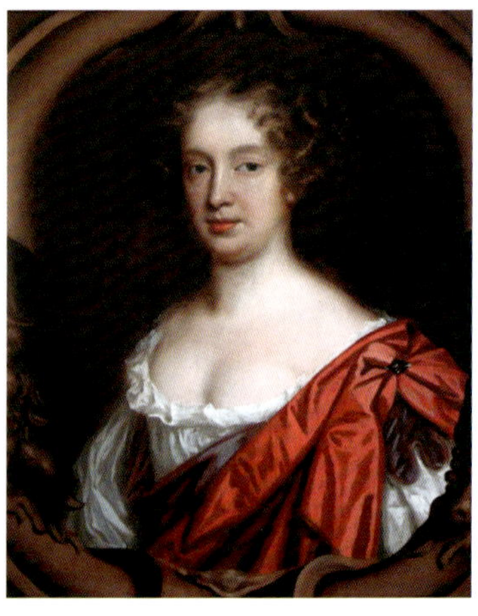

Top: Mary Beale, *Portrait of an unknown woman*, previously thought to be a self portrait, c. 1675-80

Below: Mary Beale, *Self portrait*, c. 1680

rather than the Puritan Mary Beale.

A head and shoulders of a young woman wearing a brown and cream dress, and bearing the signature Mariah Beale was formerly believed to be a self portrait but the supposition has been dismissed recently. Another self portrait has recently come to light, showing a confident woman with creamy skin and perfectly coiffed hair; such an image would have appealed to potential clients. This was painted c. 1680 on canvas, whereas Charles recorded that Mary finished 'her own face' on bed ticking in September 1677.[10] The use of ticking instead of linen canvas was an economy which reflected the resourcefulness of her husband. Bed ticking was less expensive than canvas and its texture provided a sympathetic base for oil paint. Mary Beale's last known self portrait of 1681 was likewise painted on bed ticking, 'The Picture of my Dearest Heart's owne upon ye H.L. Bedtickinge, was paintd over without oileing or varnish it But upon ye old one only querie how it settles', Charles noted.[11] The paint settled well and in this self portrait Mrs Beale appears as the *grande dame,* almost haughty, in a voluminous gown of subdued colours and with her left hand on one of the spaniels that were popular with King Charles II.

Mary Beale's self portraits show her as a wife, mother, artist, Greek goddess, shepherdess and a woman of style. They illustrate the skill and imagination of an artist who presented fashionable women with various options when they consulted her about having their portraits painted.

Sir Peter Lely and the Beales

Charles and Mary Beale invited Peter Lely to visit Mary's Pall Mall painting-room in April 1672, an important occasion that was documented by Charles Beale. Lely arrived accompanied by the artist Richard Gibson ('Dwarf Gibson') and Mr Skipwith (a mourner at Lely's funeral in 1680). Mary may have first made the acquaintance of Lely when he visited Suffolk in the 1640s – Vertue believed that Lely 'first put a pencil in her hand before she was married'.[12] The Beales and Lely were certainly on good terms by 1659 when Charles supplied Lely with colours, and by 1661 Lely had painted several pictures of the Beale family and his own self portrait for Charles and Mary. Lely's portrait of Mary, wearing a low-cut white dress and blue scarf, was exhibited at the South Kensington Museum in 1866, when it belonged to Mr George Handford.[13]

According to an excerpt from Charles Beale's almanack of 20 April 1672, 'Mr Lely was here & commended very much her (Mrs Beal), coppy that she had made after Sir Anthony Van Dyke own picture, also her coppy after our Saviour praying in the Garden &c after Anto Da Correggio'.[14] The original painting by Antonio da Correggio (1489–1539) of 'Christ in the Garden of Gethsemane' was borrowed from 'my worthy and kind friend' Dr Thomas Belke, Prebendary of Canterbury, who was sufficiently impressed by Mary Beale to commission his own portrait from her.[15] Belke also arranged for Beale to borrow Van Dyck's painting of the Porter family – the diplomat Endymion Porter had been Charles I's agent abroad and was instrumental in amassing the King's art collection. Lely thought highly of Mary's 'coppy in little after Endimion Porter, his Lady & 3 sons he commended extraordinarily & sd to use his own words, it was painted like Vandyke himself in little & that it was the best coppy he ever saw after Vandyke'. Lely also 'very well liked her two Coppyes in great of Mr Porter's little son Phil. He commended her other works. Coppyes & those from the life – both he & Mr Gibson both commended her workes'.[16]

Thomas Wentworth, 1st Earl of Strafford. An engraving of 1793 after Mary Beale who copied Sir Anthony Van Dyck's portrait of Strafford, c. 1636

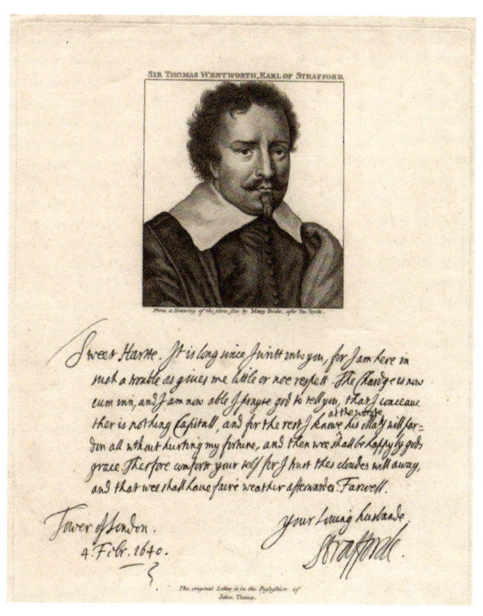

Another of Mary Beale's copies after Van Dyck was the troubled face of Thomas Wentworth, 1st Earl of Strafford (1593–1641), King Charles I's ruthless Lord Deputy in Ireland who was charged with treason by Parliament and beheaded on Tower Hill in 1641. An engraving by John Thane (1793) from Mary Beale's painting was enhanced by the replication of a touching note from Strafford to his wife, written in February 1640 while he was imprisoned in the Tower of London. Strafford's only surviving son, William (1626–1695), fled the country after his father's execution, returning in 1652. He married Lady Henrietta Mary Stanley who sat for her portrait by Mary Beale in May 1677.[17] She died childless in 1685 and is remembered by a vast monument at York Minster.

The Lely/Beale conversation of April 1672 turned to a discussion of Van Dyck's method of painting. Looking at a version of Van Dyck's portrait of Bishop Antoine Triest, Charles Beale questioned how Van Dyck could possibly finish a face in a day 'and wrought up to so extraordinary a perfection?'. Lely had heard that the artist painted it over fourteen times and confided in Beale that Nicholas

Lanier, Master of the King's Music and an art connoisseur, had posed for seven days for Van Dyck and it was this painting that inspired King Charles I to summon Van Dyck to England.[18]

Charles Beale recorded a second visit from Lely in 1677: 'Lely was at our house with Mr Wemburgh' (Gerrit Uylenburgh, a landscape artist and briefly surveyor of pictures to Charles II). The guests were shown Mary's portraits of Mrs Clarke, Dr Belke, Miss Russell, Monsieur Counsel, 'Bat's picture' (their son Bartholomew), Earl Fauconberg, Mrs Stillingfleet, Sir William Turner and an anonymous gentlewoman. Lely approved: 'He told me that Mrs Beale was very much improved in her painting' Charles noted with pride. The Beales then showed Lely 'some of the hands we had cast in Alabaster (especially many of those of my Dearest Hearts in various postures which we cast up to ye elbow'). Lely 'could hardly believe we could cast them so curiously ourselves and said we had made him greatly out of love with his own which (upon the sight of ours) he should now think very meane and poore. He advised us to cast a great many'.[19]

During the 1670s the Beales commissioned Lely for portraits of their family and friends. He charged £20 for a head and shoulders and £30 for a three-quarter length portrait, compared to Mary Beale's fee of £5 for a head and shoulders and £10 for a three-quarter length portrait. The Beales were privileged to watch Lely at work on the pictures they commissioned from him. Furthermore, Lely invited Charles Beale to bring his sons to his studio to view his collection (valued at about £10,000, he claimed). On another occasion at Lely's studio Beale showed 'Mr Wm Bonett the same excellent pictures – this person was a learner there'.[20] The Lely/Beale friendship extended to the loan of paintings from Lely's personal collection for Mary and her sons to copy and study. The Beales also borrowed from the royal collection through the goodwill of the Lord Chamberlain and William 'Backstairs' Chiffinch, a picture dealer to Charles II who arranged for the loan of Italian drawings.

'My most worthy friend Dr Tillotson' was painted by Lely for the Beales and for Dr Cradock in 1672. 'He drew them first in chalk rudely, & afterwards in colours, and rubd upon that a little colour very thin in places for the shadows & laid a touch of light upon the heightening of the forehead. he had done them both in an hours time'.[21] Tillotson sat another nine hours for Lely while the Beales watched the master at work. Charles Beale noted Lely's technique minutely. 'he apprehending the colour of the Cloth upon which he painted was too light. before he began to lay on the flesh colour he glazed the whole place where the face & haire were drawn in colour over thin with cullens earth & a little bonn black (as he told us) made very thin with varnish'.[22] At the last sitting Charles Beale noticed a change in Lely's method. 'His manner in the painting of this picture, this time especially seemd strangely different both to myself and my dearest heart from his manner of painting the former pictures he did for us. this wee thought was a more conceiled, misterious scanty way of painting then the way he used formerly, whch wee both thought was a farr more open & free, & much more was to be observ'd and gain'd from seeing him paint then, then my heart coud with her most carefull marking. learn from his painting either this, or Dr Cradock's picture of his doing – for Dr Patrick'.[23]

Sir Peter Lely was unusually generous in allowing Charles and Mary Beale to observe him at work, although he did extend the privilege to William Fever in 1673.[24] Lely and the Beales enjoyed a mutually satisfactory relationship. Lely personally encouraged Mary Beale and accepted commissions from her and her husband, while benefitting from a supply of Charles Beale's colours in part-payment. For example in 1672 Beale 'delivered to Mr Lely 1 ounce of Ultramarine at £2 10s p. ounce towards payment for Dr Tillotson's picture – for me'.[25] The price of ultramarine escalated to £4 10s an ounce in 1674 when Beale calculated that his 'Lakes & ultermarins' supplied to Lely amounted to £28 19 shillings, 'so there is due to him £1 1 shilling in full payment of the 2 forementioned pictures'.[26] One of these was Lely's portrait of Charles Beale junior which he 'dead colourd' in August 1674, then 'took a drawing upon paper after an Indian gown which he had put on his back' so as to finish the drapery.[27] Lely's portraits of Tillotson and Brook Bridges, Charles's nephew, were paid for with 'severall parcells of Lake of my own makeing whch he sent for 17 August 1671. and Ultramarine – & money £13 12s'.[28] Ultramarine blue was a colour associated with renaissance paintings of the Virgin Mary and it was a scarce commodity, made from the semi-precious mineral, lapis lazuli. Known as ultramarine because it came from beyond the sea, the mineral was originally mined in what is now Afghanistan. Charles Beale mastered the process of producing the colour for his wife and for Lely, and if Mary's clients wanted drapery painted in ultramarine, Charles charged an extra £1 for a large portrait, 10s if 'in little', and he devised his own glaze to preserve the quality of the colour.

The artist Thomas Manby (*c.* 1633–1695) was content to be given eight ounces 'of my very good Lake of my makeing and 1 ½ oz of Excellent Pink' in part-payment for his landscape background to Mary's copy of the Countess of Clare's picture in 1677[29] (Mary also painted Gilbert Holles, 3rd Earl of Clare). The artist Alexander Comer (1632–1700) shared Charles Beale's interest in experiments with colours, confiding in him 'a secret that he used a black chalk ground in oil instead of blew black and found it [a] much better and more Innocent Color'.[30]

Colonel Giles Strangways commissioned Mary Beale to paint portraits of his family and contemporaries. These were displayed at Melbury House, Dorset. Among the family portraits by Beale are (top) *Mrs James Long, née Susanna Strangways*, 1672, and (below) *Mrs Thomas Strangways, née Susan Ridout*, c. 1675

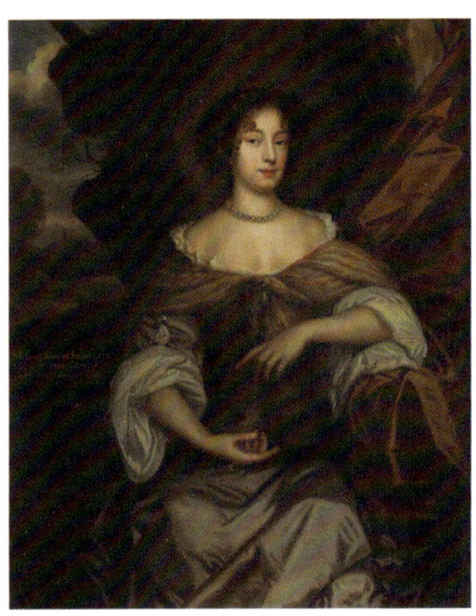

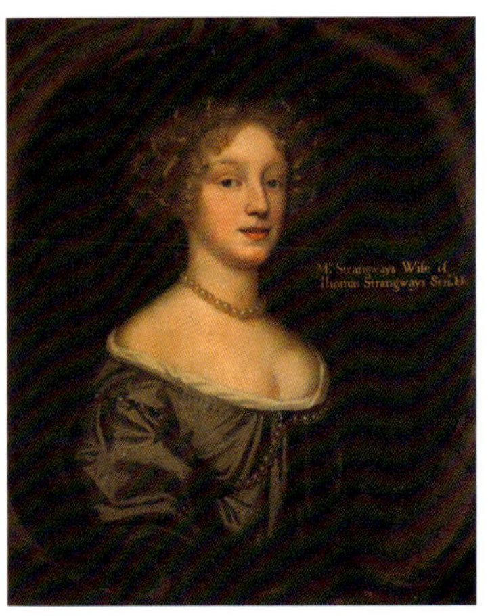

Royalist patrons

While living at Hind Court in the early 1660s Mrs Beale secured her first commissions from the clergy and this category of sitters remained her mainstay. The art historian Bainbrigg Buckeridge (writing in 1706, he could have known Mary Beale) claimed that she became acquainted with 'the greatest part of the dignify'd Clergy of her time' through her husband Charles, 'who was much in favour with that Robe'.[31] From 1670, with a studio in fashionable St James's, the range of Mary's sitters widened to include 'persons of distinction' as her husband described them.[32] These politicians, scholars, natural scientists, physicians and aristocrats who personified post-Restoration London, liked her work. Many of her sitters were key figures in the history of the seventeenth century, from parliamentarians related to Lord Protector Oliver Cromwell, to royalists who organised the Restoration of the monarchy, to the bishops who opposed King James II in the crisis that led to the accession of King William and Queen Mary in 1689. The conversations between the artist and her sitters must have been riveting, for as Samuel Woodford's memoirs recalled, Mary Beale's sessions were social occasions and those who sat for her often brought a companion and stayed to dinner.

Many of the 'persons of distinction' who made appointments with Mary Beale were fervent royalists such as the Earl of Clarendon and the Hon. Henry Coventry. Several were personally involved with King Charles II's escape into exile in 1651 and his Restoration of 1660. One cavalier who rejoiced to see the King restored to his throne was Colonel Giles Strangways (1615–1675) of Melbury Sampford, Dorset, who had raised a regiment to fight in the civil war and was consequently punished by the parliamentarians with three years in the Tower of London. After Charles II's defeat at the battle of Worcester in September 1651 he was secreted in Dorset by

Colonel Francis Wyndham and his cousin Colonel Strangways, who presented the desperate King with 300 pieces of gold. Strangways was an admirer of Mary Beale's paintings, commissioning paintings of himself, his son Thomas and his wife, and his daughter Susanna.

Horace Walpole saw a portrait of Giles Strangways at Melbury in the late eighteenth century, describing it as 'a very good half length I believe by Walker'.[33] The artist was more likely to have been Beale, who completed 'Coll Strangeways HL' in December 1672.[34] Walpole also commented on eight portraits in stone-coloured frames by Mary Beale that he saw at Melbury.[35]

An energetic politician, Fellow of the Royal Society and a devout Anglican, Strangways relied on Mrs Beale for portraits of contemporaries he admired to add to his collection at Melbury: Dr Zachary Cradock, Mary Beale's distant cousin, a chaplain to Charles II and Provost of Eton; Dr Thomas Pierce, Dean of Salisbury; Samuel Cromlehome, high-master of St Paul's School and the clerics Tillotson and Stillingfleet.[36]

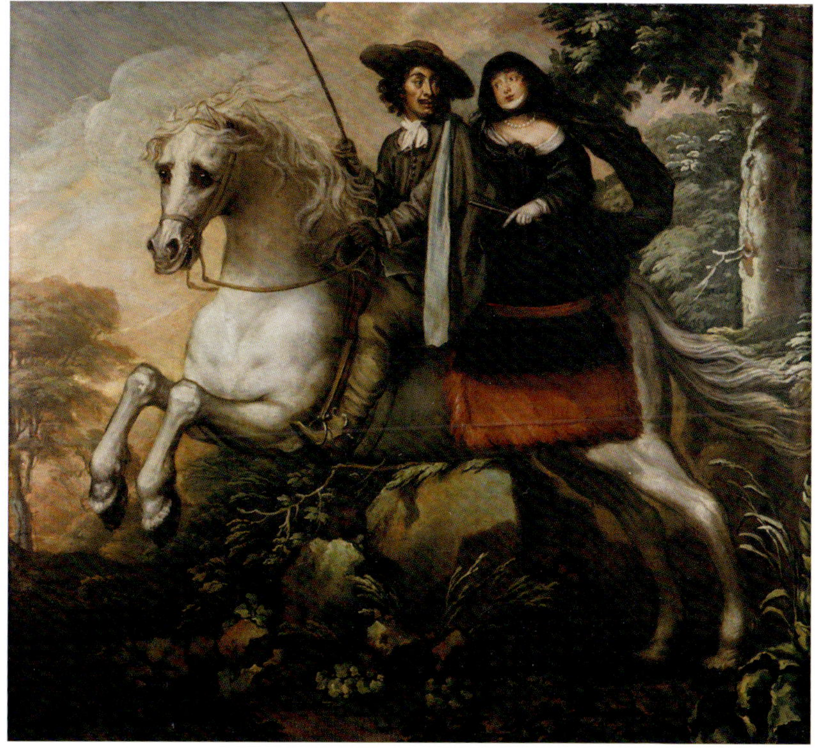

Isaac Fuller, *King Charles II and Jane Lane riding to Bristol following the King's defeat at the battle of Worcester* in 1651, c. 1660-72. Jane Lane married Sir Clement Fisher in 1663. She was painted by Mary Beale, probably in the 1670s or 1680s

King Charles II's escape in the immediate aftermath of the battle of Worcester was largely due to the courageous Miss Jane Lane, sister of Colonel John Lane who sheltered the King at Bentley Hall, Worcestershire, where the family planned the King's escape. Disguised as Miss Lane's servant, 'William Jackson', the King rode with her to Stratford-upon-Avon, where she rebuffed suspicious soldiers, thence to Bristol. Strangways and his allies eventually secured a boat to ship the King from Shoreham in Sussex to Fécamp, France. Miss Lane soon came under suspicion, so she escaped to France, to be greeted by the King with the words 'Welcome, my life'. They were joined by Colonel Thomas Blagge carrying the monarch's precious Order of the Garter badge and sash, rescued from the battlefield at Worcester. Jane Lane received her rewards at the Restoration of the monarchy: an annuity, a gold watch, a lock of the King's hair, a coat of arms featuring a sturdy horse (reminiscent of their escapade in 1651) and the motto *Garde Le Roy.* She married Sir Clement Fisher Bt in 1663. Mary Beale's portrait of Jane Lane/Lady Fisher surfaced in 1866 when it was owned by Andrew Fountaine, presumably a descendant of the art collector Sir Andrew Fountaine (1676–1753). It was catalogued as 'half length, standing near a tree' (an oak perhaps, referring to the tree that sheltered King Charles II after his flight from the battlefield?).[37]

The 1866 exhibition catalogue of portraits at the South Kensington Museum (the Victoria and Albert) listed a portrait of Anna Maria, Countess of Shrewsbury (1642–1702) by Mary Beale, owned by Earl Spencer. The Countess provoked a duel between Henry Jermyn and Colonel Thomas Howard in 1662 in which Jermyn was killed. Five years later Anna Maria's husband, the Earl of Shrewsbury, challenged another of her lovers, George Villiers, Duke of Buckingham, to fight for her. The Countess, it is said, watched the duel at Barn Elmes in January 1668 disguised as a page and holding the Duke's horse. Swords clashed and her husband died of his wounds. After retiring to France for an interlude, this doughty woman returned to England and married George Brydges MP in 1677.[38]

George, 1st Earl of Berkeley FRS (1627–1698), was one of 'the immortal seven' who travelled to The Hague in 1660 to invite King Charles II to return to England and take the throne. Berkeley was still at the forefront of politics in 1688 when a provisional government steadied the nation pending the arrival and endorsement of Prince William of Orange. Mary Beale's portrait of Berkeley celebrated his

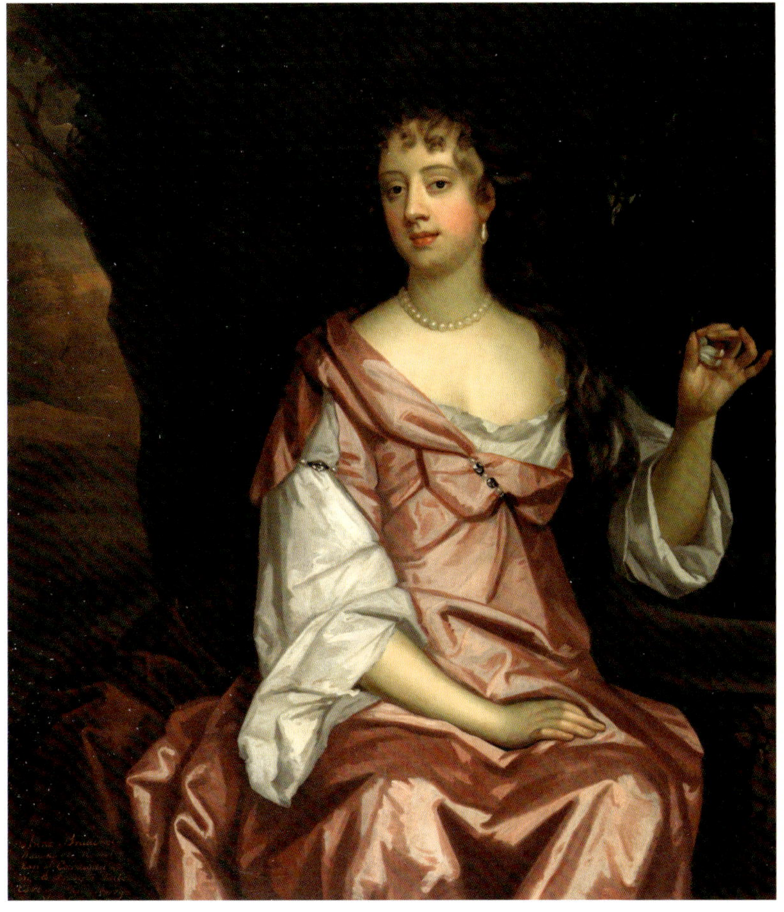

Left: Mary Beale (attributed to), *The Countess of Shrewsbury*, c. 1660. In 1866 this portrait was catalogued under Mary Beale's name; recently it has been described as by the school of Sir Peter Lely

Below: Mary Beale, *The 1st Earl of Berkeley*, probably painted in 1679, the year he was given the earldom

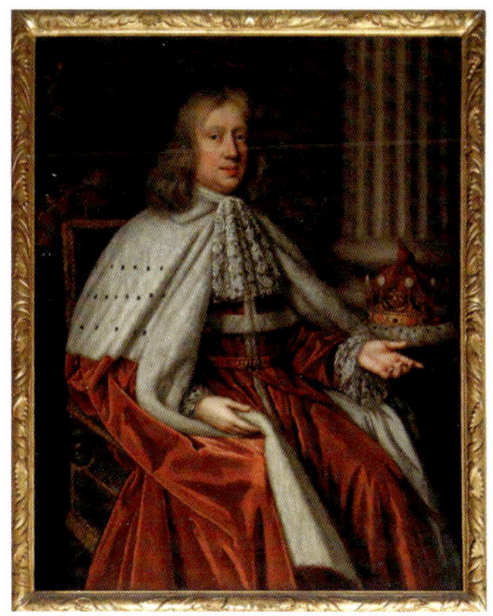

recent earldom: he chose to be painted wearing his ermine robes with his coronet to hand (he was reputed to be arrogant, coarse and unscrupulous).

Elizabeth Massingberd, daughter of the Treasurer of the East India Company, was a wealthy target for Berkeley, whose wife she became in 1646. She is said to have commissioned Mary Beale for a portrait of Margaret Blagge (1652–1678), the beautiful daughter of Colonel Thomas Blagge and Mary (née North), both descendants of ancient Suffolk families. The pious Margaret Blagge, a reluctant courtier, met the diarist John Evelyn in 1672 and they formed an inviolable friendship, a marriage of souls. Having dined with her, Evelyn escorted Margaret to Matthew Dixon's rooms in 1673 to sit for her picture, 'which I desired her to give me'.[39] Margaret deliberately

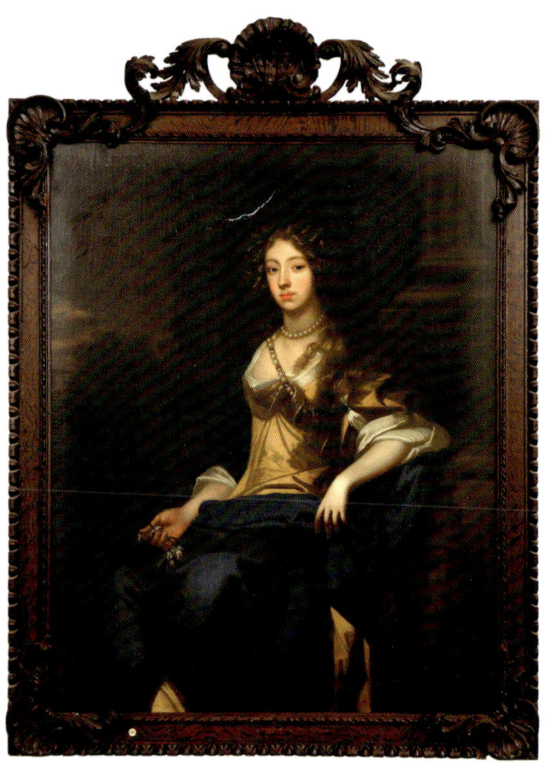

Mary Beale (attributed to), *Lady Godolphin*, 1675

chose the lugubrious posture and the composition, which featured a tombstone and sepulchral urn. The result was a melancholy portrait of Margaret with downcast eyes. Lady Berkeley, it is alleged, 'would have something more attractive',[40] so she commissioned a more conventional portrait of Margaret, elaborately dressed, holding a sprig of laurel to symbolise love and virtue and resting her elbow on a sculpture of cupid. Long believed to be from the brush of Mary Beale, one version of this portrait is at Berkeley Castle, Gloucestershire, another greets guests at West Lodge Park Hotel, Hertfordshire.

John Evelyn wrote the biography of Margaret Blagge and dedicated 'The Altar of Friendship', to 'this Miracle of a young Lady in a licentious Court & so depriv'd an age'.[41] The admirable Miss Margaret Blagge was courted by Sidney Godolphin, 1st Earl of Godolphin (1645–1712) for nine years before she agreed to marry him secretly in 1675, only to die soon after the birth of their son in 1678. Lord Godolphin's younger brother, William, was the subject of one of Mrs Beale's early portraits and the Godolphin/Berkeley network brought commissions for portraits of Mrs Ann Howard, daughter of the Earl of Berkshire and a maid of honour to the Duchess of York, and from Lord Berkeley for a portrait of his daughter, Theophilia, wife of Sir Kingsmill Lucy.

The Restoration of King Charles II was masterminded by politicians, civil servants and by General George Monck. Having been commander-in-chief of the Commonwealth army he arrived in London early in 1660 to prepare the way for the King. On the march south from Scotland, Monck contacted his relation, Sir William Morice (1602–1676), seeking his advice, and the two convened in the capital to plan an agreement with King Charles II as the basis for the Restoration. The King, writing from Brussels where he was poised for his return to England, acknowledged Morice's outstanding efforts behind the scenes. In London, Monck led his troops through the streets of the City, to the joy of its inhabitants who rejoiced at the prospect of the Restoration of the monarchy after the civil war, the execution of Charles I and eleven years of the Commonwealth.

It was an ironic turn of events, as Evelyn noted, 'and all this was done without one drop of blood shed, and by that very army which rebelled against him' [Charles II].[42]

Monck and Morice were at Dover to greet Charles II on his return to his kingdom. The King knighted Morice at Canterbury, en route for London, and appointed him Secretary of State; Monck was created Duke of Albemarle. For the King's triumphant procession through the City of London on 29 May 1660, Morice literally paved the way by ordering that the streets be specially gravelled. He sickened of politics after the humiliating raid by the Dutch fleet at Chatham and the impeachment of Lord Chancellor Clarendon in 1667. He resigned as Lord of the Treasury in 1668 'owing to his disgust with the King for breaking his promises and debauching the nation',[43] retiring to his estate at Werrington, Devon. Morice knew of Mary Beale through his personal secretary, Dr John Cooke, and she painted Morice's daughter, Lady Pole, and grand-daughter, Lady Carew.

Mary Beale found a few patrons among City dignitaries such as Alderman Hildesley, Sir Robert Viner and Sir Thomas Davies. Alderman Sir Robert Viner/Vyner Bt (1631–1688), Lord Mayor of London (1674–5), was involved with – and profited from – the coronation of King Charles II at Westminster Abbey on 23 April 1661. As the King's goldsmith, Viner supplied the new regalia (two crowns, three sceptres, orb, mace, collars, garters and plate) earning him some £30,000. Viner inherited the family banking house and became the King's largest individual creditor. Sir Robert and 'His Lady, his daughter' were painted by Mary Beale in June 1672 when Charles Beale noted with satisfaction the receipt of £30 for three pictures.[44] The daughter was Viner's ten-year-old step-daughter, Bridget Hyde (1662–1734), whose marriage to Viscount Dunblane was arranged by Viner, despite the fact that she was pledged to another. Meanwhile, Bridget was abducted at pistol point from Viner's country house, Swakeleys. She was rescued, only to be abducted a second time in 1682 by Dunblane who married her. When Dunblane inherited his father's title, the young girl who had been painted by Mary Beale in 1672 became the Duchess of Leeds.[45]

A second Lord Mayor approached Mrs Beale in the form of Sir Thomas Davies who, with his wife Elizabeth, herself an Alderman's daughter, sat for their portraits during Davies's mayoralty (1676–7). Davies was a bookseller trading from the sign of The Bible in St

Paul's churchyard, and a Master of the Stationers' and the Drapers' companies. Despite being immensely rich, he was 'a meane spirited person when he was Sheriff of London,' and regularly drunk in taverns;[46] Samuel Pepys described him as 'the little fellow'… the bookseller'.[47] A share of Davies's fortune was inherited by his daughter Mary who put it to use in founding the Grosvenor estate, London, after her marriage to Thomas Grosvenor.

The popularity of Mary Beale's portraits lay in her ability to capture good likenesses. The importance of an accurate likeness was a point made by Lord Protector Oliver Cromwell to Sir Peter Lely in 1654. 'Mr Lilly [Lely] I desire you would use all your skill to paint my picture truly like me & not flatter me at all but remark all these ruffness, pimples, warts and everything as you see me… otherwise I will never pay a farthing for it'.[48] Mary Beale did not flatter her sitters: her husband's warts are in evidence in her portraits of him and she painted Lord Halifax's double chin and long nose accurately. Her patrons wanted portraits of their family, friends and heroes, the monarchy and royal mistresses that were recognisable. Contemporaries praised Mary Beale's portraits for their likeness to the sitter and for her skilled use of colour. Her painting of Symon/Simon Patrick when Dean of Peterborough, for instance, was, her husband attested, 'one of the best pictures both for painting and likeness D Heart ever did & therefore the more fitt to be presented [to] him to whom we are so exceedingly obliged'.[49] Samuel Woodford sat for Mary in September 1664 and noted that 'she hath done it very like as all say that see it & are better judges of its likenesse than my self'.[50] Woodford watched Mary paint Auditor Bartholomew Beale and noted it was 'done very hapliy and exceeding like'.[51] When Dr John Tillotson sat for Mary in 1681, Charles Beale praised the portrait because it was 'extreamly like him and [she] coloured it exceeding rarely, made it very forcible & strong. She bestowed the whole day upon it, the most obliging Dean satt with admirable and unwearied patience being one of the readiest persons in this world to gratify & serve his friends'.[52] Clergymen such as Tillotson were content to sit patiently for Mary Beale because they trusted her to provide a good likeness. Moreover, she was pious, educated and amiable.

The majority of Mary Beale's portraits were intended as personal memorials for the sitter's family or friends. Her copies after Lely and Van Dyck were in demand because they enhanced an individual's collection of paintings of famous men and beautiful women, while her commissions from statesmen, politicians, bishops and Fellows of the Royal Society recorded the status of the subject. In the post-Restoration period, portraiture flourished by royal example and collecting portraits became important to the affluent. There was even a book, *Polygraphice* (1675), which advised on the appropriate hanging of portraits: royalty and nobility should be displayed in the dining-room, distinguished men and women were suitable for the walls of withdrawing rooms, wives and children were best placed in bedchambers. Mrs Beale's patrons preferred head and shoulder portraits which her husband, Charles, described as pictures 'in little'. They were sometimes as small as 15 by 12 inches (38.1 by 30.8 cms), otherwise 24 by 20 inches (60.96 by 50.8 cms) or 30 by 24 inches (76.2 by 60.96 cms), with variations. Mary Beale's three-quarter length portraits were usually 50 by 40 inches (127 by 101.6 cms). Full length portraits are rare but she obliged with a copy of Lely's full length picture of King Charles II for the Duchess of Newcastle, and her full length portrait of Sir William Turner was dictated by the dimensions of similar portraits hanging in the great hall at Bridewell.

Portraits of 'divines'

Never before had so many Anglican clergy posed for a female artist. Mrs Beale was besieged by commissions from 'divines' who might well have chosen one of her male contemporaries to paint their portraits but they favoured the industrious, pious Mary Beale. Soon after her return to London in 1669/70 she painted Dr William Bates (1625–1699), the nonconformist vicar of St Dunstan in the West who was known for his dislike of drinking toasts. He had known the Beales since they lived at Hind Court and he first sat for Mary Beale in 1662. When in October 1664 Mrs Beale concluded a session of painting Dr John Tillotson 'he and his wife dined here and at night we all went to see Dr Bates and his wife'.[53] Bates took part in the negotiations that formed the basis of King Charles II's Restoration and was subsequently appointed a chaplain to the King. The last few years of his life were spent as a preacher at a Hackney meeting-house and, after his death his library formed the basis of Dr Williams's library, Gordon Square, London.

Sir Peter Lely, *Bishop Symon Patrick*, 1668

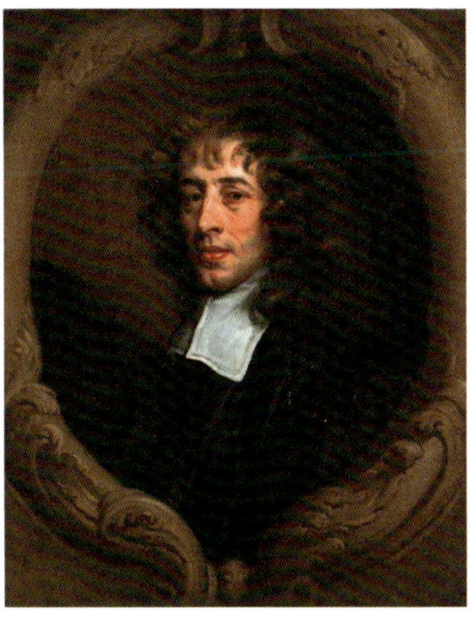

The Reverend Symon Patrick (1626–1707) was presented with the living of St Paul's, Covent Garden, by the Earl of Bedford in 1662. Patrick was a prolific author and a highly respected vicar, not least because he stayed in London to attend to his parishioners during the great plague of 1665. The plague spread from the City to Westminster in September when Patrick encountered a dismal procession in the Strand: thirty poor people carrying white sticks led by a woman on horseback with a flag proclaiming *Laus Deo* and escorted by the doctor of the pest house. Patrick dosed himself with 'plague drink', London treacle and 'Lady Allen's water', so managed to avoid the contagion. He took heart when he heard that the clapper had fallen off the great bell at Westminster (as it had towards the end of the previous plague); the return of the 'dawes' (jackdaws) to the abbey and palace was another good omen.[54] Patrick's comforting handbooks such as *The Heart's Ease* offered practical guidance to the faithful (the publication was dedicated to his patrons Sir Walter and Lady St John, whom he introduced to Mrs Beale). A heavy load fell on Patrick in November 1686 when he was summoned to Whitehall to discuss King James II's desire for the conversion to Catholicism of the Lord Treasurer, the Earl of Rochester. A secret meeting was arranged in the presence of two Roman Catholic priests and, after 'a great deal of wrangling' Rochester rejected the arguments of the King and the Catholics, to the credit of Patrick and his colleague, Dr William Jane, Dean of Gloucester.[55]

Sir Peter Lely's portrait of Symon Patrick of around 1668 is a head and shoulders set in a feigned oval frame, a device favoured by Mary Beale. Mrs Beale produced her version in 1672 and both Patrick and his wife, Penelope, sat for her in 1677. Penelope (1646–1725) had previously taken a vow of celibacy and it took years of persuasion before she agreed to marry Patrick in 1675. Mary Beale produced further portraits of Patrick as Dean of Peterborough (1681) and lastly as Bishop of Ely in the 1690s, making him one of her most frequently painted subjects, along with John Tillotson, Thomas Sydenham and Edward Stillingfleet.

Dr John Tillotson (1630–1694), who had impressed the Beales with his sermons at St Lawrence Jewry, married Oliver Cromwell's niece, Elizabeth, in 1664. Elizabeth, 'Betty', was the confidante of Mary Beale who sent Betty a copy of her 'Discourse on Friendship' (see pages 78, 85). Dr Tillotson was an acute logician and philosopher. He and his colleagues Lloyd, Patrick, Tenison and Stillingfleet were renowned in their lifetimes as 'the greatest divines we have had these forty years'.[56] Tillotson was a regular visitor to the Beales when they lived at Hind Court and their esteem for him prompted them to commission his portrait by Sir Peter Lely in July 1672.

Dr Tillotson and his contemporaries at the University of Cambridge in the 1650s – Symon Patrick, Richard Kidder and Thomas Tenison – were all painted in later life by Mary Beale. Dr Thomas Tenison (1636–1715) was promoted to office by Heneage Finch (1621–1682), 1st Earl of Nottingham and Lord Chancellor, who in 1680 presented Tenison with the living of St Martin-in-the-Fields, the church attended by the Beales until St James's, Piccadilly, was consecrated in 1684. Dr Tenison's and Dean Symon Patrick's portraits were among 'Pictures begun 1681 by My Dearest Heart for friends and upon Account of Kindness and not profitt'.[57] Mary Beale also painted Anne, Tenison's wife, and two later portraits of Tenison (1692, 1695) are attributed to her (see page 169). Tenison was a vituperative anti-papist and his views were shared by many Londoners who rioted and set fire to 'mass houses'. Charles and Mary Beale and their Protestant friends were appalled by the revival of the Queen's Chapel (1662–80) in Pall Mall, designed for the Roman Catholic Queen Catherine of Braganza, and by Wren's new Catholic chapel at Whitehall Palace (1685–6). One of Tenison's duties was to attend James, Duke of Monmouth, the illegitimate son of Charles II and Lucy Walter, as Monmouth awaited execution on Tower Hill in July 1685, condemned to death for a rebellion against the newly crowned Roman Catholic King James II. The Duke's sister, Mary Walter (b. 1651), married William Fanshawe in 1676, whose likeness was painted by Mary Beale the following year.[58]

Once King James II had fled the country in December 1688, Tenison, Patrick and Lloyd met at Stillingfleet's house to map out a policy of religious toleration for the Church of England. Tenison (whose coffin was discovered in 2017 at St Mary's church, Lambeth) succeeded Tillotson as Archbishop of Canterbury and was installed in May 1695. He was a philanthropist, founding the first public library in London and schools (Archbishop Tenison's schools continue to flourish in London and Croydon). Mary Beale's portrait of his wife hung in the Archbishop's bedroom after her death and, following the demise of the Archbishop in 1715, it was left to Archbishop Tenison's School for Girls.

Dr Gilbert Burnet (1643–1715), a friend of Charles and Mary Beale since the 1670s, was suspected of collusion with the Rye House plotters in 1683. His friends, the Earl of Essex, Lord Russell, and his cousin, Robert Baillie, were implicated in the plot which aimed to kill the King and the Duke of York. Burnet comforted Russell during his

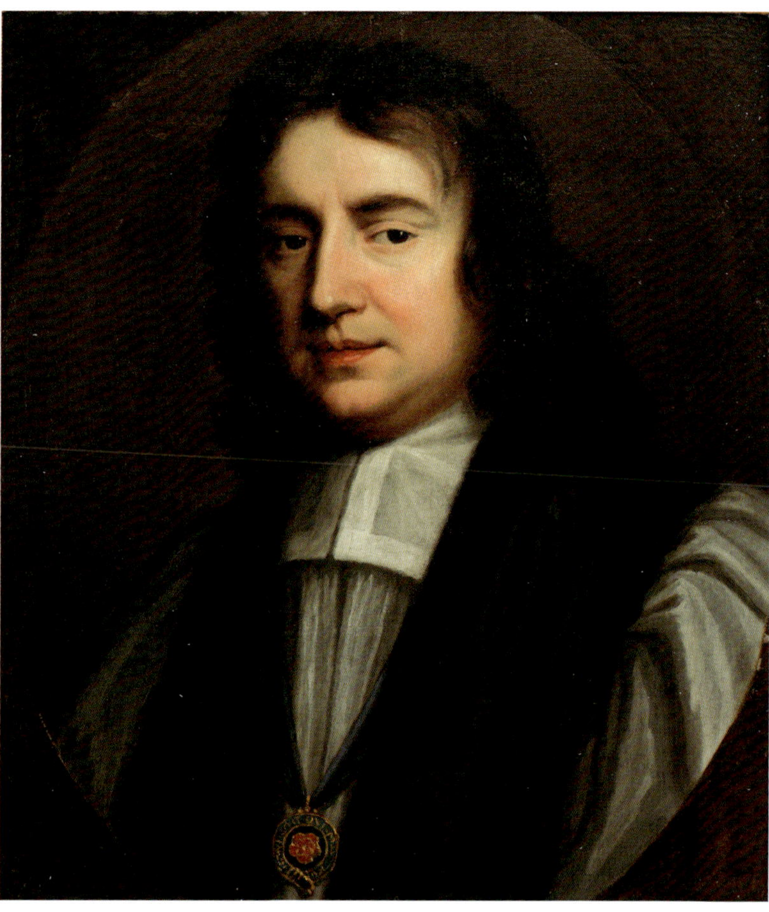

Mary Beale, *Gilbert Burnet, Bishop of Salisbury*, c. 1689-91

imprisonment in the Tower of London and escorted him to the scaffold where the condemned man presented Burnet with his watch. The Rye House Plot placed Burnet under a cloud and he spent the years of King James II's reign abroad, returning as an ally of Prince William of Orange, whom he accompanied to Torbay in November 1688.

Mary Beale painted Burnet in 1681, c. 1689-91 and c. 1691. Meanwhile Burnet requested a portrait of William Lloyd, Bishop of St Asaph, while Mary presented Burnet with her painting of Dr Edward Stillingfleet in return for Burnet's gift of the first two volumes of his *History of the Reformation* (1679, 1681). Charles Beale recognised the importance of Burnet's history and sent the 1681 volume to Prince Rupert's bookbinder to be bound in red turkey leather with gilt.[59] The preface to Burnet's classic work on the Reformation acknowledged

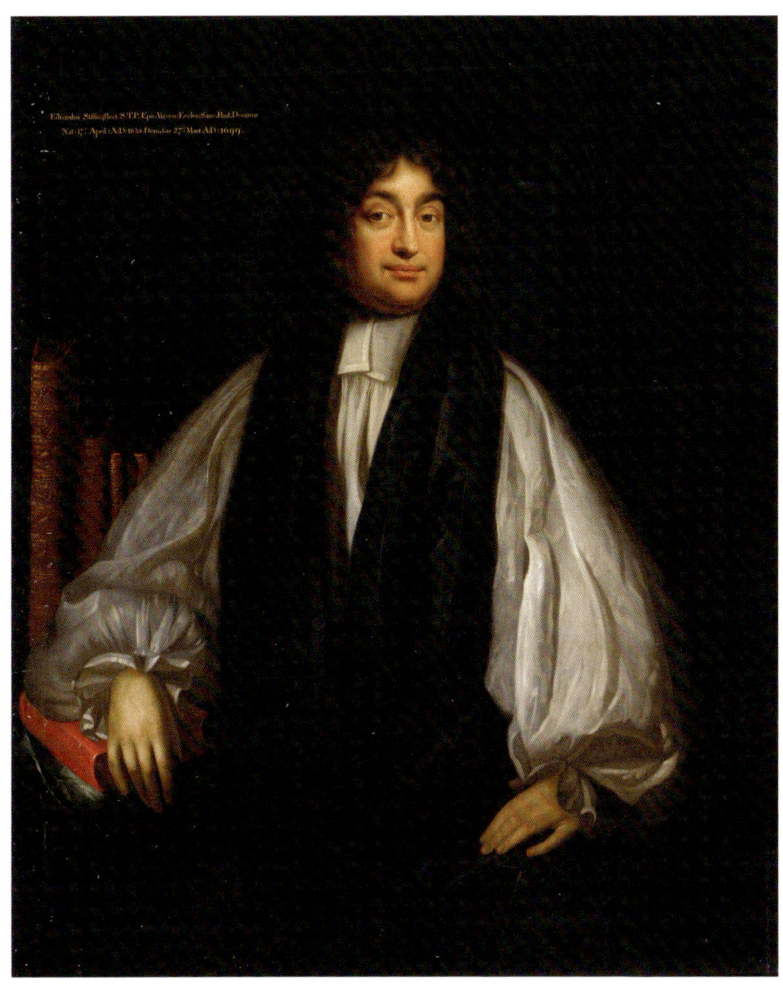

Mary Beale, *Edward Stillingfleet FRS*, painted soon after his appointment as Bishop of Worcester in 1689

the assistance of the Beales' friend, 'the famous and eminently learned Dr Stillingfleet' and the financial support of the Beales' neighbour in Pall Mall, Robert Boyle.[60] Burnet's autobiography, *History of My Own Time*, first printed in 1724, records the careers and foibles of many of Mrs Beale's circle, enlivened by opinionated comments.

Dr Edward Stillingfleet FRS (1635–1699) first sat for Mrs Beale in December 1664, shortly before his installation as rector of St Andrew's, Holborn. In Pepys's opinion he was a rising star, 'the ablest young man to preach the gospel of any since the Apostles. He did make the most plain, honest, good, grave sermon – in the most unconcerned and easy yet substantial manner that I ever heard'.[61]

Stillingfleet was blessed with charisma and good looks (he was known as 'the beauty of holiness'). As a commissioner for rebuilding St Paul's Cathedral after the great fire, he knew Sir Christopher Wren whom he persuaded to design St Andrew's, Holborn, which had escaped the fire but was dilapidated. Rebuilt between 1684 and 1687, St Andrew's was the largest of Wren's City churches.

Portraits of Stillingfleet were in demand. Mary Beale painted him at the behest of Colonel Strangways in 1672 and the Beales commissioned Lely to paint Stillingfleet in 1674.[62] She painted him again in 1681, and a portrait of him as Bishop of Worcester is attributed to her; a portrait of his eight-year-old daughter, Andrea, is also believed to be by Mrs Beale. Stillingfleet shared Charles Beale's interest in Italian art and owned some of Richard Symonds's Italian notebooks of 1649–51; his library was considered one of the best in England, as hinted by the portrait of around 1690.

Stillingfleet, Tillotson, Tenison, Patrick and Lloyd formed a pressure group to oppose King James II's religious policy and ultimately they achieved success. The King realised, too late, that he had alienated the leaders of the Church of England, the Aldermen and liverymen of the City. He attempted to redress the situation but failed. The departure of this autocratic Roman Catholic monarch and the accession of King William and Queen Mary in 1689 brought many of the Beales' friends to high office, and Mary's portraits of them confirmed their positions as leaders of the Anglican church (see chapter 7).

The most erudite of the Beales' friends was William Lloyd (1627–1717) whose career led to the bishopric of Worcester in 1699. John Wilkins remarked that Lloyd had 'the most learning in ready cash of any one he ever knew...a holy, humble, meek and patient man ever ready to do good'.[63] The Beales became acquainted with Lloyd while they were living in Hampshire and saw him more frequently during his tenure of St Martin-in-the-Fields from 1676 to 1680 (he sat for his portrait in 1677). He led the opposition to King James's religious policy, for which he was imprisoned in the Tower (see chapter 7). He lost credibility when in 1712 he announced to Queen Anne that the Church of Rome would be destroyed and Rome consumed by fire in less than four years.[64]

Fellows of the Royal Society

Mary Beale found an interesting group of sitters among the distinguished Fellows of the Royal Society. Her portraits of Fellows comprise a veritable roll-call of the natural philosophers, inventors and authors of late-seventeenth-century London. The Royal Society, granted a charter by King Charles II in 1662, aimed to foster natural philosophy, mechanical arts, inventions, physic, the survey of the heavens and 'the perfection of graving, statuary, limning, coining... and the most excellent Artists of these kinds'.[65] The horizons of the Society were limitless as its Fellows endeavoured to extend the boundaries of knowledge.

Mary Beale's introduction to Fellows of the Royal Society may have been implemented by the scientific writer, Dr John Beale (1608–1683), her husband's cousin and a Fellow from 1663. Dr Beale's interests ranged from the manufacture of ink and gunpowder to agricultural tools, and he was a pioneer of pomiculture who consulted John Evelyn about trees and garden design. The Beales had further contacts with the Royal Society through Samuel Woodford (elected a Fellow in 1664) and Thomas Flatman (elected in 1668). Woodford was proposed for fellowship by the pillar of the Society, Dr John Wilkins, and by the diplomat Sir William Godolphin (both were painted by Mary Beale). Wilkins was the Royal Society's Secretary, and his portrait by Mrs Beale brought her to the notice of other Fellows. Her portrait of 1670-72 (illustrated on page 74) remains with the Royal Society; an earlier portrait of Wilkins (1668, shortly before he left London for the bishopric of Chester) is at Wadham College, Oxford, the cradle of the Royal Society under Wilkins's wardenship, and a third is at the Bodleian Library, Oxford.

Wilkins was closely associated with the Cromwell family (he married the Lord Protector's sister) and he continued to be influential in political and intellectual circles after the Restoration of the monarchy, as vicar of St Lawrence Jewry in the City, at the Royal Society and as Bishop of Chester. He died at the Tillotson's house in Chancery Lane (Mrs Tillotson, Mary Beale's friend and correspondent, was his step-daughter).

With these contacts, Charles Beale may have aspired to be elected a Fellow of the Royal Society. He was well-read, his penmanship was elegant, his prose flowery (as was the fashion) and he conducted experiments with colours and pigments, a field which interested the Society. His lack of a university education was a hindrance, not to mention his precarious social standing after his dismissal from the Patents Office.

The physician Sir George Ent FRS (1604–1689) sat for his portrait

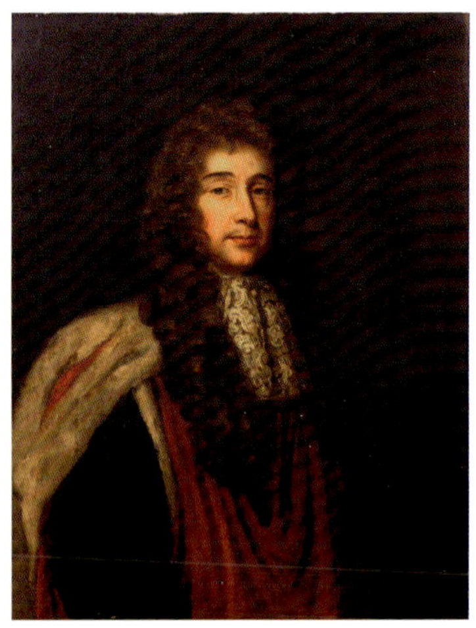

Mary Beale, *The physician William Croone FRS*, c. 1680

in 1674, as did his wife and their son, George, also a Fellow. The latter travelled on the Continent with the antiquarian and biographer John Aubrey, who commented that Ent 'puts me in mind of Plato's saying that perpetual drunkenness is the reward of virtue'.[66] Sir George, on the other hand, was celebrated as the ornament of his age. He held the first meeting of the Royal Society's anatomical committee at his house in St Giles-in-the-Fields where the lungs of a viper were dissected in order to research respiration. The subject was pursued by Dr William Croone who took a live chicken to one meeting, choked it, then revived it by blowing into its lungs. Sir George Ent was a President of Royal College of Physicians and the defender of William Harvey (1578–1657), discoverer of the circulation of the blood. It was due to Ent's determination that Harvey's work on animal reproduction, *Exercitationes de Generatione Animalium* was published in 1651.

Dr William Croone FRS (1633–1684) was a pioneer of blood transfusion, which entailed experiments on dogs (leading Samuel Pepys to speculate if the blood of a Quaker might be transferred to an archbishop). Mrs Beale's portrait of Croone, painted a few years before his death of a fever at the age of fifty-one, was presented to the Royal College of Physicians by Dr William Woodford, Croone's grandson and Samuel Woodford's godson, in 1738. It was noted that the portrait was an accurate representation of Croone: *manu perita Dnae Mariae Beal accurate depictum*. Croone's widow, Mary, married Sir Edwyn Sadleir Bt (1656–1719) of Temple Dinsley, Hertfordshire, in 1686. The couple's portraits at Sutton House, Hackney, are regarded as among Mary Beale's best. Lady Sadleir fulfilled her first husband's wishes by endowing the Croonian lectures at the Royal College of Physicians and at Emmanuel College, Cambridge.

Robert Hooke FRS (1635–1703) suffered from poor health and an awkward appearance. John Aubrey described him as 'but of middling stature, something crooked, pale-faced but his head is large and his eye full, popping and grey. He has a delicate head of brown hair and an excellent moist curl'.[67] Mary Beale painted Hooke at the peak of his career as surveyor for the rebuilding of the City after the great fire of 1666, a demanding post which Hooke combined with curatorship of experiments at the Royal Society.

In his youth Hooke had been taught to draw by the miniaturist Samuel Cooper and had served a brief apprenticeship to Peter Lely in 1648. He abandoned painting because the smell of oil paints gave him headaches (Aubrey thought it was more likely that Hooke needed

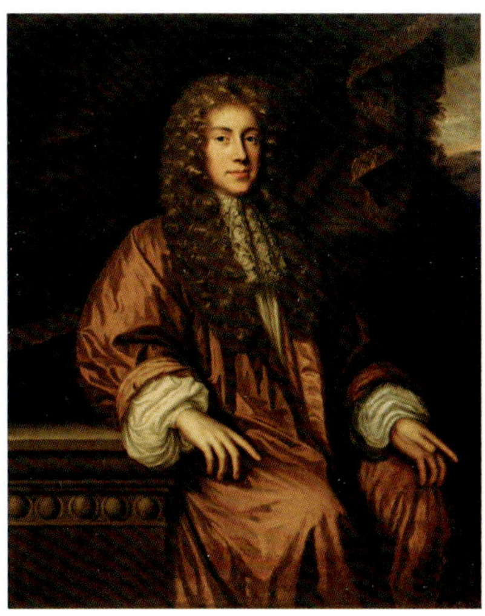

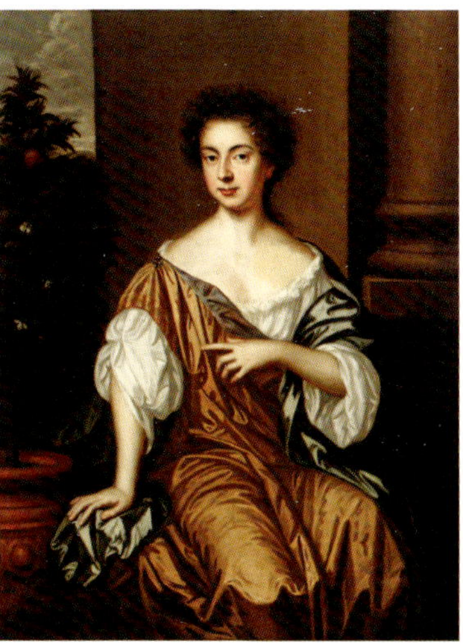

Mary Beale, *Sir Edwyn Sadleir Bt*, of Temple Dinsley, Hertfordshire, 1686–7

Mary Beale, *Lady Sadleir*, 1686–7

to retrieve his apprenticeship fee). Mrs Beale's portrait celebrated Hooke's appointment as architect for the new Bethlehem Hospital, Moorfields, a commission from Sir William Turner, who was himself painted by Beale (see page 89).

Hooke recorded in his diary for 20 April 1674 'At [Robert] Boyles. He promised eye water and to sit at Mrs Beale's. At Beale's. Shav'd and cut hair at Youngs'. Hooke also referred to 'young Beale' (most probably Charles junior) who with Harry Hunt, Hooke's assistant, was studying painting.[68] Lisa Jardine, in her biography of Hooke, traced the Beale/Hooke portrait to the Natural History Museum where it was previously thought to have been a portrait of the naturalist and theologian John Ray FRS (1627–1705).[69]

Hooke's friend, the natural philosopher Robert Boyle FRS (1621–1691), was reluctant to have his portrait painted (he had suffered a stroke in 1670) and the purpose of his visits to Mrs Beale's house in 1674 and 1675 may have been purely social. Boyle lived with his sister, Katherine Viscountess Ranelagh, in Pall Mall, where the house was a pantheon for Fellows of the Royal Society (the site is now occupied by the Royal Automobile Club). Lady Ranelagh (1615–1691) was the *éminence grise* of the Royal Society but ineligible to be elected a Fellow (the first women Fellows were not elected until 1945). She master-minded a network of correspondents at home and abroad and was herself an experimental chemist. Like Mary Beale, she blazed a trail for intellectual, artistic women; they were neighbours and quite likely friends. Charles Beale must have been fascinated by the laboratory constructed by Hooke behind Lady Ranelagh's house (1676–7). Here Boyle conducted experiments with colours using syrup of violets, juice of blue-bottles and chemicals. As he and Charles Beale recognised, 'The mixing of pigments being no inconsiderable part of the painter's art'.[70]

The nobility and aristocracy

The list of 'People of Quality',[71] politicians, nobility and aristocracy, influential women and the occasional conspirator who sat for Mary Beale constitutes a directory of who-was-who in late-seventeenth-century London. Yet, unlike Verelest, Huysmans, Lely, Kneller, Wissing, Riley, Dahl and John Michael Wright, who enjoyed royal patronage, that honour escaped Mary Beale. Nevertheless, many of her patrons were titled, some were courtiers and influential politicians. Lady Compton, Sir John Cropley Bt, the Countess of Derby (who loaned her portrait by Lely for Mary to copy), Lady Parsons, the Countess of Northumberland, and the Scots chieftain John Murray, 1st Marquess of Atholl, commissioned portraits from life and copies of originals by Lely from Mary Beale during the 1670s. One of Mary Beale's most esteemed patrons was Lady Delamer, daughter of Sir James Langham Bt, whose portrait was painted around the time of her marriage to Henry Booth, Lord Delamer, in 1670 (see page 164).

Through her friendship with Lady Backhouse, Mrs Beale obtained commissions to paint her (after her marriage to Henry Hyde, Lord Cornbury), and her husband, who succeeded as 2nd Earl of Clarendon in 1674. He inherited his father's magnificent art collection which hung at Clarendon House, Piccadilly, before its demolition. The 2nd Earl and his wife were a powerful couple: the Earl was the uncle of Queen Mary II and Queen Anne, and brother-in-law to King James II. The Countess of Clarendon was first lady of the bedchamber to Queen Anne and a rival to Sarah, Duchess of Marlborough, in the Queen's affections (the jealous Duchess commented that Lady Clarendon 'looked like a mad woman and talked like a scholar').[72]

George Vertue found a reference in Charles Beale's almanack for 1674 to '2 pictures Lady Mary Candish blew scarf £22'.[73] This was Mary Cavendish (1646–1710), daughter of the 1st Duke of Ormond who married William Cavendish (1641–1707), later the 1st Duke of Devonshire, in 1662. Mary Beale's portrait, after Lely's original, depicted the young woman who was to be the chatelaine of Chatsworth House, Derbyshire, rebuilt by her husband between 1687 and 1706. Mrs Beale received a second commission from the family, for a portrait of the Duke of Ormond in 1677.

An aristocratic art connoisseur approached Mary Beale in 1674. This was Sir William Fermor/Farmer (1648–1711), who chose her in preference to Lely or John Riley. Fermor, later Baron Leominster, was the owner of Easton Neston, Northamptonshire, a palatial house completed by the architect Nicholas Hawksmoor in 1702. Fermor filled Easton Neston with works of art, not least the Arundel marbles.

Thomas Belasyse, 1st Earl Fauconberg (1628–1700) and his wife Mary (1637–1713, née Cromwell), who were from opposite ends of the political spectrum, were among the élite to visit the Beales in Pall Mall to sit for their portraits: the Countess in 1671-2, again in 1674, and her husband in 1676.[74] Fauconberg was a dashing figure from a royalist family, nevertheless he was persuaded to marry (secondly) Mary Cromwell, third daughter of the Lord Protector – she came with a dowry of £15,000 in 1657. Her father died the following year and was buried in Westminster Abbey; the corpse was exhumed in 1661,

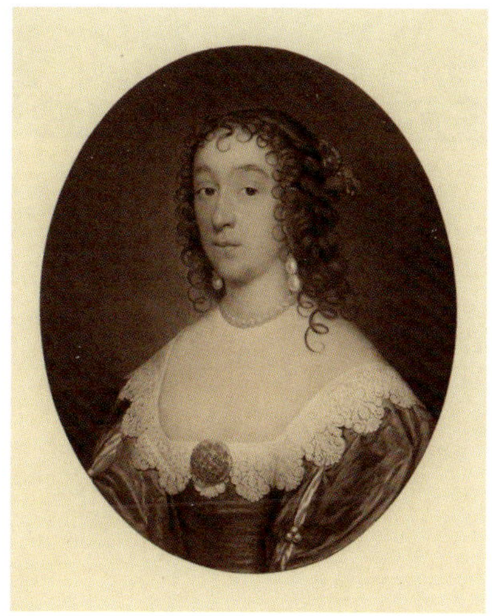

Left: Engraving by Abraham Blooteling after Mary Beale, *Thomas Belasyse, 1st Earl Fauconberg*, 1676

Right: Lithograph, nineteenth-century English school, *Countess Fauconberg, daughter of Lord Protector Oliver Cromwell*

decapitated, then hung at Tyburn gallows. Tradition has it that Mary Fauconberg had previously rescued the body intact and removed it to the family vault at Newburgh Priory, North Yorkshire, (where Mary Beale's portraits of Fauconberg and his wife can be seen). The savage reprisals of 1661 did not affect Fauconberg's appetite: he joined

Samuel Pepys and a dozen of 'his old acquaintance' at The Mitre tavern in Fenchurch Street in December of that year to enjoy 'a good Chine of beefe, which with three barrels of oysters and three pullets and plenty of wine and mirth, was our dinner'.[75]

Bishop Burnet found Lady Fauconberg 'a wise and worthy woman, more likely to have maintained the post [of Lord Protector] than either of her brothers'. In relation to Cromwell's children, the saying went that 'those who wore the breeches deserved the petticoats better, but if those in petticoats had been in breeches, they would have held them faster'.[76] It was due to Lady Fauconberg's astute management that her husband served as Privy Councillor to Oliver Cromwell, Richard Cromwell, Charles II and King William III, and he was given an earldom for his role in the negotiations that prefaced the reign of William and Mary. Fauconberg commissioned Mary Beale to paint his wife and he paid what was owing for his own portrait (£5 with an additional £3 10s for a leatherwork gilt frame) in February 1677.[77] Mary Fauconberg was renowned for her charity, piety and wit and was admired by Jonathan Swift, Dean of St Patrick's Cathedral and the author of *Gulliver's Travels*.

In the post-Restoration period Mrs Beale's patrons were generally royalists by nature, the exception being a clutch of names that will forever be associated with Cromwell and the parliamentarian/Puritan government that dominated England from 1649 to 1660, Lady Fauconberg being one. Puritan by upbringing, Mary Beale was personally affiliated to several of Cromwell's supporters: her distant cousin, the Reverend Samuel Cradock, married Honoria Fleetwood, sister of the regicide George Fleetwood (at the Restoration Fleetwood narrowly escaped the death sentence and was transported to Tangier). Dr John Wilkins, later Bishop of Chester, painted by Mary Beale in the 1670s, had been entrusted with chancellorship duties by Oliver Cromwell and was an advisor to his son, Richard. Elizabeth Tillotson, the wife of Dr John Tillotson, was Oliver Cromwell's niece and Mary Beale's dearest friend.

The parliamentarian hero Thomas, 3rd Lord Fairfax (1612–1671) is credited with the formation of the New Model Army which claimed victory over the royalists at the battle of Naseby in 1645. Fairfax married Anne, (1618–1665, née Vere), daughter of his commander in Ireland. She was an outspoken witness during the trial of King Charles I at Westminster Hall in 1649 when her remarks provoked gunfire from the floor. After the Restoration the couple retired, wisely, to

Yorkshire, but before her death in 1665 Lady Fairfax posed for Mary Beale, wearing a low-cut dress and a blue scarf/shawl.[78] An earlier portrait of Lady Fairfax, cautiously attributed to Mary Beale, shows her in a different light as a plump, dowdy woman in a brown dress. A portrait of Lord Fairfax in armour and holding a baton could well be by Beale, whose painting of Admiral Robert Fairfax is signed and dated by Mary Beale, 1685.

Henry Cavendish, 2nd Duke of Newcastle upon Tyne (1630–1691), and his Duchess were enthusiastic patrons of Mrs Beale. The Duke succeeded to the title following the death of his father in December 1676 and commissioned portraits of himself and his wife promptly.

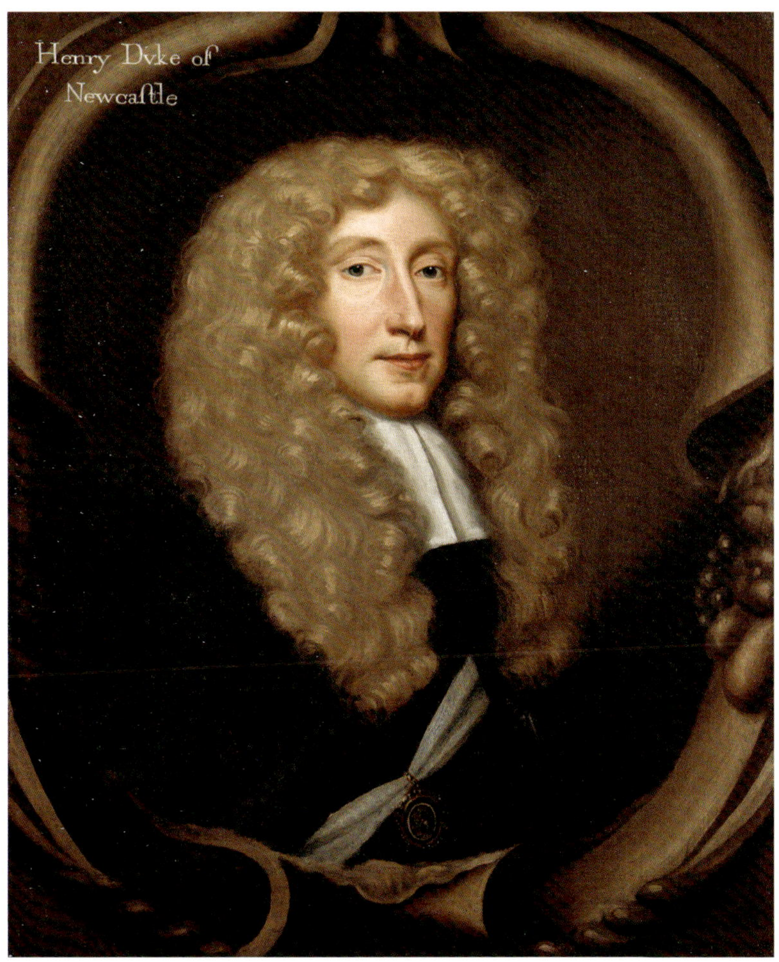

Mary Beale, *Henry Cavendish, 2nd Duke of Newcastle*, 1677. He wears the Order of the Garter which he was awarded in 1677

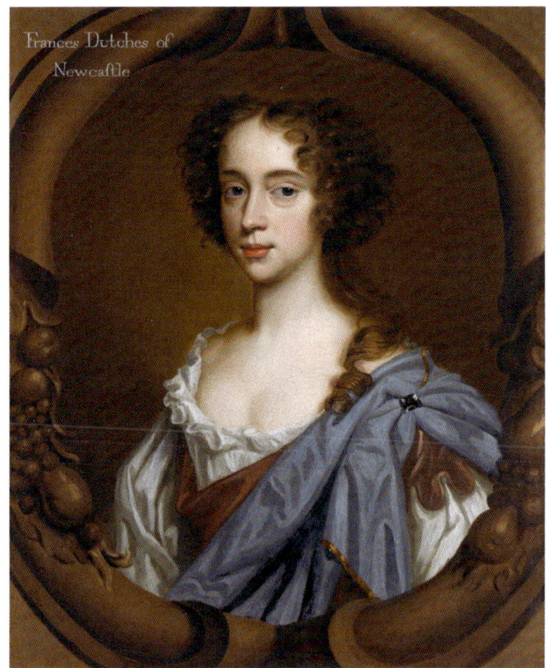

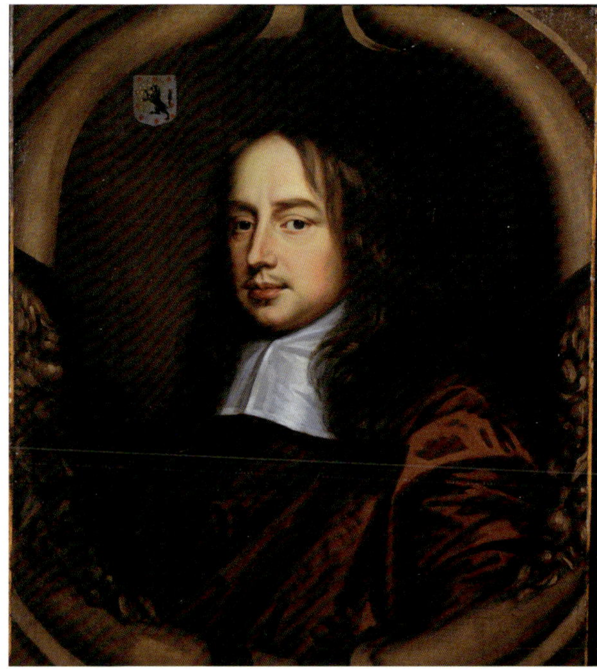

Above left: Mary Beale, *The Duchess of Newcastle*, c. 1676–7. Mary Beale also painted a half-length portrait of the Duchess in 1681

Above right: Mary Beale, *The Hon. William Pierrepont*, c. 1670–78

The Duke and Duchess, Frances (1630–1695, née Pierrepont, her unusual surname derived from Holme Pierrepont, the family seat in Nottinghamshire), knew Mary Beale through the Duchess's father, the Hon. William Pierrepont MP (1607–1678), whose portrait was painted by Beale in the early 1670s; he was another of her Cromwellian connections. Renowned as 'Wise William' on account of his political acumen during the turbulent parliaments of the 1640s, Pierrepont can be credited with establishing Oliver Cromwell's militia as the country edged towards civil war; he championed Richard Cromwell when few did and vehemently opposed the Restoration of the Stuart monarchy. 'Wise William' Pierrepont had officially retired from politics by the time he was painted by Mary Beale, nevertheless, his dislike of the Court of Charles II was overt and he was fortunate to escape retribution, managing to retain his wealth and estates in five counties.

The note 'Pierpoints' in Charles Beale's almanack for 1681 referred to commissions from the Duchess of Newcastle. The volume of work coming Mrs Beale's way was declining at this time, so she was grateful that the Duchess 'sent my Dear Heart a letter about making a faire whole length Coppy of the King's Picture after Sir

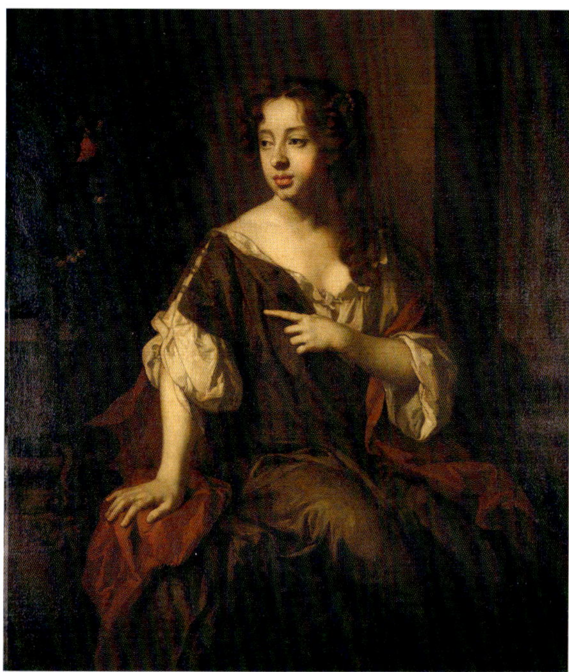

Left: Sir Peter Lely, *The Countess of Ogle*, c. 1679–80. Mary Beale made a copy after Lely, 'in little' in 1681

Peter Lely for my Lord Duke's Gallery at his house at Nottingham Castle', where the long gallery was built for the display of portraits.[79] The Duchess also approached Mrs Beale for copies of Lely's paintings of her only son, Henry Cavendish, Earl of Ogle (1659–1680), and his wife. Ogle married the heiress Lady Elizabeth Percy in 1679 and the couple were painted by Lely. With the deaths of Ogle and Lely in 1680, the Duchess turned to Mary Beale for copies of Lely's originals. This entailed nine journeys for the Beales from Pall Mall to Newcastle House, Clerkenwell, (Charles charged £21 for the copies and £1 7s for coach hire).[80] The widowed Countess of Ogle was still a prize to be won; she remarried Thomas Thynne of Longleat who was shot in Pall Mall in 1682 (see page 136).

The Bolingbroke family was doubtless introduced to Mrs Beale by the Reverend Symon Patrick, rector of St Paul's, Covent Garden, from 1662 to 1689. Patrick was also a royal chaplain from 1671 (he first sat for his portrait by Beale 1671-2) and personal chaplain to Sir Walter St John, Bt (1622–1708), the founder of St John's School, Battersea. Lady Mary St John, mother of Lord Bolingbroke, and her sisters, Lady Anne Rich and Lady Essex Finch, were painted by Mrs

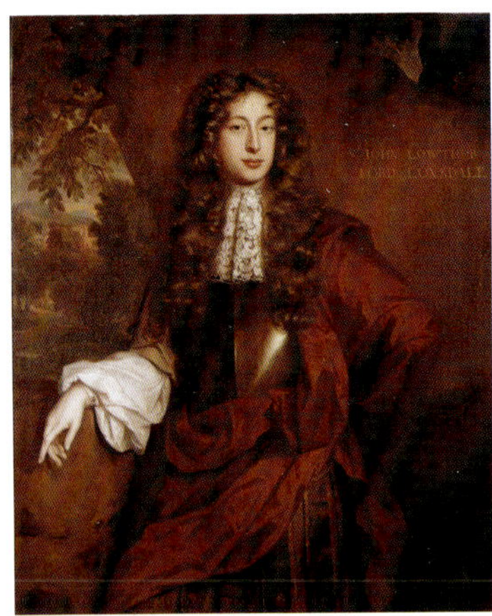

Mary Beale, *John Lowther, 1st Viscount Lonsdale*, 1677

Beale, who also copied Lely's portrait of Oliver St John, 2nd Earl of Bolingbroke (1634–1688) in 1677.

As with the Peirreponts and the Bolingbrokes, so with the Lowther family: a portrait of one member of a family invariably led to further commissions from that family and their connections. None more so than the Lowther/Thynne family who in one year alone, 1677, inundated Mary Beale with some thirty commissions. This glut of paintings of Lowthers and Thynnes originated in the marriage of Katherine Thynne to John Lowther, 1st Viscount Lonsdale, in 1674. Beginning with the portrait of Lady Katherine with her hand on a spaniel and the familiar pillar and curtains as background, Mary Beale proceeded to paint 'Old Sir John Lowther', and 'many pictures for Lowthers' and their relations, the Thynnes.[81]

The playwright Thomas Otway (1652–1685) was outside Mary Beale's usual range of patrons and it has been questioned whether the portrait of Otway might not be Charles Beale.[82] Horace Walpole was in no doubt about the sitter and the artist, crediting Mary Beale with a very interesting portrait of Otway belonging to the poet Gilbert West,[83] a claim substantiated by the South Kensington exhibition of 1866 when Earl Spencer loaned the Otway/Beale painting.[84]

Neighbours in St James's

Several illustrious neighbours in St James's found Mary Beale's Pall Mall painting-room congenial and convenient, and made appointments to have their faces painted (hands, copied from plaster models, draperies, ovals and backgrounds were executed later, generally by Mary's sons, Bartholomew and Charles). George Savile, 1st Marquess of Halifax (1633–1695), lived near the Beales when in London, occupying the grandest mansion of St James's Square, Halifax House, which boasted some fifty rooms and the luxury of river water piped into the Marquess's bathroom. He sauntered along Pall Mall to sit for Mary in April 1677 when Charles Beale noted 'Lord Halifax's face finished, he sat for about three hours',[85] in a full wig. The painting was probably at the insistence of his second wife, Gertrude Pierrepont, sister of Frances, Duchess of Newcastle (Mary Beale copied Lely's portraits of Gertrude and Frances for Halifax). Halifax possessed an astounding intellect; 'a man of a great and ready wit, full of life and very pleasant, much turned to satire', yet 'out of measure vain and ambitious'.[86]

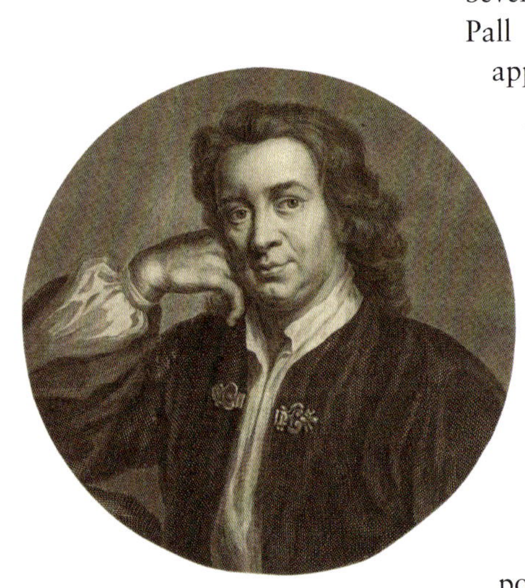

Jacobus Houbraken after Mary Beale, *Thomas Otway*, 1741

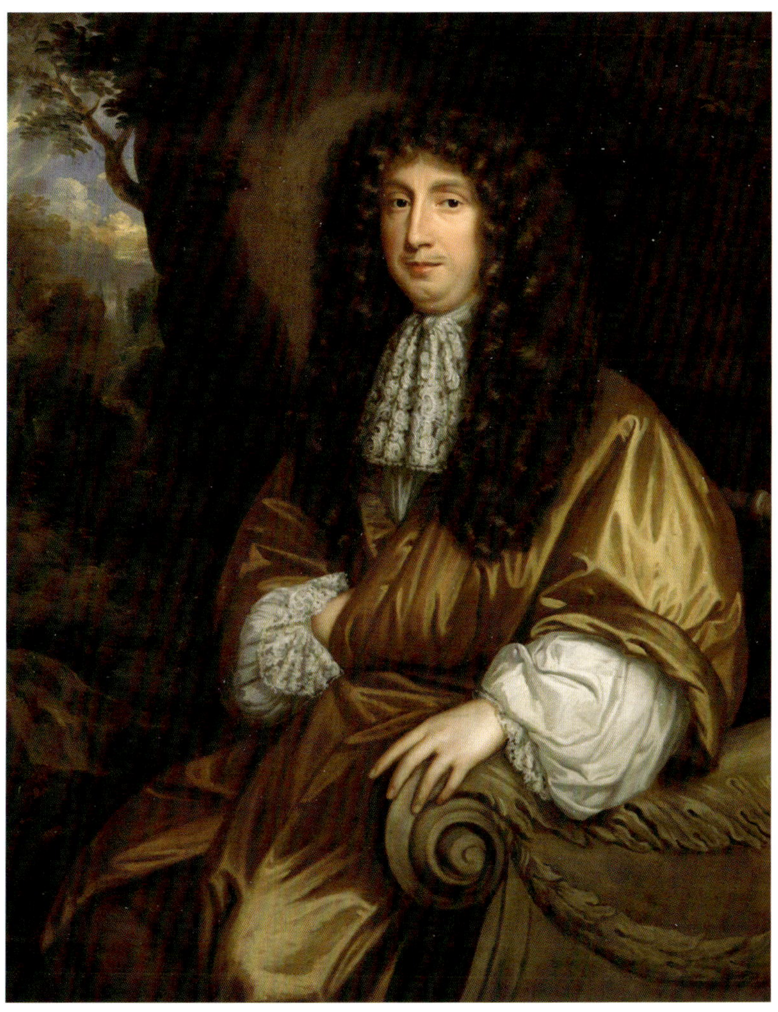

Mary Beale, *George Savile, 1st Marquess of Halifax*, 1674–6

Halifax's great-uncle, the Earl of Strafford, had been beheaded, and his father imprisoned in the Tower of London during the early stages of the civil war. Halifax upheld his family's loyalty to the Stuarts as Privy Councillor to King Charles II and chief minister from 1681. He soon fell out of favour due to his opposition to the imminent succession of the King's brother, James Duke of York. Thus, Halifax and his neighbour in St James's, the Earl of Clarendon, were denounced as enemies to Charles II. With the accession of King William and Queen Mary in 1689, Halifax returned to power as Lord Privy Seal and he personally handed the King and Queen their crowns at the coronation service.

Lord Halifax's uncle was the Hon. Henry Coventry (1618–1686), a masterful figure in the House of Commons on King Charles II's behalf and an ambassador who negotiated the Treaty of Breda with the Dutch in July 1667. The Beales' correspondent, Dr John Cooke, wearied of these negotiations and wished he was at Allbrook with them, rather than at Whitehall where no-one was as busy as he, 'unless it be the Taylors and Sempstresses who are employed in the Excellencies equipage'.[87] Once peace with the Dutch was signed, Coventry was famous: he 'hath got more fame and common esteem then [*sic*] any gentleman in England hath at this day and is an excellent

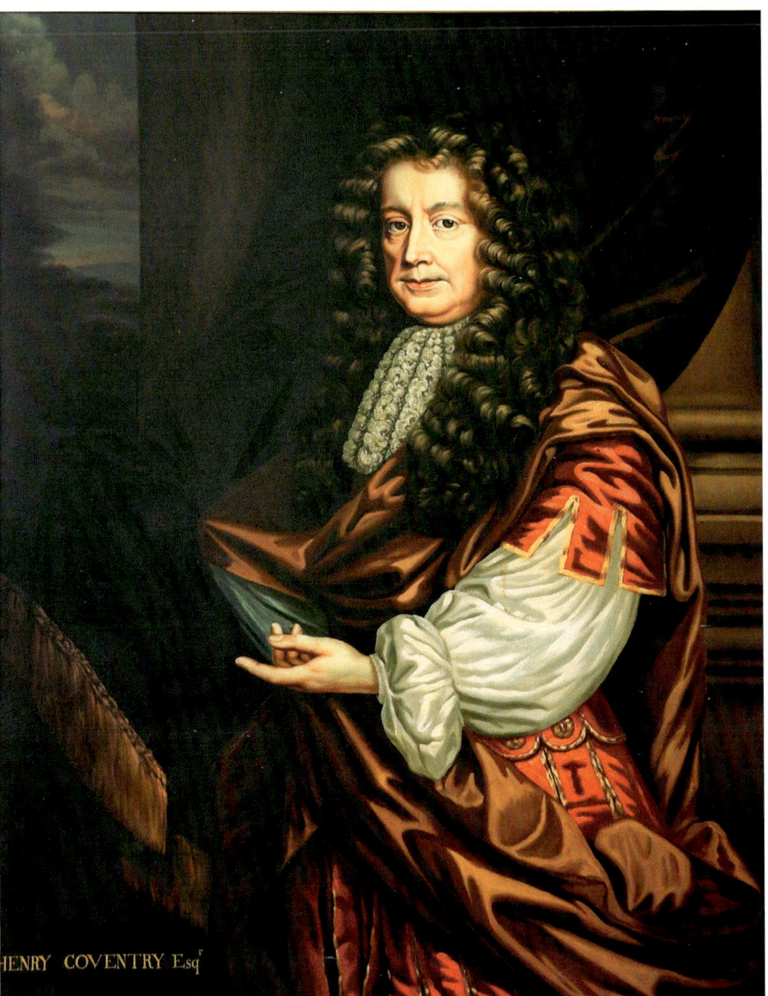

A recent copy of Mary Beale's portrait of *The Hon. Henry Coventry*, 1677

and able person'.[88] Coventry was a neighbour of the Beales in St James's, and Mary Beale captured his likeness in July 1677,[89] shortly before he succumbed to gout (the portrait is at Longleat House, Wiltshire; a copy is at West Lodge Park Hotel, Hertfordshire).

Henry Coventry's brother-in-law was Anthony Ashley Cooper, 1st Earl of Shaftesbury (1621–1683), probably the 'Lord Asheley' who sat for Mary Beale in 1674.[90] Lord Paget, a Whig supporter of Shaftesbury, commissioned a copy of Lely's portrait of Shaftesbury from Beale in 1681.[91] two years before Shaftesbury fled to the Continent. He was suspected of implication in the Rye House Plot of 1683, which aimed to assassinate the King and his brother, so he decided to escape before his treasonable offences were punished. Having spent six weeks at Wapping disguised as a Presbyterian clergyman, Shaftesbury reached Amsterdam where he died within the year.

Daniel Malthus (1651–1717) of Pall Mall, apothecary to Queen Anne and King George I, was painted by Mary Beale in 1681, 'upon Account of Kindness and not profitt'.[92] Malthus lived at The Pestle and Mortar, Pall Mall, next door to Dr Thomas Sydenham, after whom he named his son. Dr Sydenham (1624–1689), known as 'the English Hippocrates', was an early occupant of Pall Mall, living in a house on the south side until 1669 when he moved to the north side. Sydenham fought with the parliamentarian militia in his youth but his courage did not extend to the year of the great plague of 1665 when he abandoned London to devote himself to writing a medical treatise, later expanded and published as *Observationes Medicae* (1676).

The prosperous Dr Sydenham loaned his neighbour Lady Ranelagh £100 in 1666 and he regularly gave smaller amounts to Charles and Mary Beale, whose son, Bartholomew was one of his pupils. Charles Beale's notebook records his wife's first portrait of the doctor in 1672: 'Dr Sidenham's picture begun'.[93] Another portrait, showing the physician wearing an informal neck-scarf, was presented to the Royal College of Physicians by Sydenham's son in 1691, and Sydenham's grandson presented a third portrait attributed to Beale, in 1747. The Beale portrait at the National Portrait Gallery is dated 1688, the year before Sydenham's death.

King Charles II's mistress, Eleanor, Nell, Nellie or Mrs Gwyn, became a neighbour of Mary and Charles Beale in 1670 when she was installed in a house at the east end of Pall Mall with her infant,

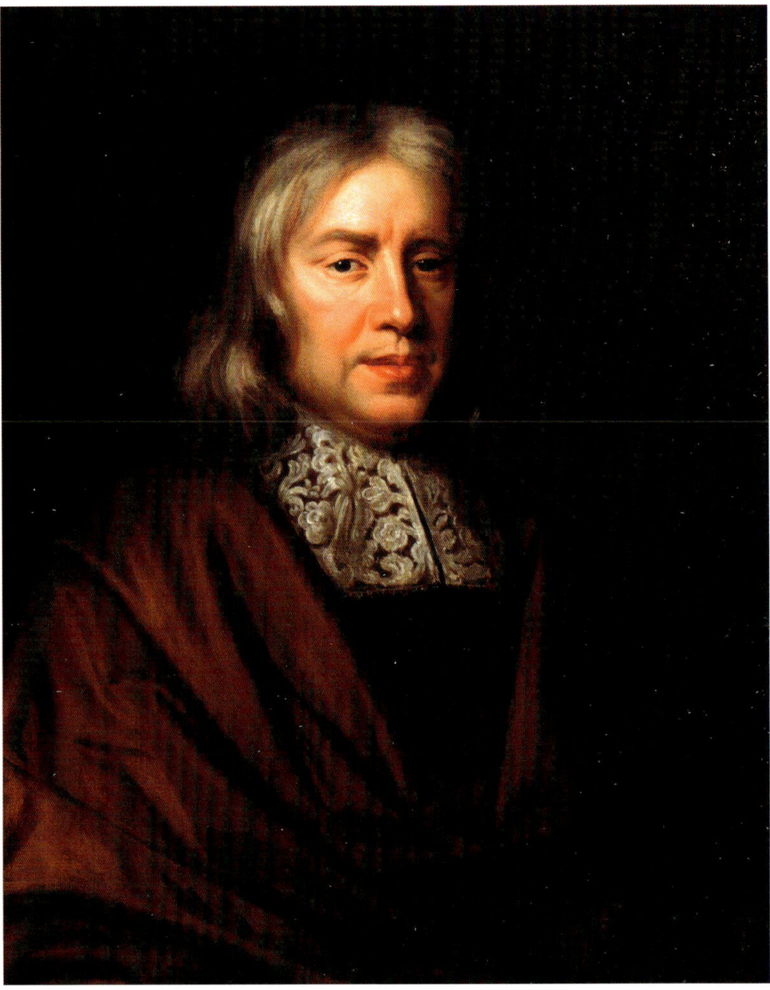

Right: Mary Beale, *Dr Thomas Sydenham*, 1688

Opposite: Sir Peter Lely, *Nell Gwyn*, c. 1675

the King's illegitimate son (later the Duke of St Albans). In the spring of 1671, John Evelyn overheard 'a very familiar discourse' taking place between the lovers in Pall Mall, 'She looking out of her Garden on a Terrace at the top of the Wall, and the King standing on the greene Walke Under it. Thence the King walked to the Duchess of Cleavelands, another Lady of Pleasure & curse of our nation'.[94] King Charles later granted Nell the freehold of a superior residence at the west end of Pall Mall, on the south side overlooking the park and closer to the Beales. Here Nell Gwyn lived in style from 1676 until her death in 1687. Gilbert Burnet disapproved of the publicity she

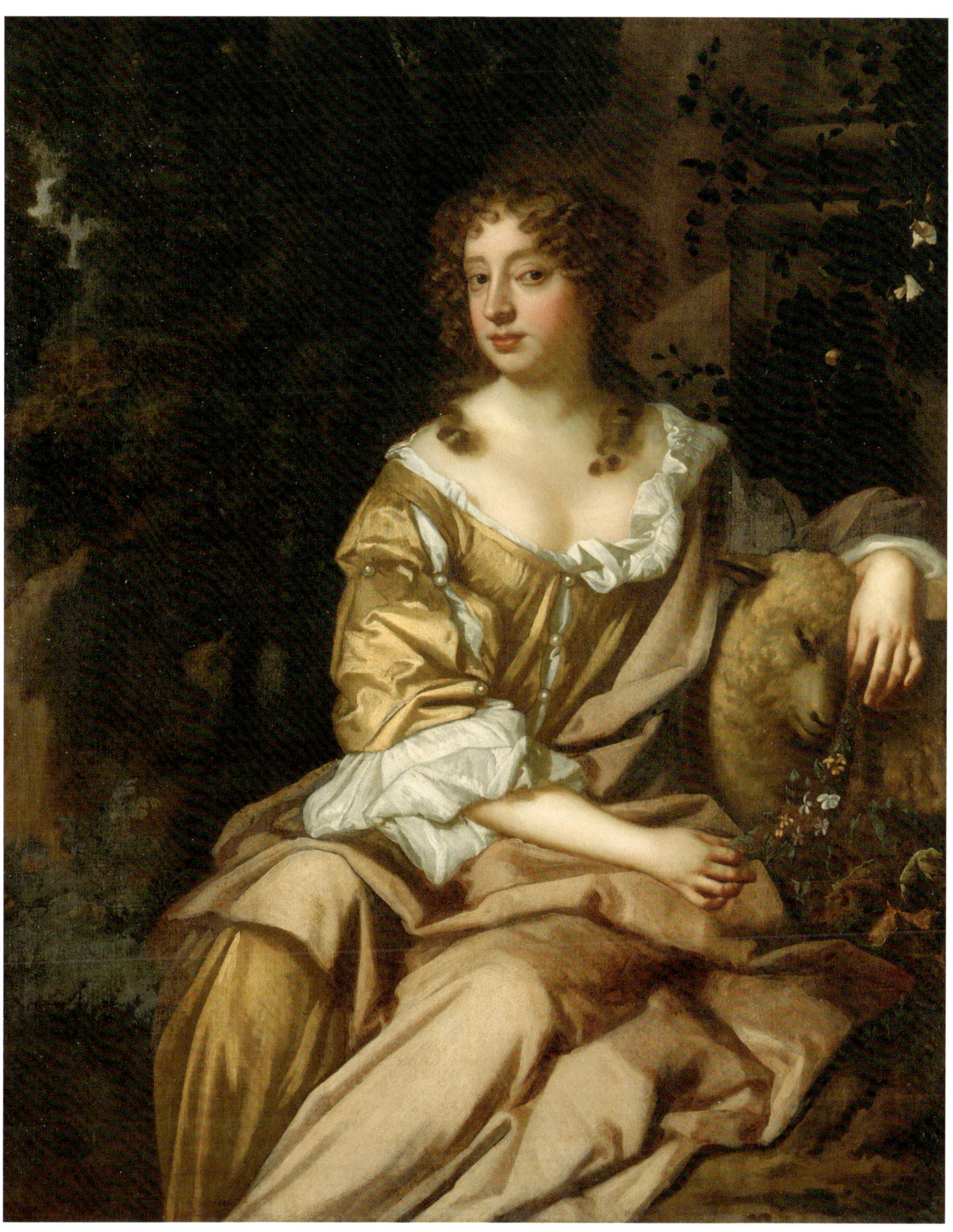

attracted, describing her as 'the indiscreetest and wildest creature that ever was in a court, yet continued in favour to the end of the King's life and was maintained at a vast expense'.[95] The self-described 'Protestant whore' was painted by Mrs Beale, after Lely, 1676–7.

Pictures of King Charles II's mistresses were in demand. Samuel Pepys and his superior at the Navy Office, the Earl of Sandwich, hankered after portraits of Barbara Villiers, the King's first mistress and the wife of Lord Castlemaine; she was created Duchess of Cleveland in 1670. The demand was such that thirteen unfinished portraits of the Duchess were found in Lely's studio after his death. The Beales viewed a collection of paintings of the King's mistresses at the Whitehall lodgings of Mr Babington May (brother of Hugh May, the surveyor) in April 1677,[96] and arranged to borrow several for Mary to copy. Thus she obtained access to Lely's portraits of Louise de Kéroualle (created the Duchess of Portsmouth in 1673 and the King's mistress until his death), 'Mrs Gwinn with ye lamb', 'Mrs Davies with ye gold pott' (Moll Davis, a predecessor to Nell Gwyn in the King's affections), Barbara Villiers, (a copy after Lely has surfaced in Hertfordshire but the attribution to Mary Beale is questionable). The Beales also viewed a portrait by Henry Anderton (1630–1667, a pupil of Robert Streeter) of 'La Belle Stuart', Frances Teresa Stuart, Duchess of Richmond and Lennox (1647–1702). Acknowledged as the most beautiful woman at Court, 'La Belle Stuart' fought off the King's advances and married the Duke of Richmond in 1667. She was the model for medals cast to commemorate the Peace of Breda (1667) and for the figure of Britannia on the copper coinage introduced in 1672.

Contrasting with Mary Beale's head and shoulder portraits of a single subject set in an oval surround, was a double portrait 'in little' of Richard Maitland, 4th Earl of Lauderdale (1653–1695) and Anne, his Countess, daughter of the 9th Duke of Argyll. They married in 1678 and the painting shows them leaning towards each other over a decorative urn. The same year saw Lauderdale appointed a general of the Mint and a Privy Councillor, so Mrs Beale's portrait celebrated achievements in three fields. Another member of the family, Lady Mary Maitland (1645-1702), daughter of the 1st Duke of Lauderdale, married Lord John Hay in 1666 at a ceremony attended by King Charles II. Lord Hay of Yester chose to be painted by Gerard Soest in 1670, but his wife preferred Mary Beale. The result was purchased by Richard Jeffree and featured in the exhibition *Mrs Mary Beale, Paintress* at the Manor House Museum, Bury St Edmunds (1994).

Opposite: Mary Beale, *Lady Mary Maitland Hay*, c. 1680

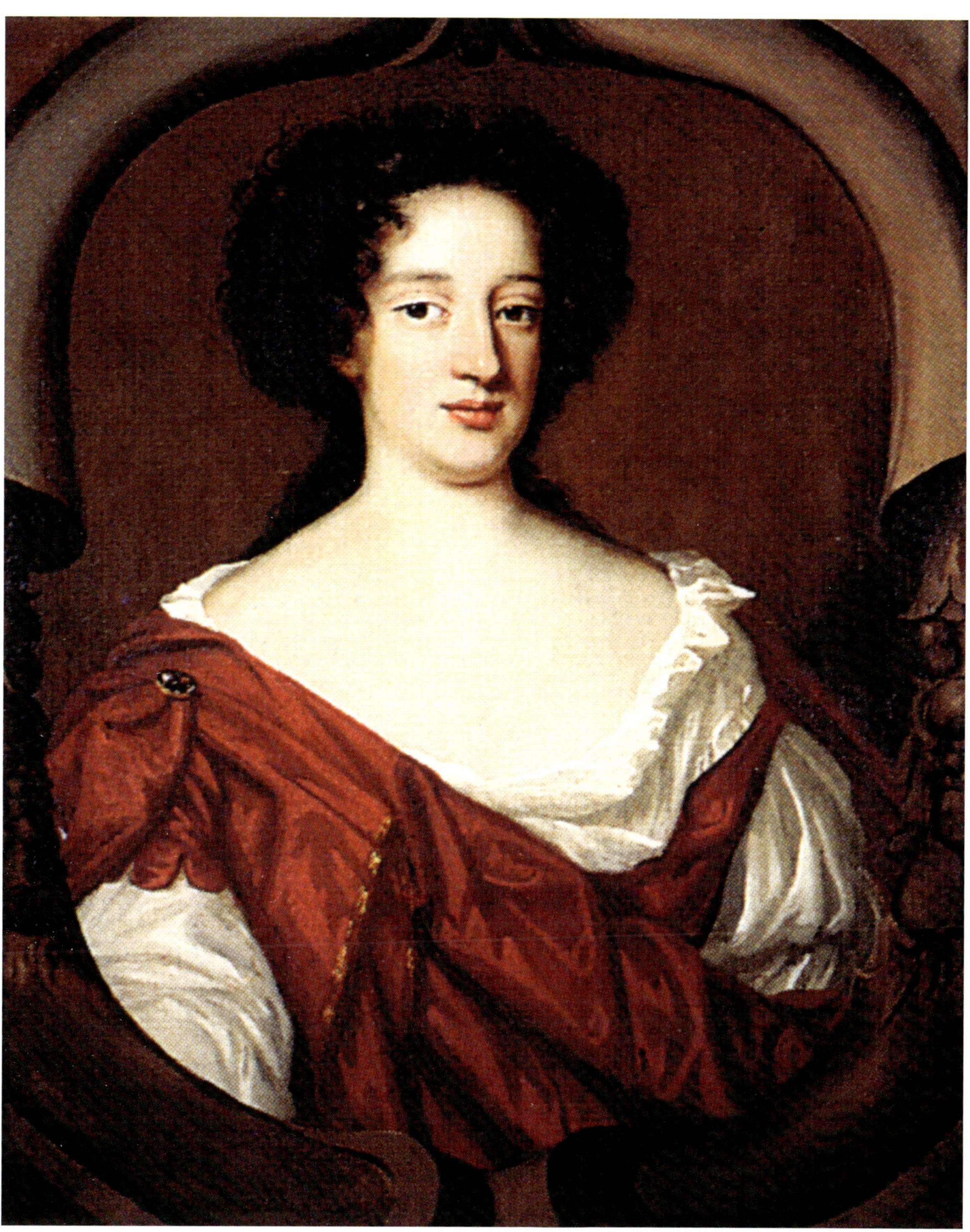

When Hay succeeded as 2nd Marquess of Tweeddale in 1697, Mary became a Marchioness.

In February 1682 the inhabitants of Pall Mall and St James's were shocked by the murder of Thomas Thynne (1648–1682) of Longleat House, Wiltshire, who with Sir Henry Frederick Thynne Bt (1615–1680) and Lady Thynne had been painted by Mrs Beale in 1677. Thynne's previous dalliance with Mary Trevor, a maid of honour to Queen Catharine of Braganza, resulted in her pregnancy and departure from Court in 1678. Mary Trevor's portrait, apparently by Mary Beale, must have predated her disgrace.

In 1680 Thynne married the widowed Countess of Ogle (1667–1722, née Lady Elizabeth Percy). Elizabeth Ogle was fourteen at the time and a reluctant bride who fled to the Netherlands to escape her elderly husband, known as 'Tom of Ten Thousand' on account of his wealth. Thynne was the victim of *un crime passionnel* in February 1682: he was shot and mortally wounded in his coach as it was driven along Pall Mall (some accounts say St James's Street). The motive was jealousy: his wife had caught the eye of a Swedish nobleman, Count Königsmark, who employed three assassins to kill Thynne. As the victim lay dying he was comforted by the Duke of Monmouth (who had been in the coach with him minutes before the crime) and by Dr Tenison, ministering consolations. Thynne was buried in Westminster Abbey where a macabre tombstone illustrates the murder. The three assassins were executed at the scene of the crime (having been visited in prison by the Beales' friend, Gilbert Burnet). Count Königsmark was arrested at Gravesend, disguised as a woman; he was tried at the Old Bailey and acquitted (he claimed Thynne's death resulted from a duel). Lady Elizabeth Percy/Ogle/Thynne then married Charles Seymour, 6th Duke of Somerset, and bore him thirteen children.

Mary Beale has been criticised for her 'average Lelyesque performance' and her 'plodding and incessant' production of portraits.[97] It is true that dozens of her paintings were copies of Lely's originals and dozens more exude his influence. Her best pictures are sensitive, honest portraits from life; she captured gravity on the faces of clerics and sweetness in the expressions of children. Her numerous portraits of 'people of Quality' and 'persons of distinction',[98] provide a unique historical and visual record of those who occupied centre stage on the vibrant political, religious and intellectual scene of late seventeenth-century England.

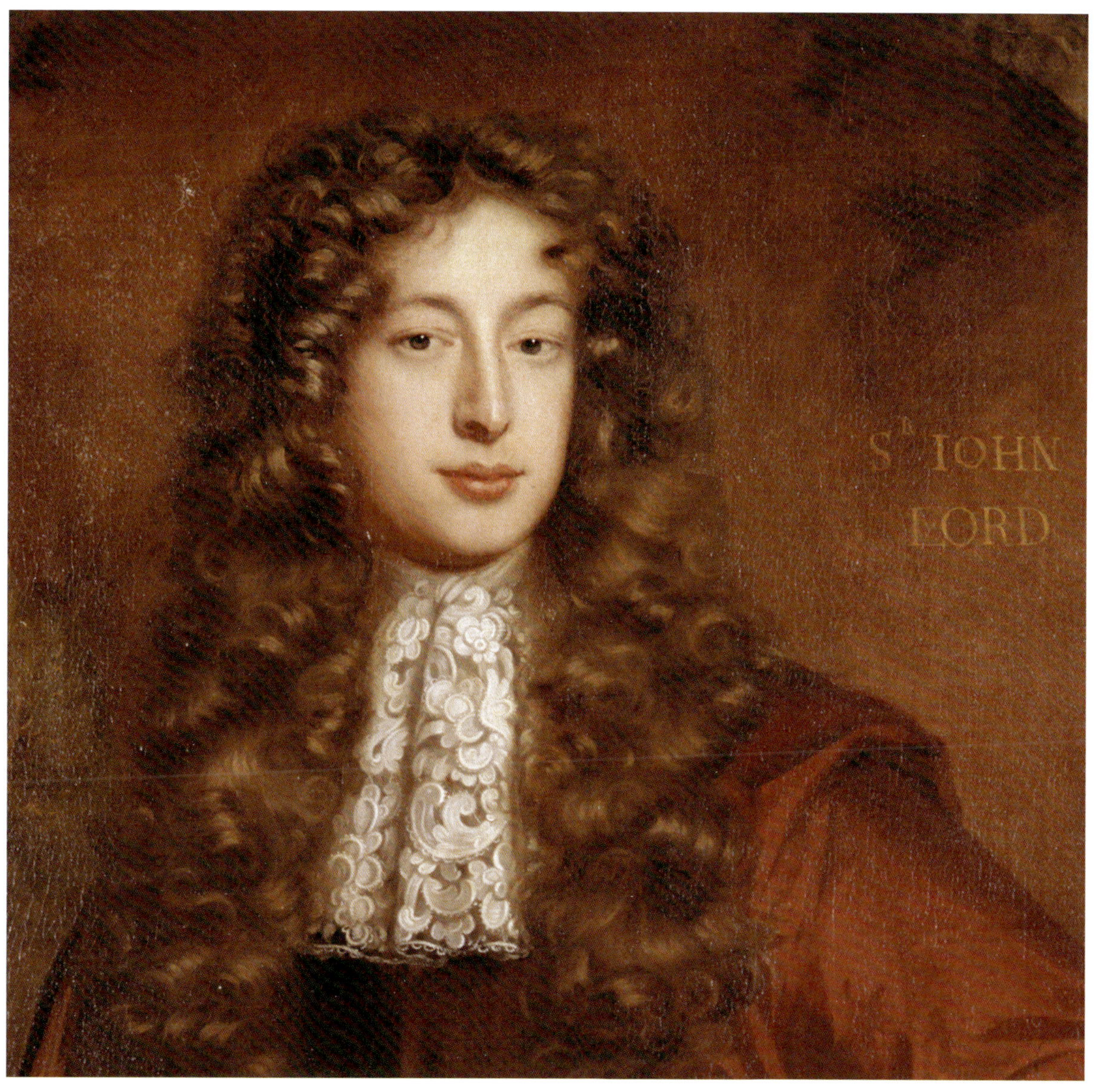

Detail of Mary Beale's portrait of *John Lowther, 1st Viscount Lonsdale*, 1677

NEXT TO THE GOLDEN BALL, PALL MALL: NOTES

1. Rent Roll, Earl of St Albans, Add Ms 22,063, f. 18, BL. Charles Beale listed as resident 1670–99, see *Survey of London. The Parish of St James Westminster*, (1960), XXX, p. 547

2. CBA 15 January 1680, 19 February 1681

3. Charles Beale paid the parish poor rate for St Martin-in-the-Fields, 1669. Poor rate ledger 1669, F1112, WCA

4. CBA 1677

5. Rawlinson 104, 12 September 1672

6. *A Description of the Villa of Mr Horace Walpole at Strawberry Hill near Twickenham, Middlesex with an inventory*, (1842). See also Peter Hill, *Walpole's Art Collection*, (1997). According to a letter from M. Martin, Yale editor of Walpole's correspondence, to E. Croft Murray, Walpole gave the original self portrait by Beale to Richard Bull for use in the illustrated *Description of Strawberry Hill*, (1786). Letter enclosed with Charles Beale's sketchbook, 1679, British Museum Prints and Drawings

7. GVCBA 22 July 1672

8. Lely painted Lady Castlemaine as Minerva, the Roman equivalent of Pallas

9. This point was made by Dr Keith Cunliffe in *Women by Women. Catalogue 2009*, St Edmundsbury Borough Council, (2009)

10. CBA 25 August, 6 September 1677.

11. CBA 13 July 1681

12. 'Vertue Note Books I', *Walpole Society* 18 (1930), p. 105

13. *Catalogue of the First Special Exhibition of National Portraits ending with the reign of King James II on loan to the South Kensington Museum*, (1866), pp. 143-4

14. GVCBA 20 April 1672

15. CBA 20 February 1672

16. GVCBA 20 April 1672

17. CBA May 1667

18. GVCBA 20 April 1672

19. CBA 6 January 1677

20. GVCBA 30 September 1672

21. *Ibid.*, 24 April 1672

22. *Ibid.*, 5 June 1672

23. *Ibid.*, 1 August 1672

24. William Gandy, 'Notes on Painting 1673-99', Add Ms 22,950, BL. See Mansfield Talley, *Portrait Painting in England: Studies in the Technical Literature before 1700*, (1981), pp. 316, 332, 334, 336, 338

25. GVCBA 1 August 1672

26. *Ibid.*, August 1674

27. *Ibid.*

28. *Ibid.*, 1 October 1672. Mary Beale copied Lely's portrait of Brook Bridges in 1681, CBA 15 January 1681

29. CBA 16 February 1677

30. CBA 4 June 1677

31. B. Buckeridge, 'An Essay Towards an English School of Painters', in Roger De Piles, *The Art of Painting and the Lives of the Painters*, (1706), p. 403

32. GVCBA 1676-7

33. Paget Toynbee, 'Horace Walpole's Journals of Visits to Country Seats', *Walpole Society* 16 (1927-8), p. 47

34. GVCBA December 1672

35. Paget Toynbee, *op. cit.*

36. CBA 23 July 1672

37. *Catalogue of the First Special Exhibition of National Portraits, op. cit.*, p. 131

38. *Ibid.*, p. 150

39. Evelyn, IV, p.13, 13 June 1673. Dixon, active from 1671, died in 1701. Little is known about his work

40. W.G. Hiscock, *John Evelyn and Mrs Godolphin,* (1951), p.112

41. Evelyn, III, p. 628, 29 May 1660

42. *Ibid.*

43. W. Marston Acres, 'The Morice family of Werrington', *Notes and Queries* 192 (1947), pp. 178-80

44. GVCBA June 1672. A second note cites £20 paid for Viner's lady and daughter and a copy of Sir Robert's picture. Sir Robert and Lady Viner, their son and Lady Viner's daughter were painted as a family group by John Michael Wright, 1673

45. A book of her recipes and cures is at the Wellcome Library, London

46. *Gentleman's Magazine* 39 (1769), p. 516

47. Pepys VIII, p.497, 23 October 1667

48. 'Vertue Note Books I', *op. cit.*, p. 91

49. CBA 17 October 1681

50. S. Woodford, *Liber*, 28 September 1664

51. *Ibid.*, 29 December 1664

52. CBA 27 April 1681

53. S. Woodford, 'Memoirs', 19 October 1664

54. *The works of Symon Patrick DD including his autobiography,* ed. by Rev Alexander Taylor, (1858), IX, pp.578, 584

55. *Ibid.*, pp. 491-95

56. GB 1 pt 1, pp. 335,338

57. CBA 1681

58. *Ibid.*, 14 July 1677

59. *Ibid.*, March 1681

60. GB, *History of The Reformation,* (1820 edition), I, p.xiii

61. Pepys, VI, p. 87, 23 April 1665

62. GVCBA August 1674

63. GB 1 pt 1, pp. 337-8

64. *Ibid.*

65. Thomas Sprat, *History of the Royal Society,* ed. by Jackson I. Cope and Harold Whitmore Jones, (1958), p. 149

66. Ruth Scurr, *John Aubrey. My Own Life,* (2015), p. 251

67. *Ibid.*, p. 137

68. *Diary of Robert Hooke,* ed. by Henry W. Robinson and Walter Adams, (1935), pp. 98, 99, 163

69. Lisa Jardine, *The Curious Life of Robert Hooke. The man who measured London,* (2003), pp.17, 19

70. Robert Boyle, 'The Experimental History of Colours', I, pt 2, pp. 668-788, in *The Works of the Hon Robert Boyle with a life by Thomas Birch,* (1744)

71. GVCBA 1677

72. *The Correspondence of Henry Hyde, Earl of Clarendon,* ed. by S.W. Singer, (1828), I, p. 238

73. GVCBA 1674

74. *Ibid.*, 1671–2, 1674. CBA 14 February 1677 when Fauconberg paid what was owing for his portrait and £3 10s for a leatherwork gilt frame

75. Pepys, II, p. 241, 30 December 1661

76. GB I, pt I, p. 149

77. CBA 14 February 1677

78. *Catalogue of the First Special Exhibition of National Portraits, op. cit.*, no.701

79. CBA April 1681. Commissions from the Duchess of Newcastle led to Beale's portrait of Elizabeth, (1653–1709, née Egerton), wife of the 4th Earl of Leicester (at Penshurst Place, Kent)

80. *Ibid.*, July-August 1681

81. GVCBA 1676–7

82. John Ingamells, *Later Stuart Portraits 1685–1714,* (2009), p. 19

83. Horace Walpole, *Anecdotes of Painting in England,* (1862), III, p. 540

84. *Catalogue of the First Special Exhibition of National Portraits, op. cit.*, no 937

85. CBA 30 April 1677

86. GB 1, pt 1, p. 484

87. Rawlinson 113, 18 April 1667

88. Pepys, VIII, p.533, 16 November 1667

89. CBA 14, 19 July 1677

90. GVCBA 1674

91. *Ibid.*, 1681

92. CBA 1681

93. GVCBA July 1672

94. Evelyn, III, p. 573, 1 March 1671

95. GB I, pt 1, p. 474

96. CBA 21 April 1677. Mrs May sat for Mary Beale in 1681

97. C. H. Collins Baker, *Lely and the Stuart Portrait Painters,* (1912), II, p. 39

98. GVCBA 1676–7

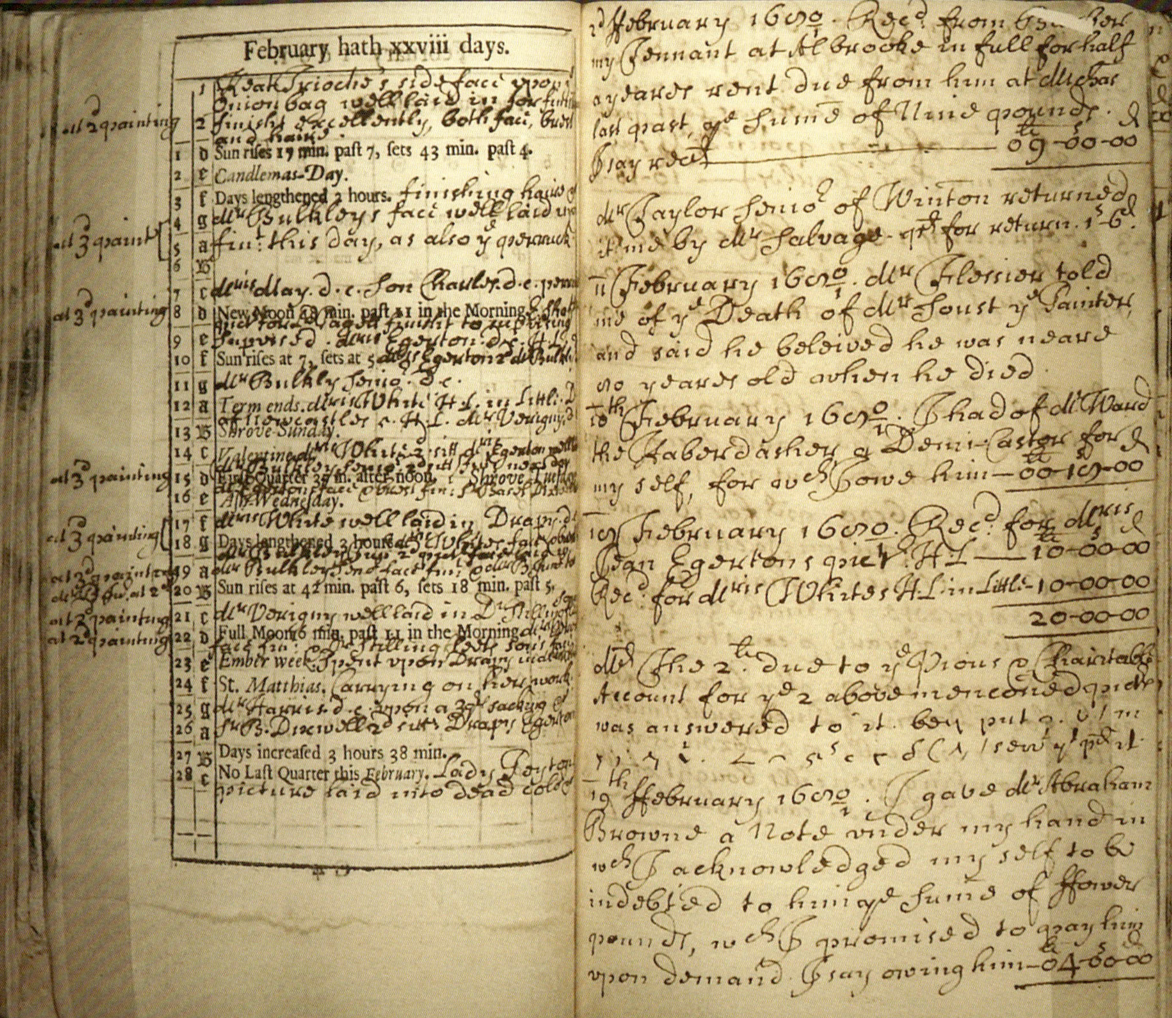

February hath xxviii days.

1		Mr Sprinks sid face upon Onion bag well laid in for first finisht excellently, both face, body and hands.
2		
1	D	Sun rises 17 min. past 7, sets 43 min. past 4.
2	c	Candlemas-Day.
3	f	Days lengthened 2 hours. finishing hair of
4	g	Mr Bulkley's face well laid in
5	a	fin: this day, as also ye [illegible]
6	b	
7	c	Mris May. d. c. son Charles d. c. [illegible]
8	D	New Moon 43 min. past 11 in the Morning. [illegible]
9	e	[illegible] Mrs Egerton's d. c. H.L.
10	f	Sun rises at 7, sets at 5. Mrs Egerton's d. c. Bulkley
11	g	Mr Bulkley junr. d. c.
12	a	Term ends. Mris Whites H.L. in little.
13	b	Shrove-Sunday. Newcastle. H.L. Mr Vovigny
14	c	Valentine. Mris Whites [illegible] Mrs Egerton [illegible]
15	D	First Quarter 34 min. after noon. [illegible]
16	e	Ash-Wednesday.
17	f	Mris Whites well laid in. Drapery
18	g	Days lengthened 3 hours. [illegible]
19	a	Mr Bulkley's 2nd face fin: [illegible]
20	b	Sun rises at 42 min. past 6, sets 18 min. past 5.
21	c	Mr Vovigny well laid in. Dr Stillingfleet
22	D	Full Moon 6 min. past 11 in the Morning. [illegible]
23	e	Ember week. [illegible] Drapery
24	f	St. Matthias. Carrying on housework
25	g	Mr Harris d. c. upon a 3d sacking of [illegible]
26	a	[illegible] Drapery Egerton
27	b	Days increased 3 hours 38 min.
28	c	No Last Quarter this February. Lady [illegible] picture laid into dead colour

Margin notes: at 2 painting; at 3 paint; at 3 painting; at 3 painting; at 3 painting; at 2 painting; at 2 painting.

2d February 1670. Rec'd from [illegible] my Tennant at Albrooke in full for half a yeares rent due from him at Michas last past, ye summe of Nine pounds. I say rec'd — 09-00-00

Mr Taylor junr of Winton returned [illegible] by Mr Salvage — pd for return 1s 6d.

11 February 1670. Mr Flessiour told me of ye Death of Mr Soust ye Painter, and said he believed he was neare 80 yeares old when he died.

10th February 1670. I had of Mr Wand the Haberdasher a Demi-Castor for my self, for wch I owe him — 00-16-00

19 February 1670. Rec'd for Mris Jean Egerton's pict H.L. — 10-00-00
Rec'd for Mris Whites H.L. in little — 10-00-00
20-00-00

Mr Chas 2d due to ye Pious & Charitable Account for ye 2 above mentioned pictures was answered to it. [illegible]

19th February 1670. I gave Mr Abraham Browne a Note under my hand in wch I acknowledged my self to be indebted to him ye summe of Foure pounds, wch I promised to pay him upon demand. I say owing him — 04-00-00

6. CHARLES BEALE'S ALMANACKS

Charles Beale's almanacks were pocket-book diaries printed by William Lilly from 1644. They were popular for the astrological predictions and tables they provided: Beale, Flatman, Aubrey, Ashmole and many of their contemporaries were fascinated by the occult, horoscopes and astrology. From 1647 Lilly's almanacks bore the title *Merlini Anglici Ephemeris* and they sold up to 30,000 copies annually; Charles Beale purchased one every year for some thirty years until the year of Lilly's death and the end of the almanacks in 1681. Beale used the blank pages as a diary to record his wife's career and the 1681 almanack ends with two pages written in a secret cipher similar to Samuel Pepys's diaries (the two families were related).

The art historian George Vertue (1684–1756) was interested in Charles and Mary Beale. He planned to write a history of the arts in England (his notes fill some forty volumes) and he made excerpts from Charles Beale's almanacks which he described as 'Small Almanack pocket books – wherein he daily writ many affairs of business & family accounts &c. but the most remarkable is the daily imployments of his ingenious wife Mrs Beal [*sic*] concerning her painting & drawing from the life, or from famous paintings. he every day minutely mentions what she was imployd in and what parts of a picture she did daily – likewise his accounts of his own affair in the sale & making up of Ultramarine Colour to whom sold, what price & degrees – also Lakes, pinkes (& pd for frames), his own & childrens accounts, rents, expences, besides other occurrences so as yearly to fill up mostly the blank leaves of one of each of these small books'.[1]

Vertue borrowed several of Beale's almanacks from Dr Richard Rawlinson who collected Beale memorabilia. However, possibly as many as thirty-three almanacks with Charles Beale's papers and books had been inherited by Mr Carter, colour supplier to the Beales. 'Many others were at the same time sold to Rev Mr Brooke. These Mr Carter says, were all his in custody from 1711 – he lent them to a Scrub painter to read, whose goods being seiz'd on were lost and sold away'.[2]

Opposite: Charles Beale, a page from his almanack for 1681. The almanacks recorded Mary Beale's appointments with her patrons, the materials she used and the suppliers, household expenses and family events

Two of Charles Beale's almanacks survive: one for 1677 surfaced at the sale of the 2nd Earl of Oxford's library after his death in 1741 and is now is at the Bodleian Library, Oxford, where it was discovered by Elizabeth Walsh in the course of her research into Mary Beale. The other, for 1681, was acquired from a Birmingham bookseller by George Scharf, Director of the National Portrait Gallery 1857–95, who deposited it with the gallery's archives.

Charles Beale's almanacks provide a unique insight into the professional and personal affairs of the family. Charles recorded the names of those who made appointments to have their portraits painted; he noted his purchases of artists' equipment and experiments with materials and techniques. He took responsibility for household expenditure and debts, all the while encouraging 'My Dearest Heart' to pursue her career.[3] Charles was an artist manqué with a special interest in Italian art; he planned to translate into English the lives of ten Italian masters including Correggio, Michelangelo, Leonardo da Vinci, Giorgione, Raphael and Marietta Robusti, daughter of Tintoretto.[4]

Hoping perhaps, to secure a commission for his wife or encouragement for his own plans (above), Charles Beale pursued Prince Cosimo de' Medici, Grand Duke of Tuscany, who visited London in 1669 to acquire works of art and meet artists. The Beales were living in Hampshire at the time of the Duke's visit and their approach was unproductive.[5] Nor did Charles have success with his petition to the Board of the Green Cloth in 1677 (the officers of the Board recommended appointments to the royal household). By that date Mary's productivity was such that Charles abandoned personal ambitions in order to devote himself to organising and supporting the career of 'My Dearest Heart'.

Charles Beale junior, *Carter, the colour seller*, c. 1680

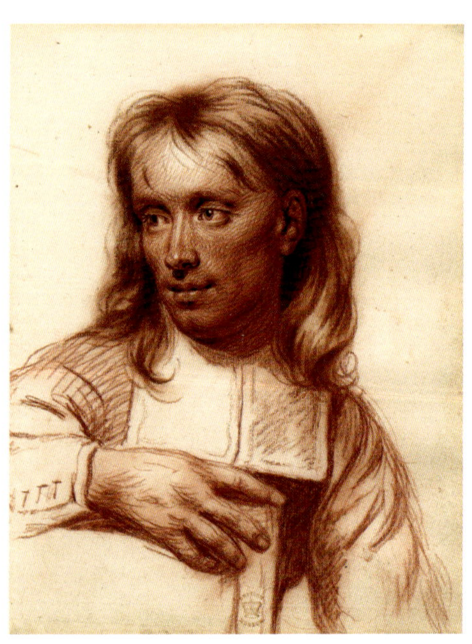

The almanacks reveal Charles Beale's knowledge of pigments, colours and the technicalities of oil painting. He noted the components of Mary's paintings such as the different types of cloths he sized and primed for her to paint upon: canvas, sacking (coarse woven material), bed ticking (a dense linen twill), Dutch cloth, onion bags (made from jute or hemp), and flaxen cloth, with the suppliers. He was a customer and friend of the Carters, father and son (one of whom was George), colour sellers he relied upon for pigments. 'Mr Phiner' or 'Phenne' (John Fenn)

of Fleet Bridge was another colour seller used by Beale; he supplied Beale with 2lbs of 'excellent deep Terra Vert at 4s 6d a pound... extraordinary good as ever I saw.',[6] for example. Fenn also primed canvases and provided the Beales with black chalk, Flemish linseed oil, Spanish cakes (a mix of chalk and alum), smalt (a cobalt pigment made from finely ground blue glass), umber, 'blew black' (from charred vegetable matter) and ceruse (white lead or a mixture of it).[7] Fenn was expert in grinding the yellow pigment called 'pinke' made from greenweed. Charles Beale's own experiments in making 'Green pink' dated from the summer of 1654 and he was still trying to perfect the colour in 1663. His experiments with this and other processes required persistence and physical strength. The grinding, sorting and mixing the ingredients in the correct proportions, boiling the concoctions in a heavy brass kettle and pouring it into pails was laborious, while the priming of canvases needed space and patience. Charles agonised over his efforts during the summer of 1677: 'There was some mistake in the colour of this primer for after I mixt it, I found it to cast so very much too Redish yellow', so he tempered it with some 'blew black' and a little cullen's earth (a reddish black derived from peat), hoping this would be suitable for portraits of men with swarthy complexions.[8]

Charles Beale found that the apothecaries' shops of Bucklersbury in the City of London were the best sources of natural cinnabar (vermilion) and cochineal. He purchased at least one batch of cochineal from a relative, the apothecary Samuell Symons, at a cost of £7 15s.[9] Dried cochineal beetles were imported from the West Indies and Mexico and when the derivative was mixed with chalk and alum it produced a rich, strong-bodied red colour. Charles conducted eleven trials using cochineal in pursuit of the best red lake before achieving success with a recipe which consisted of 'bundles of the best sort of Spanish cakes and one ounce of the best Cochinel to which I put in 3 ounces and ¼ of chalk. It produced 4 ounces of Lake. Mr Lely allowed me 6 shillings an ounce for it. The rest of it my Deare Heart used herself'.[10] More 'extraordinary' was Beale's scarlet India lake. In the summer of 1677 he ground '2 pellets of India Lake which was put into a Bladder for my dearest heart's use upon extraordinary occasions'.[11] Beale's colours were ground and mixed with linseed or poppy oil, then stored in pigs' bladders until needed – Mary used some of the India lake 'in finishing my face' (her portrait of Charles, 1677).[12]

Mr Williams of Snow Hill provided 'very good Cullen's Earth'. John Dod, a linen draper at Ye Queen's Head, Cornhill, supplied canvas to Charles Beale. Mr Sprignell also provided canvas, while Royston sacking came from Owen Buckingham at Ye Swan in Bread Street. Beale exchanged with Adrian Henny, a painter, half an ounce of ultramarine for four ounces of pale blue smalt (used for skies, and when mixed with white lead, for landscapes). Charles thought Henny's smalt was 'the best and finest smalt that ever came to England'.[13] Another specialist supplier was Mr Smaley from whom Beale purchased six dozen duck-quilled black pencils and five dozen small 'pointing pencils' (brushes) for Mary at a cost of 7s 6d (1681).[14]

Beale offered his wife's patrons a choice of fifteen different frames for their portraits, leatherwork gilt being the most expensive. John Norris of Long Acre was one frame-maker used by the Beales (he might have been the joiner who made Sir Peter Lely's coffin for £6 in 1680).[15] The name Flessier appears frequently in Charles Beale's accounts as a maker of gilt frames; he was to be found near the Fountain Tavern in the Strand (Mary painted Tobias Flessier and his grand-daughter). Mr Godbolt, carpenter and frame-maker, specialised in ebony frames such as the one he made for Dr Stillingfleet's portrait in 1681, and he made a desk and table with large drawers for the aspiring young artist, Charles Beale.

'Cousin Beale's paynting-roome'[16]

At the house in Pall Mall Mary Beale's painting-room developed into a professional studio that could accommodate students, fellow artists and distinguished sitters. Her sons assisted their mother in her painting-room and their father was diligent in paying them for their work on draperies and the oval surrounds in which Mary liked to place head and shoulder portraits. Their eldest son, Bartholomew 'Barth' or 'Batt', was working on the drapery for his mother's self portrait on bed ticking in September 1677 (he was soon to abandon art for a career in medicine). The younger son, Charles, worked on thirty pictures during the year 1676–7, 'ovals, copies and his mother's originals'.[17] He showed promise as an artist so was sent to Thomas Flatman in 1677 to be instructed in miniature painting.

Sarah Curtis (1676–1743) joined Mary Beale as a pupil at a young age and later pursued a career as a professional artist near Covent Garden. Through her neighbours, the two Misses Hoadly, mantua makers, she met their brother, the Reverend Benjamin

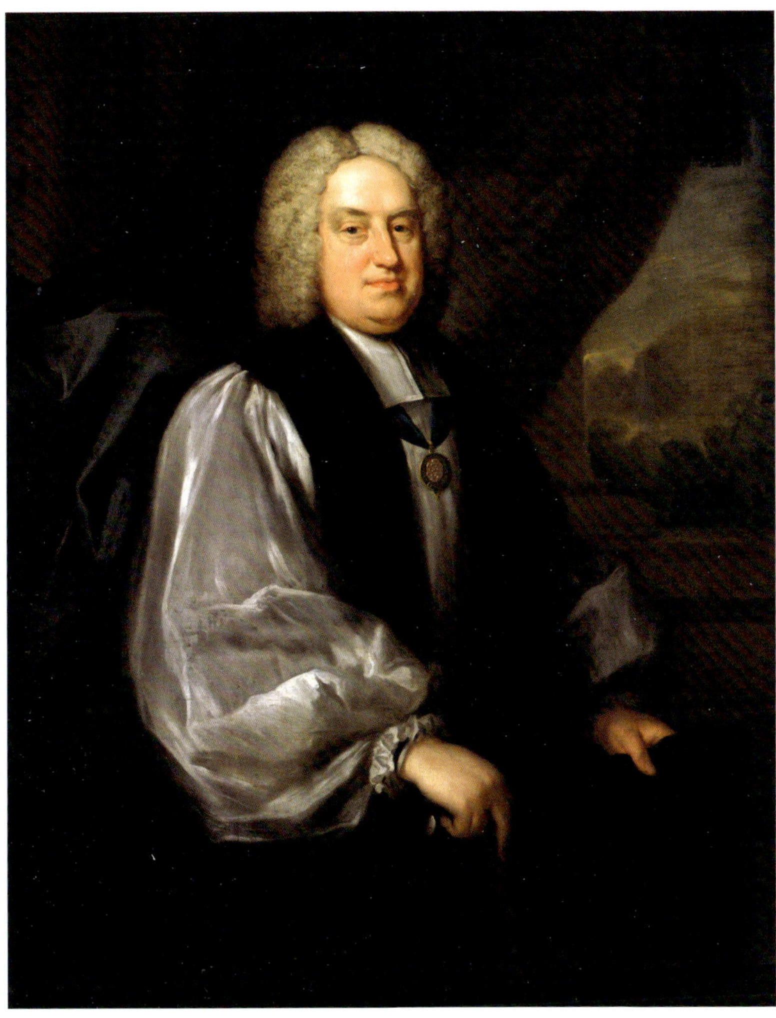

Sarah Curtis, *Bishop Benjamin Hoadly*, c. 1726–43. Sarah was a pupil of Mary Beale

Hoadly, whom she married in 1701. Hoadly (1676–1761), a cripple since his youth, carved a successful, controversial path in the Church. His wife, Sarah, was free to paint as and when she chose, taking into account that she bore seven children and moved the household from Bangor to Hereford, then to Salisbury and lastly to Winchester as her husband's career dictated. Sarah Hoadly inherited at least one of Mary Beale's patrons, Bishop Gilbert Burnet, whose portrait was engraved by William Faithorne for the frontispiece for Burnet's *History of My Own Time*. Sarah also painted the theologian William

Whiston (1667–1752), and her husband when he was Bishop of Salisbury.

The landscape artist Thomas Manby (*c.* 1633–1695) worked occasionally in Mary Beale's painting-room, for instance he filled in the background for 'ye copy of Countess of Clare's picture' in 1677.[18] The Countess (d. 1683), wife of the 2nd Earl of Clare, may have been impressed by Mary Beale's portrait of Lady Delamer, a distant relation. Then having sat for her own portrait, she persuaded her son, Gilbert Holles (1633–1689, the 3rd Earl), to make an appointment with Mrs Beale. The 3rd Earl's daughter married Christopher Vane, Lord Barnard of Raby Castle, County Durham, and Lady Barnard's portrait was painted by Mary Beale in 1681. Thus Mary's portraits of the family spanned three generations.

Thomas Manby, Henry Cooke and William Moore were content to work alongside Mary Beale in her painting-room. Mrs Beale was the principal artist and these men respected her. Cooke (*c.* 1642–1700) worked on drapery for the Earl of Shaftesbury's portrait (Mary's copy after Lely) in January 1681. After an insulting experience with a difficult sitter, Cooke abandoned portraiture and took up history painting. He was commissioned by King William III to repair the precious Raphael cartoons, and by the Duke of Marlborough to make copies from them (Cooke's work was later banished to the attic at Blenheim Palace). William Moore, brother of Bishop John Moore (1646–1714), sat for his portrait by Mrs Beale in 1677 and may have assisted her; he was evidently an artist – he purchased canvases and

Left: Mary Beale, *Portrait of a young girl*, c. 1681

Right: Mary Beale, *The Penitent Magdalene*, c. 1672

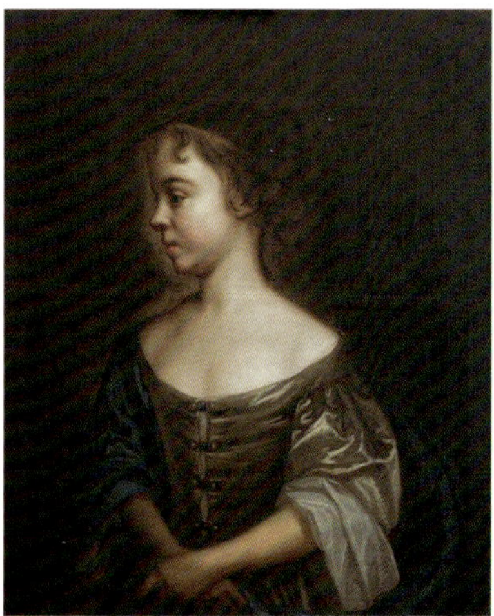

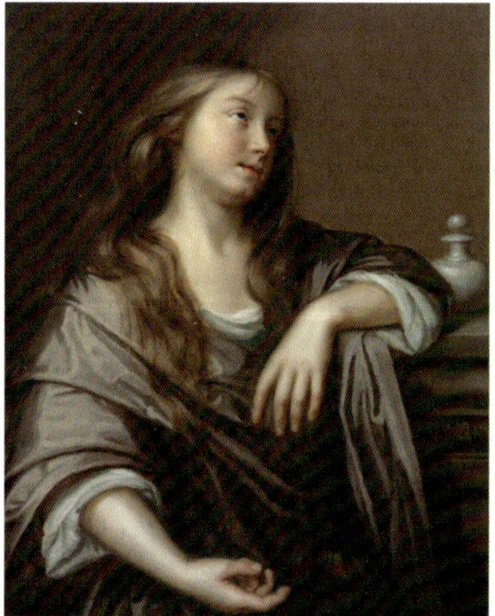

pigments from Charles. Mary was commissioned for portraits of the Moores' parents, Thomas and Elizabeth, in 1681.[19]

Keaty/Kate and Moll Trioche were regularly at Mary Beale's painting-room, Moll as a model, Kate as a student/model (they may have been the daughters of Charles Beale's relative, Canon Richard Trioche). Kate has been tentatively identified as the beguiling girl Mary painted 'side face' in the summer of 1681.[20] She was a keen student artist who could afford to pay Charles Beale £1 10s for an ounce of ultramarine.[21] Moll Trioche posed for Mary as the penitent Mary Magdalene in 1671-2. According to the gospels, Mary Magdalene repented of her dissolute life and followed Jesus, witnessing his crucifixion, burial and resurrection; her pre-eminence as a female disciple inspired Caravaggio's 'Magdalene' (1594-5). Mary Beale's version was painted two years before Moll's death at the age of sixteen. She was buried in the cemetery at St Martin-in-the-Fields where a sentimental epitaph, attributed to Charles Beale, expressed the family's affection for Moll.

Sweetest Creature, here she lies,
Snatch'd early from our wandring Eyes;
Why should Mortals , prize this Light,
Since here's' obscur'd in envious Night
Beauty, Wit and Modesty?
All charming things (tho' born to die)
If these perish, what can save
The most accomplish'd from the Grave?
In pity, courteous Reader, hast away,
Thy foot ne'er trampl'd on such lovely Clay.
Amicitiae doloris ergo, Lubens Coatcus posuit.[22]

Coincidentally, or perhaps not, Charles Beale's brother, Bartholomew, threw himself out of a window at his house in Hatton Garden on 8 May 1674, the day after Moll's death. The coroner's inquest decreed that he had 'cast himself out of his upper window... he died worth a great estate in lands and moneys'. It was concluded that he perished by 'throwing himselfe downe in his frantick fitt'.[23] Bartholomew left Charles Beale £450; his widow Elizabeth, who had been painted by Mary Beale in 1664, was the main beneficiary.

In addition to assistants and models, Mary Beale needed a porter to run errands, transport frames and deliver pictures, one Thompson Norris (possibly a relative of Norris/Norrice, a framer and joiner).

He was provided with a livery and was sketched by Charles Beale junior. The household also included a maid called Mary, succeeded by Susan Gill who was paid £3 10s annually; she too was drawn by Charles Beale junior with the family cat, 'Poor Puss Bun', (illustrated on page 180).

Mary Beale's god-daughter, Alice Woodford, stayed with the Beales for long periods after her father's second marriage in 1667, preferring to live in London rather than in Hampshire with her father, step-mother and their young children. She 'came to us ye second time' in February 1677 at the age of fifteen,[24] and she joined the Beales again in 1681 when she was painted by Mary.[25] Alice spent a further two years in London prior to her marriage to a country vicar in 1689.

Mary Beale worked in her Pall Mall painting-room every day except Sunday when there were church services and sermons to be attended. Her schedule of appointments was unremitting, for example in February 1677.

'1st Mr Moore, third sitting two hrs. Feb. 3rd Mrs Twisden's picture. Feb. 5th Mrs Fitzjames fourth sitting. Feb. 6th Mrs Fitzjames face and breast finished. Feb. 7th Mr Rog Twisden's face carried a good way. Feb. 8th Mrs Twisden third sitting. Feb. 9th Countess of Derby face in little well laid in. Feb.10th Countess of Derby face and breast. Feb. 12th Countess Derby scumbled and re-touched. Feb 13th Mrs Twisden's face laid in for finishing'.

And so on until the end of month when there were sittings for Sir Stephen Fox's sons, William and James. Sir Stephen Fox (1627–1711) had accumulated a fortune as Paymaster to the King's guards and was himself painted by Lely. His son James died soon after Mary Beale completed his portrait and William died in 1680. Sir Stephen's daughter, Jane, who sat for her portrait in March 1677,[26] fared better by marrying the Earl of Northampton in 1686. Mary Beale's schedule for February 1677 was interrupted only by the death of Charles's 'Deare Cousin Katherine Smythe'. She then resumed work, finishing the portraits of the Countess of Derby and Mrs FitzJames.[27]

While Mary worked, Charles was often 'about town' purchasing artists' materials for her use. On one occasion in 1677 he diverted from such tasks to visit the Monument, recently completed by Sir Christopher Wren and Robert Hooke to commemorate the great fire of 1666. He 'went to ye very top of the Pillar in New Fish Street Hill' to enjoy the view.[28] On an expedition with their son, Charles,

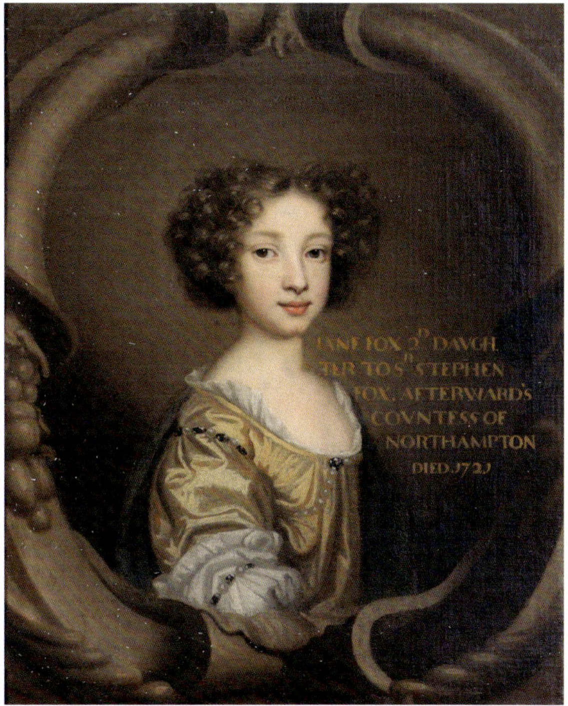

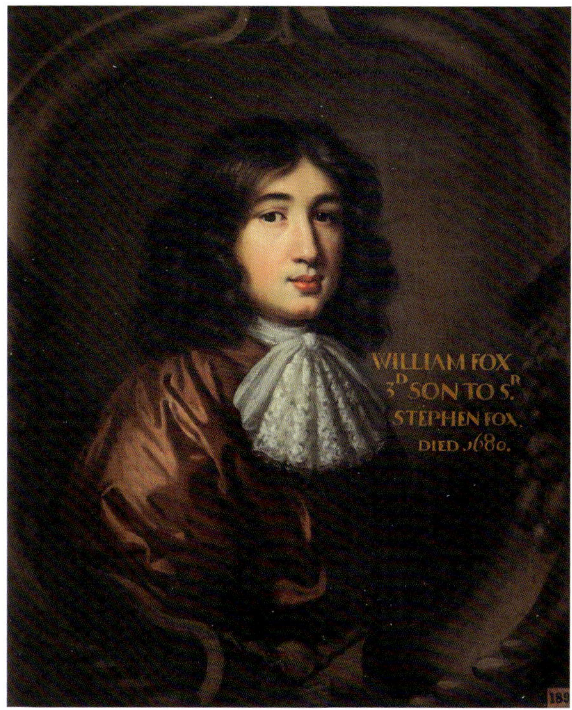

Left: Mary Beale, *Jane Fox*, later Countess of Northampton, 1677. Jane had five sittings for this portrait, at the age of eight

Right: In 1677 Mary Beale painted Jane Fox (above), William Fox (above right), and James Fox for their father, Sir Stephen Fox, Paymaster to the King's guards

the Beales visited Parry Walton of Lincoln's Inn Fields. Walton was a dealer, picture restorer, artist and Keeper of the King's pictures (he restored paintings for the Beales' patrons and Mary painted his son). At Walton's house the Beales admired his collection, especially the portrait by Van Dyck of Lady Carnarvon which captured her 'most rare faire complexion...exceeding fleshy'. Walton also showed the Beales 'a rare head by Holbein of Lord Thomas Cromwell'.[29]

Charles's almanacks record family occasions such as the marriage of 'my deare niece Betty, only daughter to my Deare Bro Bartholomew Beale Esq deceased' to Edward Partheriche at St Lawrence Jewry in 1681,[30] and a family dinner at the Hunts (Charles's sister-in-law, Elizabeth, was the daughter of Colonel Thomas Hunt).[31] He noted the deaths of contemporary artists such as John Greenhill (1676), Samuel Cooper (1672) and Gerard Soest (1681) and lamented the death at the age of forty-seven of Dr Isaac Barrow FRS in 1677. 'That most pious, learned and eminent Divine' died of a 'malignant fever' at lodgings in the Strand (Barrow's attempt to cure his fever by fasting and taking opium proved fatal).[32] Descended from a Suffolk

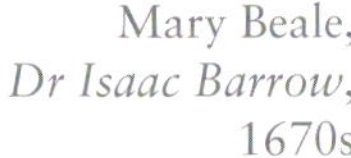

Mary Beale,
Dr Isaac Barrow,
1670s

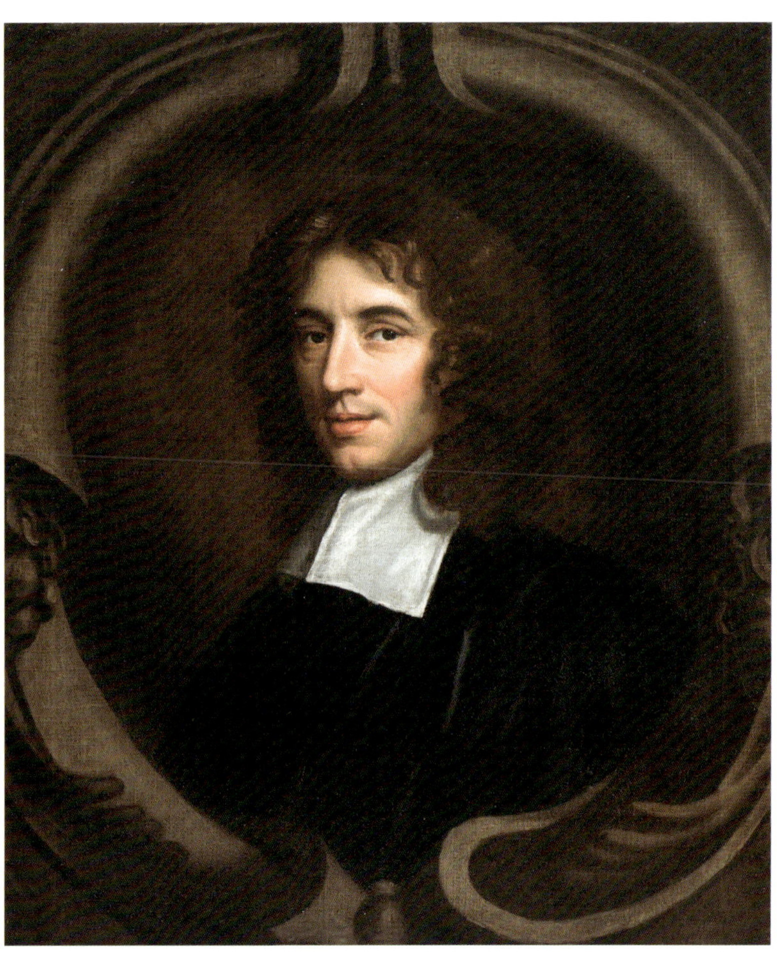

Opposite:
Top: Mary Beale,
Dr Hezekiah Burton,
c. 1674

Centre: Mary Beale,
Dr William Owtram,
1672

Below: Mary Beale,
Dr Benjamin Whichcote,
1682

family, Barrow was a brilliant mathematician and theologian, Master of Trinity College, Cambridge, and a benefactor of the College library (he persuaded his friend Sir Christopher Wren to design the new library, 1676-84, and Wren concurred without charge). Barrow's career had been promoted by the Beales' mutual friend, John Wilkins and, in his turn, Barrow nurtured Sir Isaac Newton (1642-1727). Barrow was averse to having his portrait painted (possibly because he was lean, pale and of an uncouth appearance) 'but his friends contrived to hold him in conversation while a Mr Beale [sic] took it without his knowing'.[33]

Charles Beale was likewise saddened by the demise at the age of forty-nine of Dr Hezekiah Burton (1632–1681), rector of St George's

Southwark, from 1668 to 1680. 'That most Pious learned, good natured worthy reverend and excellent divine died of a fever at his house at Barn Elmes'.[34] He had been painted by Mary in or around 1674 and the subsequent engraving by Robert White was used as the frontispiece to Burton's *Several Discourses* (1684).

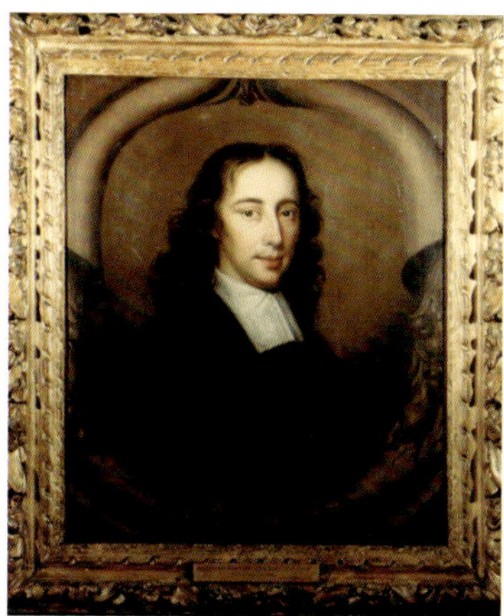

Robert White was an engraver of Bloomsbury specialising in engravings from portraits by Lely, Kneller, Riley and Mary Beale (who painted Mr and Mrs White in 1681).[35] White's engravings after Beale provided frontispieces for publications such as Dr William Owtram's *Twenty Sermons* (1682), for the Reverend Edmund Trench's autobiography (1693), David Clarkson's *Sermons and Discourses on Several Divine Subjects* (1696), the Reverend Benjamin Whichcote's *Several Discourses* (1701) and Dr Anthony Horneck's *Sermons* (1706). Owtram (1627–1679) was the rector of St Mary Woolnoth in the City of London, advancing to St Margaret's Westminster and, at the time of Mrs Beale's portrait of him, he was a Prebendary of Westminster Abbey. Clarkson was a dissenting minister and a colleague of Mary Beale's cousin, the Reverend Samuel Cradock. The latter may himself have been painted by Mrs Beale – his portrait was engraved by White for the frontispiece to *Knowledge and Practice* (1702). Whichcote (1609–1683), a man 'of a rare temper, very mild and obliging',[36] was one of the Cambridge Platonists, a philosopher and theologian whose *Moral and Religious Aphorisms* (1703) was a source of pithy quotations, one of the briefest being 'There is no better way to learn than to teach'. Whichcote's wife, Rebecca, was the widow of the City merchant and colonialist, Matthew Cradock, an ancestor of Mary Beale. Her portrait of Dr Whichcote is at Emmanuel College, Cambridge, where he founded fellowships and scholarships; another version is at Lambeth Palace.

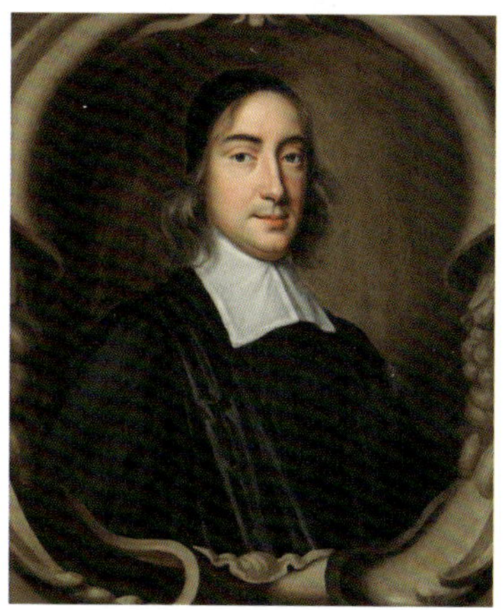

Engravings from Mrs Beale's portraits were also published by Abraham Blooteling (1634–1690) who came to England in 1673 (Charles Beale was one of his customers). He engraved Mary Beale's portrait of Dr Thomas Sydenham, providing the frontispiece for *Observationes Medicae* (1676), arguably Sydenham's most important work. Blooteling made engravings of Beale's portraits of Earl Fauconberg and Bishop Wilkins 'very probably by Mrs Beale's desire'.[37] Her portrait of Dr Tenison when he was vicar of St Martin-in-the Fields was engraved by Peter Vanderbank (1695). In the mid-eighteenth century Thomas Chambars/Chambers published an engraving of a self portrait of Mary Beale with a head and shoulders

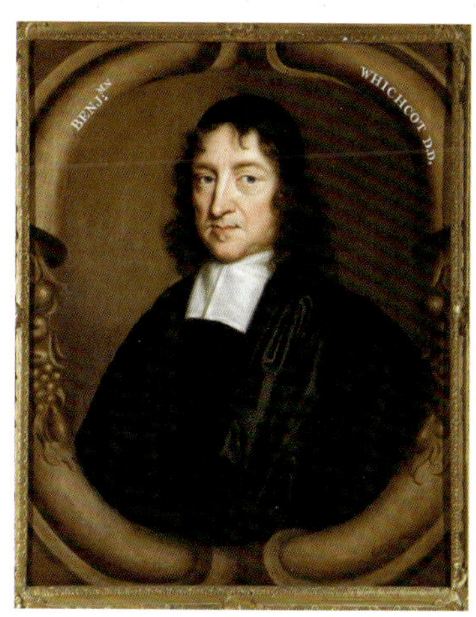

of her adult son Charles alongside; 'Mary Beale pinxit' testified to the originals. They hung in Horace Walpole's green closet at Strawberry Hill, Twickenham, and were listed in the 1774 sale catalogue as 'Mrs Beale and her son Charles's, heads in water-colours by her'.[38] Walpole also owned Mary Beale's portrait of Anne Hyde, Duchess of York, after Lely, and several paintings by Charles Beale (see page 179).

Post Lely

The London art market was shocked by the death of Sir Peter Lely who suffered an apoplectic fit while finishing a portrait of the Duchess of Somerset on 30 November 1680. He died as a result, at the age of sixty-three and was buried at St Paul's, Covent Garden, where a white marble monument featured an epitaph to *Petrus Lelius* by the Beales' friend, Thomas Flatman. The sale of Lely's art collection was organised by his solicitor and executor, Roger North (1651–1734), a lawyer and art collector from Suffolk who in 1677 owed Mary Beale £3 8s for his portrait.[39]

Prior to the sale, Charles Beale returned paintings he had borrowed from Lely's studio. Parry Walton varnished Lely's last works and former assistants in the studio put finishing touches to pictures. John Baptist Gaspars ('Lely's Baptist' as he was known) and Prosper Henry Lankrink compiled an inventory and valued the collection. Lely's former pupil, Frederick Sonnius, took up residence at the house in Covent Garden so as to complete unfinished portraits and safeguard the premises. The dispersal of Lely's materials and 'the utensils of painting' was left to colour sellers and artists to organise (Charles Beale purchased some sacking for Mary's use). The sale of sculptures and pictures (575 by Dutch, Flemish and Italian masters and some 300 by Lely and his pupils) was held in April 1682. Charles Beale was there bidding for portraits of Lady Norris, a half-length of an unknown woman described as 'mazarine' (indicating perhaps, the deep blue colour of her dress), a three-quarter length portrait of a girl, 'a Pannell design of a Family' and more panels (seven lots cost him £8 15s). On the second day he purchased a marble sculpture of a woman for £5 10s and a woman's head on cloth for 12s. [40]

Mrs Beale may have hoped to fill the void left by the deaths of John Greenhill (1676), Joan Carlile (1679), Sir Peter Lely (1680), Gerard Soest (1681) and William Wissing (1687). Greenhill was a disciple of Lely and a promising artist, 'a very forward Ingenius young man that at the age of twenty he made a copy after Vandyke'.

So ingenious was Greenhill that 'Sir Peter Lely grew jealous of him'.[41] Greenhill's career was cut short when he fell into the company of actors 'they so debauch'd him from his study that he went as farr backwards'. After a bout of drinking he was carried to Parry Walton's house in Lincoln's Inn Fields where he died.[42]

Greenhill's death inspired an elegy written by the novelist, playwright and spy, Mrs Aphra Behn (1640–1689, née Amis). Aphra's husband, of Dutch extraction, died in 1665 and because of her contacts in the Low Countries, Aphra was commissioned to gather intelligence in Antwerp during the Dutch wars: her warning of a Dutch raid to the Thames went unheeded, resulting in the catastrophe of 1667. Returning to London, poverty-stricken, Mrs Behn dedicated herself to writing novels, plays, poems and stories (her works fill six hefty volumes). Mrs Behn's plays and personal amours were scandalous but brought her success and admirers. Thomas Otway wrote the prologue to her comedy *City Heiress* (1682) and he may have recommended Mary Beale to her. The 2nd Duke of Buckingham (1628–1687), an enthusiast for plays, owned Mrs Beale's portrait of Mrs Behn, which was sold at the Stowe sale of 1848 to J. S. Caldwell. Aphra Behn's biographer, Montague Summers, traced the painting to the Heath Caldwell family of Linley Wood, Staffordshire, from whom it passed to Miss M.V. Wakefield-Richmond, another biographer of Mrs Behn, and she presented the portrait to St Hilda's College, Oxford. Aphra Behn and Mary Beale were like-minded women who overcame traditional prejudices towards women in the arts; as Virginia Woolf put it, 'all women together ought to let flowers fall upon the tomb of Aphra Behn' at Westminster Abbey.[43]

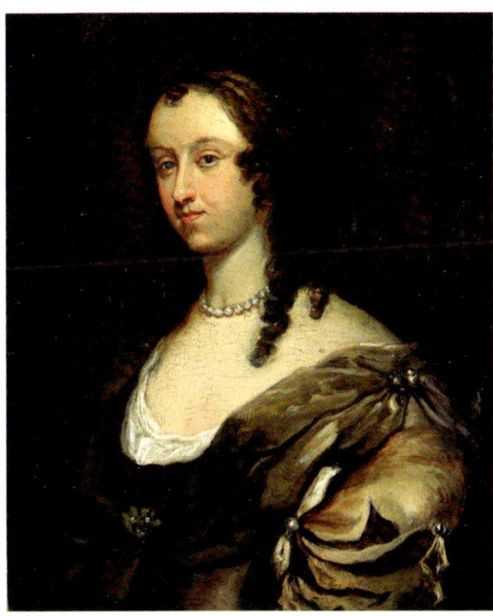

Mary Beale, *Aphra Behn*, playwright and novelist, 1670s

The deaths of several London portraitists augured well for Mary Beale, were it not for the dominance of Sir Godfrey Kneller Bt (1646-1723). Kneller's portrait of King Charles II (1679) led to his appointment as Court painter in succession to Lely, a position he held onto during the reigns of James II, William and Mary and King George I. For a time Kneller shared this position with John Riley (1646–1691), and William Wissing (1656–1687) was poised to challenge Kneller had it not been for his early death. The Swedish artist Michael Dahl (1659–1743) settled in London in 1689 and was encouraged by Kneller. David Paton (*c.* 1660–1709) was highly regarded by the Scottish aristocracy – his double portrait of the Duke and Duchess of Lauderdale is at Ham House, Richmond.

The supremacy of Kneller and competition from a younger generation of portrait painters was not to Mary Beale's advantage. However, the death of Lely brought an increased demand for copies of his portraits, for which she was already renowned: in 1676 she had painted fourteen copies of Lely's originals.[43] Copies of masterly portraits of royalty, illustrious figures and the King's mistresses were de rigueur and provided an artist such as Mary Beale opportunities to learn in the process. After Lely's death Mary copied many of his originals, such as the Earl and Countess of Ogle, the Countess of Northumberland and King Charles II in armour. She was at the same time copying Van Dyck's royal portraits: Charles Beale recorded the 'King's face finished in little after Van Dyke' and the Princess of Orange's face, ditto, in September 1681.[44] Mary Beale's version of Lely's portrait of Queen Catherine of Braganza was in the Hengrave Hall sale of 1897 and her copy of Van Dyck's portrait of King James II was formerly at Minley Manor, Hampshire. Mary Beale also studied the Italian masters: her husband's almanacks referred to 'several paintings of Italian Masters copyd by Mrs Beale. After old Palma. St John. St Katherine' ('old Palma' being Palma Vecchio c. 1480–1528, a Venetian artist also known as Jacopo Negretti).[46]

'Our great want of money'[47]

A lull in the London art market after Lely's death, a general rise in prices, the prominence of Kneller and the challenge of younger artists brought a decline in the number of Mary Beale's commissions. According to her husband's almanacks, she had completed eighty-three portraits in 1677, compared to thirty-nine in 1681, with a corresponding drop of income from £429 4s in 1677 to £209 17s 6d for 1681.[48] One factor in Mrs Beale's decline in productivity was the threatening political situation: potential patrons, especially politicians and clergy, were preoccupied. The prospect of the accession to the throne of King Charles II's brother, the Roman Catholic Duke of

York, and in the meanwhile the King's intolerable policies, made for instability. London, particularly the City, was a hot-bed of party politics and anti-papist plots, riots and fires. Two of the capital's most popular preachers, Gilbert Burnet and William Lloyd, were vehemently anti-Catholic. Addressing the Lord Mayor and citizens in September 1680, Burnet warned of the dire effects of popery, while Lloyd stirred anti-Catholicism from the pulpit of St Martin-in-the-Fields. The Titus Oates plot of 1678, the Rye House Plot of 1683, the arrests of the City Aldermen and the King's *Quo warranto* proceedings against the City were not conducive to patronage of the arts.

The Beales' 'disappointment of money'[49] was due in part to the failure of some clients to pay promptly and in full: six pictures were unpaid for in January 1677 and it was four years before payment was received for the Marchioness of Dorchester's portrait. Charles Beale accepted part-payment for a portrait and he would have found it embarrassing to chase important clients who were in arrears. Financial problems first surfaced in 1677 when, despite Mary's earnings of £429 4s for the past year, £50 was owed in debts. So Charles Beale borrowed £5 from Francis Knollys on security of his gold watch.[50] Increasingly desperate, Charles took 'a 20 shillings piece of gold of Oliver Cromwell's' to a goldsmith in Covent Garden and received £1 in exchange.[51]

Thereafter Charles Beale called upon loans from relatives and friends habitually, and was grateful for a few guineas. He borrowed £5 from 'my true and most kind friend' Thomas Slater, Clerk to the Brewers' Company, in 1681.[52] The family's physician, Dr John Browne, contributed 5 guineas, while Cousin Auditor Bridges (Charles's nephew) obliged with £10 'in our great straites and disappointment of money'.[53] Fortunately 'My Deare Sister Mrs Elizabeth Beale' paid a generous £20 once Mary had finished 'ye face of her Picture, this day' in June 1681.[54]

Despite 'Our low condition' there were no economies in the Beale household. On the contrary, Charles purchased books from Jolivet (one of Mary's sitters) and from Mr Rogers, and he indulged in two new prayer-books for himself and Mary.[55] He had a weakness for prints and early seventeenth-century engravings and owed the print-seller George Baker money. Nor did he economise on clothes: his tailor's bills suggest he was vain about his appearance. He purchased two yards of rich flowery Venetian silk for a waistcoat, black ribbon for his hat,[56] new shoe buckles, garters and Cordoba gloves.[57] He ordered four cravats, 'a coate and breeches in the best broad cloth' with nine dozen silk buttons for his son Charles's coat, and a livery coat, breeches and cap for the porter, Thompson Norris. More essential was a new painting apron for Mary, made from six ells of cloth which cost 13s (an ell measured 45 inches), cambric painting sleeves and a pair of shoes from Sampson the shoemaker.[58] Household purchases included eighteen pewter plates which were engraved with the Beale coat of arms,[59] sixteen china cups of 'unusual fashion', six cane-bottomed chairs and one armchair. In August the family took advantage of the cherry crop to distil cherry brandy which required twenty-four pounds of black cherries, two gallons of the best brandy at 3s 4d a gallon, oranges, cinnamon and mace.[60] New outfits, furniture, pewter, china and a plentiful supply of cherry brandy indicated that the Beales continued to entertain patrons and friends at the Pall Mall house, as they had done at Hind Court. Although finances were strained, Charles made regular donations of 10s from his 'pious and charitable account'.[61]

In the spring of 1681 Charles admitted to be 'in such pressing need yt we had but only 2s 6d left us in the house against Easter'.[62] Under these circumstances he praised God that Lady Pierrepont paid for the Marchioness of Dorchester's picture 'done long since'. This was a half-length portrait of Catherine, daughter of the Earl of Derby and the second wife of Henry Pierrepont, 1st Marquess of Dorchester. 'Our most Gratious God sent us in this supply when we were in deep and sad distress for want of money for which adored be his sacred name'.[63] A further blessing was bestowed by Bishop William Lloyd who excused Charles Beale from his duties as a collector of the parish poor rate, a tedious and potentially costly task.[64]

As the number of commissions dwindled, Mrs Beale occupied herself with portraits of herself, her son Charles, Keaty Trioche, Edward Stillingfleet, the Flessiers and Alice Woodford, 'upon account of study and improvement'.[65] Experiments with cheaper materials – onion bags, bed ticking and Royston sacking in lieu of linen canvas – were overseen by Charles who recorded the innovations. In July 1681 Alice Woodford's picture was painted on onion bag 'done over before she finish't it with white poppy oile, as thin done over as she could', an experiment watched closely by her husband.[66] Not one to sit idle, Mary painted eleven friends 'upon Account of Kindness and not profitt'.[67] These included a portrait of Dr Stillingfleet for Dr Gilbert Burnet, Charles Beale's cousin, Nicholas Smythe, the Earl of Ogle for Mr Browne, Symon Patrick when Dean of Peterborough, Mary Tillotson (daughter of John and Elizabeth), and Lady Barnard for Mr Crawford. She repaid favours with paintings of Thomas Flatman, Parry Walton's son, and Mrs May's picture was given to Dr Cooke.

Portraits of the 1680s

Mrs Beale's loyal clients, the clergy, provided welcome commissions during lean years. In 1681 William Lloyd, Bishop of St Asaph, requested a portrait of Gilbert Burnet and another of his librarian and protégé, William Wotton. Lloyd paid £5 for Wotton's picture with an additional £1 10s for an ebony frame and 3s 6d for a deal case.[68] Dr John Cooke wanted paintings of his daughters. Dr John Nicholas of Winchester sat for Mary in 1681; in the same year, Dr John Batteley, chaplain to Dr Tillotson, made an appointment. The scheming Earl of Shaftesbury sat for his portrait when aged sixty in 1681, and John Dawnay of Wykeham Abbey, North Yorkshire, commissioned portraits of himself and his wife, Dorothy, to mark his elevation to the peerage as Viscount Downe; his seventeen-year-old heir, Henry, sat for Mary Beale the following year.

Mary Beale, *Catharine Sedley, Countess of Dorchester*, c. 1683. This portrait was exhibited in 1866 under Mary Beale's name; it has recently been attributed to Sir Godfrey Kneller

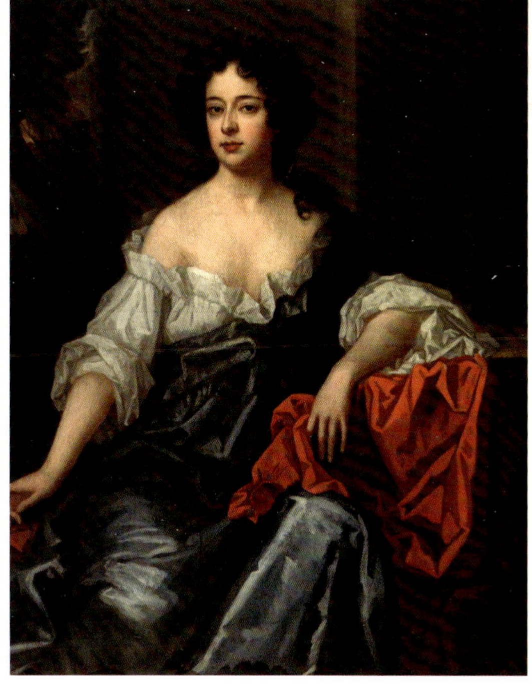

King James II's mistress, before and after his accession to the throne, was Catharine Sedley (1657–1717), created Countess of Dorchester by the King in 1686, and after her marriage to the Earl of Portmore she became the Countess of Portmore. King James installed her at 21 St James's Square where Catharine indulged her taste for sculpture and paintings. Mary Beale's portrait of her neighbour showed Catharine seated, wearing a low-cut dress with red drapery;[69] she was also the subject of one of Mary's rare miniatures. After the King's departure to France in 1688 the Countess remained a determined Jacobite and was long remembered for her sharp tongue. Outrageous to the end, when she encountered the Duchess of Portsmouth and the Countess of Orkney in a drawing-room at Windsor, she exclaimed 'God! Who would have thought that we three royal whores should meet here?'.[70]

Some of Mary Beale's most perceptive portraits were of the old and the young. For example in 1682 she painted the philosopher/theologian Dr Benjamin

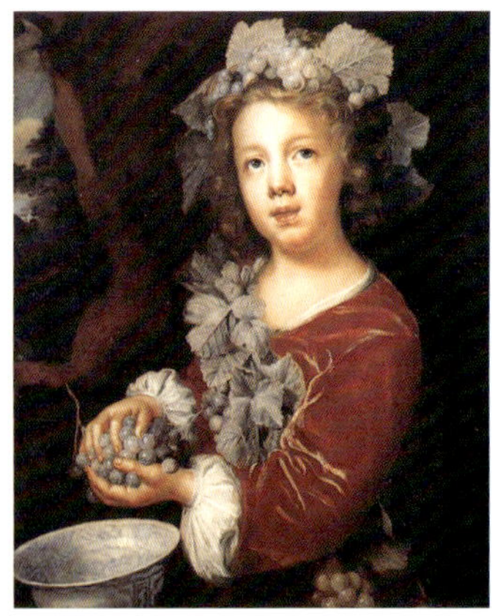

Whichcote when he was seventy-three, looking pensive (he died the next year). The portrait of her neighbour, sixty-four-year-old Dr Sydenham, conveys his profound, compassionate character (1688). She painted children and youths with sympathy, beginning with her own sons, progressing to an enchanting young Bacchus, the arrogant Master Newdigate, a boy with a spaniel, the eight-year-old Jane Fox and the sorrowful eighteen-year-old Heighes Woodford whose mother had died soon after giving birth to him. Indulgent parents commissioned portraits of the Hon. Thomas Twisden as a teenager, and sixteen-year-old Basil Dixwell (later the 2nd Baronet). The serious Caleb Bankes (1659–1696) was painted by Mrs Beale while he was at the University of Cambridge.

Above: Mary Beale, *The Young Bacchus*, c. 1660–65

Right: Mary Beale, *Caleb Bankes*, 1675

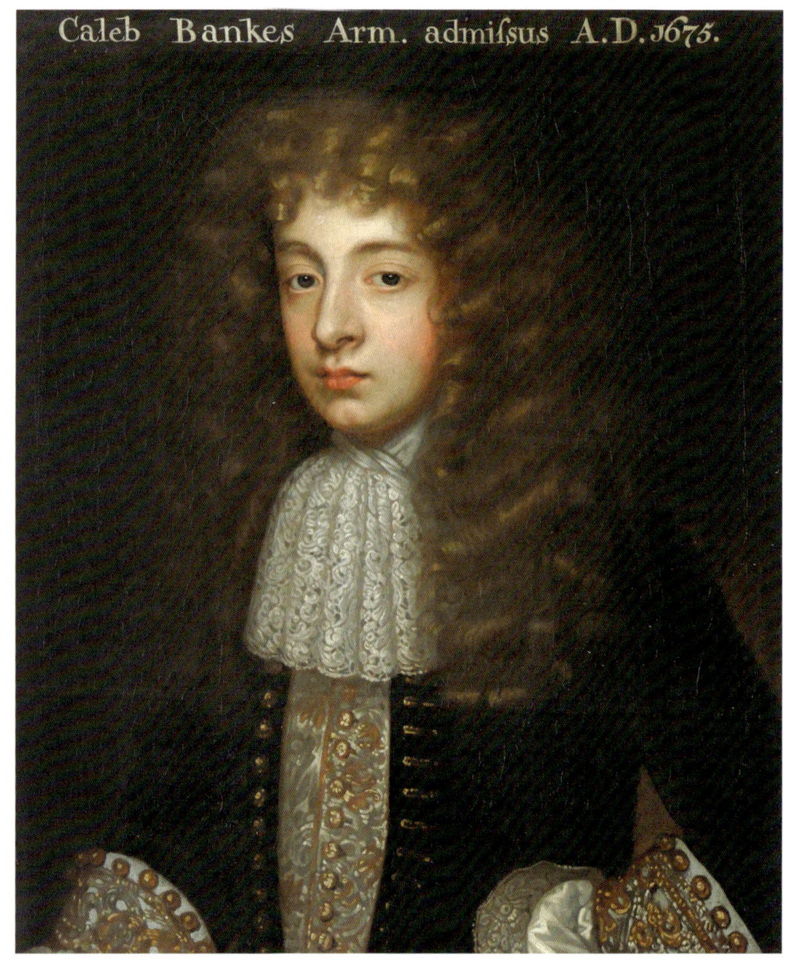

Neither Charles Beale's almanacks, George Vertue's excerpts nor personal correspondence relating to the Beales survive after 1681.[71] This is not to say that Mary abandoned her profession. On the contrary, she was still painting in the 1680s and her last known works date to the 1690s. Some of her later portraits are signed and dated; pictures for the Twysden/Twisden family were completed in the 1680s and 1690s and others can be dated approximately from the appearance of the sitter.

Mary Beale's portraits of the Twisden family, Charles Beale's distant relations, began with Lady Twisden (1610–1702), her eldest son, Sir Roger (1640–1703), and his wife, Margaret, commissioned in 1677. The Twisdens were Kent landowners and may have been

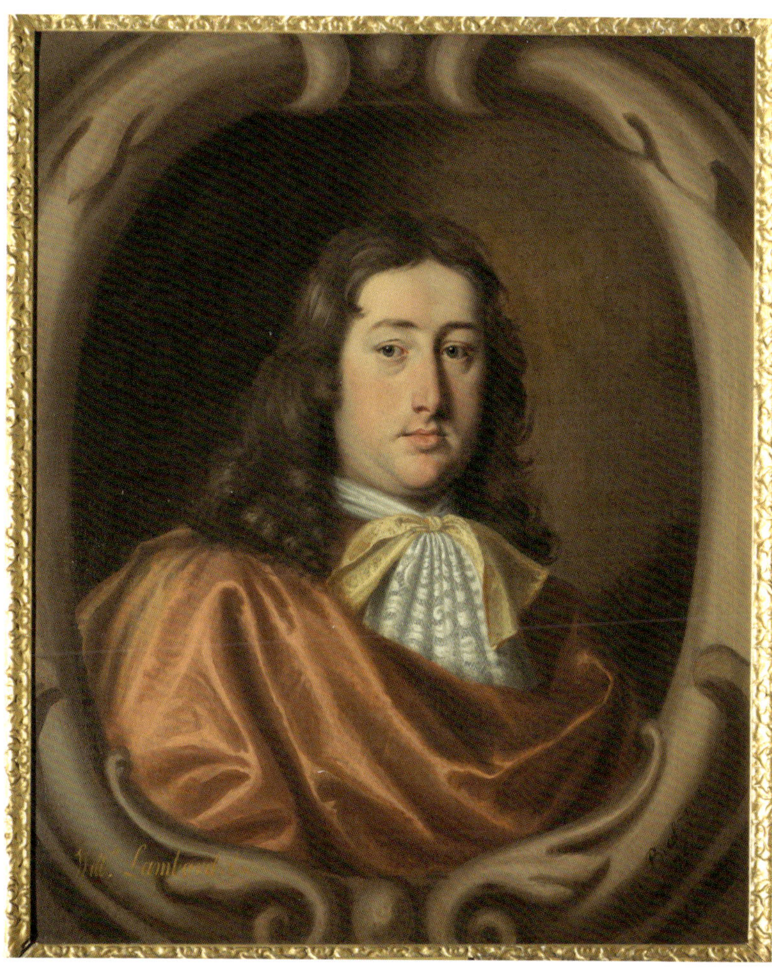

Mary Beale, *William Lambarde*, 1676

impressed by Mary's portrait of William Lambarde (1644–1711) whose family also came from Kent. Lambarde was the great-grandson of the Elizabethan antiquary and benefactor of the Drapers' Company. Mary Beale's head and shoulders of Lambarde set in an oval surround has puzzled experts due to the inscription 'Ann Beal Pinx 1676', however 'Ann' seems to be a flourish to the initial M.

Sir Thomas Twisden Bt (1602–1683) and Lady Twisden had been drawn by John Greenhill, and for Mary Beale's oil painting Lady Twisden wore the same black lace veil and pearls. Her brother, Colonel Matthew Tomlinson, was present at the trial of King Charles I on the day the death sentence was passed in January 1649 and he had the dubious honour of accompanying Charles I to his execution three days later. Lady Twisden's husband, Sir Thomas, a judge and politician, was present at the trial of the regicides, following the Restoration of the monarchy in 1660. Their son, Sir Roger, replaced Bartholomew Beale, Charles Beale's brother, as an Auditor of the Imprests in 1674 and succeeded as 2nd Baronet Bradbourne in 1683. The younger generation of the Twisden family visited Mrs Beale's studio in 1682 to have their portraits painted: the Hon. Thomas Twisden (1667–1728) was accompanied by his aunt, Lady Style (1647–1718). Mary Beale's portrait of the attractive Lady Style was acquired by Richard Jeffree, who led the revival of interest in Mary Beale from the 1970s.

The Hon. Thomas Twisden was fifteen when he sat for Mary Beale. Three years later she painted another young man, believed to be William Cavendish (1672–1729). His father had recently inherited the peerage as Earl of Devonshire, thus William became Lord Cavendish (and later the 2nd Duke of Devonshire). A politician throughout the reigns of Queen Anne and King George I, Cavendish is best remembered for his art collection at Devonshire House, Piccadilly, and at Chatsworth in Derbyshire.

Mary Beale's portrait of Robert Fairfax (1666–1725) is dated 1685, the year he returned from serving on a merchant ship in the Mediterranean. Scion of a parliamentarian family (his grandfather was killed during the civil war of the 1640s), Fairfax was nineteen when painted by Beale, looking remarkably mature in armour. He was present at the battle of Beachy Head in 1690, when control of the English Channel fell into the hands of the French, causing panic in England for fear of an invasion. Fairfax was involved in several skirmishes with the French before he retired as Rear Admiral.

The war against France was pursued vigorously by King William and Queen Mary, joint monarchs from 1689. William persuaded parliament that it was the duty of a Protestant nation to confront the expansionist policy of the Catholic King Louis XIV. In contrast to the extravagant Court of Charles II and the riotous reign of James II, William and Mary established a godly, Protestant ethos. A few days after succeeding to the throne, the King named Gilbert Burnet as Bishop of Salisbury, and several of the Beales' friends – Tillotson, Stillingfleet, Lloyd, Patrick, Moore and Tenison (the King's spiritual adviser) were promoted. With the accession of the pious William and Mary, Mrs Beale came to the fore as portrait painter to the episcopacy and these paintings celebrated the revival of the Anglican Church at the end of the seventeenth century.

Left: Mary Beale, *Lady Twisden*, 1677

Right: Mary Beale, *Lady Style*, 1682

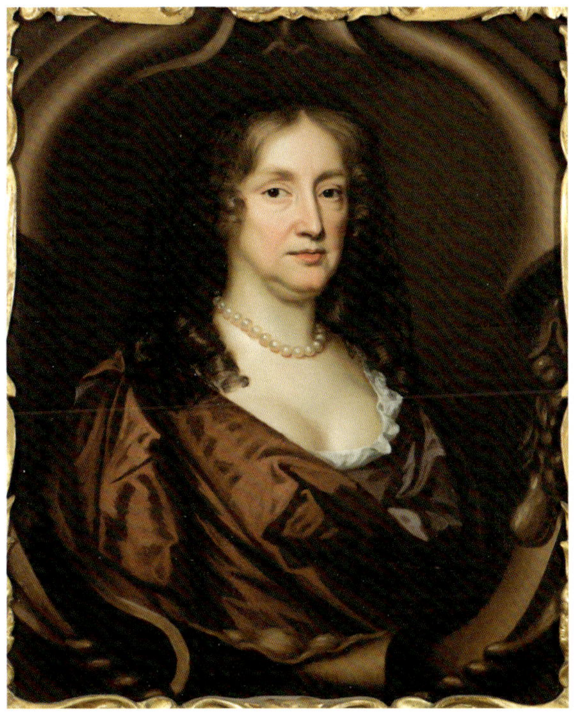

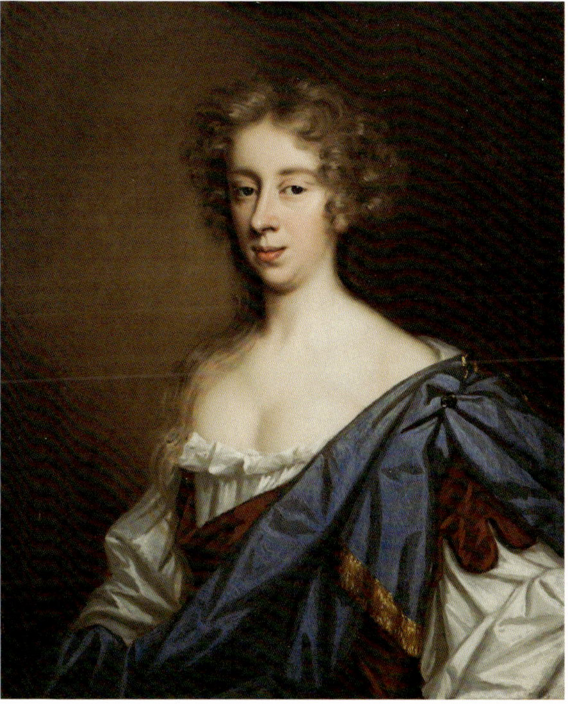

CHARLES BEALE'S ALMANACKS: NOTES

1. 'Vertue Note Books IV', *Walpole Society* 24 (1936), p. 168. Vertue mentions having seen seven almanacks. His published excerpts cover six years: 1661, 1672, 1674, 1676, 1677, 1681. His friend, Dr Richard Rawlinson FRS (1690–1755), bequeathed his collection of Beale memorabilia to the Bodleian Library, Oxford

2. 'Vertue Note Books IV', *op. cit.*, pp. 14-15

3. Charles Beale referred to Mary as 'My Dearest Heart' or 'My D. Ht' throughout the almanacks

4. GVCBA 26 May 1676. William Aglionby's *Painting Illustrated. Together with the Lives of the Most Eminent Painters, (*1685), superseded Beale's project

5. Dr John Cooke requested a copy of a letter to the Grand Duke of Tuscany on behalf of Charles Beale, *State Papers Domestic,* 23 November 1671, p. 582

6. CBA 14 February 1677

7. *Ibid.*, June–July 1677

8. CBA 29 August 1677

9. *Ibid.*, 8 December 1677

10. Charles Beale, 'Experimental Secrets found out in the way of Painting', (1647–63), July–September 1659

11. CBA 25 August 1677

12. *Ibid.*

13. GVCBA 3 May 1676

14. CBA 24 February 1681

15. Add Ms 16,174, f. 7v, BL. Henry and John Norris, father and son, made frames for the aristocracy and in 1689 John was appointed joiner to the Privy Council

16. S. Woodford, *Liber*, 23 January 1665

17. CBA 1676–7

18. *Ibid.*, 16 February 1677

19. *Ibid.*, 3 May 1681

20. *Ibid.*, 13 July, 8 September 1681

21. *Ibid.*, 4 June 1681

22. Edward Hatton, A *New View of London,* (1708), II, p. 821

23. Camden Society 44 (1849), p. 120

24. CBA 9, 14 February 1677

25. *Ibid.*, 14 July 1681

26. *Ibid.*, 15, 21 February, 12 March 1677

27. *Ibid.*, February 1677

28. *Ibid.*, 27 March 1677

29. *Ibid.*, 16 November 1681

30. *Ibid.*, 9 March 1681

31. *Ibid.*, 22 March 1681

32. *Ibid.*, 4 May 1677

33. DNB (1885-1901), I, p. 1223

34. CBA 5 September 1681

35. *Ibid.*, June 1681

36. GB I, pt 1, p. 331

37. GVCBA 9 February 1676

38. *A Description of the Villa of Horace Walpole…with an inventory,* (1774), p. 33

39. CBA 15 January 1677

40. Diana Dethloff, 'The executors' account book and dispersal of Sir Peter Lely's collection', *Journal of the History of Collections* 8 (1996), pp. 15-51

41. 'Vertue Note Books I', *Walpole Society* 18 (1930), p. 30

42. *Ibid.*

43. Virginia Woolf, *A Room of One's Own,* (1929), p. 69

44. GVCBA 1676

45. CBA September 29, 30, 1681

46. GVCBA 1674

47. CBA 10 December 1681

48. The sums are verified by Beale's almanacks. The number of commissions was calculated by Richard Jeffree and Elizabeth Walsh, see *The Excellent Mrs Mary Beale,* (1975), p. 15

49. CBA 25 January 1681

50. *Ibid.*, 3 February 1677

51. *Ibid.*, 26 April 1677

52. *Ibid.*, 25 January 1681

53. *Ibid.*, 1 April

54. *Ibid.*, June

55. *Ibid.*, 10 November 1677

56. *Ibid.*, 2, 10 July 1677

57. *Ibid.*, 26, 30 July 1681

58. *Ibid.*, 20 February 1677, 2 October 1677, 23 February 1681

59. *Ibid.*, 24 November 1677

60. *Ibid.*, 5 August 1681

61. *Ibid.*, May 1681

62. *Ibid.*, 1 April

63. *Ibid.*, 6 August

64. *Ibid.*, 12 April 1677

65. *Ibid.*, December 1681

66. *Ibid.*, 14 July

67. *Ibid.*, December

68. *Ibid.*, 21 June

69. CBA May 1677. The portrait belonging to Earl Spencer was exhibited in 1866, see *Catalogue of the First Special Exhibition of National Portraits ending with the reign of King James II on loan to the South Kensington Museum,* (1866), p. 171

70. ODNB

71. An undated, suicidal letter from Flatman to Charles Beale may be the exception

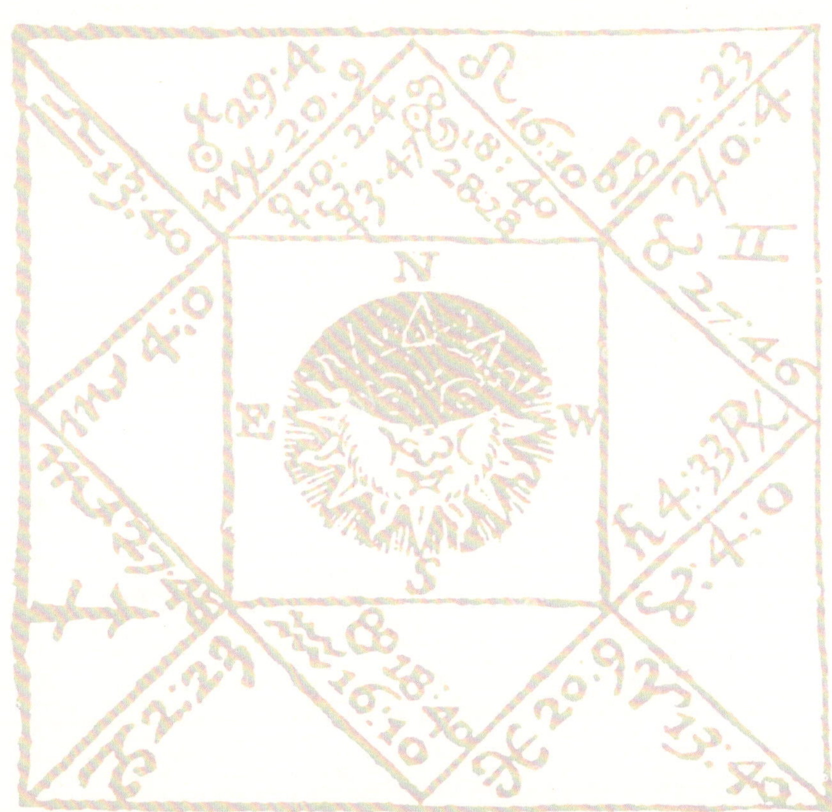

A woodcut from William Lilly, *The Starry Messenger*, 1645. Lilly's astrological chart predicted the death of King Charles I

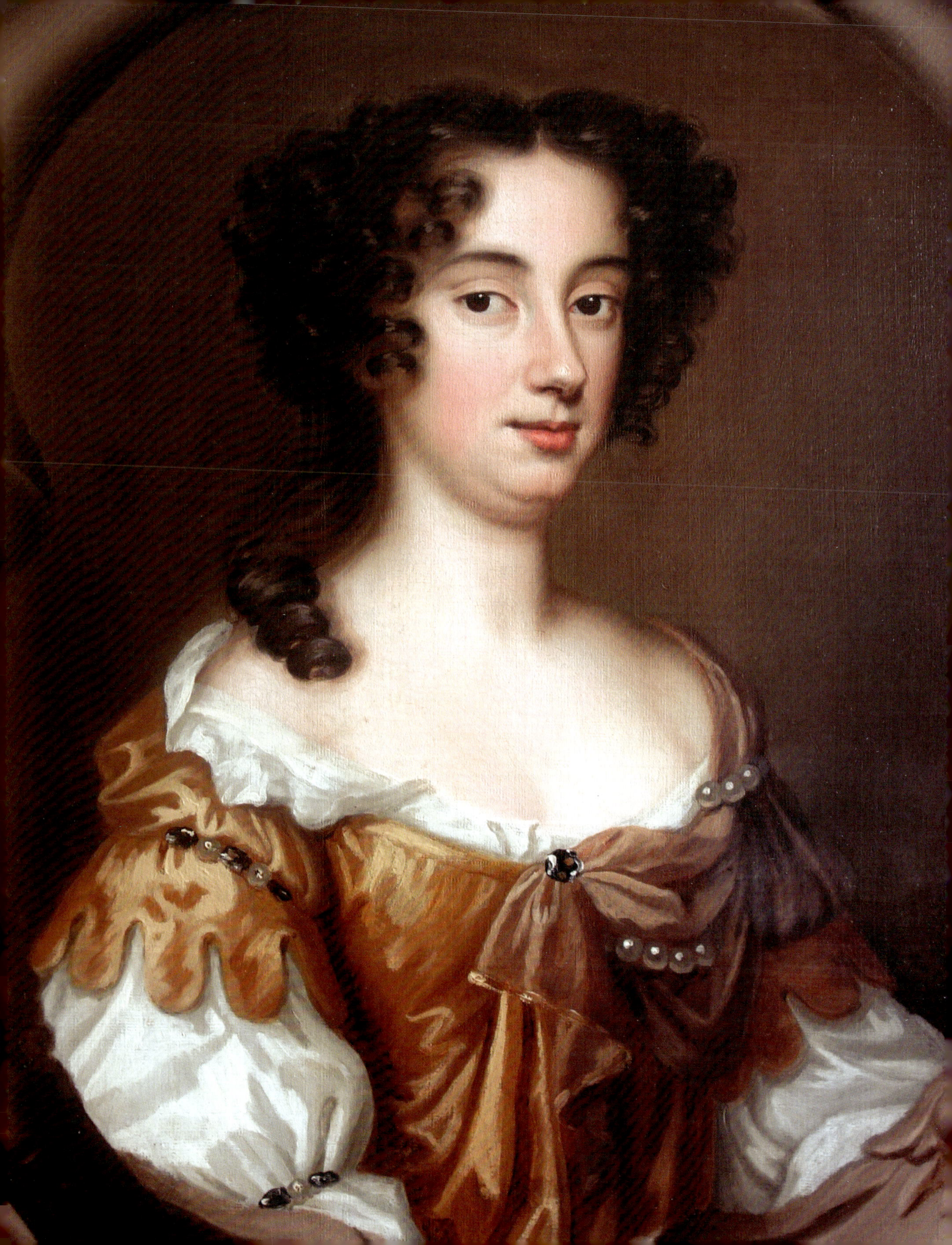

7. 'THE EXCELLENT MRS MARY BEAL'[1]

AFTER THE VICISSITUDES OF KING JAMES II'S REIGN, the last ten years of Mary Beale's life commenced in 1689 with the 'glorious revolution' that brought many of her friends and patrons to positions of power. As the invasion by Prince William of Orange loomed, Henry Booth, Lord Delamer (1652–1694) raised a small army in Cheshire to support the Prince. His service was rewarded with the chancellorship of the Exchequer and in 1690 he was created the Earl of Warrington. His wife, Mary, (1652–1691, née Langham) was painted by Mary Beale, around the time of her marriage in 1670.

Mary, the only surviving child of Sir James Langham Bt, was the beloved of Sir John Nelthorpe Bt (1614–1669) of Scawby Hall, Lincolnshire, (where there are three portraits attributed to Mrs Beale). Nelthorpe died unmarried, leaving Miss Langham his diamond ring, gold watch, thirty-one gold coins, a knife set with agate and diamonds and a jewel worth £500 to be inscribed 'Love's Paraphrase' and worn 'in memory of him who did truly love her'. A year after Nelthorpe's death Mary married Lord Delamer; she was to see him imprisoned three times on charges of treason and she witnessed his trial at Westminster Hall by the infamous Lord Chancellor, George Jeffreys, recently returned from conducting the Bloody Assizes in the west country. Jeffreys was outwitted by Delamer and found solace in drink. Delamer's memorial in the church of St Mary the Virgin, Bowdon, Cheshire, records that he was a 'person of unblemished honour…tried for his life upon false accusations of high treason'. His wife Mary was eulogised as the epitome of virtue, 'a lady of ingenious parts, singular discretion, consummate judgement, great humility, meek and compassionate temper, extensive charity, exemplary and unaffected piety'.

No courtier was closer to King James II during the dénouement of December 1688 than Thomas Bruce, 2nd Earl of Ailesbury (1656–1741), gentleman of the bedchamber to the beleaguered King. Ailesbury married Elizabeth (1656–1697, née Seymour) in October 1676 and their portraits by Mary Beale were painted the following

Opposite: Mary Beale, *Lady Delamer*, c. 1670

Opposite: Unknown artist, *The seven bishops committed to the Tower of London, 1688*, c. 1689. Four of the bishops had previously been painted by Mary Beale: William Sancroft, Archbishop of Canterbury, (centre) in 1677, William Lloyd, Bishop of St Asaph, (top left) 1677 and 1681, Francis Turner, Bishop of Ely, (top right) c. 1683-8, and John Lake, Bishop of Chichester, (middle row left) in 1685

year.[2] Ailesbury's memoirs recall his dash to Faversham where James II had been recognised and apprehended as he attempted to leave the country. Ailesbury accompanied the King back to the capital on 15 December 1688 and wished him adieu when he finally embarked for France a few days later. Ever loyal to the exiled King, Ailesbury plotted to overthrow King William III, for which he was imprisoned in the Tower of London in 1696 (Elizabeth died in childbirth while he was there). On gaining his freedom, Ailesbury settled in Brussels, married an heiress and wrote his memoirs.

The departure of James II heralded the reign of King William III and Queen Mary II, James's eldest daughter who had married Prince William of Orange in 1677. Princess Mary's maid of honour was Elizabeth Villiers (1657–1733), the Prince's mistress and later the Countess of Orkney. Mary Beale painted 'Mrs Villiers' before her departure to the Continent,[3] also her sister, Anne, and she had previously copied Lely's portrait of their cousin Barbara Villiers, King Charles II's mistress.[4] Despite her acquaintances at the Court of William and Mary, Mary Beale failed to obtain royal patronage. Sir Godfrey Kneller (1646–1723) was in prime position as portrait painter to the royal family and the aristocracy, lauded in the 1690s for his 'Hampton Court Beauties' (portraits of ladies of the Court). John Riley (1646–1691) who charged an extortionate £40 for a full length portrait, competed for commissions and was appointed Court painter to William and Mary in 1689. Antonio Verrio (1636–1707), in England from 1672, more famous for murals than portraits, also commanded attention. Nevertheless, Mary Beale maintained her position as the favourite portraitist of the Protestant clergy. The 'great disappointment of money'[5] which had forced Charles and Mary Beale into debt during the previous decade must have been alleviated after 1689, judging by Mary's commissions for portraits of three archbishops, ten bishops, King William's chaplains and from country gentry such as the Carew family of Cornwall, Thomas Fountayne of Yorkshire and the Reverend Robert Cremer of Norfolk.

The Protestant establishment

Opposition to King James II approached its climax in April 1688 with the King's second Declaration of Indulgence suspending all laws against Roman Catholics and Dissenters. This was intolerable to the Anglican clergy: Archbishop William Sancroft and six bishops organised a protest. Bishop William Lloyd hastened to London

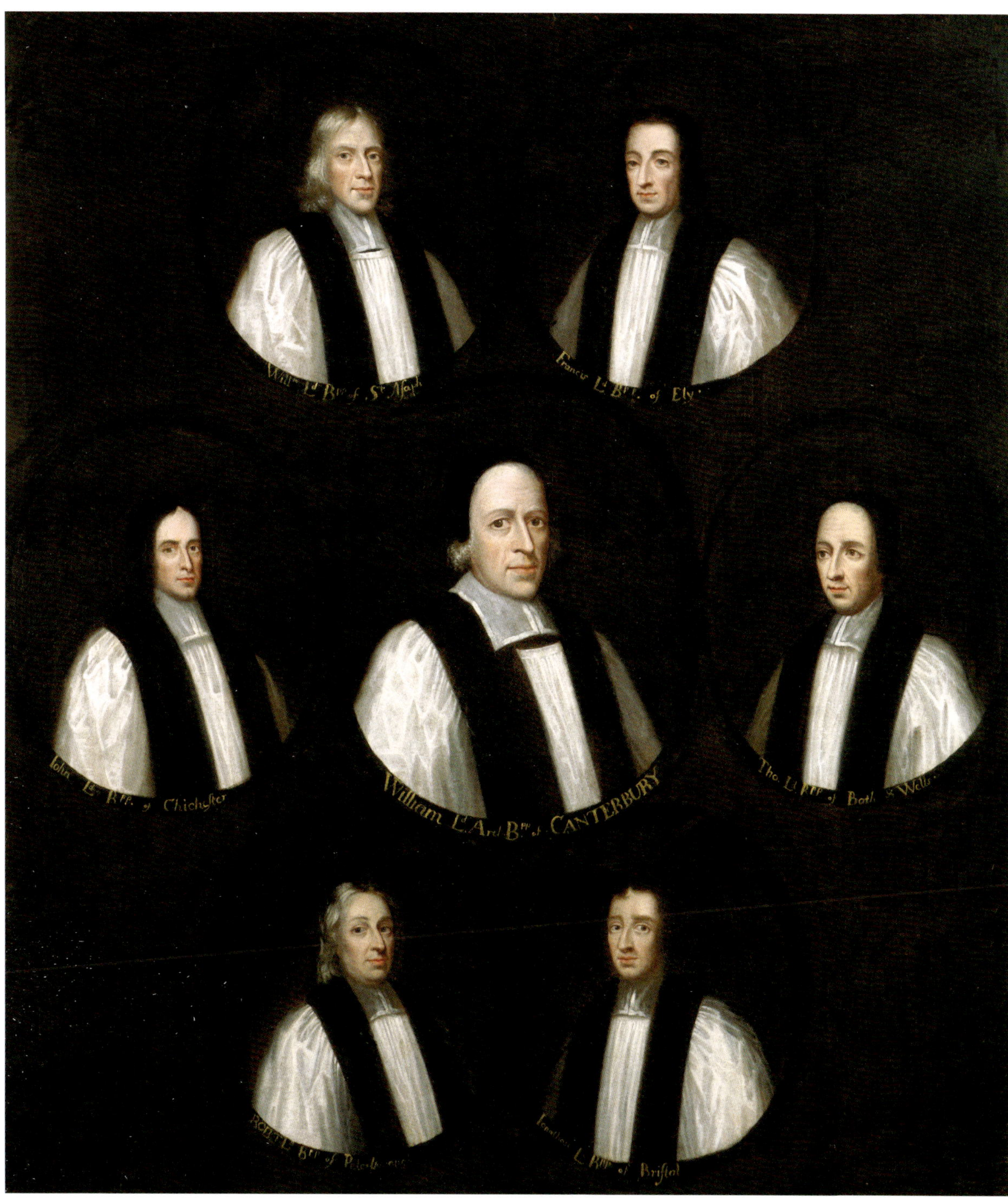
Willm Ld Bp of St Asaph
Francis Ld Bp of Ely
John Ld Bp of Chichester
William Ld Arch Bp of CANTERBURY
Tho. Ld Bp of Bath & Wells
ROBT Ld Bp of Peterborough
Jonathan Ld Bp of Bristol

from Wales and the bishops of Peterborough, Ely, Bath and Wells, Bristol and Chichester descended from their dioceses. Lloyd was their spokesman, personally submitting a petition to the King, who regarded the bishops' objections as an act of rebellion. Lloyd denied this, 'We would lose the last drop of our blood rather than lift up a finger against your Majesty', he averred.[6] News of the bishops' protest spread like wildfire, delighting Londoners who were shocked when the King ordered the arrests of the bishops on charges of seditious libel.

Lloyd, Sancroft, Turner, White, Lake, Trelawny and Ken found themselves in the Tower of London (Lloyd, Sancroft, Turner and Lake sat for their portraits by Mary Beale at various dates). The bishops' trial by jury gave a verdict of not guilty, so after their brief imprisonment the bishops were freed, to be greeted by jubilant crowds in New Palace Yard, Westminster. Lloyd was rescued from the fracas by the Earl of Clarendon's coach and driven to Clarendon's house in St James's Square.

The invitation to Prince William of Orange to take the throne was extended in the spring of 1688 and as a result the Prince landed at Torbay on 5 November. King James II attempted to escape on 11 December and finally embarked at Rochester a week later. Bishops Turner and Lloyd, with the Earls of Berkeley and Clarendon were among the peers of the realm assembled at the London Guildhall on 11 December to maintain national stability during the transitional period between the flight of James II and the accession of William and Mary in February 1689. Henry Hyde, Earl of Clarendon, uncle of the new Queen, was one of the first to support Prince William on his march towards London; Lloyd assisted at the coronation of William and Mary in April 1689 and in 1700 was promoted to the see of Worcester in succession to Bishop Edward Stillingfleet.

Eight bishops declined the call to the House of Lords in 1689, demonstrating their refusal to take the oath of loyalty to King William and Queen Mary. However, Gilbert Burnet was a steadfast supporter and was personally appointed by the King to be Bishop of Salisbury (his second portrait by Mary Beale was commissioned soon after his appointment, a third around 1690–91). Bishop John Tillotson, first painted by Mary Beale in 1664, was especially favoured by Queen Mary and was promoted to Archbishop of Canterbury in 1691. Symon Patrick, who had sat for Mary Beale in the 1670s and in 1681 was again painted by her as Bishop of Winchester in 1689, returning to her painting-room in 1693 when he was Bishop of Ely. Thomas

Tenison was first painted by Mary Beale 'upon Account of Kindness and not profitt',[7] when he was vicar of St-Martin-in-the-Fields in 1681. He was consecrated Bishop of Lincoln in 1692, prompting a second portrait by Beale, and a third, attributed to Beale, is inscribed 'Thomas Cantuar' with the Archbishop's coat of arms (he was enthroned at Canterbury Cathedral in May 1695).

The careers of Burnet, Tenison, Lloyd and Bishop Richard Kidder were advanced through the influence of Daniel Finch FRS (1647–1730), 2nd Earl of Nottingham, Earl of Winchilsea and Secretary of State to King William and Queen Mary. His father, Lord Chancellor Heneage Finch (1621–1682), was the stepson of Elizabeth Cradock,

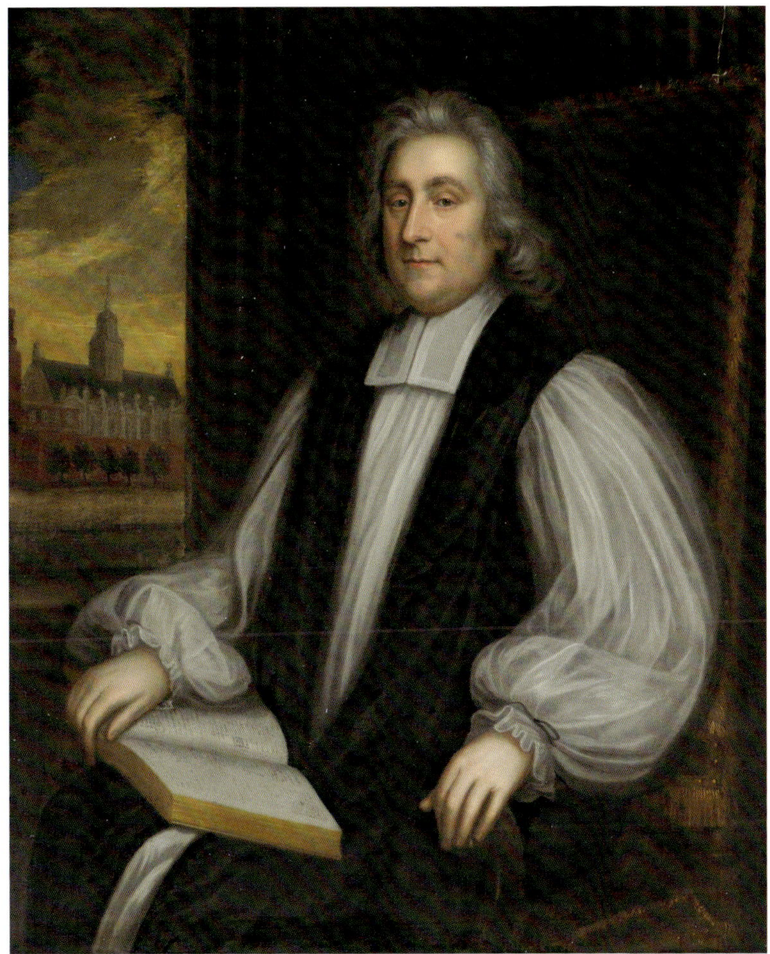

Mary Beale (attributed to), *Dr Thomas Tenison, Bishop of Lincoln*, 1692. King William III nominated Tenison to the see of Lincoln in 1691 and he was installed in 1692. He was consecrated Archbishop of Canterbury in 1695

daughter of William Cradock of Staffordshire, and the relationship brought Mary Beale commissions. In 1677 she completed portraits of Daniel Finch (known as 'Don Dismal', he was a tall thin man with a swarthy complexion) and his wife. When Lady Finch died in 1684, Daniel mourned the loss of 'one that I loved as myself and that loved me more than herself…I once had the best woman in the world', he wrote to the Countess of Warwick.[8] The Cradock/Finch connection led to Mary Beale's portraits of Lady Finch's sisters, Lady St John and Lady Rich, Lady Maidstone, wife of William Finch Viscount Maidstone, and Dr Leopold Finch, Warden of All Souls College, Oxford.

Another Cradock connection was with Richard Kidder (1635

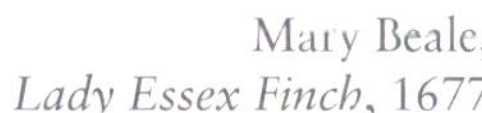
Mary Beale, *Lady Essex Finch*, 1677

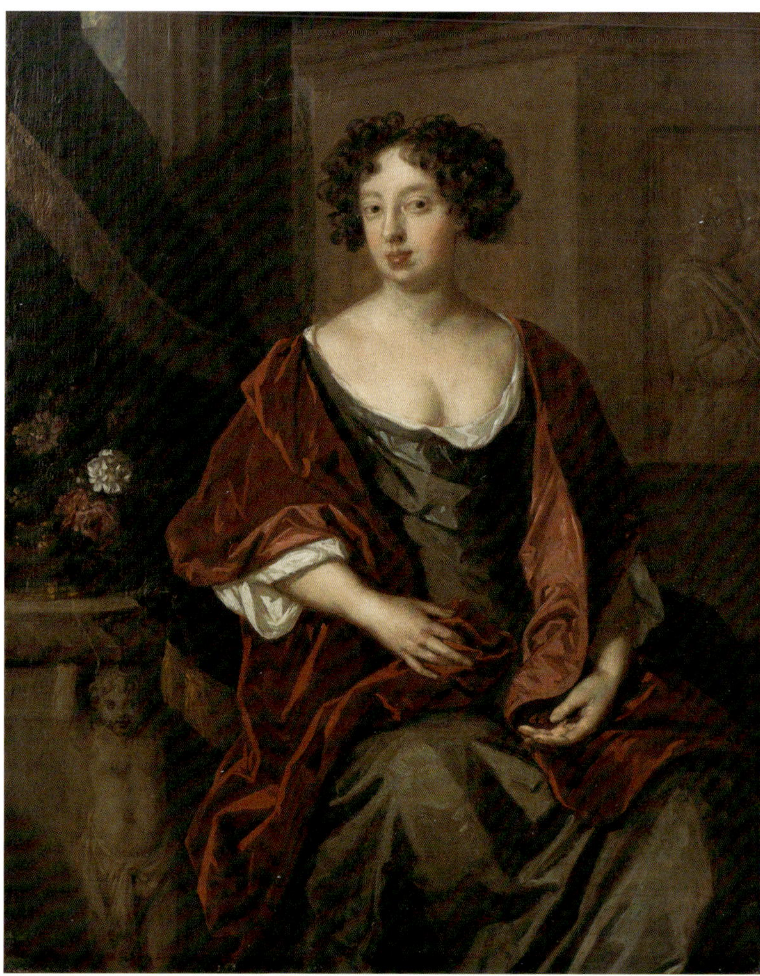

–1703), chaplain to William and Mary, Dean of Peterborough from 1689 and Bishop of Bath and Wells from 1691 until his tragic death. Kidder had been nurtured at Emmanuel College, Cambridge, by the Reverend Samuel Cradock, a distant cousin of Mary Beale. 'Mr Cradock I can never forget. He was very tender of me, and the greater part of my subsistence was owing to him', Kidder remembered. 'Tis hardly possible that one man can owe to another more than I do to him'.[9] Kidder's portrait by Beale, painted while he was Bishop of Bath and Wells, is at Emmanuel College, Cambridge, with that of his colleague, Dr George Thorp (1638–1719). Kidder and his wife were killed during the night of 26-27 November 1703 when a violent storm caused a chimneystack of the bishop's palace to collapse, crushing the sleeping couple.

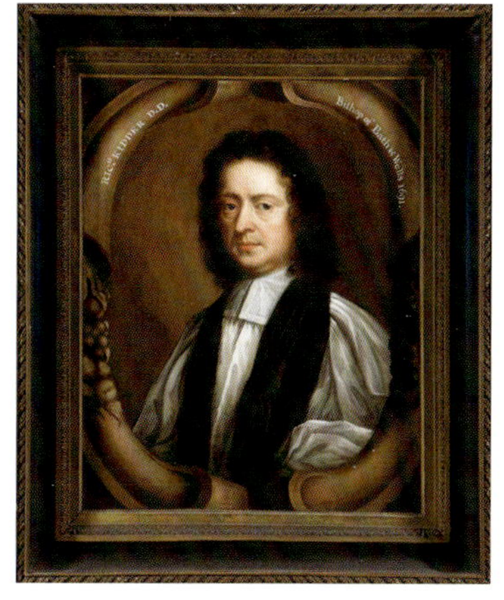

Mary Beale, *Bishop Richard Kidder*, possibly 1691 when he was installed as Bishop of Bath and Wells

Two more bishops came Mrs Beale's way: Bishop Humphrey Humphreys (1648–1712) was painted soon after his appointment to the see of Bangor in 1689. Similarly, she painted Bishop James Gardiner (1637–1705) at the time of his promotion to the bishopric of Lincoln in 1695.

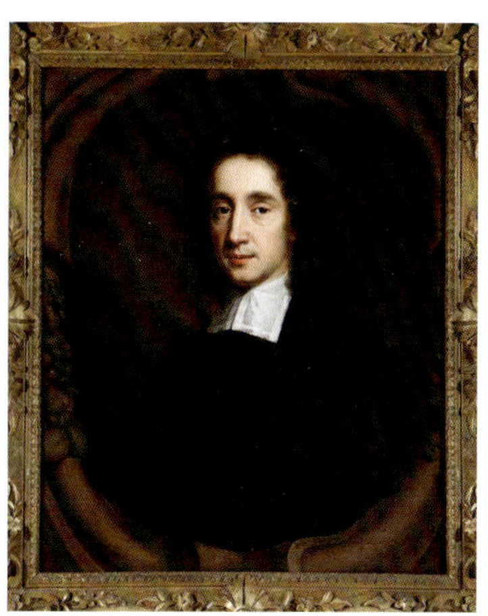

Mary Beale, *Dr George Thorp*, c. 1682

Jacobites

The accession of King William III and Queen Mary II was not welcomed by all. The King was obsessed with the war against France and was regularly threatened by Jacobite intrigues that focussed on 'the king across the water'. Mary Beale's brother, the Reverend John Cradock (1643–1714) was an outspoken Jacobite, which may explain why there is no mention of him in Charles Beale's almanacks, nor is there evidence that he was painted by his sister. John Cradock had been educated at King Edward VI's grammar school, Bury St Edmunds, and at Emmanuel College, Cambridge. After ordination he maintained his family's connection with Suffolk where he was Rector of Rickinghall from 1673 to 1712. Cradock received £900 from King Charles II in the early 1680s, for 'secret services' rendered to the crown.[10] A decade later, his support for Charles's brother, the exiled James II, brought him to the attention of the authorities.

In 1691 the Reverend John Cradock with Thomas Thurlow a cleric, Henry Rayner an apothecary, a vintner, and four other gentlemen were charged with riotous and treasonable offences. It was claimed that they 'did riotously assemble themselves at Bottersdale and did consult and what ways and means they might bring back King James'. Cradock and the apothecary Rayner who had been in contact with King James during the summer, were heard singing a bawdy song,

William and Mary, a son of a whore,
Who turn'd his father out of door,
William and Mary, George and Anne,
The Devill himself loved such a one.

A conspiracy was suspected: Cradock and his fellow Jacobites were reported to have drunk King James's health and sworn 'Damnacion to King William and Queen Mary and their army'.[11] Trouble was averted; John Cradock amended his behaviour and remained rector of Rickinghall until two years before his death.

Bishops, peers of the realm and country clergy were threatened with imprisonment and the loss of livelihood if they failed to take the oath of allegiance to King William and Queen Mary. In these circumstances, ardent Jacobites such as Mary Beale's patron, the 4th Earl of Lauderdale, chose to follow King James II to France. The 2nd Duke of Newcastle (painted by Beale in 1677) refused to take the oath; Lord Charles Murray (whose portrait was painted by Beale in 1676) was imprisoned by order of King William III, whereas it was Queen Mary who instigated the arrest of her uncle, the Beales' neighbour and patron, the Earl of Clarendon. He was confined to the Tower of London, accompanied for a time by his wife, who had entertained Charles and Mary Beale at Swallowfield in 1668.

Mary Beale, *Bishop Francis Turner*, c. 1683-8

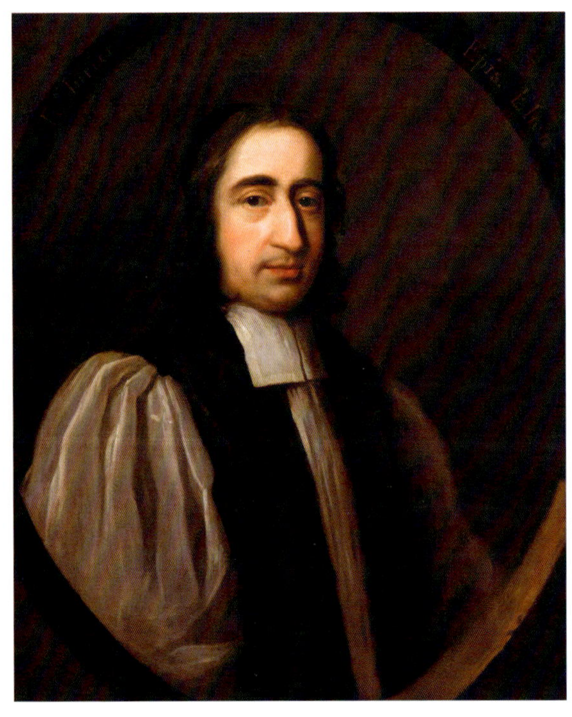

Clergy who refused to take the oath of allegiance were suspended from their livings. The legality of their position was defended by the lawyer and politician, Roger North, himself called before the House of Lords regarding prosecutions during the two previous reigns. North's family lived near Bury St Edmunds and with his brothers, Roger attended the same school as Mary Beale's brother. Roger North sat for his portrait by Mary Beale in 1677;[12] and he must have introduced her to Dr George Hickes (1642–1715), antiquary and author, painted by Mrs Beale that year. Hickes was suspended as Dean of Worcester in 1689 and sheltered from the authorities by North.

Bishop Francis Turner (1637–1700), Master of St John's College, Cambridge, from 1670 was an infamous Jacobite conspirator who was arrested, then went into hiding during the reign of William and Mary. Bishop John Lake (1624–1689) was twice imprisoned for refusing to sacrifice his principles, once by the parliamentarians (he fought for King Charles I at Basing House and Wallingford prior to his ordination in 1647). Secondly, Lake found himself in the Tower in 1688 with Lloyd and their fellow bishops. His portrait by Mary Beale commemorated his appointment to the see of Chichester in 1685, from which he was suspended by the new regime in 1689.

Mary Beale's last portraits

It was probably through Sir William Morice, who in 1651 purchased Werrington Park and the manor of Launceston in Cornwall from Sir Francis Drake Bt, that Mary Beale was introduced to local families. She painted Morice's daughter, Anne, wife of Sir John Pole 3rd Bt, his grand-daughter, Lady Carew, and a portrait of Morice exhibited in 1866 may be by Beale. Lady Pole's father-in-law was the cavalier

Left: Mary Beale, *Sir Courtenay Pole Bt*, signed and dated 1670

Right: Mary Beale, *Lady Pole*, c. 1670

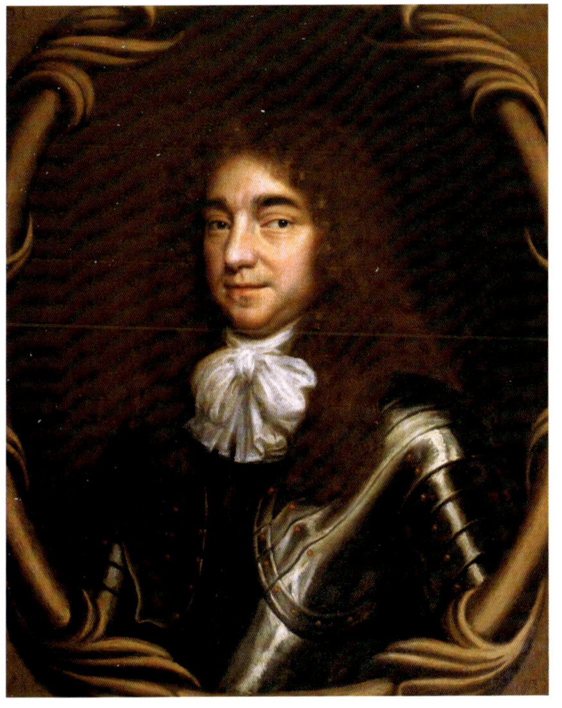

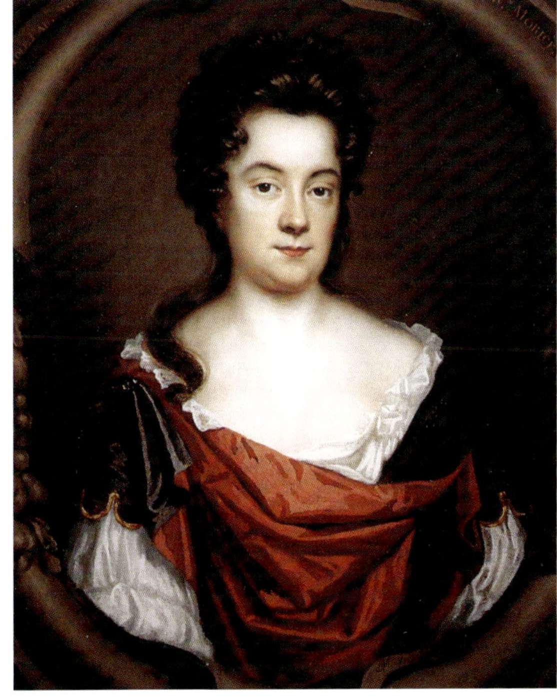

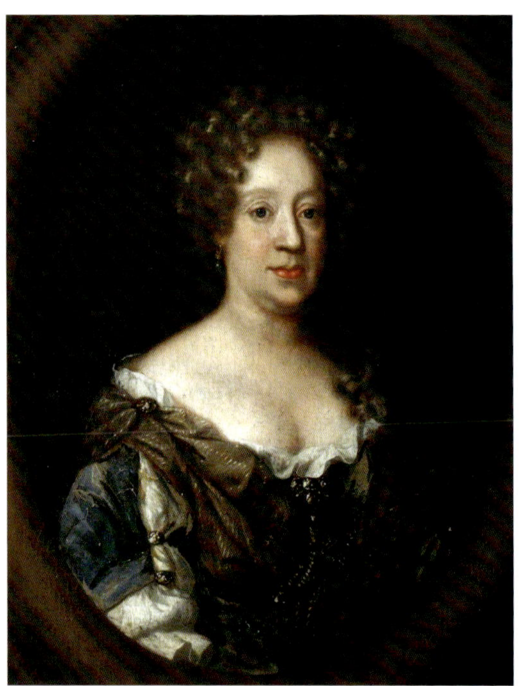

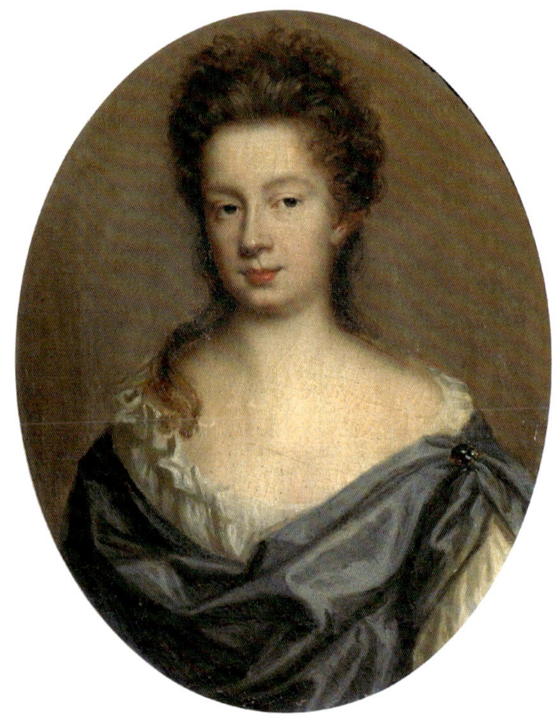

Left: Mary Beale (attributed to), *Mrs John Buller of Morval, née Anne Goode*, c. 1675-85

Right: Mary Beale, *Lady Carew*, c. 1685-90

Sir Courtenay Pole Bt (1619–1695) of Shute House, Colyton, who chose to be painted in armour (1670). Pole's main achievement was the introduction of the hearth tax in 1662, for which he was called 'Sir Chimney Pool'. His portrait is at Antony House, near Saltash, Cornwall, along with a portrait of Anne Goode (b. 1639, daughter and heiress of John Goode of Morval, later Mrs Buller), attributed to Mary Beale. Sir John Carew 3rd Bt (1635–1692) of Antony married three times. His third wife, Mary (née Morice), and two daughters by his first wife, Jane and Rachel, and the Reverend William Carew sat for Mary Beale. Her portrait of Rachel Carew, who married Ambrose Manaton of Kilworthy, is said to have inspired Daphne du Maurier's novel, *My Cousin Rachel* (1951). The claim is supported by the fact that Rachel's sister, Jane, was the second wife of John Rashleigh of Menabilly House, Fowey, leased from Philip Rashleigh by du Maurier from 1943 to 1969. Menabilly was the inspiration for the romantic house called Manderley in du Maurier's novels.

Mary Beale completed her last portraits in the 1690s. These pictures of familiar subjects are some of her best, for example Stillingfleet (1690), Burnet (1691), Kidder, (1691), Woodford

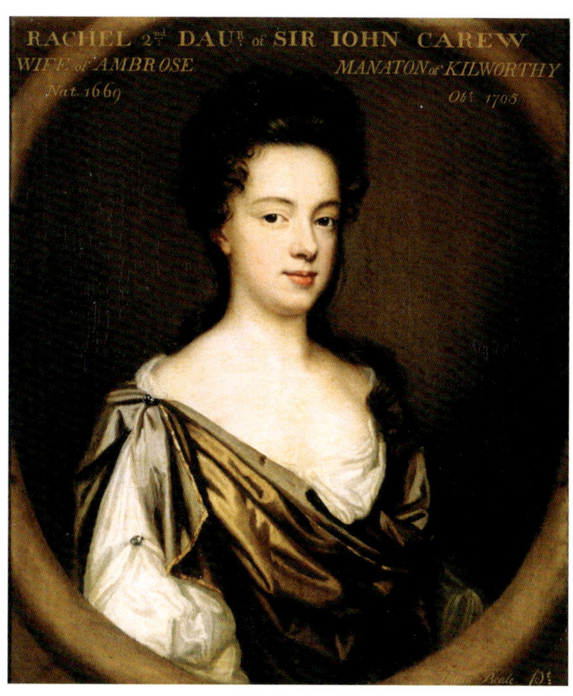

Mary Beale, *Mrs Ambrose Manaton of Kilworthy, née Rachel Carew*, c. 1692–5

Top: Mary Beale, *Reverend William Cremer*, c. 1692

Below: Mary Beale, *Thomas Fountayne*, 1690s. The inscription lower left refers to his death in 1708

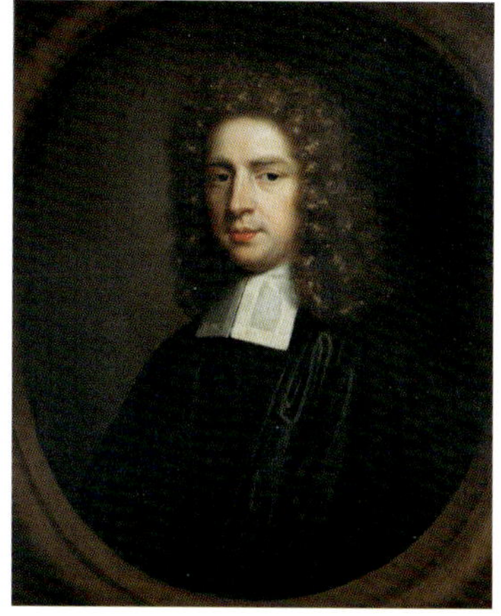

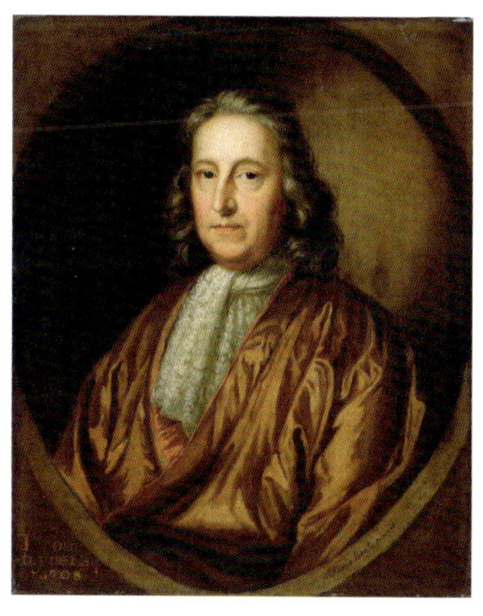

(1692), Gardiner (1695) and the portrait of Tenison as Archbishop of Canterbury is attributed to her (1695). Her portrait of the Norfolk vicar, the Reverend William Cremer, is signed, and has been dated to around 1692. Thomas Fountayne (1641–1709) a barrister of Melton, Yorkshire, was also signed 'Maria Beale' and painted during this last bout of her activity; Fountayne knew Mary Beale through Bishop Symon Patrick, whose son married Fountayne's daughter.

Post mortem

Mary Beale died aged sixty-five in 1699 at the family's house near the sign of The Golden Ball, Pall Mall, and was buried below the communion table at St James's Piccadilly, on 8 October. Belatedly, in 2001, a memorial plaque to her was erected on the north wall of the church, near one remembering the botanical artist Mary Delaney (d. 1788), also of Pall Mall.

With the death of his 'Dearest Heart', Charles Beale lost his *raison d'être*, emotionally and professionally, and went to live with his eldest son, Bartholomew (1656–1709) in Coventry, where he died in 1705 at the age of seventy-three. Bartholomew had chosen medicine as a career and qualified from Clare College, Cambridge, in 1682. He practised as a physician in Coventry where he had inherited a property called Pannyer from his great uncle, John Beale (1587–1643) of the Stationers' Company. Dr Bartholomew Beale was the author of an ambitious treatise dedicated to Robert Harley, Earl of Oxford, which attempted to fathom the 'true causes of all disease proceeding from vicious bloods' (1706). He was survived by his widow Ann (d. 1726), and their daughter, Ann Keeling.

George Vertue recorded that at the time of Mary Beale's death one self portrait was in the hands of Mr Minshull of Lincoln's Inn Fields and another belonged to Dr J. Harris FRS.[13] In 1722, a small half-length portrait of her 'painted by Sir Peter Lilly in his best manner' was on the market and was purchased by Mr Raynard for £16 10 shillings in the sale of Peter Cross's collection.[14] A double portrait of Charles and Mary Beale by Lely was inherited by Mrs Wilson of Ormond Street, the widow of Wilson the banker (Charles Beale junior was lodging with them at the time of his death and owed them money).[15]

In a working life of some forty years Mary Beale completed no less than 160 oil paintings with at least another forty attributed to her. In addition, she was a competent painter of watercolour miniatures. Only a few of these have been traced: the earliest, signed and dated 1674 is of Henry Somerset, 1st Duke of Beaufort. A miniature self portrait of 1679, last seen in the United States of America, is inscribed on the reverse 'Mrs Mary Beale a famous woman for painting ye head, in the Pall Mall. Died at ye age of...years in the year 1698 (this sold for 1,800 guineas in 1971). A miniature of Catherine Sedley, Countess of Dorchester, described as 'somewhat coarse' is initialled MB, so could be by Mary Beale.[16]

On his visits to country houses during the second half of the eighteenth century, Horace Walpole saw at Melbury House, Dorsetshire, Mary Beale's portrait of the house's former owner, Colonel Giles Strangways (Walpole thought the artist was Robert Walker). Walpole also saw at Melbury 'eight heads in Stone-coloured frames of a Master and fellows of a college in Oxford by Mrs Beales, among them are Tillotson and Stillingfleet'. He noted that her portrait of the Hon. Henry Coventry, Secretary of State, was at Longleat House, Wiltshire, where he also saw 'Two Lady Thynnes, much dressed' (Mary Thynne, Coventry's sister, and Frances Thynne, Viscountess Weymouth, were painted by Beale in

1677). 'Mr Lovibonde of Hampton has several pictures that were Mrs Beales; twenty small copies of Sir Peter Lely among which are two of Mrs Godfrey [Arabella Churchill, mistress of the Duke of York prior to her marriage to Colonel Charles Godfrey], Cowley with a flute and a crook, a copy of the same in Indian ink by Charles Beale (initialled). Sir Palmes Fairborne the Admiral by Mrs Beale',[17] (Fairborne, 1644–1680, was a governor of Tangier). Walpole coveted Edward Lovibond's collection and purchased several portraits at the Lovibond sale in 1776.

Charles Beale junior (1660–1714 or 1726)

The Beales' younger son, Charles, was a gifted draughtsman whose early promise was blighted by declining eyesight. He trained in his mother's studio and received instruction in miniature painting from Thomas Flatman. 'I sent my son Charles to Mr Flatman's', his father wrote in 1677, 'in order to his beginning to learn to limne of him. This same time I set my son Barth's picture upon a yard Cloth done extremely well by my Dearest Heart for Charles to make his first Essay in Colour in water upon'.[18] Sixteen miniatures by Charles Beale and about a dozen of his oil paintings were traced by Richard Jeffree during his researches.[19]

Charles Beale's miniatures being 'inconsistent in style, technique and quality and with different monograms', are difficult to identify with certainty.[20] They date from 1679 to 1688, beginning with a luminous portrait of his mother and a copy of Sir Peter Lely's self portrait.

Charles Beale junior painted miniatures copied from the portrait of Bishop Antoine Triest owned by his parents, from their painting of 'Venus and Cupid' by Hanneman, portraits of

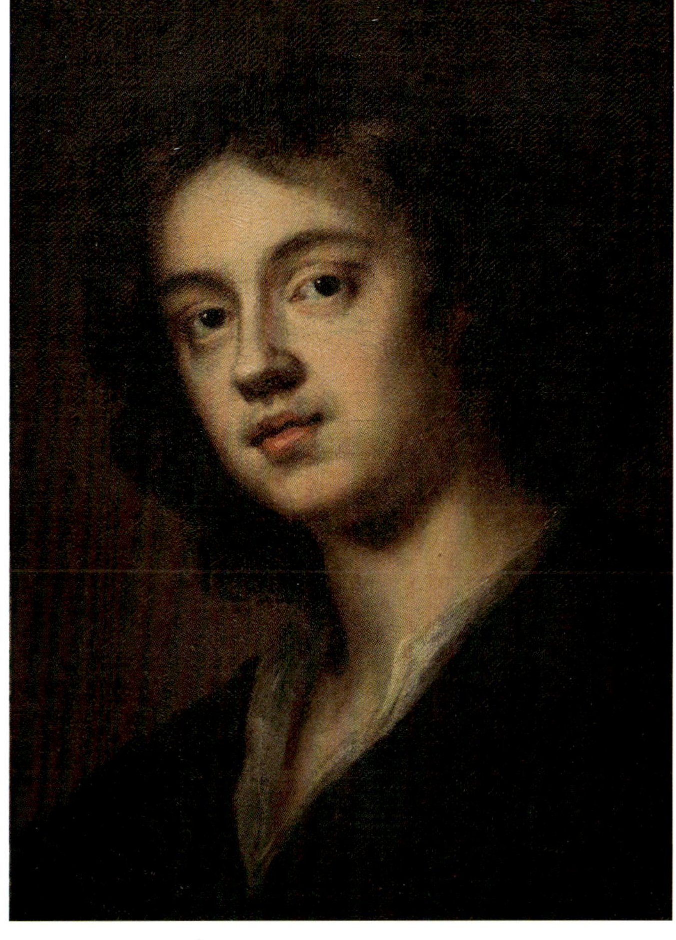

Mary Beale, *Charles Beale junior*, c. 1681

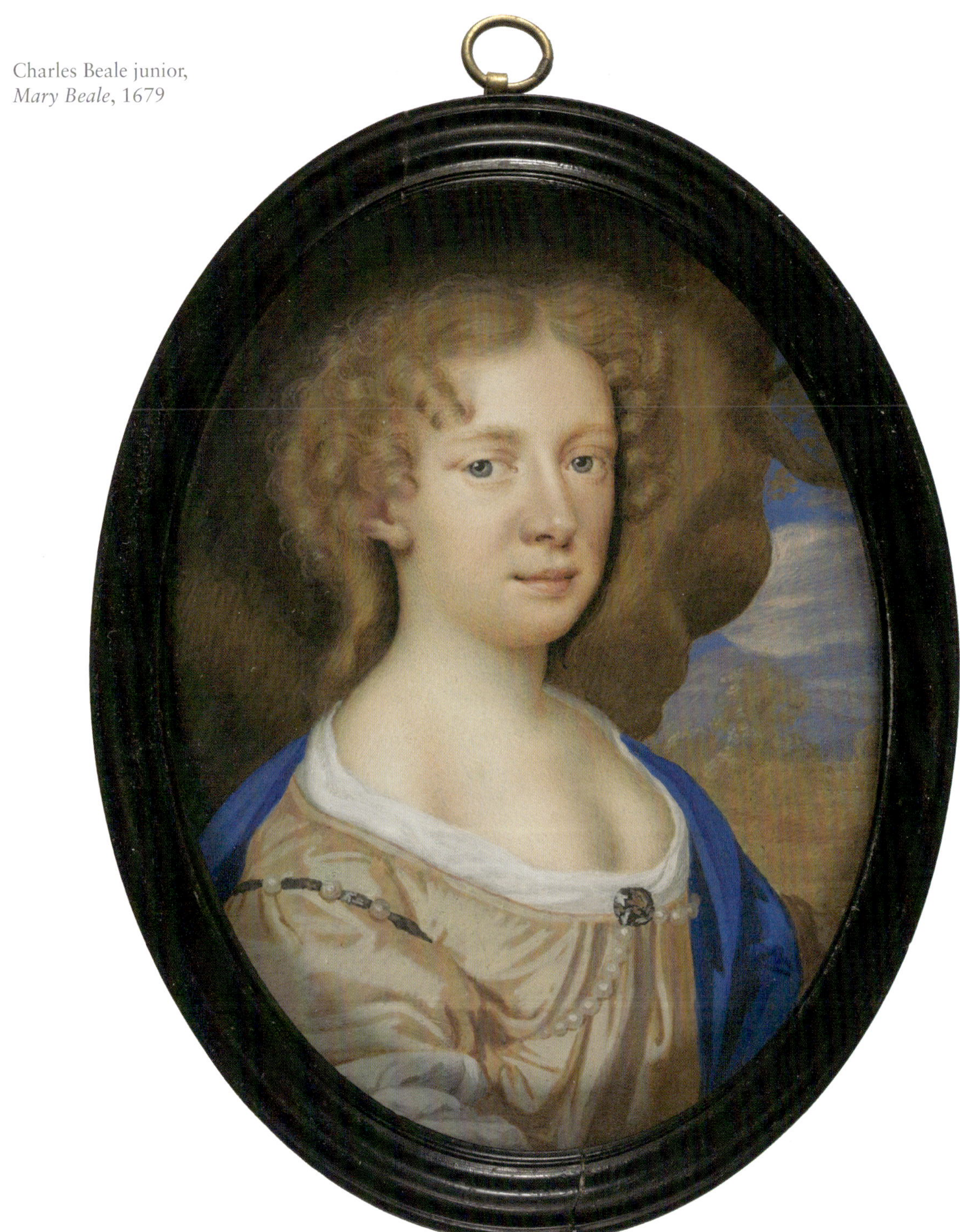

Charles Beale junior,
Mary Beale, 1679

the 4th Earl of Lauderdale and his wife, and Hezekiah Burton and Edward Stillingfleet, whom his mother had painted. Similarly, his miniature of John Tillotson, judged by Vertue as 'tollerable',[21] now in the collection of Her Majesty the Queen, was probably based on one of Mary Beale's portraits of the Archbishop. Charles Beale junior has also been credited with miniatures of Sir Isaac Newton, Samuel Pepys, the Reverend Charles Whalley and a man thought to be the poet John Dryden (1693).[22]

That inveterate collector, Horace Walpole, admired the work of Mary Beale and her son, and paintings by both adorned the walls of his Gothic villa, Strawberry Hill, Twickenham. Walpole chose six miniatures by Charles Beale for his bedchamber, while Mary Beale's paintings were in the green closet and the gallery.[23] At Earl Waldegrave's sale of the contents of Strawberry Hill in 1842, miniatures by Mary Beale of herself and her son, Charles, were still *in situ*. Mary's copy of Lely's portrait of Anne Hyde, Duchess of York, was displayed in a prominent position in the magnificent gallery, set into a gilded canopy above the entrance door, and the self portrait of Lely copied by Charles Beale junior from the original belonging to his parents, hung in the yellow bedchamber. Charles Beale's miniatures of Charles II, James Duke of York and Mary Princess of Orange as children, copied from Van Dyck's originals, were for sale, also Charles's miniature of Elizabeth Wriothesley, the Duchess of Montagu (one of Lely's 'Windsor Beauties'), and 'nineteen small heads in oil of the court of Charles II except Saccharissa [the Countess of Sunderland] copied by Jarvis and bought at his house at Hampton by Mr Lovibond'.[24] These 'nineteen small heads in oil' seem to have been copied by Charles Jarvis/Jervas from the 'twenty small copies of Sir Peter Lely' by Mary Beale, which Walpole had seen at Lovibond's house.

Hundreds of Charles Beale's red chalk drawings are preserved at the Department of Prints and Drawings of the British Museum. Previously attributed to his mother, they are 'unlike almost any other British drawings that have survived from the seventeenth century, with the possible exception of Samuel Cooper'.[25] The drawings, some in the original sketchbooks, others individually mounted, range from spontaneous sketches to worked-up portraits of sleeping children, young women, friends and servants: these characters and cats add a warm, personal dimension to the Beales' household. Girls known as 'Buttermilk', 'Mumping Nan', and Thompson Norris the porter can be identified as the Beales' servants, artisans and friends.

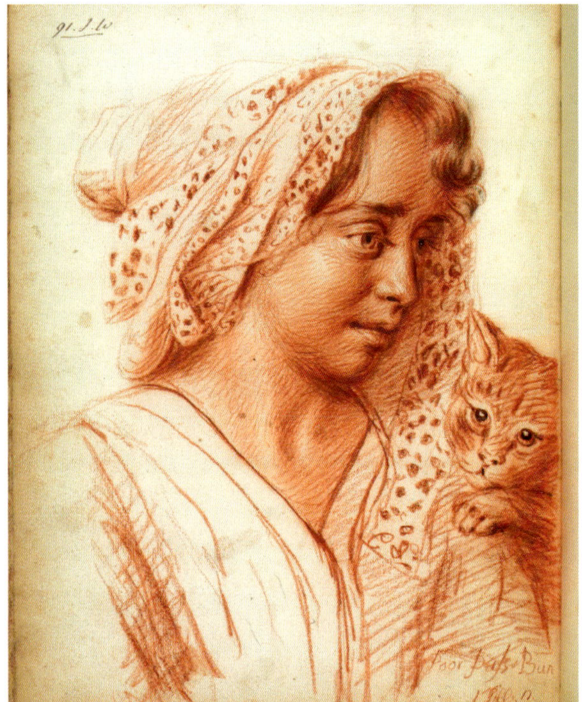

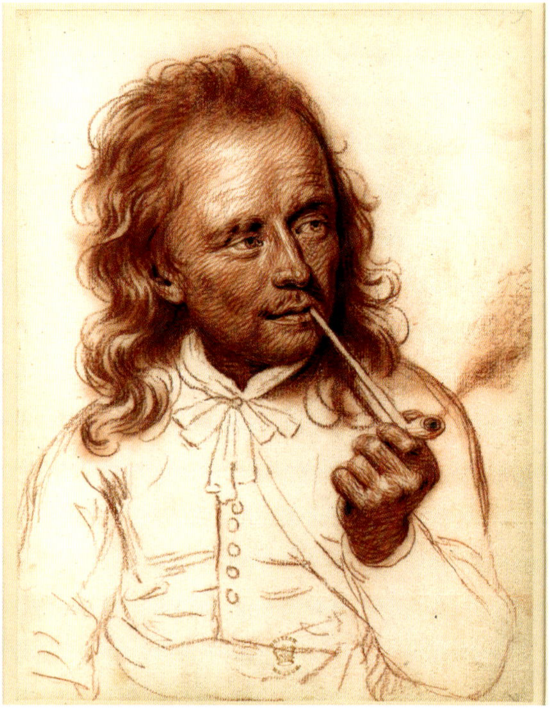

Above left: Charles Beale junior, *Susan Gill, with 'Poor Puss Bun'*, 1680

Above right: Charles Beale junior, *Tom Norris*, 1680

Charles drew the Carter family, Susan Gill the maid, Moll Trioche who modelled for his mother, young Sampson, son of the family's shoemaker, the daughter of their landlord, Symons, and a boy who was probably one of the sons of Dr Thomas Sydenham, the Beales' neighbour in Pall Mall.[26]

Latterly, Charles Beale junior turned to oil painting. A portrait of the Hon. Robert Cecil (1667–1717) at Hatfield House is signed Carolus Beale and dated 1689. His other portraits in oils include Charles Fox (son of Sir Stephen Fox, one of Mary Beale's patrons), Henry Barwell, a Leicestershire lawyer, and his wife (1693), and the seductive Jane Bohun, one of three sisters who inherited the franchise of Spitalfields Market, London, from their father, George Bohun MP (1642–1705). In 1712 Jane married Colonel George Lucy of Charlecote Park, Warwickshire, where her portrait remains (Mary Beale had painted Lady Lucy, Colonel George's mother, 1673–4).

Country gentlemen such as Peter Foulkes and Sir Charles Holte Bt sat for Charles Beale, also a flamboyant young man of the Packer family. Two oval portraits of Charles Beale's cousins, Mr and Mrs

Bartholomew Beale of Shropshire, signed and dated 1693, were discovered by Richard Jeffree in the 1960s and form part of his bequest to St Edmundsbury Borough Council.

The date of Charles Beale junior's death has been disputed. Vertue reported that he died in 1714 in Long Acre where he lodged. However, one of Beale's sketchbooks, 'the 3rd Book 1680', is inscribed 'Charles Beale's Book. Anno Domini 1721', indicative of his activity at that date but the note may not be his own handwriting. To add to the uncertainty, a Charles Beal/Beale was buried at St Martin-in-the-Fields in 1726.

Descendants

Charles Beale junior died unmarried and childless. His elder brother, Dr Bartholomew Beale of Coventry, predeceased him in 1709, leaving a widow and a daughter. Mary Beale's brother, the Reverend John Cradock, married Elizabeth (d. 1700) and secondly Mary; of his nine children, two sons were clergymen: John, rector of Layham 1754–6, and William, rector of Rickinghall in Suffolk 1723–42. Charles Beale's nephew, Bartholomew (1651–1724) purchased Bildeston Hall, Suffolk, and Bartholomew's daughter Jane (d. 1764) married Jacob Brand of Polstead Hall. Thus the Beale/Cradock roots in Suffolk were nurtured into the eighteenth century.

The Beales' connections with Buckinghamshire, however, did not last beyond the seventeenth century. The manor house, north-west of St Michael's church, Walton, had been acquired by John and Bartholomew Beale in 1622. After the deaths of Bartholomew and his wife, the brothers Bartholomew Beale junior and Charles (Mary Beale's husband), Richard Gilpin and others settled the manor on George and Thomas Gilpin in 1668 (the Reverend Theodore Beale's daughter, Dionysia, married George Gilpin). The Gilpins secured their hold on Walton manor and estate before selling it to Sir Thomas Pinfold (1638–1701), who demolished the manor house. Walton is now dominated by the buildings of the Open University, set in verdant gardens and parkland. Despite modern development, the deconsecrated St Michael's church survives, complete with its splendid monument to Charles Beale's parents, Bartholomew and Katherine.

The other substantial Beale property, Heath House, a seventeenth-century mansion at Leintwardine, Herefordshire, was, with Hopton Castle in Shropshire, the seat of Charles Beale's brother Bartholomew

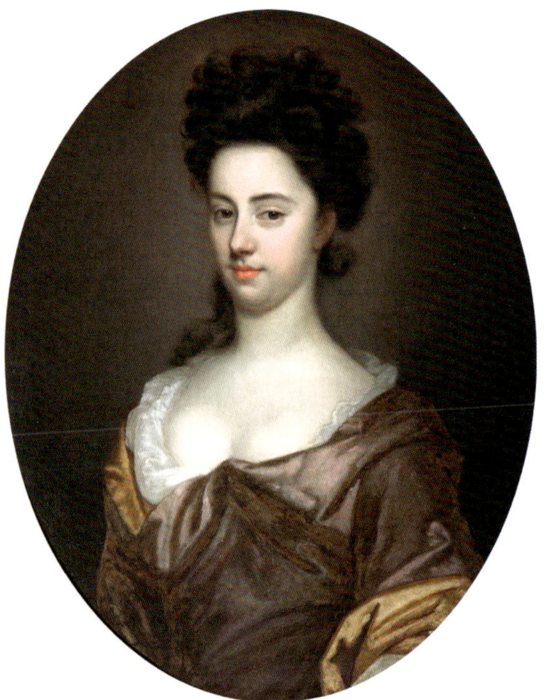

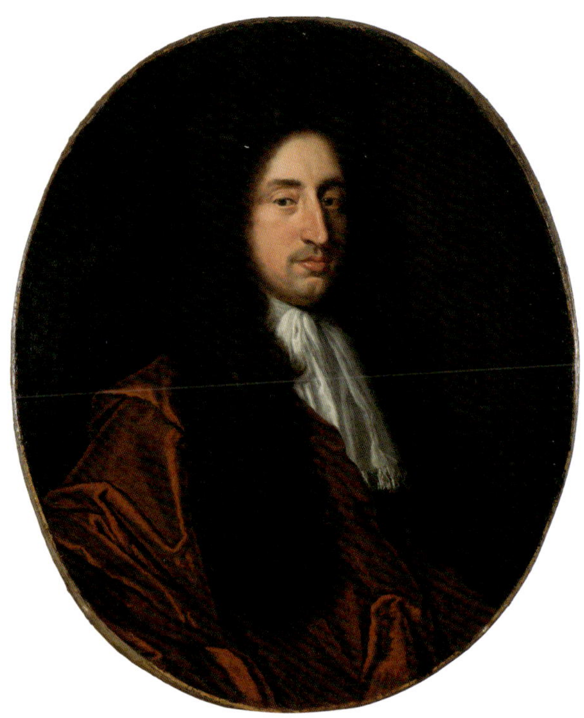

Above left: Charles Beale junior, *Jane Bohun*. The portrait may mark her marriage to Colonel George Lucy in 1712

Above right: Charles Beale junior, *Bartholomew Beale*, 1693

and his wife Elizabeth. The Herefordshire/Shropshire properties were inherited by Thomas Beale (1787–1845) who married Catherine Salwey of Moor Park, Shropshire. Heath House remained in the possession of the Beale family until it was sold with its contents in the late nineteenth century. The medieval Hopton Castle, besieged by royalist forces in 1644, had been acquired by the Beales in 1655 and was sold in 1890 (the ruined castle has since been preserved and is open to the public).

Charles Beale's sister, Margaret, married John Brydges/Bridges in 1636. Their eldest son, John, purchased the manor of Barton Seagrave, Northamptonshire, where he died in 1712. One of his sons, Charles (1672–1747), was a portrait painter who emigrated to Williamsburg, Virginia, where he painted eminent families. John and Margaret Bridges' second son, Brook (1644–1717), whose portrait Mary Beale commissioned from Lely in 1671 and which she later copied,[27] was an Auditor of the Imprests from 1672 to 1705. He purchased Goodnestone Park in Kent in 1700, where the house was rebuilt by his son, the 1st Baronet Bridges FRS (1679–1728).

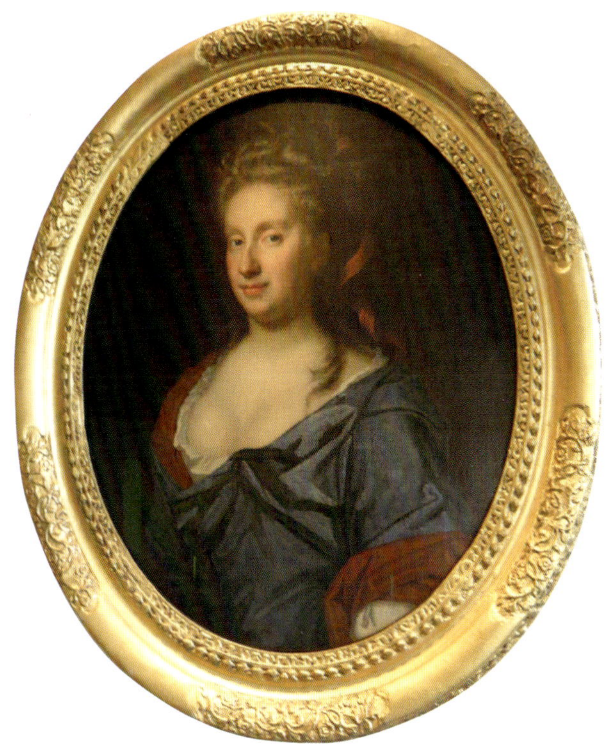

Charles Beale junior,
Elizabeth Beale, 1693

Elizabeth Bridges, daughter of the 3rd Baronet, married Edward Austen (1767–1852), Jane Austen's brother. The author stayed at Goodnestone and, either during or soon after her visit of 1796, she wrote *Pride and Prejudice*. Goodnestone remained the family seat of the Bridges until the end of the nineteenth century.

The Beale family of Birmingham, eminent lawyers, businessmen and politicians, believed they were descendants of Charles and Mary Beale. Accordingly, Sir William Phipson Beale Bt (1839–1922) MP for Ayrshire, acquired one of the younger Charles Beale's sketchbooks. Likewise, his sister, Miss Helen Mary Beale, owned a Charles Beale sketchbook, stored in a box inscribed 'Mrs Mary Beale's Sketches Anno Domini 1665 to 1675'. Hugh Beale also claimed to be a descendant of Mary, and was the proud owner of a self portrait of Mary dated to 1681.

The Beale family of West Lodge Park Hotel, Hertfordshire, have a connection with Mary Beale through her patron, the Hon. Henry Coventry, Secretary of State to King Charles II, who acquired the West Park estate in 1673. Trevor and Andrew Beale, owners of the hotel,

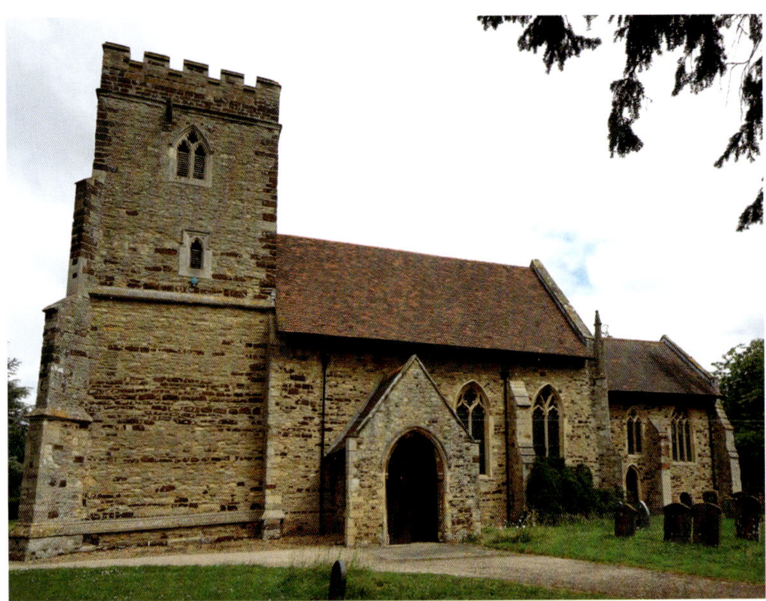

Left: St Michael's church, Walton, Buckinghamshire, the parish church of the Beale family in the seventeenth century

do not appear to be related to the Beales of Buckinghamshire (their ancestors were from Hertfordshire). Nonetheless, Andrew Beale is enthusiastic about Mary Beale, and at West Lodge Park Hotel the Mary Beale restaurant opened in 2009. It forms a sympathetic setting for portraits collected by Andrew Beale's family, supplemented by several on loan from the Richard Jeffree bequest. Jeffree died in 1991 aged sixty-one, having studied Mary Beale for some thirty years. He left fourteen portraits by her and two by her son Charles to the National Art Collections Fund with the request that they should join four Beale portraits already owned by St Edmundsbury Borough Council. An exhibition of the collection, dedicated to *Mrs Mary Beale, Paintress* was held at The Manor House Museum, Bury St Edmunds, in 1994. When that Museum closed in 2006, the portraits were transferred to the Moyses Hall Museum, a twelfth-century building at Cornhill, Bury St Edmunds. The museum at Bury St Edmunds, Mary's market town when she lived at Barrow in the seventeenth century, boasts the largest collection of her work under one roof.

1. Samuel Woodford dedicated his poem 'Belisa', published in *A Paraphrase Upon the Canticles and some Select hymns of the New and Old Testaments with other occasional compositions in English verse,* (1679), to 'The Excellent Mrs Mary Beal'. The title of the exhibition catalogue of Mary Beale's work (1975) amended the spelling to Beale

2. CBA 1677. Bartholomew and Charles Beale junior painted the drapery

3. *Ibid.*, 10 May 1677

4. CBA April 1677

5. *Ibid.*, 25 January 1681

6. Agnes Strickland, *The Lives of the Seven Bishops committed to the Tower in 1688,* (1866), p. 61

7. CBA 1681

8. Charlotte Fell Smith, *Mary Rich, Countess of Warwick (1625–78). Her Family and Friends*, (1901), pp. 302-3

9. Amy Edith Robinson, *The Life of Richard Kidder DD, Bishop of Bath and Wells, written by himself*, (1924), p. 4

10. *Moneys received and paid for Secret Services of Charles II and James II 1679-1688,'* Camden Society 52 (1851), pp. 49, 78

11. Harley Ms 6853, ff.10, 12, 16, 17, 61, 231, BL

12. CBA 29 December 1677

13. 'Vertue Note Books I', *Walpole Society* 18 (1930), p. 54

14. *Ibid.*, pp. 105, 107-8

15. 'Vertue Note Books IV', *Walpole Society* 24 (1936), p. 65

16. G. C. Williamson, 'Mr Francis Wellesley's Collection of Miniatures and Drawings', *Connoisseur* 51 (1918), p. 69

17. Paget Toynbee, 'Horace Walpole's Journals of Visits to Country Seats', *Walpole Society* 16 (1928), pp. 45, 47, 69

18. CBA 5 March 1677. This picture of Bartholomew, 'done extremely well' by his mother and copied in watercolour by his brother, Charles, may be the portrait formerly thought to be Abraham Cowley

19. Jeffree and Walsh research notes (*c.*1970-90), 2/1, Ms 128, Heinz Archive and Library, NPG

20. John Murdoch, *Seventeenth-Century English Miniatures in the Collection of the Victoria and Albert Museum,* (1997), p. 251

21. 'Vertue Note Books IV', *Walpole Society* 24 (1936), p. 65

22. R. W. Goulding, 'The Welbeck Abbey Miniatures', *Walpole Society* 4 (1915), p. 16

23. *A Description of the Villa of Horace Walpole...with an inventory*, (1774), pp. 33, 69, 123-4, 133

24. *A Description of the Villa of Mr Horace Walpole at Strawberry Hill, near Twickenham, Middlesex with an inventory*, (1842), pp. 11, 15, 26. Charles Jervis/Jervas (1675–1739) was an Irish portrait painter and collector. His estate and art collection were acquired by Edward Lovibond (1724–1775)

25. Lindsay Stainton and Christopher White, *Drawing in Early Stuart England from Hilliard to Hogarth,* (1987), p. 214

26. Elizabeth Walsh, 'Charles Beale's 3rd Book 1680' , *Connoisseur* 149 (1962), pp. 248-52

27. CBA 15 January 1681

GALLERY OF NEW IMAGES

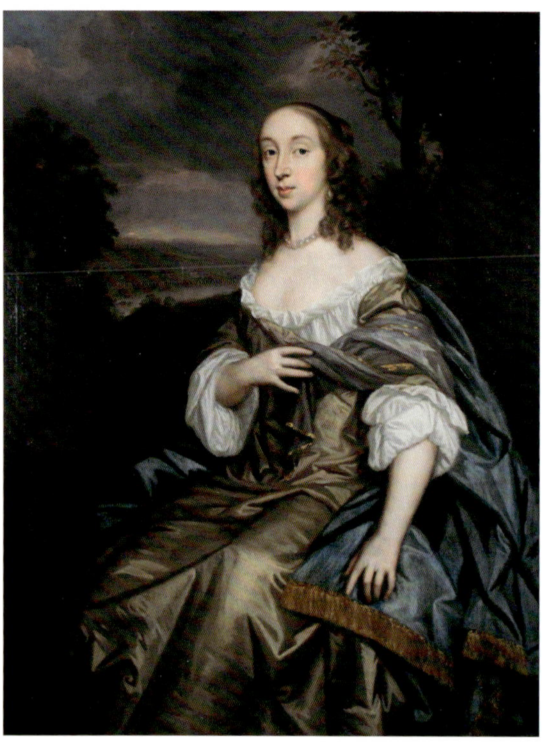

Frances Vaughan, Countess of Carbery (1621-1650). Copied by Mary Beale in the 1670s from an earlier portrait by Sir Peter Lely

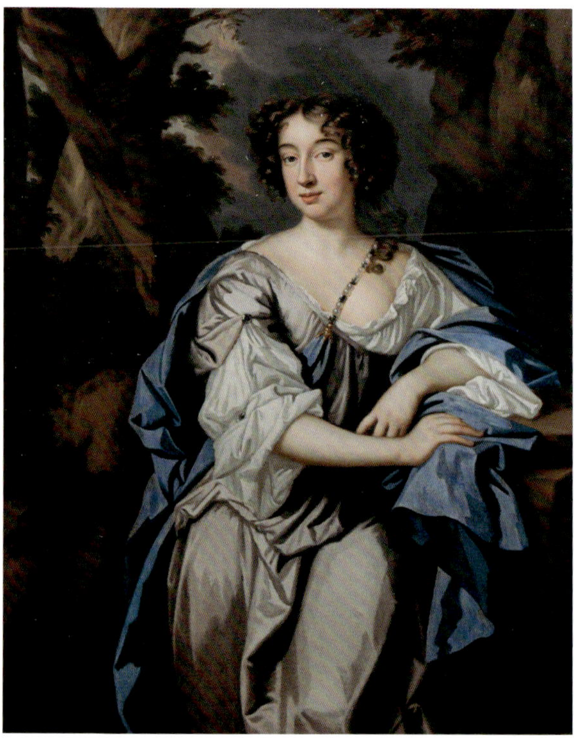

An unknown woman, possibly Mary Cavendish, Duchess of Devonshire, (1646–1710), 1670s. Mary Beale painted Lady Mary wearing 'a blew scarf' in 1674 and again in 1676–7. Charles Beale charged extra for his blue pigment

Opposite: *Dr Samuel Woodford FRS (1636–1700).* He married Alice, Charles Beale's cousin, and the couple lived with the Beales in London from 1661 until 1663. After Alice's death in 1664, Samuel found solace with the Beales. His mournful countenance may date the portrait to that year. He wrote a poem to 'The Excellent Mrs Mary Beal' in 1664, and she painted him again in 1692 when he was a Prebendary of Winchester Cathedral

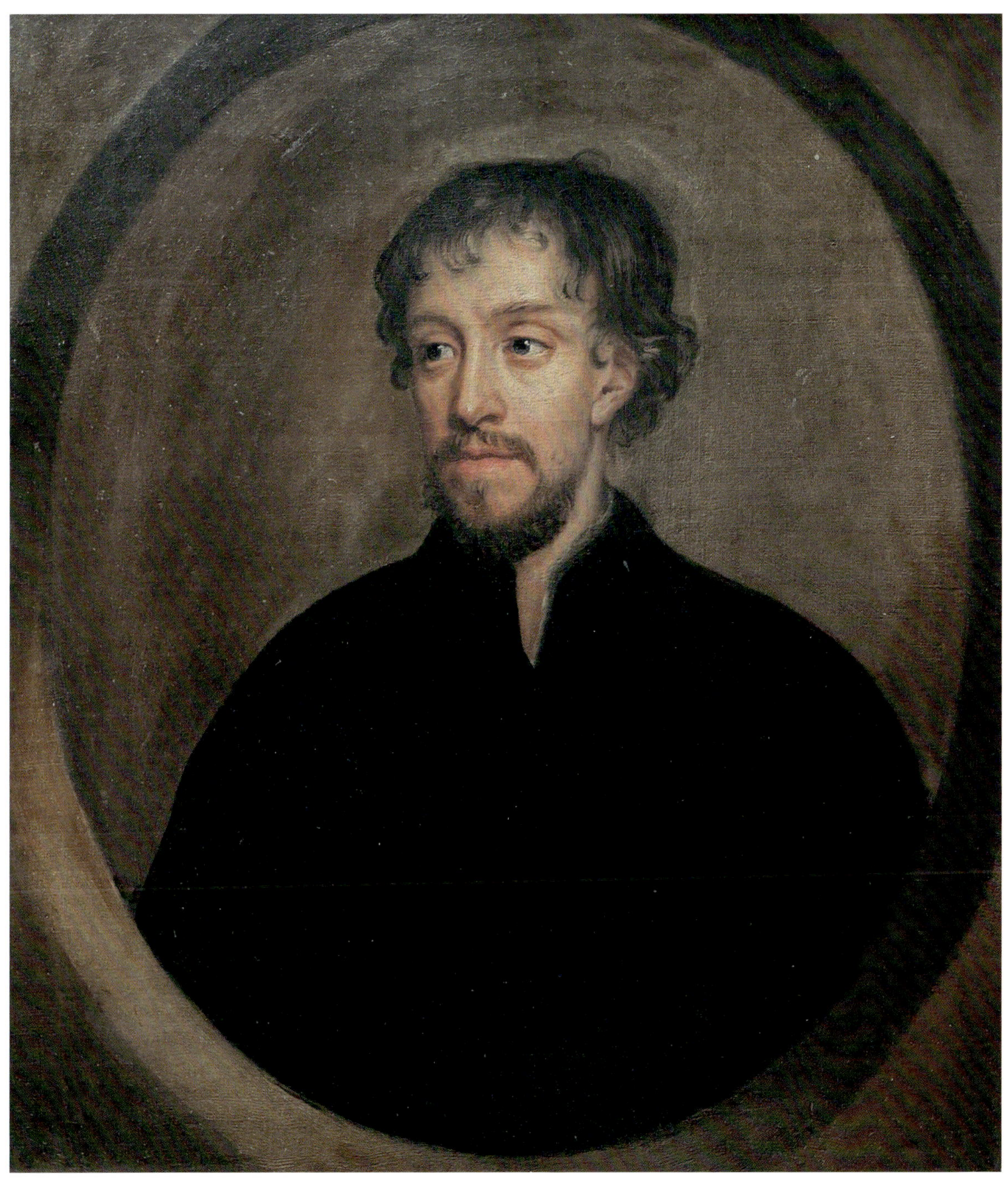

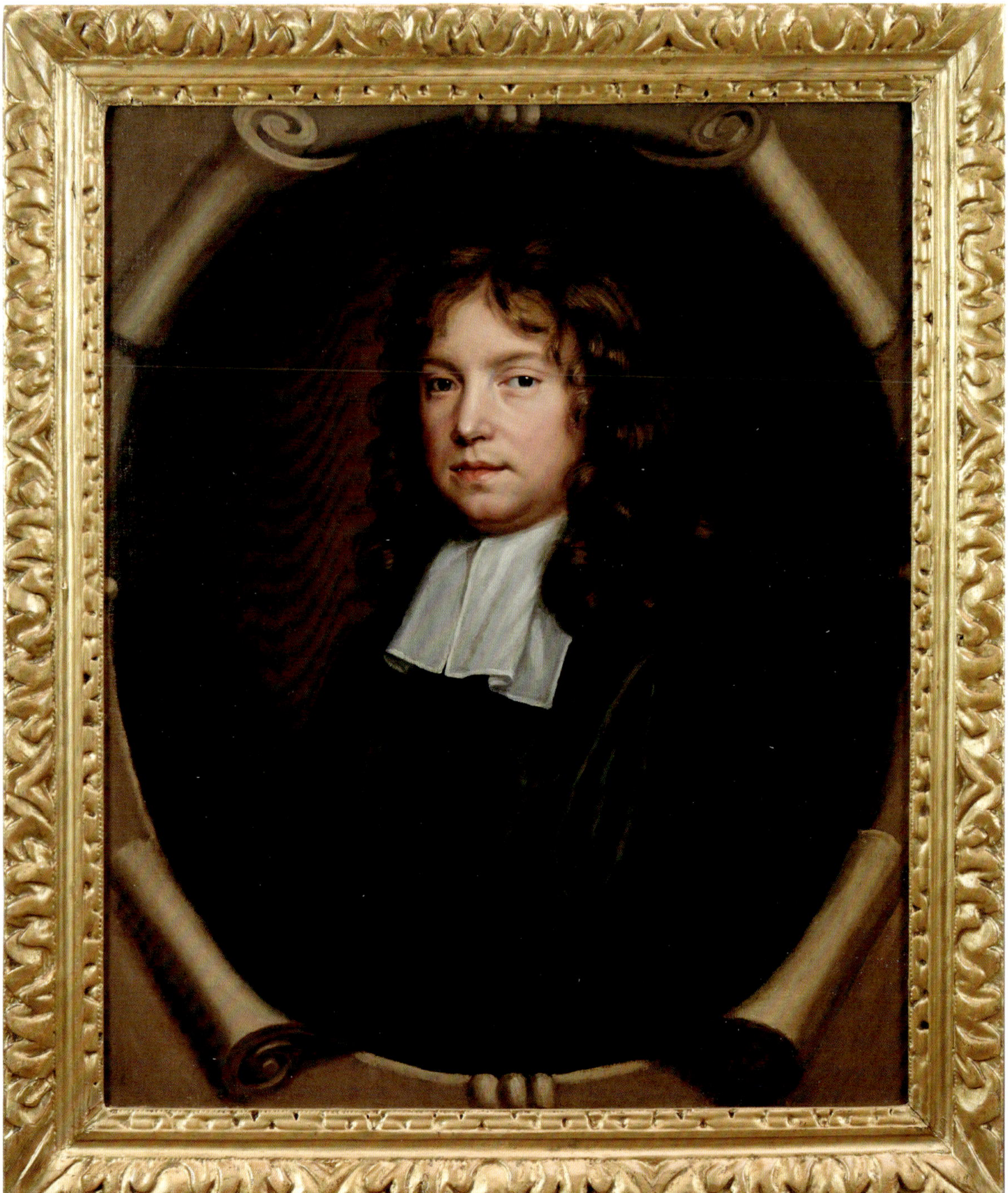

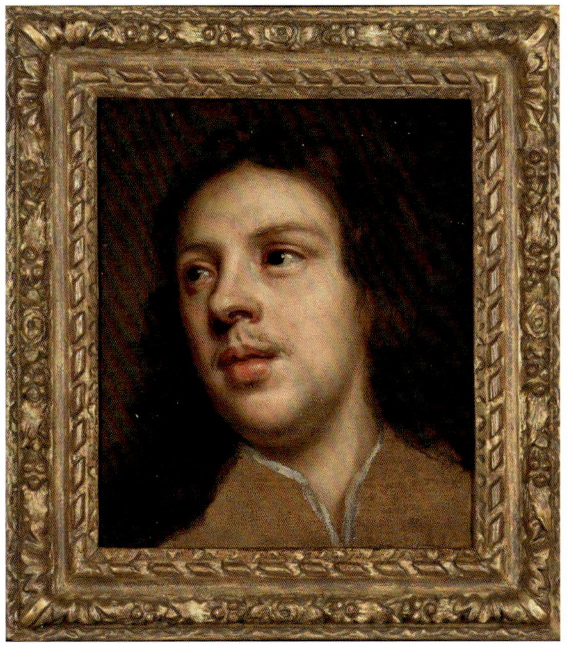

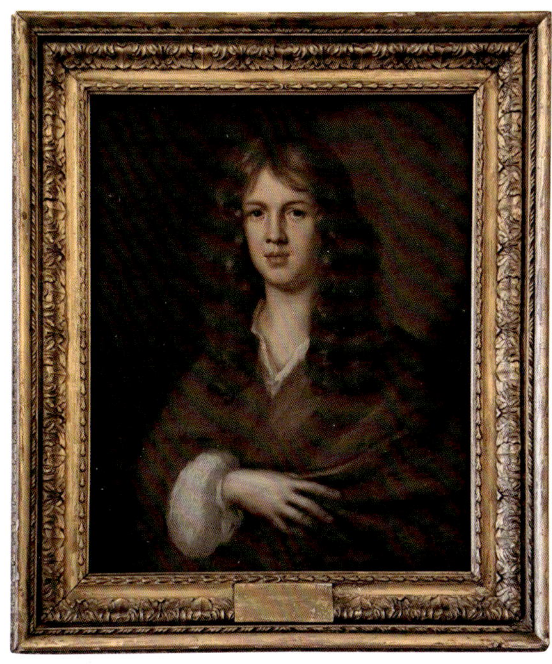

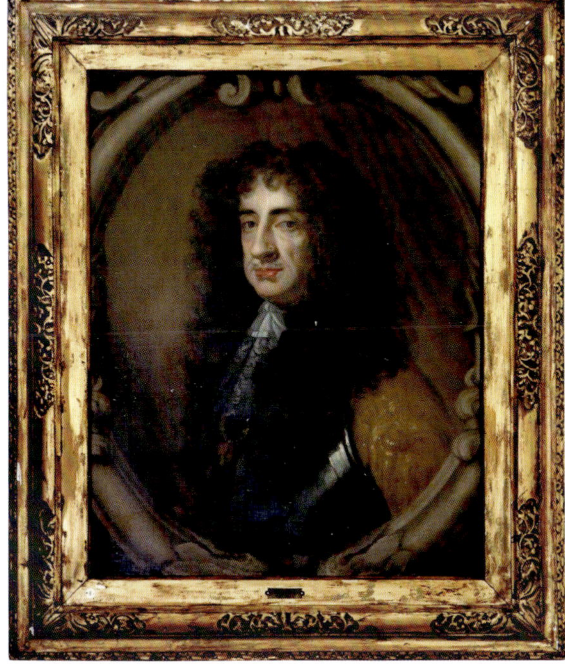

Above left: *Charles Beale (1632–1705)*, the artist's husband, c. 1660

Above right: *Bartholomew Beale, Charles and Mary's eldest son (1656–1709)*, painted c. 1676–80

Left: *King Charles II (1660–1685)*, copied from Sir Peter Lely's portrait which the Beales borrowed from him. Charles Beale recorded that Mary 'finished Charles II' in November 1677

Opposite: *The Reverend Jeremy Taylor (1613-1667)*, c. 1662, Chaplain in Ordinary to Charles I and the Bishop of Down and Connor after the Restoration. He wrote a 'Discourse on Friendship' (1662), a subject taken up by Mary Beale in 1667

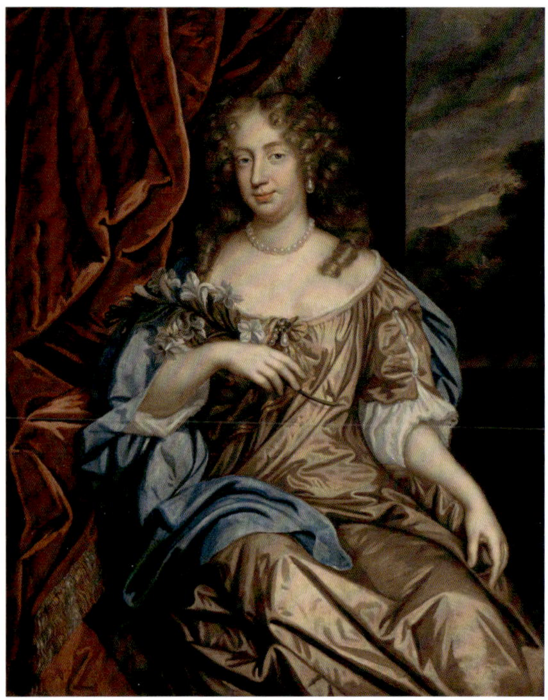

Gertrude Savile, Marchioness of Halifax (1641-1727). Mary Beale painted the Marques of Halifax in 1676/77, and the Countess c. 1679. Their London house was in St James's Square, close to the Beales in Pall Mall

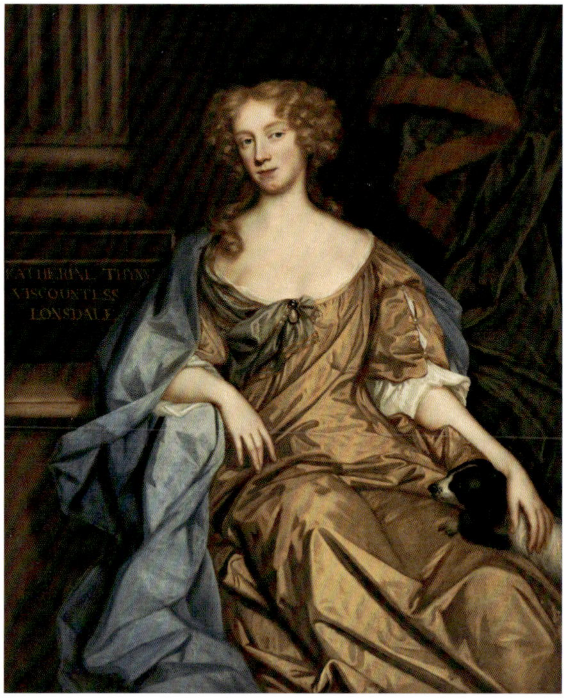

Katherine, Viscountess Lonsdale, née Thynne (1653–1713). In 1677 she married John Lowther (1655–1700), later Viscount Lonsdale of Westmorland. After his death she managed the family estates and was a patron of the Whig party. She was one of some thirty members of her family painted by Mary Beale in 1677

Opposite: *Bishop Henry Compton (1631–1713)*, probably painted on his appointment as Bishop of London in 1675. He was an Anglican royalist who established the gardens at his residence, Fulham Palace, London

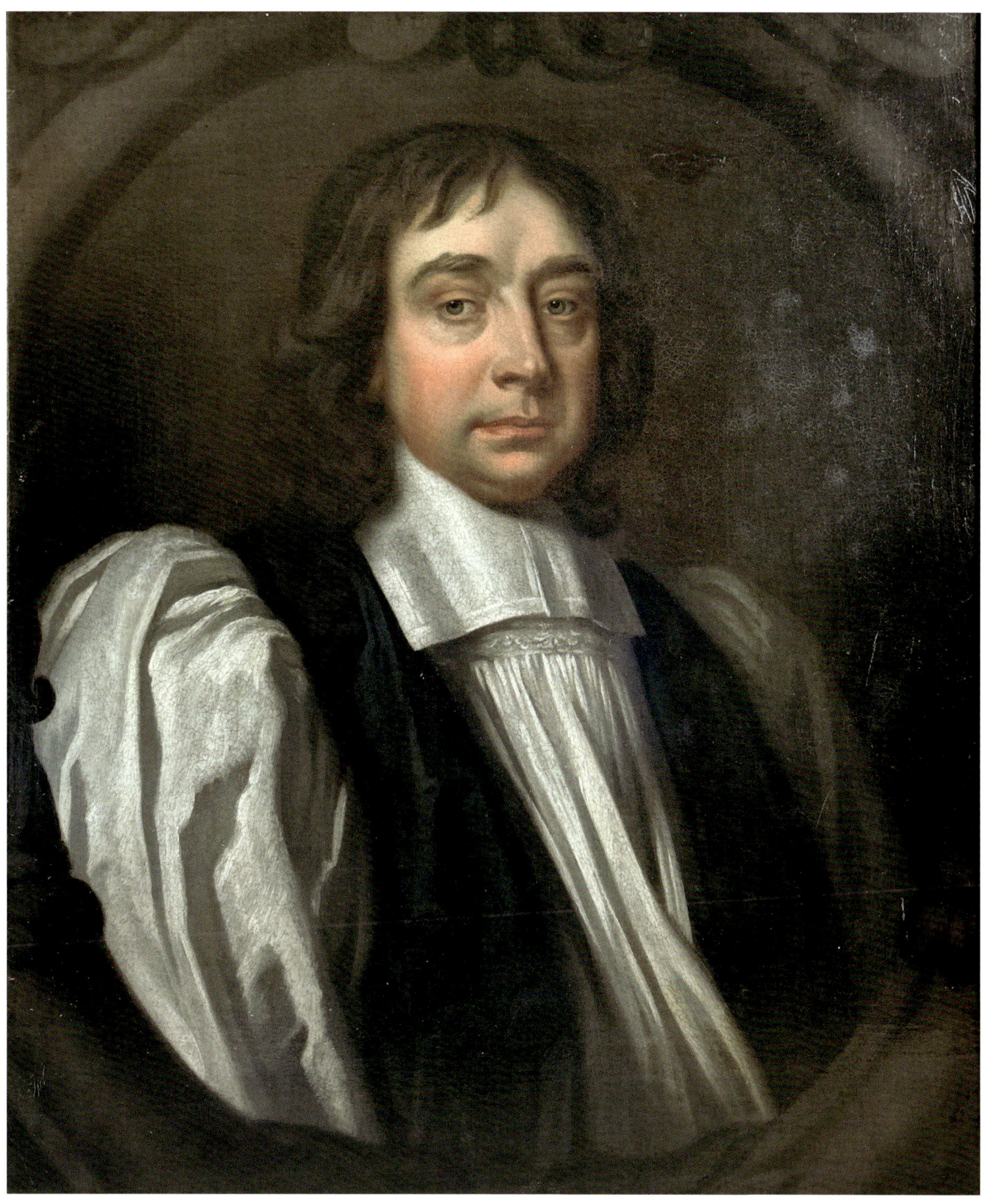

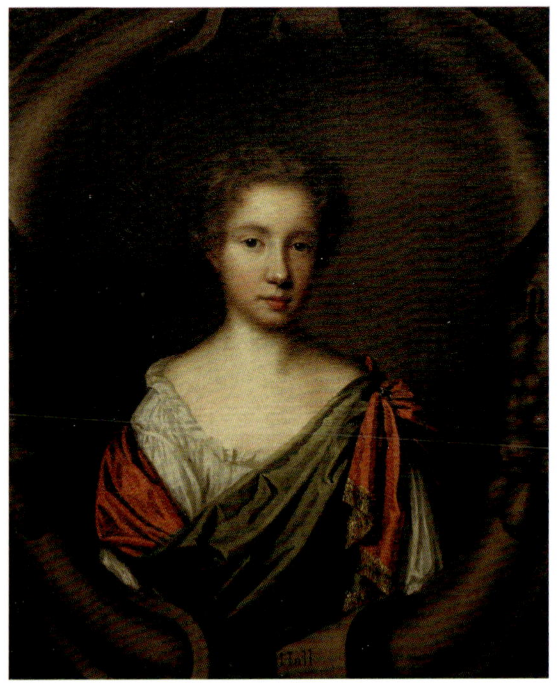

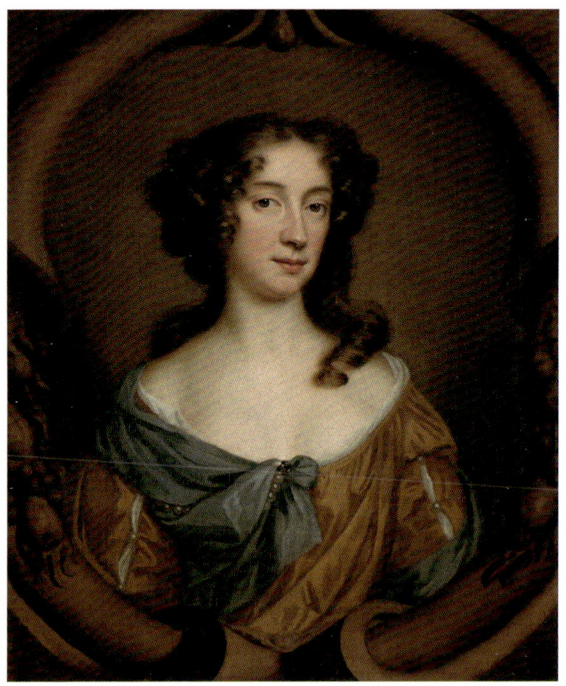

Above left: *Lady Sarah Hall (c. 1677).* The portrait was unpaid for in January 1677

Above right: *An unknown woman in a brown dress*, c. 1680

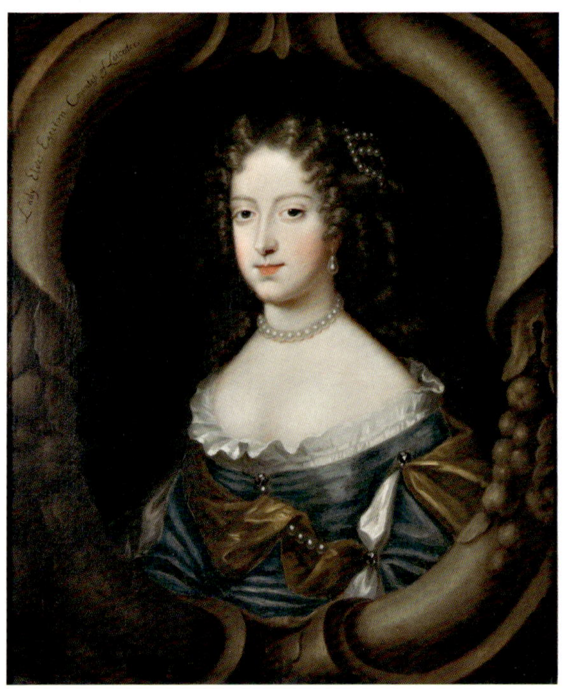

Right: *Lady Elizabeth Egerton (1653-1709)*, wife of Robert Sidney, Earl of Leicester (1649–1702). Charles Beale noted 'Mistress Egerton's face and breast finished' in January 1681

Opposite: *Bartholomew Beale (1656–1709)*, Mary Beale's eldest son, painted c. 1660. Another portrait of Bartholomew at about the same age is on p. 55

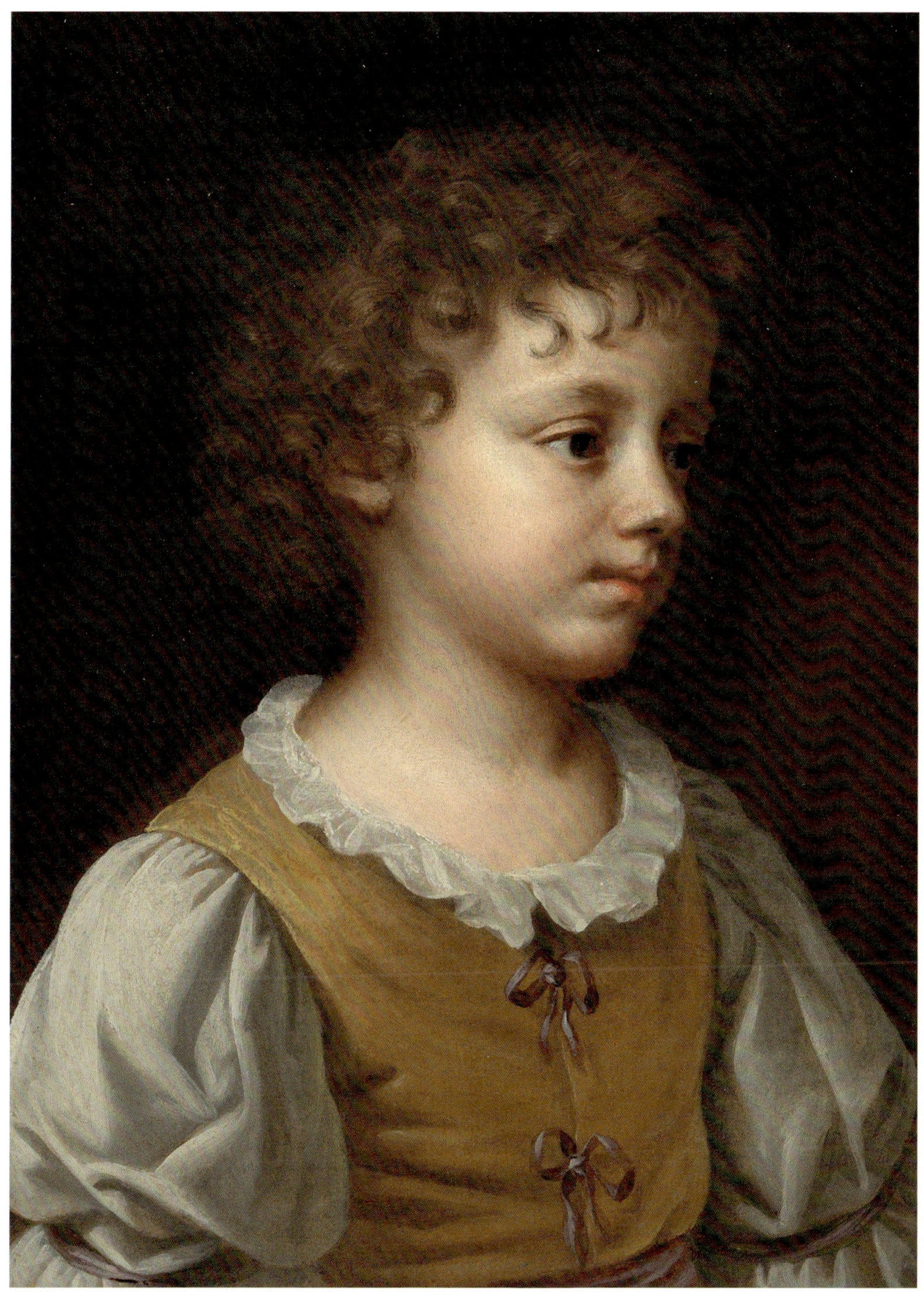

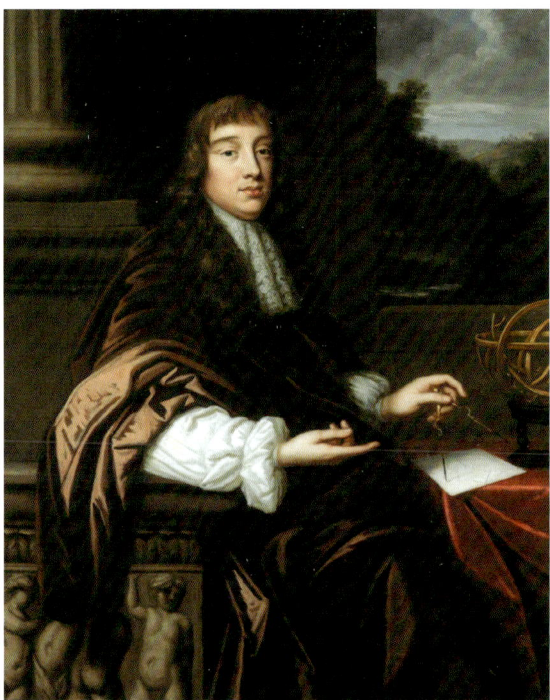

Above left: *The Hon. Henry Coventry MP (1618–1686)*, a diplomat and Secretary of State to Charles II from 1672 to 1679. 'Mr Secretary Coventry' sat for Mary Beale twice in July 1677

Above right: *The mathematician, natural philosopher, inventor and architect Robert Hooke FRS (1635-1703)*. On the table is his prototype of an orrery, a mechanical model of the solar system, and he points to his drawing of elliptical motion. Hooke was Curator of Experiments at the Royal Society from 1662 and a lecturer at Gresham College. The stand carved with putti appears in other paintings by Mary Beale. It has been suggested that the background shows Lowther Castle and Church. Mary Beale painted many members of the Lowther family, and Hooke produced designs for the castle and church. Hooke's diary records a visit to the Beales in April 1674

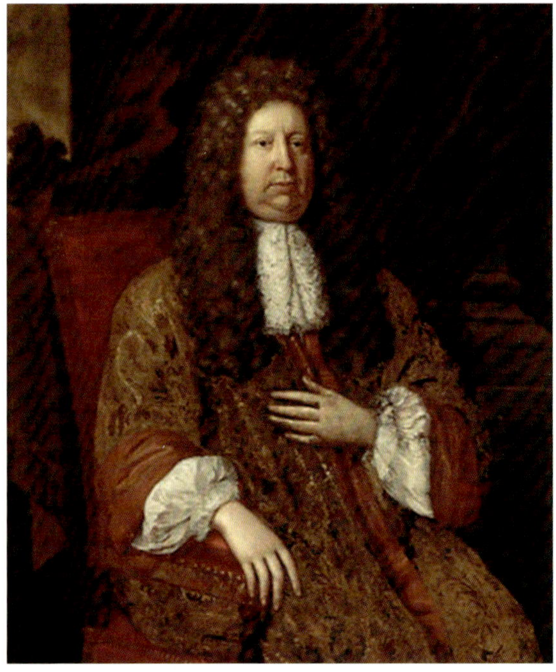

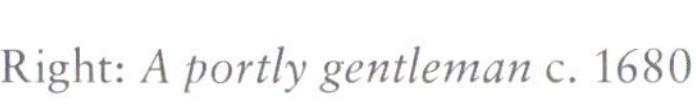

Right: *A portly gentleman* c. 1680

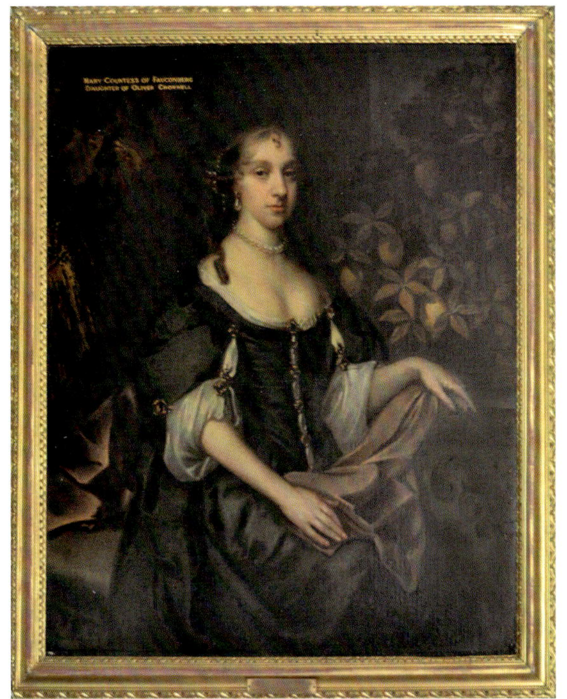

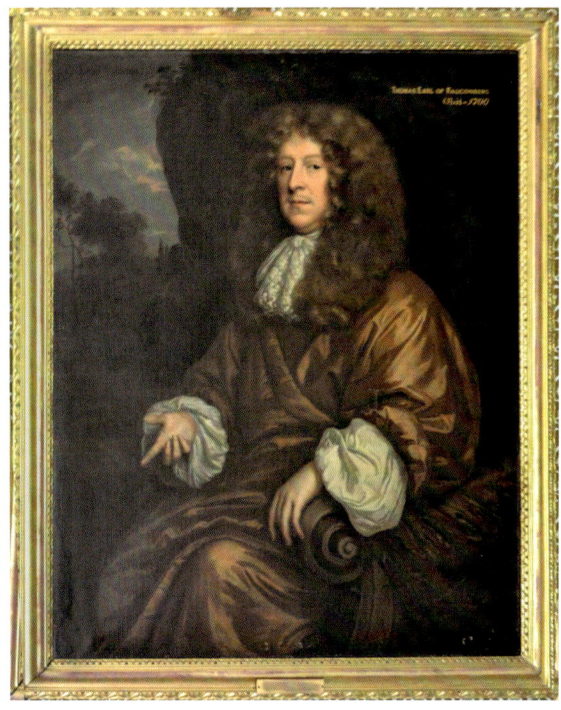

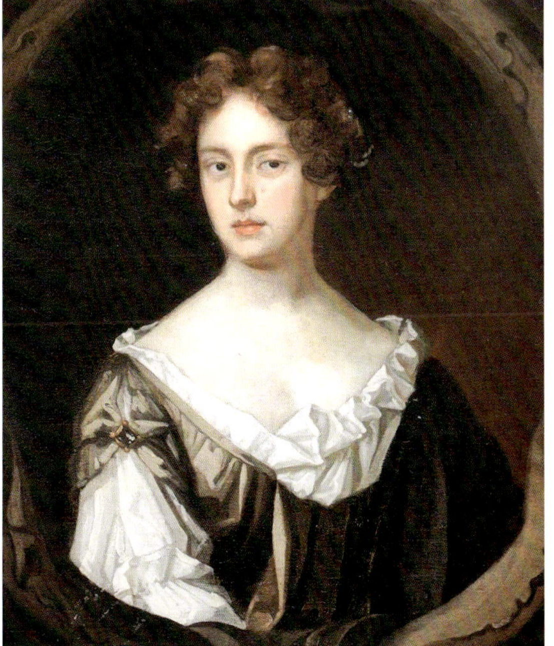

Above left: *Mary, Countess Fauconberg, née Cromwell (1637–1713)*, painted by Mary Beale in 1671 or 1672. The countess is believed to have rescued the corpse of her father, Lord Protector Oliver Cromwell, from Westminster Abbey

Above right: *Thomas Belasyse, Earl Fauconberg (1678–1700)*. He married Mary Cromwell, the Lord Protector's third daughter in 1657. Painted by Mary Beale in 1676 or 1677

Left: *A woman, possibly of the Williams family*, c. 1680

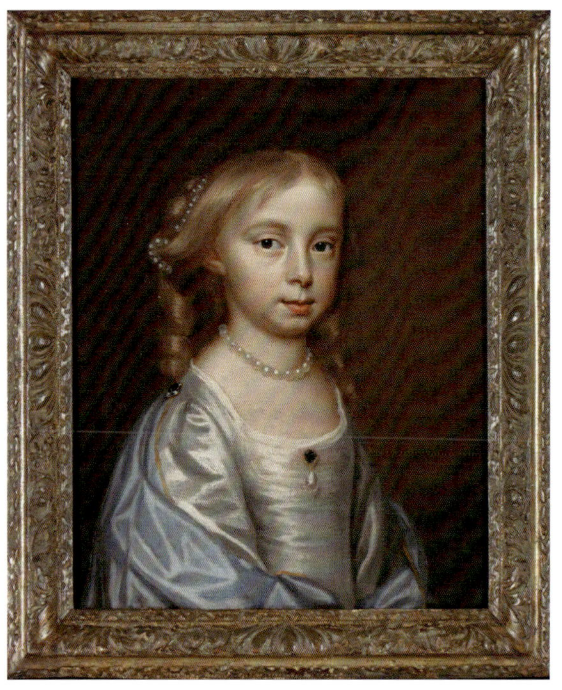

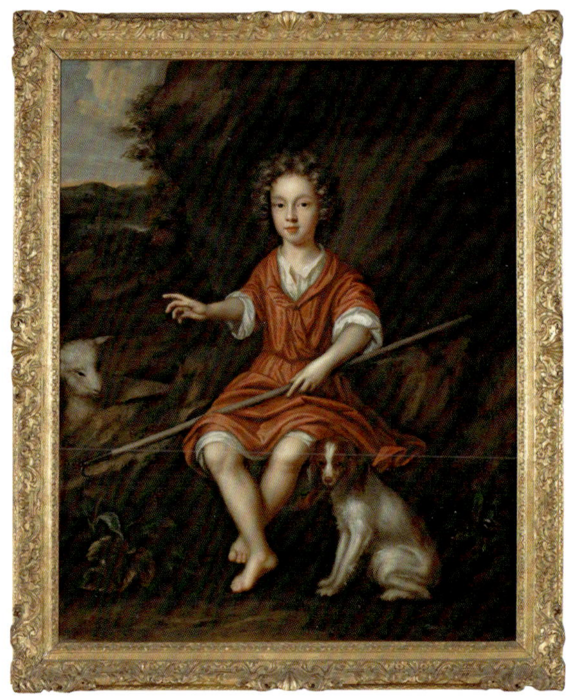

Above left: *Elizabeth Jones (c. 1664–1681)*, painted in the early 1670s when she was about eight. She was the daughter of Sir William Jones, appointed Attorney General in 1675. Mary Beale painted a Mrs Jones in 1671/72, who may have been Elizabeth's mother

Above right: *Charles Beauclerk (1670–1726)*, the illegitimate son of Charles II and Nell Gwyn. In 1676 he was created Baron of Heddington and Earl of Burford. The portrait may have been painted that year, when he was six. The king gave him the title the Duke of St Albans in 1684

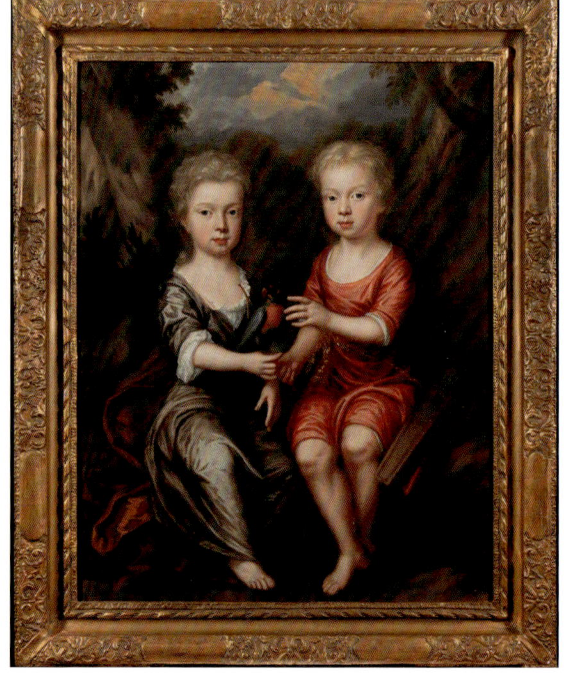

Right: *Two children in a landscape*, 1680s

Opposite: *Richard Goulston (1669-1731)* of Wyddial, Hertfordshire. His marriage was arranged in 1677 when he was eight which might have prompted this commission. He was Member of Parliament for Hertford in the early eighteenth century

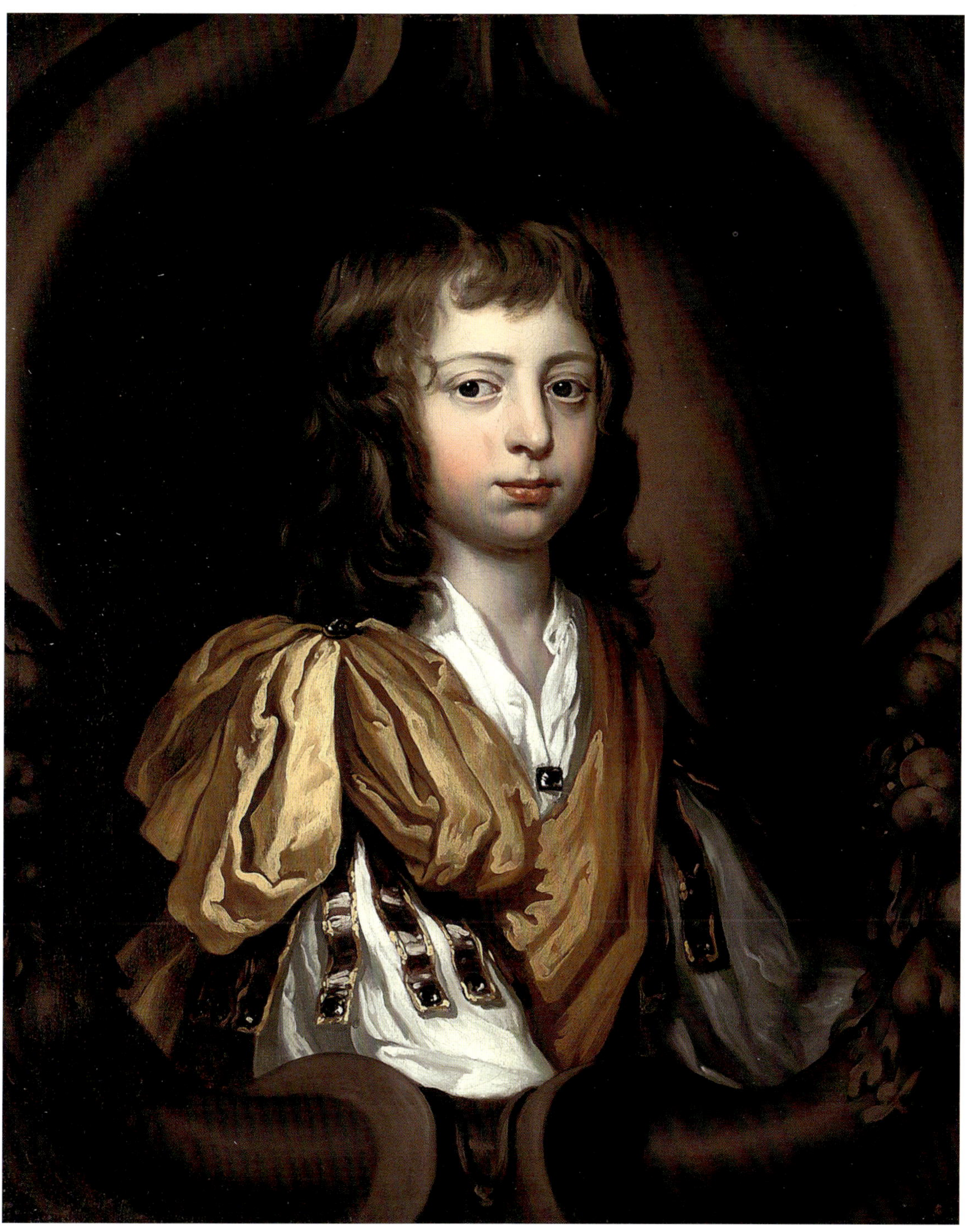

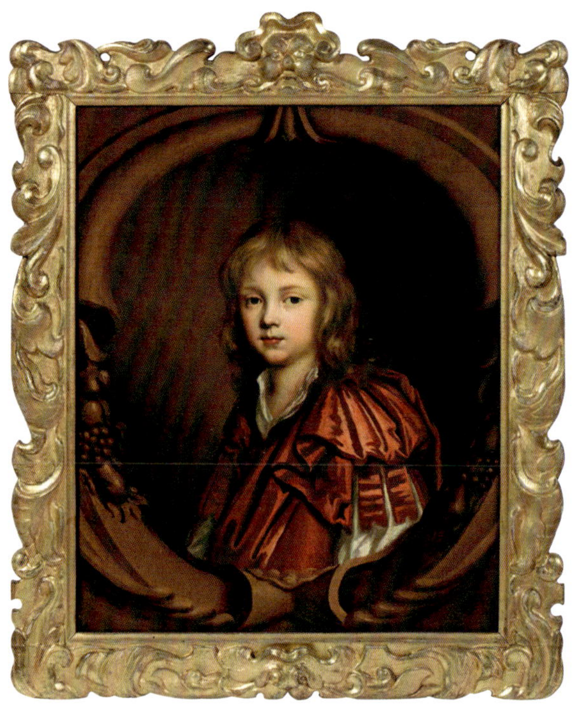

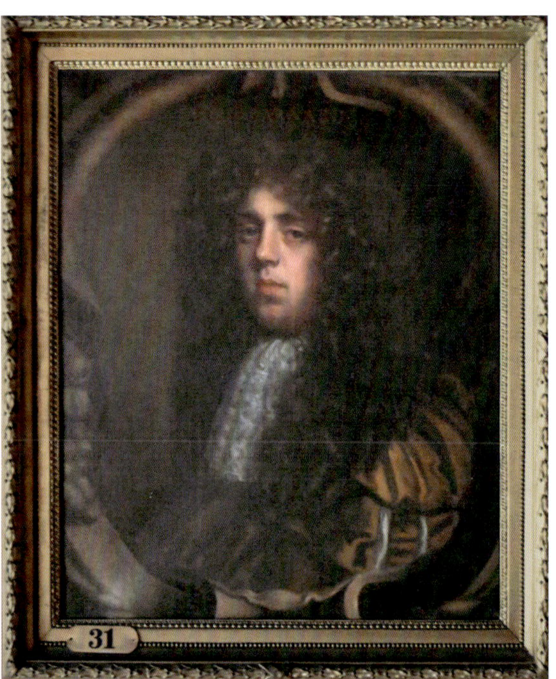

Above left: *A young boy* c. 1682. Signed 'M. Beale pint'

Above right: *Christopher Vane (1653–1723)* created Baron Barnard by William III in 1689. He married Elizabeth Holles in 1676. The couple opposed their son's marriage and attempted to deprive him of his inheritance, Raby Castle, leading to a lawsuit in 1716, which saved Raby from destruction

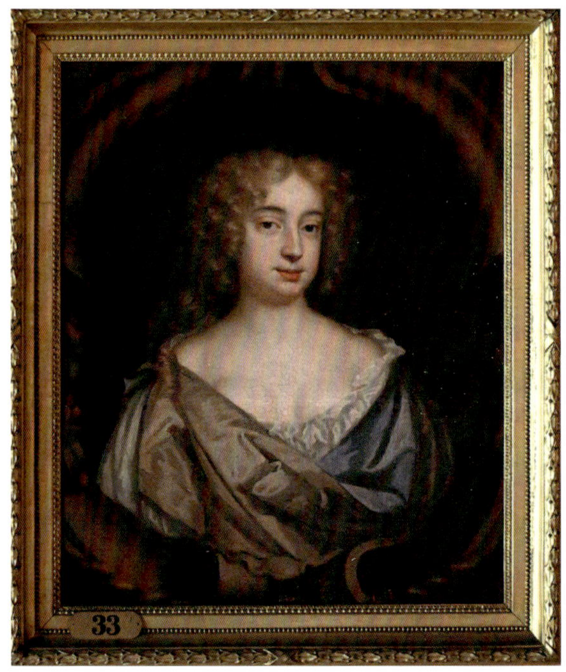

Right: *Elizabeth, Baroness Barnard, née Holles* (c. 1657–1725). Her part in the dispute with her son earned her the nickname 'Old Hell-Cat'. Charles Beale's almanack records 'Lady Barnard's face and breast finished', in July 1681

Opposite: *Elizabeth Adams, née Hirst or Hurst as a shepherdess*, late 1660s. She married Conrad Adams (1621–1691) in Barbados in 1663

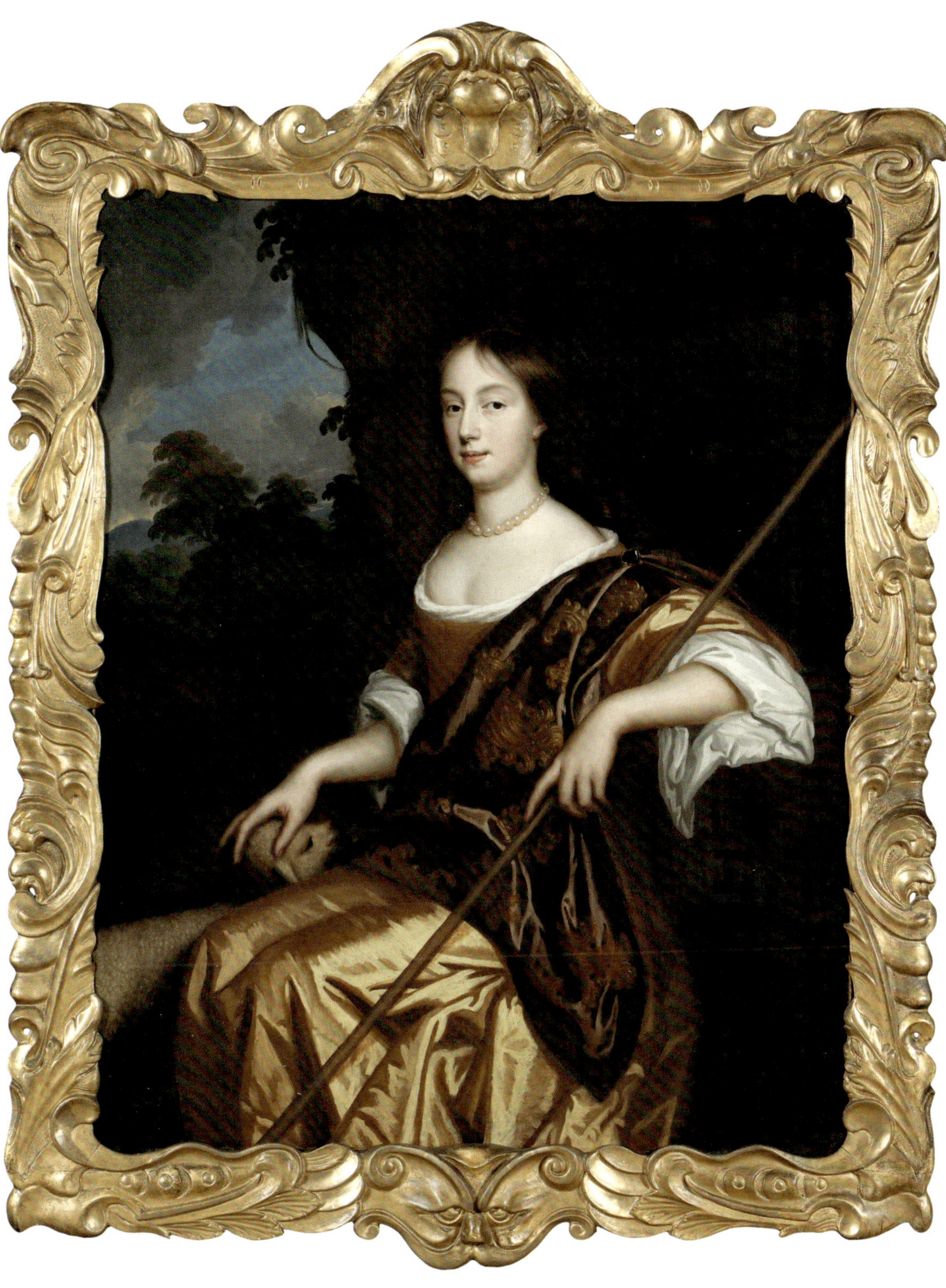

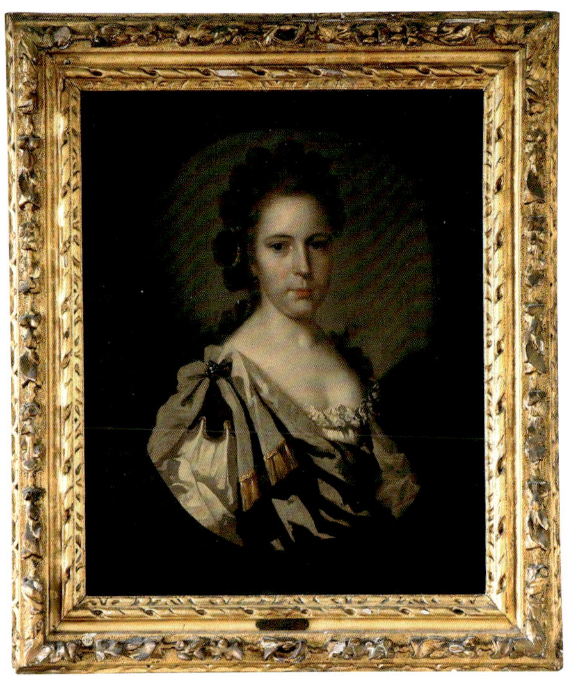

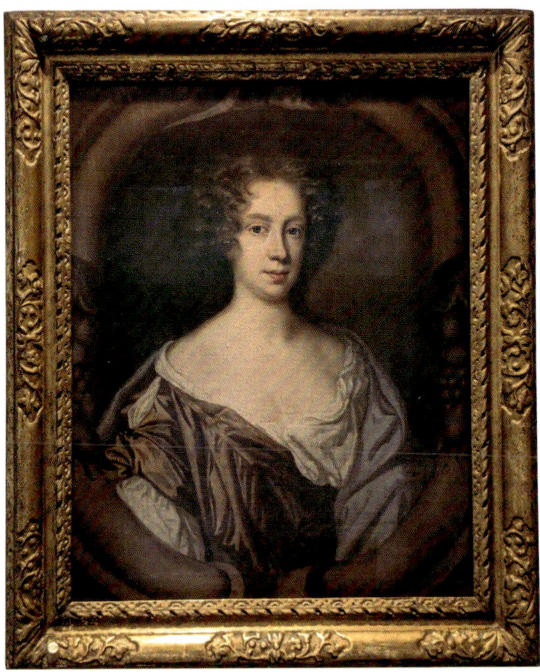

Above left: *A woman with jewels in her hair*, c. 1670

Above right: *A woman in a brown dress*, c. 1670. This was previously thought to be a self-portrait of Mary Beale. It is signed Mariah Beale on the bottom right of the oval frame

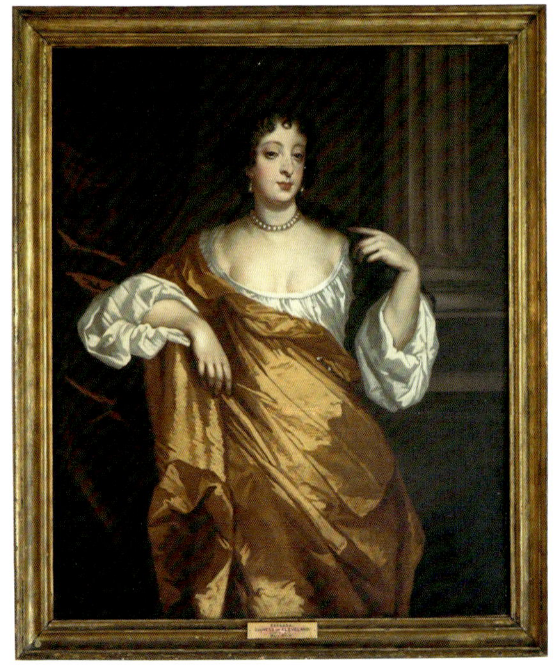

Right: *Barbara, Countess Castlemaine, Duchess of Cleveland, née Villiers (1640–1709)*. She was one of Charles II's mistresses and bore him five children. Mary Beale copied Sir Peter Lely's portrait of 1672

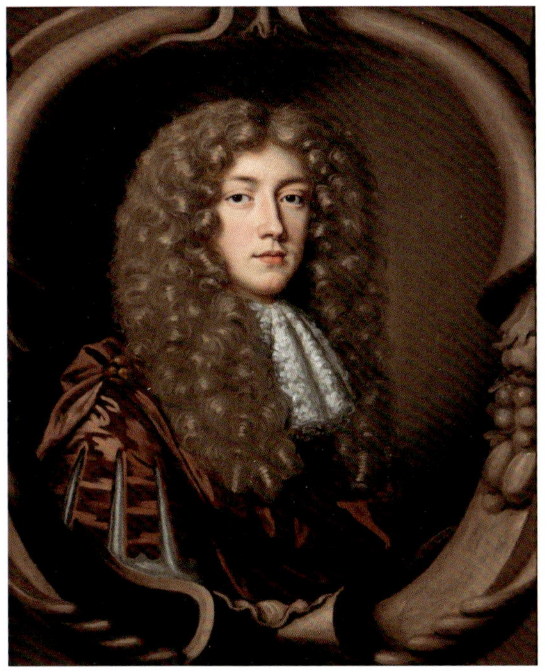

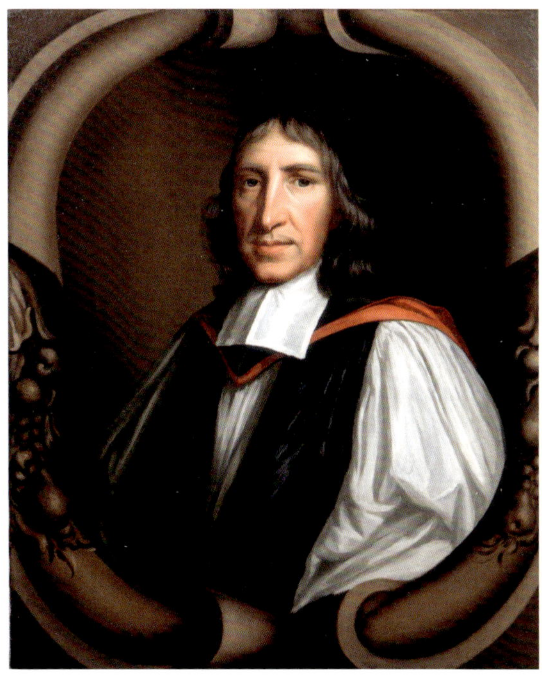

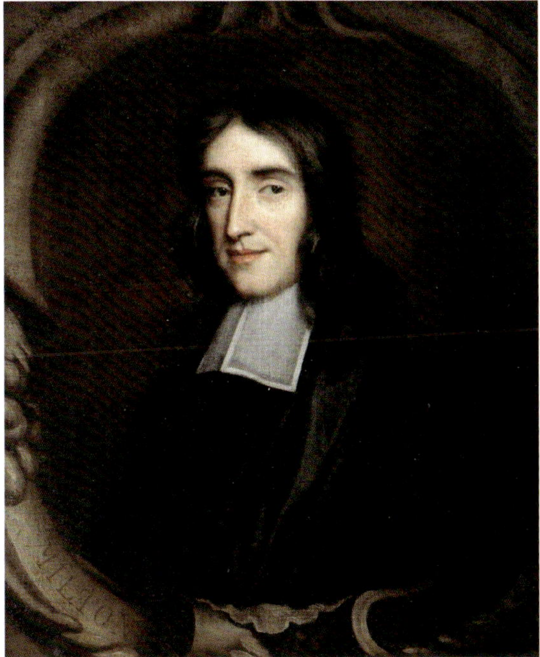

Above left: *Portrait of a gentleman*, traditionally considered to be the Duke of Monmouth (1649–1685), c. 1670s

Above right: Bishop John Lake (1624–1689), Bishop of Bristol in 1684, Bishop of Chichester from 1685 when he sat for Mary Beale. He refused to accept the succession of William III and Queen Mary in 1689, so was suspended from office

Left: *A member of the Milton family*, 1670s. The oval frame is inscribed 'Milton' but this cannot be the poet John Milton who was blind from 1652 and died in 1674 aged sixty-six. The subject might be the poet's younger brother, Sir Christopher Milton (1615–1693), a judge

TRANSCRIPT OF MARY BEALE'S 'DISCOURSE ON FRIENDSHIP', 1667

THIS TRANSCRIPT is from Harley Ms 6828 ff. 510-523 at the British Library where Mary Beale's handwritten Discourse is to be found. It is prefaced by a covering letter addressed to Mrs Elizabeth Tillotson, niece of Lord Protector Oliver Cromwell, who married Dr John Tillotson, later Archbishop of Canterbury, in 1664 (Mrs Beale has much to say about marriage). Elizabeth was at first reluctant to accept Dr Tillotson's proposal but was persuaded by her step-father, Dr John Wilkins, who married the couple. Mary Beale painted Tillotson five times, Elizabeth, and their daughter, Mary, once, and Wilkins sat for two portraits. Mary Beale was also commissioned for portraits of Elizabeth Tillotson's cousin, Mary (née Cromwell, Countess Fauconberg) and her husband, Earl Fauconberg, in the 1670s.

At the time of writing the 'Discourse on Friendship' Mary Beale was living in Hampshire with her husband, Charles, and their two young sons. Charles Beale had been dismissed from his post as Deputy Clerk of the Patents Office in 1664 whereupon the family moved from London to Hampshire. Few commissions came Mary's way during the five years she spent in the country, leaving her time to reflect and write.

John and Elizabeth Tillotson had known Charles and Mary Beale since at least 1664 when John Tillotson sat for his first portrait by Mary. In 1672 the Beales commissioned Sir Peter Lely to paint Tillotson's portrait and in 1677 Mary Beale's portrait of Tillotson was 'for ourselves'; he sat for two more portraits in the 1680s. The Tillotsons and the Beales were close: Charles Beale regarded John Tillotson as his 'most worthy friend' while Mary referred to Elizabeth as 'My Deare ffriend'.

Dr Tillotson was an influential preacher at St Lawrence Jewry and Lincoln's Inn during the 1660s; he was appointed Dean of Canterbury in 1672, Archbishop in 1691. He gave most of his income to charity, leaving his widow in penury after his death in 1694. King William III showed his high regard for the late Archbishop by granting Elizabeth an annuity for life (she died in 1702, two daughters having predeceased their parents). Elizabeth educated her husband's nephew and her three grandchildren, and she ensured that her husband's sermons were published, in fourteen volumes dedicated to the King.

Mary Beale's letter to Mrs Tillotson (illustrated on pages 78, 85) is dated 9 March 1666 (1667 according to the new calendar). Mrs Tillotson's response to Mary Beale's Discourse is unrecorded.

Illegible words and queries are indicated in this transcript by question marks.

Discourse on Friendship

Friendship is the nearest Union which distinct Souls are capable of; (and is as rare to be found in sincerity, as it is excellent in its qualities) though next to the glorifying our Creator, man seems to be made for nothing more. For when God had at first created him, it is not fitt said hee, that Man should be alone, so then he gave him Eve, to be a meet help, and what can that imply but that God gave her for a ffriend as well as for a wife. A wife and friend but not a slave; For we find her not in the beginning made subject to Adam, but alwaise of equall dignity & honour with him, till by her own great modulity, sinning her self & then seducing her husband, she lost her share in that rule which before they had in common, and as a just reward of her transgression had both her desires & person subjected to him. A curse which she not only procured to her self, but intaild upon all her female posterity, except a small number who by ffriendships interposition have restored this marriage bond to its first institution.

Now Friendship which is so excellent in its nature, cannot be without order, & must be governed by Lawes proper to it self. For as Kingdoms & Commonwealths without a due administration of Justice, and an awfull observance of Statutes become barbarous, & salvage; so Friendship without a right Rule soone degenerates into vice & becomes most destructive to the good of Mankind, which it was designed chiefly to sustaine. For if instead of Religion & Moralitie sense shall there command, & if in place of reason, the passions shall direct, & solely bear sway, it is no longer Friendship, but a confederency in evil doing, & though the name may still remain, yet its operations shall instead of yielding the wholsom fruits of peace bring nothing but mischief & confusion.

That Friendship therefore be established, and its Laws inviolably kept, it is necessary that my self, or any who are industrious to enter into this alliance, consider both my own temper & theirs in whom I choose to repose this trust.

And first I ought to make a serious enquiry and pass an impartiall censure on my self that so I may the better understand how farr I am qualified for so sacred a bond, & learning thence my owne imperfections, may be able to strive against & restrain them, both by Religion & reason. Effectual meanes both, but especially the former. For if Socrates could by the improvement of his reason only in the misteries of Philosophy, chang the badd inclination of his mind into a temper perfectly argreeable, How much better may we be able to regulate ours by Religion, which is the highest reason, & a more unerring guide than Philosophy.

After a severe judgement past upon myself in this particular, I shall be inabled to direct my choice, to such a person as will be best suit with me. I meane not that I should choose a friend always of my owne humor and constitution, such a choice being many times attended with very ill consequences. For where any one passion is predominant in a man, the like proportion of it in another, seemes oft times very distastefull, and frequently a grain or two of the contrary proves very agreeable. For example, two melancholique persons can never be desirable friends, supposing their melancholy runns in the same channell, for if there be not upon all occasions distrusts & jealousies, with a taking those things in evil part, which were never intended, so there will be at best but a feeding one an other with such disconsolate conversation as shall at once impaire their strength and increase their burthen; two things than which nothing can be more contrary to the nature of true friendship. Whereas to a melancholique person a cheerfull friend who has a truly good nature is certainly in my opinion most consonant; For the cheerfulness of the one, if prudently managed will be the best antidote against the dejection of the other.

An other care of those who would bee admitted members of this Society, ought to be a sober inquiry into the nature of it, what it is, & wherein Friendship consists, least through ignorance thereof they give this sacred name to that which true Friendship most of all abhors; Flattery & dissimulation which is but a kind of mock Friendship, though for the same reason that the appearances of vertues had alwayes had more followers than the reall vertues themselves, it hath found best acceptance in the world.

Between ffriends words & actions must always be allowed the best & most candid construction. For if we give our selves once the liberty of harsh and unkind thoughts, twice doing so will beget an habit & evil habits usher in badd affections, which oft times end in disunion. Or if the breach be made up againe, it seldom becomes so firm, or looks so beautifull as before. A mutuall bearing therefore with one anothers infirmities and conforming to those dispositions which beare sway in such we love, as it is a great part of wisdome & so it is one of the surest signs & clearest evidences of Friendship. For if we seriously consider our selves, we shall find soon by what occurs there, the necessity of some allowance to be made for the constitution & temper of those with whom we converse. Not that this should incourge any to indulg themselves in those unpleasant humors and inclinations, with which many times their lives are chequered, upon pressumption that true friendship can & must beare with them. But let such know, that if there be not striveing on their part, as well as a forebearace on ye other, their friendship is by no means reciprocall, and amounts to little more than half & most imperfect ffriendship.

The name of ffriend has certainly in it more charmes than that of any other relation in the world. Solomon sayes there is a Friend that is nearer than a Brother; and sure it is, the nearest relations of blood and affinity, without this cement are easily disjoynted & becom very indifferent & almost insignificant. For I should add that such have turned greatest Enemies each to other. I could easily be furnisht with authoritie to confirm my assertion. For how oft has the dividing of an Estate separated Bretheren, & the selling of a Jointure alienated the love of a husband or wife. Whereas true friendship on all such occasions says Mephibosheth ? In another case to David, Let him take all. For that friendship which has only consanguinity or self interest for its ffoundation, will assuredly run to ruin, if there be once an unsuitableness of thoughts in the one & a fayling of the expectations in the other.

Now that ffriendship which is truly noble in itself, cannot be base in its endes for then it ceases to be friendship & is changed into some deformed & ugly passion, unworthy of so excellent a name. For as the best things corrupted become most loathsome so ffriendship vitiated degenerates into the worst of evils.

As touching the ends of ffriendship, self love must not be wholy excluded from being one; though but sparingly to be used. For that seems to be the center from which all the lines of ffriendship are drawn. For did I not love myself first I could scarce be capable of loving my friend; & were it not that I propounded a great satisfaction to my self by gaining an interest in him, & in his virtues, I could never heartily desire it.

This is requisite therefore for the beginning

of Friendship, but as that grows more perfect the love of myself is swallowed up in the love of my ffriend. I then becom more sollicitous for his good than for my owne; & am more delighted with the good things he enjoys, than distrest with the evils my self suffers; on all occasions preferring him, & contenting my self, like Jonathan, with the second place of authority in that Kingdom of ffriendship where he absolutely rules.

True friendship hates envy, yet always abounds with Emulation & friends are ever striving who shall out do other in offices of kindness; It looks on expression as an insipid kind of Fruit unless with actions which speake more effectually.

It satisfies not itself with the superficies of a slight courtesy, but is best pleased when employd in such affairs where the difficulty of accomplishing, as well as the advantages, render them most acceptable, & this it performs without ostentation; rightly esteeming the exercise of ffriendship more worthy than the prayse. Neither is it discouraged with that danger or disgrace which it often meets with, and as the occasions which present themselves are the greater, so are its effects more extraordinary. Tis then it appears most beautifull as being in its most proper season. Since tis an easy thing for ffriendship to beare up when it hath a quiet sea, & full sayles, when all the wind that is stirring does but serve to drive it forwards to its desired haven, but then is the truth & power of it seen when it is able to make its way through mounting Deeps & tempestuous storms, neither can be swallowed up by the impestuousness of the one, or driven back by the violence of the other. And that person who is not willing to share with his friend in all conditions & lows not at all times, is unworthy to be admitted into this society, & to be honoured with so illustrious a title.

So much for Friendship in the general. I shall now treat of it a little more particularly. From the beginning therefore, & carrying on a Friendship, how different so ever the conditions and outward estates of the persons are, it is necessary that their minds beare a like proportion to each other. For if this be wanting it will be impossible to maintain that freedom in converse, without which this relation would be insignificant and incapable of exercising its most noble acts. This being the perfecion of Friendship, that it supposes its professors equall, laying aside all distances, & so levelling the ground, that neither hath therein the advantage of other. Not that this either do or should take away that respect, which is in ffriends, through Friends, or to those whome providence hath placed in an higher rank. For true ffriendship will be alwayes tender of withdrawing from those they love that which as their birthright they may lay claim to, without urging it upon them, as that wherein they count themselves honoured. But by this I meane a removall only of that which any such inequalities may be apt & not seldom is wont to produce it ? A thing very necessary & materiall in Friendship. For till this be effected there will unavoydably be on the one part too great a propensity to exercise that authority which the advantage of Birth & Condition have given them, whereby insensibly they become forward in imposing their owne opinions as Laws, esteeming themselves injured if not punctually obeyd, & looking on those favours which they ambitiously dispense, as too great & impossible to be requited, because done to those whom they account so much below them. On the other side, they whose apprehensions make them too scrupulously sensible of their distance, become exceeding timorous in discharge of such offices, as the Laws of ffriendship both respect & command from them. For instance in one for all; in administring counsell & advice, such will be divided between what is good and pleasant, fearing least the one should not please & the other not profitt & how inconsistent both those tempers are with the nature of true Friendship, I leave to their judgements, in whose breasts this generous flame has been once kindled.

Beside where there is this distance, there can never be a freedom in communications, thoughts & weightiest concernments. This being the product of a more than ordinary familiarity, and an argument where it is freely used of the interest Friendship as that wherein Friends give their hearts mutualy in hostage for the truth of their affections.

My discoverys therefore to my Friend, should be free & open without any veile drawn over them, suddain & unconstraind, not concealing them so long till my countenance betrays them, & never thinking any concernment of my own lesse a secret because communicated to him. Thus must I do in all things which relate to myself, but in the affaires of a third person I must use a great deale more caution, and be always very tender of revealing them (for as one very well sais the secrets of my ffriend are not my owne). Least whilst I thereby think to oblige the one, I betray the other, & give him to whom I imparted the secret, occasion to distrust, that in some like circumstance I will do ye same by him. Neither must I only beware of an open & absolute discovery of them, but in things wherewith I am entrusted, take heed also of giving the least occasion of suspicion by any doubtfull word or action, either inconsiderately, or on purpose, thrown out and imediatly wrested to the divulging of that which I would either still indeed have kept as a secret, or was bigg with till well delivered. Many there are who take a pride in the latter, & out of an ambition which they have to be taken notice of as persons intrusted with no small matters, baulk not the opportunity of discovering by circumstances & dark speeches that which by their open discourse they would persuade you they would not tell for all the world. But if a wise man can from the glance of an eye, or an unusuall demeanour of the body, draw probable conjectures of the occasion, how much more may such indiscreet hints give light to those things which were never intended for subjects of publique discourse. Now it matters not whether the things intrusted to me be of great, or less, importance. For I am not to measure my fidelity by the greatness of the thing but my faithfull performance of the charge. And as I must endeavor by all care, & silence, to manifest my sincerity in such particulars, as are deposited in my breast, under the seale of secrecy, so where I am left at liberty I must be sure not to betray my owne discretion and love, in the fond discovery of such affaires, the concealment of which may make for my ffriends greater advantage.

Now the admirable effects that arise from this Divine relation, & are insepable & as it were continuall with it, are infinite, because they interpose on all occasions that either are or can be offered. For not only when anything that is extraordinary & unusuall befalls us, but also in our most common affaires, the assistance of ffriends is truly necessary; though where the circumstances offerd are greater, its actings likewise appear more illustrious.

I shall only mention a few particulars and those such as are most familiar to us, by which the excellency of this relation may from surer consequences be deduced, than the proportion of Hercules his body was, from the length of his foote. I shall in the first place treat of Counsell & faithful advice, which must be lookt upon if not as the only, yet as the main result of that which before I hinted, the revealing my most secret thoughts to my ffriend & communicating to him those concernments which are lockt up to all the world beside. Counsell therefore & advice, when they are to be given, should be suited not only to the person, but to his condition. For if in counsell respect be had only to the person requiring it, without consideration of what the effects may be, all the advice that is tendered may by accident prove like the over hastey healing of an old wound, which though skind over for the present is in continuall danger upon the least accident, to break out with worse circumstances. Counsell, therefore should be rather safe than pleasant, though where they may be joyned it becomes more acceptable. Beside it should be alwaise free, and candid as to the manner, wholesome & considerate, as to the occasion. For if in obtaining it, I am forced to use passionate intreatys, the advice that is so gained will seem rather an object of my persuasion, than interest of my ffriendship & will imediatly beget a distrust, that I have pitched upon an unfitting person for the opening of my mind to, who is more willing (it may be) to know my disease, than to prescribe a remedy for its cure.

Wherefore it is an unfallible discovery of the vertue of ffriendship, imediatly to interpose with suitable counsell, according to the present juncture of affaires that shall be offered. For there must not only be a sympathizing between friends but a deliberate consultation, whichever of the two is fittest to promote, who only wants that share of the present troubles which his concernment for his friend, layes on him. From a measure of troubles, so be the party especially engaged, renders a man less capable of directing himself than otherwise he would be. So that nothing can be more gratefull at such a season, than a suddain closing with the opportunity, rendering such proposalls as from ffriendship, acted by a sober judgement, and proceeding from an unbyassd principle, shall upon good ground appeare of as most likely for the attaining its ends. For in this case, empty wishes are too effeminate & become not that masculine spirit that should be in ffriends, & great souls have pitty, as being a kind of Medium that only represents their griefs more formidable. Job indeed calls for pitty from his friends, but it seemes in that place opposd to the harsh usage he received from them; and where he saith, that to him that is afflicted pitty, should be show'd from his friend, it may rationally (in my poore opinion) be understood of such a pitty as is joynd with endeavours to comfort & assist him. This therefore is one & none of the smallest advantages of ffriendship; which will the better appeare if we consider the grand obstruction of it in its course, is when those who profess it cannot, because one or others faithfull advice, is contrary to their particular designs. And this is the defect of many excellent persons who though they desire counsell, yet are impatient & reject it, if it runns not in ye same streame with their present apprehensions. Now in this they seem not so much to seek advice, as confirmation in their own opinions and where this unruly humor reigns, it shutts out the most generous offices of ffriendship. For so prone is the mind of man to make returns in hand, that it is not likely that they who will heare no counsell from others, should be heard themselves, though they proffer it with the greatest sincerity & affection; by which means this bulwark of ffriendship is blockt up on both sides, & of how great concernment this is, none can so well judg as those who have experienced the advantages that come by faithfull counsell & advice. This being one of the greatest supports of life, which in all states & conditions we shall have more or less occasion to repaire to. By this we are instructed how to avoid dangers, or else couragiously to meet them if they are inevitable; How to secure our persons, or highten our reputation, Attain our designs & prudently to use them, or at least contentedly to beare up under the disappointment. By counsell we are upheld under the greatest afflictions & temperd in the chiefest of our enjoyments, for in embracing it we do not only see with others eyes beside our owne, but as through a Telescope behold things at further distance, & becom enabled to make better discoverys than otherwise we could have done; things by this meanes appearing distinct, which otherwise seemed formless & confused.

An other advantage of ffriendship is incouragement, to which I shall joyne reproofe, being both of them the legitimate & twin Daughters of counsell, though of different complexions & contrary aspects.

Incouragement therefore of ffriends, has a great influence upon ingenious minds. It raiseth a person above himself, lessens difficulties, heightens expectations, increases hope, depresses feare & putts him many times into a fair possesssion of the things he seeks after, by making them appear possible to be attaind & within his reach. For in things which we either extreamly desire, or feare, we can with more satisfaction build upon the opinion of our friends, than our own apprehensions. The reason of which I conceive to be, Because we look on them as persons unprejudiced by those passions which govern us on such occasions. & therefore being less concernd, suppose they may make a better judgment of our undertakings, or conditions, whereas our being so nearly engaged & having our thoughts so strongly fixt upon the thing desired or dreaded, must necessarily stirr up in us many passions with disorder & subjecting us to some one or more of them, which oppose our designs, entayle on us a greater debility than nature it self has. Tis this causes us to looke on all opposition as invincible & upon all advantage as deceitfull. But the judicious incouragement of ffriends answers both these, reconciling us first to our selves (whereby at once our strength is increasd and opponents rendered inconsiderable) & then by solid argument, & not airey fancies, seting before us the probability of our successe, and liklihood of attaining our ends, if we be not our owne greatest hindrance. But as true ffriends should never be backward to incourage those they love, to such things as are prayseworthy, worthy & beneficiall, so on the other side, they must be carefull not to spurr them on to such hazardous adventures, where either ruin seems to be the most certain reward, or disgrace the likelyest crowne of all their labours, though where those ominously threaten us or are already become unavoydable, incouragements to beate them nobly must necessarily be the best cordiall to keep up our sinking spirits. For tis often seen a man needs as much incouragement to dy well, as to fight well, to suffer couragiously as to overcome bravely.

Nor is reproof in its place either less beautifull or necessary than incouragement and when performed in love, & so received there is not a more excellent & generous fruit of ffriendship. But here is the mischief, as there are few that can give it after a right manner, & duly time it, so there are few that will as they ought, receive it. Now those who would be rightly qualified for so great a work, must lay aside feare & anger. For by the one they are deterrd from doing it at all, by the other wont to over do it. For Reproof being a thing naturally unpleasant to the mind of man, it ought to be managed with all imaginable sweetness and prudence. Blunt reproofs may possibly sometimes reform, but they seldom oblig, this being a favor which we may receive from an enemy. Wherefore in this affair it is requisite to be thoroughly acquainted with the temper of the person, before we adventure on this so often thankless part of ffriendship. Tis true there are some who may be dealt with in a free & open way, who can hear their actions condemned without being displeased with any but themselves for giving the occasion, and can receive the reprimands of a friend with the same affection that they are dispenced, esteeming such wounds as given in faithfulness & looking on them as ye noblest badges of this relation. For when I praise a man I would be thought his friend but if I reprove him with such candor as I ought I justify my self to be so indeed, & I am encouraged to that office, because I think he is such to me. But there are others that must be treated in a quite different way and soe they can swallow this bitter pill, must have it well gilt. Their good deeds must be extolld & their accomplishments magnified, soe you can speake a word of their infirmities, which it may be if they are brought up in this ?, will not be taken so much amiss. For hence they will be convinced that you mention them not from any meane thoughts you had entertained of them, but only from a desire of their further advance in those things that might render them more excellent. An other sort of men there are who though like forward Children they can never be persuaded to drink the potion though the brims of the cupp be never so well sweetened, esteeming it a thing intollerable to beare exprest in their own persons, yet without offence they can hear the views which themselves are guilty of condemned in the person of another. Now why reproof is so distasteful both to these and the greatest part of mankind (if I mistake not) the reason may easily be drawn from that pride which abounds in their natures, for though they can be content to own a generall defection yet they are unwilling to be chargd with particular miscarriage, esteeming that more to their disparagement & which imediatly points at them, though of less concernment than the universall imperfection in which all are involved. And though they cannot but be conscious of their own frailties, yet they are impatient to find such witnesses of them as will thereupon take the confidence severely, but most firmly, to reprove them. But before we leave this subject of reproof one thing must not be forgot. That when tis directed to any one in his own person, as it should be performed in love

& meekness, so it must be done with ye greatest secrecy; least otherwise while you think to wipe off the blot, you only spread it, by making others take notice of that which possibly might be only seen by your self before. Beside which we lay a disobligation upon a man to inform by letting the world know the wisper of it which otherwise might have been thought to have proceeded from his owne prudence. Wherefore I think that saying of Solon maybe now fitly applied.

Thy friend in private chide, in Publique prays.

I conclude this paragraph with a pleasant encounter betwixt Socrates and Plato which I think will not be much from my purpose. Socrates as he one day at dinner reproved one of his ffriends something harshly, Plato said to him, had not this been better told in private? Socrates imediatly answered, and had not you done better if you had told me so in private?

An other advantage of ffriendship is a generous emulation which it provokes and stirrs up; an affection as different from envy as love is from hatred & true ffriendship from a combination in evils. Tis this excites us to out do our selves, as well as others, not from a desire to be the alone excellent, but that others by our example may be excited to pursue those things that are truly worthy a noble spirit. Besides this emulation is so far from repining at those advantages which nature or education has bestowed upon others, whereby they proceed with greater facility to the exercise of generous and virtuous actions, securing their names from the rough usage of time that it feeles in it self a true joy to see virtue embraced & improved to such performances as may be serviceable to the glorifying their Creator & advancing the interest of ffriendship & the common good of mankind. For none can be true ffriends who have not first espoused vertue & become as firmly united to that as to the persons of those they love & where this happy conjunction is once made, tis as great a pleasure to see it enthrond in our friend, as to find it rooted in our selves; And it will be equally desirable to have a friend worthy our invitation, as that our selves should be examples fitt for others to follow. Vertue is a Jewell to be admired in an Enemy, praised in a Friend and desired by our selves; & it is impossble we should envy others virtues & be virtuous our selves; for that envy cannot proceed from a love of virtue but out of those advantages it brings which hereby we are apt to think fall amiss when they light not on us. Emulation betweene friends I take to be this, when from beholding their virtues and the beauties of their minds, we are awakend from that sluggishness which confines our desires and enchaines within the narrow limmitts of unprofitable wishes, & provoked to an eager pursuit of such things as may not only render us like those we love, but fitt patterns to be imitated by them: & without this emulation I think I may boldly say it is as rare to find virtue as to see a river without streames, or the sun divested of its rays. Tis this putts life & spirit into all our actions and makes us carefull to perform them well. Tis the excellence of vertue itself that makes us love it, but tis the consideration of what others therein have done & the many eyes which are upon us, that makes us jealous of our selves in ye exercise of it, that so we may not by our imprudence, or by any uncomly dresse, deform so divine a Beauty. And if such reflexions in the generall are so prevalent with us, what influence then must this additionall consideration have, that whatever we do, or say, & I had almost said, think, is more visible to the eyes of our ffriend, than they possibly can be to others. For they only can compare our actions with our intentions, whilst others from what they see can only form ends of their owne according to what themselves would design from such performances. And how tender must this make every generous spirit, who has contracted ffriendship with virtuous persons, not to do anything which may make them less worthy of that sacred union; Like that souldier who being overcome by his Enemy, entreated him to give his life a passage through his breast, least his ffriend seeing a wound on his back should be ashamed of him.

Now reall friendship as it is the greatest promoter of vertue in its followers, so it is a powerfull motive to persuade others for ye love of it. For though vertue may be admired by some when found in a single person, yet it becomes more splendid when united in an excellent and numerous Society of ffriends, where their severall vertues make up one perfect concert and beget in others an admiration if not a desire, of so noble an alliance. The Theben or Holy Band mentioned by Plutarch were not so famous for their valour (though even that was without any example) as for their love. For it was their ffriendship which animatd their courage, & made them worthy King Philip's warres & had that not given a kind of Eternity to their memory, they like many other excellent

Warriors might at an hour have slept in the dust & been buried in oblivion. Of examples in this kind History is prodigiall; but I briefly hint what would be argument for a mighty volume.

Then, for contentment, where can it be found if not among ffriends; all other enjoyments are like great shaddows without any substance if ffriendship be wanting. For if a man can be truly said to enjoy either himself or what ever the world has put any value on, who has not a friend to partake with him, who may assist him in his undertakings and be a witness of his felicities. This being the necessary fate of all, that we must borrow the apprehensions of others to think ourselves happy & looke further than our owne breast if we would ever hope to find true contentment. [Lord Bacon is noted in the margin of the above paragraph].

Lastly, ffriendship is the most genuine light to discover vertue by, as being that by which it is neither discoloured nor obscured; whereas when vertue is taken up & made subservient to politick accounts, arising from a too much love of our selves, which stirrs up in us indecent desires either after profit, greatness or fame, it then appears as through coloured mediums which are so farr from beautifying it, that at best they unhansomly shaddow it, or which is wors, make it suffer a totall eclips, whereas ffriendship displayes it like ye Sun in its brightness; makes us like the Deity, love vertue for itself & endeavour the propagating it in others; is the principall support of this life, & the happiness of the next.

Mary Beale

SOURCES

Charles Beale, Almanack, 1677, Rawlinson Ms 8o 572, Bodleian Library, Oxford. Transcript and notes, 2/16, 4/6A, Ms 128, Heinz Archive and Library, NPG

Charles Beale, Almanack, 1681, CB (formerly Ms 18). Transcript Ms 19. Notes 2/13, 4/6B, 6/26, Ms 128, Heinz Archive and Library, NPG

Charles Beale, 'Experimental Secrets found out in the way of Painting', 1647–63, Ferguson Ms 134, Glasgow University Library. Transcript 1/18, Ms 128, Heinz Archive and Library, NPG

Charles Beale junior, sketches, 'Ist book, 1679', Morgan Library and Museum, New York. Photocopies 1952.9.27.2 (1-73), British Museum Prints and Drawings

Charles Beale junior, sketches, *c.* 1680-1714, G.g.5.9, British Museum Prints and Drawings

Charles Beale junior, sketches, '3rd book 1680', 1981.0516.15.1-94, British Museum Prints and Drawings

Charles Beale junior, sketches, *c.* 1680-1714, 1981.0516.16.1-72, British Museum Prints and Drawings

Mary Beale, 'Discourse on Friendship', 1667, Harley Ms 6828, ff.510-523, British Library

John Cooke's letters to Charles Beale, 1663–8, Rawlinson Letters 113, Bodleian Library, Oxford. Transcript 2/19, Ms 128, Heinz Archive and Library, NPG

Thomas Flatman's letters to Charles Beale, 1666–72, Rawlinson Letters 104, Bodleian Library, Oxford. Transcripts 2/19, 6/26, 7/16, Ms 128, Heinz Archive and Library, NPG

Richard Jeffree and Elizabeth Walsh, Art Research Papers, *c.* 1970–90, 211 files including genealogical material and catalogue of Mary Beale's paintings, Ms 128, Heinz Archive and Library, NPG

Francis Knollys's letters to Charles Beale, 1666–70, Rawlinson Letters 104, 108, Bodleian Library, Oxford. Transcripts 2/19, Ms 128, Heinz Archive and Library, NPG

Samuel Woodford, '*Lib. primus*', 1662, Osborne b41, Beinecke Rare Book and Manuscript Library, Yale University

Samuel Woodford, '*Liber Dolorosus*', 1663–5, Ms Eng. Misc.381, Bodleian Library, Oxford. Transcripts 2/7, 6/23 Ms 128, Heinz Archive and Library, NPG

Samuel Woodford, 'Memoirs of the most remarkable Passages of my Life long since collected', annotated copy of *A Paraphrase Upon the Psalms of David,* 1678, Ms 9494, New College, Oxford. Transcripts 2/7, 6/26, Ms 128, Heinz Archive and Library, NPG

Woodford family correspondence, 6/23, Ms 128, Heinz Archive and Library, NPG

BIBLIOGRAPHY

Baker, C. H. Collins, *Lely and the Stuart Portrait Painters. A study of English portraiture before and after Van Dyck,* (1912)

Barber, Tabitha, *Mary Beale. Portrait of a seventeenth-century painter, her family and her studio.* Exhibition Catalogue, Geffrye Museum, (1999)

Beale, Trevor, *The Portraits. West Lodge Park,* (2015)

Chappell, Edwin, *Eight generations of the Pepys family 1500-1800*, (1936)

Cheney, Liana, et al., *Self Portraits by Women Painters*, (2000)

Croft Murray, Edward, and Hulton, Paul, *Catalogue of British Drawings vol 1; xvi and xvii centuries, British Museum,* (1960)

Cullum, Gery Milner-Gibson, 'Mary Beale', *Suffolk Institute of Archaeology and Natural History* 16 (1918), pp. 229–51

Cunliffe, Keith, *Women by Women.* Exhibition Catalogue, Moyse's Hall Museum, (2009)

Dabbs, Julia K., *Life Stories of Women Artists 1500–1800. An Anthology,* (2009)

De Piles, Roger, *The art of painting and the lives of the painters. To which is added An Essay towards an English School by Bainbrigg Buckeridge,* (1706)

Dolman, Brett, *Beauty, Sex and Power. A Story of debauchery and decadent art at the late Stuart Court 1660–1714,* (2012)

Draper, Helen, 'Mary Beale (1633-1699) and her Objects of Affection', in *Writing the Lives of People and Things AD 500–1700,* ed. by Smith, Robert F.W, and Watson, Gemma L., (2016), pp. 115-41

Edmond, Mary, 'Limners and Picturemakers', *Walpole Society* 47 (1978-80), pp. 60–217, and 'Bury St Edmunds. A Seventeenth Century Art Centre', *Walpole Society* 53 (1987), pp. 106–18

Farrer, Edmund, *Portraits in Suffolk Houses (West)*, (1908)

Foskett, D., *A Dictionary of British Portrait Painters*, (1972)

Fraser, Antonia, *The Weakest Vessel. Women's lot in seventeenth-century England,* (1999)

Fresnay, C. A. du, *The Art of Painting,* (1716)

Glaze, Delia, *Dictionary of Women Artists,* (1997)

Greer, Germaine, *The Obstacle Race. The fortunes of women painters*, (1979)

Harley, R. D., *Artists' Pigments c. 1600–1835*, (2001)

Harris, Frances, *Transformations of Love. The Friendship of John Evelyn and Margaret Godolphin*, (2002)

Ingamells, John, *Later Stuart Portraits 1685–1714,* (2009)

Jeffree, Richard, and Walsh, Elizabeth, *The Excellent Mrs Mary Beale.* Exhibition Catalogue, Geffrye Museum and Towner Art Gallery, Eastbourne, (1975)

BIBLIOGRAPHY *continued*

Newfield, Fabien, *Mary Beale. 101 Paintings*, (2015)

Norgate, Edward, ed. by Martin Hardie, *Miniatura or the Art of Limning,* (1919)

Reeve, Christopher, *Mrs Mary Beale, Paintress 1633–1699*. Exhibition Catalogue, Manor House Museum, Bury St Edmunds (1994)

Parker, Rozsika, and Pollock, Griselda, *Old Mistresses. Women, Art and Ideology,* (2013)

Piper, David, *The English Face*, (1957)

Singh, Frederick Duleep, ed. by Farrer, Edmund, *Portraits in Norfolk Houses,* (1928)

Wendorf, Richard, *The Elements of Life. Biography and Portrait-Painting in Stuart and Georgian England*, (1999)

Whinney, Margaret, and Millar, Oliver, *English Art 1625–1714,* (1957)

Williamson, George C., *The History of Portrait Miniatures,* (1904)

Woodforde, Dorothy Heighes, ed., *Woodforde Papers and Diaries,* (1932)

Wright, Christopher, Gordon, Catherine, and Smith, Mary Peskett, *British and Irish Paintings in Public Collections,* (2006)

INDEX

Numbers in italics indicate illustrations.
Titles of paintings are in italics.